St. John's and St. George's
Parish Registers
1696-1851

Henry C. Peden, Jr.

HERITAGE BOOKS
2006

HERITAGE BOOKS
AN IMPRINT OF HERITAGE BOOKS, INC.

Books, CDs, and more—Worldwide

For our listing of thousands of titles see our website at
www.HeritageBooks.com

Published 2006 by
HERITAGE BOOKS, INC.
Publishing Division
65 East Main Street
Westminster, Maryland 21157-5026

Copyright © 1987 Henry C. Peden, Jr.

All rights reserved. No part of this book may be reproduced or transmitted in any form or by any means, electronic or mechanical, including photocopying, recording or by any information storage and retrieval system without written permission from the author, except for the inclusion of brief quotations in a review.

International Standard Book Number: 978-1-58549-099-7

INTRODUCTION

Baltimore County, which contained present day Harford County, was laid off in three parishes by the Act of 1692, passed by the Maryland Assembly. The parishes were named Copley (now St. John's), St. Paul's and St. George's. The parish churches were located in Joppa (later Kingsville), Baltimore City and Perryman (Michaelsville), respectively. The parish boundaries are shown on the accompanying map. Harford County was established in 1773, taken entirely from Baltimore County. As shown in the map, Harford County consisted of St. George's and part of St. John's.

This compilation of records was taken from a transcribed copy held by the Maryland Historical Society. Judging from the date, 1888, and the handwriting, it was apparently done by the indefatigable and reliable, Lucy H. Harrison. This collection of vital records does not represent all that are available for St. George's parish. There is another, distinctly separate, collection of parish registers, 1681-1799, 1834-1841, 1834-1903 and 1845-1881. It is planned that these will be published as a supplement in the near future.

Oft times the early handwriting was difficult to read; effort has been made to transcribe the data as accurately as possible. An occasional note by the compiler has been made in the text for clarification when an obvious error was made in recording a name or date. A surname index has been prepared which refers to the page number of the transcribed copy held by the Maryland Historical Society - and NOT to the page of this book.

Many of the ancestors of the present residents of Harford and Baltimore Counties went to school or attended church meetings at either St. George's or St. John's Parishes. The names of Hall, Taylor, Rigdon, Osborn, Smith, Clark, Paca and Jay are among those listed as vestrymen. Many of the signers of the famous Bush Declaration (the first "Declaration of Independence") were members of St. George's Parish when it was signed on March 22, 1775. This declaration antedated the Declaration of Mecklenburg, North Carolina by more than two months, and that at Philadelphia of July 4, 1776, by nearly sixteen months!

Henry C. Peden, Jr.
Bel Air, Maryland
March 1, 1987

A MAP OF ST. JOHN'S AND ST. GEORGE'S PARISHES, BALTIMORE & HARFORD COUNTIES, MARYLAND
by Henry C. Peden, Jr., 1987

KEY:
1 - Patapsco River
2 - Back River
3 - Middle River
4 - Gunpowder River
5 - Bush River
6 - Susquehanna River
7 - Spesutie Island

St. John's and St. George's Parish Registers, 1696-1851

Page 1

_____Paca, son of Aquila Paca and Martha, born Oct. 28, 1703.
Mary Paca, daughter of Aquila Paca and Martha, born Sep. 14, 1701.
Susanna Paca, daughter of Aquila Paca and Martha, born May 5, 1705.
Mary Paca, daughter of Aquila Paca and Martha, died Sep. 17, 1709.
Joseph Mead, son of Joseph and Eleanor Meade, born May---, 1717.
James Mead, son of Joseph and Eleanor Meade, born Jan. 6, 1719.
Elizabeth Meades, daughter of Joseph and Eleanor Meads, born
    Dec. 31, 1719.
Selby Meades, son of Joseph and Eleanor Meads, born Apr. 4, 1726.
_____Meads, son of Joseph and Eleanor Meads, born Apr. 22, 1728.

Page 2

_____and Hannah York was married in 1727.
William Bozley, son of Walter and Mary Elizabeth, born Mar. 11,
    1711/12.
Rachel Yoark, daughter of James and Rachel, born Jan. 12, 1713.
Hezekiah Day and Alce Bonney Day married July 12, 1713.
Isack Brown and Elimor Campell married July 13, 1713.
Thomas Walters and Elizabeth Stout married July 13, 1713.
Sarah Pickett, daughter of Wm. and Sarah, born June 16, 1713.
Elizabeth Butteram, daughter of John and Elizabeth Butteram,
    born Sept. 6, 1713.
James Cammel, son of John and Elimor, born Jan. 1, 1703/4.
Philis Cammel, daughter of John and Elimor, born Nov. 7, 1707.
Elizabeth Robinson, daughter of Wm. and Elizabeth, born Feb. 17,
    1711.
John Insor, son of John Insor and Elizabeth, born Aug. 15, 1711.
John Hichcock, son of Wm. and Mary Hichcock, born Aug. 30, 1712.
Nicolas Harbert died in Aprill, 1713.
Matthew Green was drowned in Aprill, 1713.

Page 3

Richard Preston, son of James Preston and Elizabeth, born
    Feb. 28, 1713.
Isack Groos, son of Jacob and Sarah Groos, born Jan. 18, 1712.
Rachell Groos, daughter of Jacob and Sarah, born Nov. 25, 1708.
Sarah Groos, daughter of Jacob and Sarah, born Feb. 15, 1710.

George Yoark, son of George and Susannah Yoark, born------1712.
Mary Mecomas, daughter of John and Ann Mecomas, born Feb. 4,------.
Edward Mead and Darcass Ewins married Oct. 13, 1713.
Thomas Cutchin and Jane Hicks married Oct. 28, 1713.
Temperance Roller, daughter of Archable and Rebecka Roller,
    born Aug. 9, 1713.
Rebeckah Petete, daughter of John and Elizabeth Petete, born
    Oct. 9, 1712.
Mary day, daughter of Nicholas and Elizabeth Day, born Oct. 23, 1713.
Elecksander Mecomas and Elizabeth Day married Nov. 19, 1713.
Christopher Cox died Nov. 15, 1713.
Joseph Cox died Nov. 20, 1713.
Ann Roberts, daughter of John and Mary Roberts, born Aug. 20, 1713.

Page 4

Robertt Clark, son of Robertt and Sarah Clark, born Oct. 13, 1708.
William Collason and Susanah Addams married Dec. 3, 1713.
Samuel Sicklemore and Ruth Camell married Dec. 8, 1713.
John Hopkins and Ann Hickambottom married Dec. 27, 1713.
Richard Robinson and Elizabeth Slade married Jan. 12, 1713.
William Slade, son of John and Elizabeth Slade, born Nov. 5, 1710.
Robert Slade, son of John and Elizabeth Slade, born June 30, 1712.
John Chamberlaine, son of Thomas and Mary, born Dec. 17. 1713.
George Presbury, son of James and Martha, born Aug. 18, 1710.
Mary Presbury, daughter of James and Martha, born Feb. 22, 1712/13.
George Berry and Mary Cox married February 6, 1714.
John Roberts and Ann Richarson married February 7, 1714.
John Bonadee died October 10, 1713.
Sarah Legett, daughter of John and Unity Legett, born Nov. 30, 1713.
Jane Quine, daughter of William and Elizabeth, born June 20, 1713.
John Whittacar, died November 30, 1713.
William Bond, son of William and Mary Bond, born Sept. 23, 1709.
Sarah Bond, daughter of William and Mary Bond, born Mar. 13, 1713.

Page 5

Mary Deaver, daughter of Richard and Mary Dever, born Feb. 23, 1713.
Elizabeth Cole, daughter of Elizabeth Cole, born Feb. 7, 1714.

Abraham Taylor and Dinna White married the 20 day of-----------.
Richard Rodes, son of Richard and Magdalen, born Dec. 1, 1713.
John Bond, son of Thomas and Ann Bond, born Nov. 10, 1712.
Rebecka Deson, daughter of William and Mary, born Mar. 9, 1712.
Clemency Taylor, daughter of Martin and Sarah, born Apr. 14, 1714.
Samuel Grinin and Ann Twine married March 1, 1714.
Catherine Peake died January 15, 1714.
John Roggers and Receckah Stevens married April 25, 1714.
Sarah Lough, daughter of William and Temperance, born Mar. 22, 1714.
John Whitacar and Ann Dadd married April 27, 1714.
Rachell Muckelderoay, daughter of John and Francis Muckelderoay,
    born Aug. 6, 1714.
Isack Herrington, son of Corneluis and Rachell, born May 5, 1705.
Thomas Norris, son of John and Ann Norris, born Nov. 27, 1713.
Sarah Lough, daughter of John and Elizabeth, born Jan. 23, 1714.
John Penrice died June 19, 1714.

Page 6

Charles Boseley, son of Walter and Elizabeth, born May 13, 1714.
Elizabeth Butteram died May 7, 1714.
William Hicks, son of William and Ann, born Mar. 10, 1714.
John Walker and Mary Cox, widdow, married June 12, 1714.
William Thrist, son of Richard and Mary, born June 14, 1714.
Simon Pearson, son of Simon and Emm, born May 7, 1714.
Emm Pearson, wife of Simon Pearson, died June 7, 1714.
George Simons, son of Charles and Hannah, born July 4, 1714.
Jacob Robinson and Mary Whitacar, widdow, married July 5, 1714.
Sarah Matthews, daughter of Henery and Sarah, born Apr. 25, 1702.
Elizabeth Matthews, daughter of Henery and Sarah, born July 10, 1708.
Abraham Ranasbey born May 10, 1711.
John Armstrong and Rebeckah Hicks married August 26, 1714.
John Butteram and Jane Mayer married September 8, 1714.
William Right and Juliana Benbo married September 5, 1714.
Mary Downes, daughter of Jeremiah and Mary, born Oct. 24, 1714.
John Deson, son of William and Mary, born Sept. 25. 1714.
Bartholomew Davis, son of George and Mary, born Oct. 25, 1714.
Sarah Mecomass, daughter of Elecksander and Elizabeth Mecomas,
    born Oct. 5, 1714.

Page 7

Jacob Taylor, son of Abraham and Dinnah, born Oct. 5, 1714.
Richard Ward, son of Joseph, born March 15, 1713.
Marget, the servant woman that liveth with John Rollans had a bastard baring child, February 1, 1714.
John Derbin and Abrillah Scott married August 20, 1715.
Symon Person and Sarah Schaw married July 23, 1715.
Henry Fuller, son of John and Sarah, born Feb. 2, 1713.
Jeames Denton, son of William and Sarah, born Feb. 15, 1707.
Rebecca Denton (even though the record indicates "son"), daughter of William and Saray, born April 14, 1708.
Sarah Denton, daughter of William and Sarah, born Oct. 1, 1709.
Jeane Denton born March 10, 1710.
William Denton, son of William and Sarah, born Jan. the last, 1712.
Daniel Scott, son of Danell Scott Jr. and Elizabeth, born Feb. 23, 1712.
Martha Schott, daughter of Danell Scott Jr. and Elizabeth, born Feb. 27, 1714.
Ann Harrit, wife of Oliver Harrit, died May 13, 1716.
William Williams and Jeane Asshe married May 26, 1716.
Ruth Saray Sickemore, daughter of Samevell Sickemore and Ruth, born Dec. 23, 1715.

Page 8

William Demitt (Dernit), son of William and Elizabeth, born June 1, 1715.
Thomas Smith, husband of Mary Smith, died August 24, 1716.
Ann Norris, daughter of John and Ann, born September 7, 1717.
Sarah Sickemore, daughter of Sutton and Constant, born Mar. 20, 1717.
William Smith, son of William and Rachel, born-------------.
Joseph Cooley, son of James and Elizabeth, born Feb. 28, 1721.
James Hatch, son of Sarah and John, born May 3, 1716.
Elizabeth Denton, daughter of William and Sarah, born July 10, 1716, and died October 1, 1716.
Robert Burkit and Mary Wharton married October 1, 1716.
Frances Whithead Jr. died December 22, 1716.
Mary Taylor, daughter of Martin Taylor, born October 9, 1716.
Moses Person, son of Simon and Sarah Person, born May 21, 1716.
Archiball Rollar, son of Archeball and Rebekaha, born Jan. 11, 1716.

Jeames Henly, son of Edward and Mary, born _____ 3, 1716.
Elizabeth Ward Sr. died December 13, 1716.
Leporah Cole, daughter of Thomas and Elizabeth, born Jan. 17, 1716.

Page 9

Elizabeth Merrica, wife of Joshua Marrica, died December 17, 1716.
William Hitccock and Ann Jones married September 7, 1716.
Samevall Scickemore and Katerne Herrington married Sept. 12, 1716.
Thomas Johnson and Mary Enlove married Sept. 3, 1716.
John Cammeron and Marget Macckelltons married Dec. 12, 1716.
John Day, son of Nicklous and Elizabeth, born Sept. 7, 1716.
Robert Bond, son of John and Mary, born Oct. 11, 1717.
William Armstron, son of John and Rebecka, born Nov. 24, 1716.
William Waylon, son of Partrick and Katern, born May 10, 1717.
Thomas Charmbelin, son of Thomas and Mary, born May 7, 1717.
Rebecka Scott, daughter of Daniell Scott Jr. and Elizabeth, born
        January 20, 1717.
Jude Elliot, daughter of Thomas and Sarah, born March 29, 1709.
Thomas Elliott, son of Thomas and Sarah, born Nov. 18, 1711.
William Elliott, son of Thomas and Sarah, born June 18, 1715.
Elizabeth Garland, daughter of Nicholes and Sarah, born Sep. 12, 1717.

Page 10

Susannah Petit, daughter of John and Elizabeth, born Feb. 8, 1715.
Abraham Petite, son of John Eptet and Elizabeth, born June 20, 1717.
Welthy Herington, daughter of Cornelius, baptized August 17, 1718.
Jeames Yorke, son of Jeames and Rachell, born August 11, 1718.
Mary Yorke, daughter of Jeames and Rachell, born Nov. 28, 1716.
Abraham Ditto, son of Jeames Ditto, baptized Sept. 14, 1718.
Jacob Johnson, son of Thomas and Mary, born March 15, 1718.
Comfort Person, daughter of Simon Person and Sarah, born Sep. 23, 1718.
John Nelson and Frances Roades married January 12, 1718.
William Roades and Mary_____ married January 17, 1717.
Oliver Harrett and Susannah Morrow married October 13, 1717.
Mary Rhodes, daughter of Richard and Magdelen, born Feb. 5, 1715.

Ann Rhodes, daughter of Richard and Magdelen, born Apr. 22, 1722.
Joseph Ward, son of Joseph and Bridget, died the last of June, 1717.
Mary Ward, daughter of Joseph and Bridget, born July 1, 1717.

Page 11

Elizabeth Denton, daughter of William and Sarah, died Oct. 1, 1716.
William Perdue, son of Walter and Jeane, born December 3, 1716.
Mary Perdue, daughter of Walter and Jeane, born Jan. 17, 1715.
Ann Yorke, daughter of George and Hannah, born Apr. 2, 1717.
William Dottridge and Lettis Taylor marrried Sept. 18, 1717.
Ruth Sickemore, daughter of Somevill Sickemore, died Sep. 22, 1717.
John Berton, son of Thomas and Abigall, born June 28, 1715.
Elizabeth Berton, daughter of Thomas and Abigall, born Jan. 25, 1717.
Joshua Marrikin and Dinah Day married June 24, 1718.
Jeames Isinn (Lsinn) and Elizabeth Robinson married---------------.
Thomas Barton, son of Thomas and Abigal, born June 27, 1710.
Elizabeth Ward, daughter of Joseph and Bridget, born May 1, 1707.

Page 12

John Ward, son of Joseph and Bridget, born Nov. 22, 1711.
Richard Ward, son of Joseph and Bridget, born March 1, 1714.
Sarah Downes, daughter of Jeremiah Downes and Mary, born Jan. 7, 1716/17.
Mary Downes, wife of Jeremiah Downes, died Feb. 1, 1717/18.
William Barton, son of Thomas and Abigall, born Dec. 15. 1718/19.
Cammeron Marget died January 1, 1718/19.
Robert Maxwell was buried January 12, 1718/19.
Abel (Asahel) Hatchcock (Hitchcock), son of William and Ann Hitchcock, was born April 26, 1719.
Sarrah Norris, daughter of John and Ann, born April 22, 1719.
William Jones, son of Benjamin and Jane, born May 11, 1716.
Comfort Person, daughter of Simon and Sarah, born Sept. 19, 1718.

Page 13

John Bradshaw, son of John and Mary, born Nov. 27, 1719/20.
Sarah Norris, daughter of John and Ann, baptized Apr. 24, 1720.

William Raven, son of Luke, born Feb. 13, 1696, died Mar. 24, 1718.
Esther Raven, daughter of Luke, born Dec. 8, 1718, buried Oct., 1719.
William Raven, son of Luke, born June 25, 1719, buried Feb., 1719.
William Howerd died January 29, 1718.
Peter Wittame, son of John and Ann Wittam, born May 6, 1715.
John Bond, husband of Mary, buried April 17, 1720.
Sarah Whayson, daughter of Patrick and Katerne, baptized May 8, 1720.
Rachel Denton, daughter of William and Sarah, baptized May 8, 1720.
Mr. Aquila Paca Sr. died September 10, 1721.

Page 14

Thomas Armstrong died April 12, 1722.
Sarah Baker, daughter of Charles and Avarilla, born Aug. 23, 171--.
Theophilous Baker, son of Charles and Avarila, born Nov. 2, 1701.
Elizabeth Baker, daughter of Charles and Avarila, born Sep. 17, 1724.
Birdget Baker, daughter of Charles and Avarila, born July 27, 1727.
John Frissil and Providence Dallatude married in November, 1721.
John Frissil, son of John and Providence, born in August, 1724.
Joshua Merrken, Clark of the Register in May, 1720, for St. John's
    Parrish.
Providence Frissil, daughter of John and Providence, born in
    September, 1726.
Providence Frissil, wife of John, died November 20, 1727.
John Dawney and Lydia Swift married in March, 1716.

Page 15

John Simons, son of Charles and Hanah, born March 2, 1718.
William Raven, son of Luke, born February 13, 1696/7.
William Raven died March 24, 1718.
Easter Raven, daughter of Luke, born December 8, 1712.
Easter Raven died in October, 1719.
William Raven, son of Luke, born June 25, 1719.
William Raven died in February, 1719.
Mary Roades, daughter of William and Mary, born March 2, 1719.
Henry Wheylon, son of Patrick and Catherine, born Aug. 6, 1712.
Margertt Wheylon, daughter of Patrick and Catherine, born Feb.17,1715.

Page 16

Rebeckah Taylor, daughter of John and Judith, born in August, 1719.
Sephiah Meeds, daughter of Edward Meeds and Dorcas, born Mar., 1717.
John Presbury, son of James and Martha, born October 18, 1716.
Martha Presbury, daughter of James and Martha, born Oct. 27, 1718.
Joseph Bradford, son of William and Elizabeth, born Jan. 15, 17--.
John Oliver married Sarah Smith, daughter of Edward, July 14, 1720.
Silvestine Jones married Mary Hinton in November, 1719.
Benjamin Norris and Sarah_____ married October 8, 1719.
John Nellson and Frances_____ married November 15, 1715.

Page 17

John Cameron and Sarah Crofford married June 21, 1720.
George York and Lettice Dawdridge married May 7, 1721.
James Durham and Reneckah Anderson married February 12, 1720.
John Bradshaw and Mary Callmack married June 20, 1719.
John Obryan married Ellinor Jackson, widdow, Sept. 24, 1721.
William Wright Jr. married Ann Howles September 24, 1721.
John Wiseley married Mary Bond, widdow, October 20, 1721.
Richard Atherton and Susanah Norriss married Nov. 1, 1721.
Joseph Bradford, son of William Bradford and Elizabeth, died
      February 28, 1718.
William Bradford sworn in Clark and Register for St. John's Parrish
   and Clerk to the Vestry for one year ensuing the date Apr. 28, 1722.

Page 18

Robert Taylor, son of Abraham and Dina, born Oct. 13,-----.
Ann Taylor, daughter of Abraham and Dina, born Mar. 29, 1712.
Rachell Taylor, daughter of Abraham and Dina, born Oct. 9, 1717.
Joseph Taylor, son of Abraham and Dinna, born Oct. 20, 1720.
Jacob Taylor, son of Abraham and Dinna, born Oct. 6, 1714.
Sutton Thrift, son of Richard and Mary, born Oct. 26, 1705.
Sarah Thrift, daughter of Richard and Mary, born Oct. 20, 17--.
Mary Thrift, daughter of Richard and Mary, born Jan. 8, 1720.
Benjamin Hanson, son of Benjamin and Sarah, born in 1722.
Leah Denton, daughter of William and Sarah, born Oct. 24, 1720.

Page 19

Lewis Puttee and Catherine Green married June 12, 1722.
Robert Roberson and Sarah Taylor married Nov. 9, 1721.
John Cockin and Alice Wells married May 22, 1722.
John Boice and Elizabeth Jephs married Nov. 30, 1721.
Edward Day and Averilla Taylor married May 22, 1722.
Joseph Galloway of Annarrundel County and Susanna Paca
    of Baltimore County married Oct. 18, 1722.
Thomas Richardson and Sarah Standove married May 20, 1720.
John Frissell and Providence Dallerhide married Oct. 25, 1722.
Jane Norrinton, daughter of Jno. and Elizabeth Norrinton,
    born December 20, 1721/22.
Abraham Wittacre and Ann Puttee married July 15, 1725.

Page 20

Elizabeth Dandy, daughter of Ralph and Mary, born June 25, 1720.
Thomas Richardson and Sarah his wife had a daughter Mary born
    May 26, 17--.
Sarah and Ann Greer, twins, daughters of John and Sarah Greer,
    born February 15, 1721.
Thomas Simmons, son of Charles and Hannah, born Sept. 5, 1719.
Thomas Preston married Elizabeth Deever, December 9, 1721.
James Preston, son of Thomas and Elizabeth, born Feb. 2, 1721/22.
Richard Thrift, son of Richard and Mary, born Jan. 20, 1722.
Mary Jean York, daughter of James and Rachell, born Apr. 25, 1723.
John Norris, son of Benjamin and Sarah, born March 4, 1722/23.
John Bevins Jr. and Sarah_____married December____,1723.
Joseph Presbury married Mrs. Elinor Ca------, July 11, 1723.
John Bond, son of William and Mary, died September 11, 1723.

Page 21

Aquila Scott, son of Daniel Scott Jr. and Elizabeth, born Sep., 1722.
Sarah Bull, daughter of Jacob and Rachell, born January 15, 1722.
Abraham Bull, son of Jacob and Rachell, born January 6, 1723.
Ann Sheaperd, daughter of William and Margaret Sheppard, born
    November 30, 1723.
Isaac Miles, son of Thomas and Catherine, born February 14, 1723/24.

Susanna Bradford, daughter of William and Elizabeth, born June 7, 1724.
William Hendon, son of Josias and Hannah, born December 1, 1723.
Daniel Scot Sr. died February 15, 1723/24., buried the 20th.
Joseph Presbury died June 7, 1724.
Rebecca York, daughter of James and Rachel, born August 1, 1724.
Hannah Herrington, daughter of Jacob and Hannah Herrinton, born
    March 31, 17--.
Samuel Durram and Elinor Smithson married January 15, 17--.

Page 22

Mary Merrikeen, daughter of Joshua and Dinna, born April 24, 17--.
Ann Person, daughter of Simon and Sarah, born December 15, 17--.
Sarah Fugate, daughter of James and Ann, born November 11, 172--.
Giles Steven and Alice Gudgeon married in 1722.
William Stevens, son of Giles and Alice, born August 13, 1721.
Samuel Stevens married_____on Shrove Tuesday, 1723.
Edward York, son of George and Lettice, born May 24, 1721.
Hannah Preston, daughter of James and Sarah, born May 9, 1723.
John Durrma, son of Samuel and Ellinor, born October 8, 1723.
Benjamin Legoe and Jean Taylor, widdow, married December 11, 1723.

Page 23

Margaret Allen, daughter of James, born July 15, 1724.
Robert Nairne and Ann Larman married October 29, 1724.
Joseph Foresight and Mary Willson married December 28, 1724.
Sarah Day, daughter of Edward and Averilla, born March 11, 1725.
Ann Meades, daughter of Edward and Darky, born April 18, 1725.
Mary Devans, daughter of John and Sarah, born April 9, 1724.
John Nelson, son of John and Frances, born December 23, 1723.
Ann Preston, daughter of James and Sarah, born July 20, 1725.
Solomon Armstrong, son of John and Rebecca, born April 19, 1723.
Joshua Merrikeen died November 8, 1723.
William Lowe, son of William and Sarah, born August 6, 1727.
Ann Masey, daughter of Aquila and Sarah Massey, born Feb. 1, 1725/6.

Page 24

Josias Simmons, son of Charles and Hannah, born March 19, 1728.
Aquila, the first son of Daniel and Elizabeth Scott, died July 13, 1724.
Aquila, the second son of Daniel and Elizabeth Scott, born November 18, 1724.
Sarah Denton, wife of William, died March 26, 1724.
William Denton and Sarah Dallerbride married Febeuary 17, 1725.
Providence Denton, daughter of William and Sarah, born Feb., 1725.
Sarah Darram, daughter of Samuel and Ellinor, born June 2, 1725.
Elizabeth Armstrong, daughter of John and Rebecca, born March 7, 1725/26.
Samuel Crabtree, son of William, born July 25, 17--.
John Day, son of Edward and Averilla, born in April, 1723.
Peter Carlile, son of David and Mary, born January 15, 1723.
Henry Witheral and Mrs. Mary Chamberlain married Dec. 20, 172-.

Page 25

Henry Witheral, son of Henry and Mary, born October 6, 1723.
Mary Witheral, wife of Henry Witherall, died November 6, 1723.
Henry Witherall, son of Henry and Mary, died November 12, 1723.
Henry Witherall and Mrs. Ellinor Presbury, widdow, married December 20, 1724.
Elizabeth Witherall, daughter of Henry and Ellinor, born November 20, 1725.
Peter Wittacre, son of Abraham and Ann, born July 7, 1726.
John Foy, son of Thomas and Rebekah, born January 18, 1726.
Laban Day, son of Nicholas and Elizabeth, born April 2, 1726.
Samuel Darram, son of Samuel and Elinor, born Feb. 18, 1726/27.
Mrs. Eleanor Maccomus died August 4, 1727.
Ann Massey, daughter of Aquila and Sarah, born Feb. 1, 1725/26.

Page 26

George Lorden, son of George and Dinah, born April 12, 1727.
Averila Day, daughter of Edward and Averilla, born Oct. 23, 1727, and died in July, 1734.
Sarah Assher, daughter of Anthony and Susannah, born July 6, 1727.

Jacob Grove died April 9, 1728.
Ann Wright, wife of William, died September 12, 1722.
William Wright and Elizabeth Barton married May 7, 1727.
John Kersey, son of John and Eleanor, born May, 1723.
Henry Kersey, son of John and Eleanor, born November, 1726.
Eleanor Kersey, daughter of John and Eleanor, born April 1, 1729.
James Darram, son of Samuel and Eleanor Darram, born Jan. 1, 172-.
Archibald Rollo, son of Captain Archibald and Mrs. Rebecca Rollo,
    died September 13, 1728.
John Watson and Jean Scott, widdow, married May 12, 1729.

Page 27

William Galloway and Priscilla Carr married August 9, 1725.
William Galloway, son of William and Priscilla, born Feb. 2, 1728/9.
Thomas Cook and Elizabeth Cooley married July 15, 1728.
Ann Carlile, daughter of David and Mary, born May 2, 1729.
Mary Gillins, daughter of Thomas and Elizabeth, born in May, 1725.
Susanna Gillins, daughter of Thomas and Elizabeth, born Nov., 1727.
Barnerd Preston, son of James and Sarah, born January 13, 1727/8.
James Preston, Barber, died June 19, 1729.
Rebecca Grover, wife of George Grover Sr., died in May, 1727.
George Grover and Magdelen Kelley married in July, 1727.

Sarah Grover, daughter of George and Magdelen, born in September,
    1728, and died in September, 1728 "living but one week."

Page 28

Catherine Dewson died in March, 1728.
Samuel Foster, son of Thomas and Elizabeth, born April 8, 1727.
Esther Preston, daughter of Thomas and Elizabeth, born Dec. 24, 1724.
John Preston, son of Thomas and Elizabeth, born December 28, 1725.
Thomas Preston, son of Thomas and Elizabeth, born May 22, 1727.
Josias Hobbs, son of John and Susanna, born in December, 1724.
Sarah Rice, daughter of William and Rachel, born February 23, 1725.
Elizabeth Rice, daughter of William and Rachel, born May 1, 1728.
Mark Swift and Ann Lockeord married December 2-, 1725.
John Swift, son of Mark and Ann, born May 15, 1718.
Elizabeth Swift, daughter of Mark and Ann, born December 23, 172-,
    and died February 1, 1726.

Page 29

John Thrift and Rebecca Blacklidge married in May, 1728.
John Thrift, son of John and Rebecca, born in October, 1729.
Prudence Thrift, daughter of Richard and Mary, born Jan. 1, 1724.
Martha Debruler, daughter of George and Esther, born March 6, 1727/8,
    and died March 16, 1728.
Francis Debruler, son of George and Esther, botn September 20, 1729.
William Hill and Martha Green married in September, 1724.
John Hill, son of William and Martha, born September 8, 1727,
    and died in September, 1728.
Mary Hill, daughter of William and Martha, born October 3, 1729.
Martha Burney, wife of William Burney, died in March, 1727/8.
May Alen, daughter of Nathaniel and Frances, born April 23, 1727.

Pages 30-31

Christopher Divas and Frances Hill married December 10, 1728.
John Eueings Mead, son of Edward and Dorcas, born Dec. 18, 1714,
    and died in December, 1715.
Elizabeth Meads, daughter of Edward and Dorcas, born Sept. 17, 1721.
Ann Meads, daughter of Edward and Dorcas, born April 7, 1724.
Dorcas Mead, wife of Edward, died January 5, 1727.
Thomas Legoe and Sarah Clark married December 19, 1728.
Ruben Legoe, son of Thomas and Sarah, born September 5, 1729.
James Cowdrey and Ann Green married in September, 1723.
John Cowdrey, son of James and Ann, born March 10, 1724,
    and died in May, 1725.
Mary Cowdrey, daughter of James and Ann, born September 11, 1726.
Sarah Cowdrey, daughter of James and Ann, born June 25, 1729,
    and died October 2, 1729.
Benjamin Legoe and Jane Taylor married November 4, 1723.
Thomas Armstrong, son of Thomas and Frances, born July 11, 1721.
Frances Armstrong, daughter of Thomas and Frances, born Mar. 13, 1722.
James Armstrong, son of Thomas and Frances, born May 2, 1725.
William Groves and Sarah Dallahide married in January, 1721.
Jemima Groves, daughter of William and Sarah, born March 9, 1723.
Mary Groves, daughter of William and Sarah, born Nov. 2, 1725.
Frances Groves, daughter of William and Sarah, born April 2, 1729.
Sarah Dawney, daughter of John and Lydia, born May 28, 1718.

Page 32

John Dawney, son of John and Lydia, born February 7, 1722, and died in March, 1724.
Ann Dawney, daughter of John and Lydia, born October 9, 1727.
James Preston and Elizabeth Pritcherd married in October, 1713.
James Preston, son of James and Elizabeth, born in 1716, and died in September, 171-.
Elizabeth Preston, daughter of James and Elizabeth, born in March, 1718, and died in April, 1718.
Thomas Preston, son of James and Elizabeth, born Oct. 12, 1717.
James Preston and Averila Norvel married July 17, 1726.
Jane Preston, daughter of James and Averila, born Aug. 25, 1727.
Averila Preston, wife of James, died in December, 1727.

Page 33

Jane Preston, daughter of James and Averila, died in Sepy., 1728.
Nehemiah Armstrong, son of John and Rebeca, born Feb. 25, 1729.
Robert Gudgeon died March 30, 1728.
Josias Midlemore and Frances Bochley married October 9, 1720.
Josias Middlemore, son of Dr. Josias and Frances, born Oct. 21, 1726.
William Davis, son of William and Elizabeth, born February 9, 1727.
Catherine Nelson, daughter of John and Frances, born Dec. 13, 1726.
Rebeca Rhodes, daughter of Richard and Magdelen, born Mar. 20, 1723.
William Rhodes, son of Richard and Magdelen, born in September, 1726.
Benjamin Rhodes, son of Richard and Magdelen, born November 16, 1729, and died November 22, 1729.
William Rhodes, son of Richard and Magdelen, died in Sept., 1729.

Page 34

Lewis Pottee, son of James and Elizabeth Potee, born Oct. 23, 1722.
Catherine Potee, daughter of James and Elizabeth, born Nov. 2, 1725.
James Potee, son of James and Elizabeth, born July 2, 1728.
Elizabeth Gallyhampton daughter of Thomas and Elizabeth, born June 3, 1723.
John Gallyhampton, son of Thomas and Elizabeth, born Aug. 26, 1725.
Catherine Gallyhampton, daughter of Thomas and Elizabeth, born October 6, 1727.
John Badam, son of Richard and Sarah, born March 30, 1724.
Susanna Westwood, daughter of Elisha and Mary, born July 10, 1729.
John Westwood, son of Elisha and Mary, born April 13, 1726.

Abraham Hayes, son of Edmund and Mary, born May 20, 1722.
Jacob Hayes, son of Edmund and Mary, born April 2, 1724.

Page 35

Elizabeth Hayes, daughter of Edmund and Mary, born Feb. 14, 1726.
Mary Hayes, daughter of Edmund and Mary, died January 12, 1704.
Eleanor Hayes, daughter of Edmund and Mary, died May 9, 1719.
James Hayes, son of Edmund and Mary, died December 4, 1724.
Rebecca Puttee, daughter of Lewis and Catherine, born Dec. 9, 1722.
Ann Puttee, daughter of Lewis and Catherine, born October 5, 1727.
John Harris and Dorothy Rogers married in December, 1721.
Elizabeth Harris, daughter of John and Dorothy, born June 22, 1721.
John Harris, son of John and Dorothy, born September 30, 1724.

Mary Maccomus, daughter of Alexander and Elizabeth, born May 8, 1722.
Benjamin and Mary Harris, son and daughter of John and Dorothy, born
    in March, 1727, and both died in the same month.

Page 36

William Crabtree and Mary Pyke married February 17, 1725.
William Crabtree, son of William and Mary, born December 22, 1726.
Elizabeth Crabtree, daughter of William and Mary, born Nov. 5, 1728.
Thomas Bond and Elizabeth Scott married April 13, 1725.
Ann Bond, daughter of Thomas and Elizabeth, born April 13, 1726.

Elizabeth Bond, daughter of Thomas and Elizabeth, born Nov. 2, 1727.
Sarah Walters, daughter of Edeard and Mary, born December 30, 1726.
Elizabeth Walters, daughter of Edward and Mary, born May 5, 1726.
Thomas Walters, son of Edward and Mary, born January 10, 1728.
John Longman, son of Mary Long, now bound to John Bowen, born
    February 21, 1728.
James Richardson, son of Thomas and Sarah Richardson, born
    January 5, 1723.

Page 37

Thomas Richardson, son of Thomas and Seray, born May 16, 1726.
Catherine Bull, daughter of Jacob and Rachel, born Jan, 1, 1718.
John Richardson, son of Thomas and Sarah, born January 17, 1728/9.

Hugh Lowe and Mary Freeman married June 5, 1729.
Charles Beck, son of Matthew and Mary, born June 23, 1729.
Judah Taylor, wife of John Taylor, died in January, 1723.
James York died in December, 1724.
John Taylor and Rachell York, widow, married in April, 1726.
John Taylor, son of John and Rachel, born January 19, 1727.
Henry Taylor, son of John and Rachell, born in March, 1729,
    and died in March, 1729 "being but two days old."
Nicholas Bowles and Rachel Norris married January 21, 1728.
Rebecca Norris, daughter of John and Ann, born Sept. 15, 1729.

Page 38

Rebecca Grover, wife of George Grover Sr., died in May, 1727.
George Grover Sr. and Magdelen Kelley married in July, 1727.
Sarah Grover, daughter of George and Nagdalen, born in September,
    1728, and died the same month.
Catherine Dewson died in March, 1728.
Alexander Maccomus and Hannah Wittacre, spinster, married
    August 23, 1728.
John Powell and Philis Temple married in September, 1725.
John Hutchings and Elizabeth Wright married May 9, 1726.
Elizabeth Hutchings, daughter of John and Elizabeth, born July 22,
    1727, and died March 25, 1728/29.
John Hutchings, son of John and Elizabeth, born March 1, 1729/30.
Solomon Maccomus, son of William and Hannah, born Sept. 21, 1729.

Page 39

Salathiel Galloway, son of William and Catherine, born Jan. 3, 1730/1.
Dennis Dulany, son of Thomas and Sarah, born May 28, 1731.
Isaac Hitchcock, son of Isaac Hitchcock and Elizabeth Ward, born
    August 14, 1730.
Mary Hill, daughter of William and Martha, born August 13, 1728.
Richard Hill, son of William and Martha, born May 22, 1732.
James Cowdray died December 26, 1728.
Thomas Dawney and Ann Cowdrey married in 1730.
Frances Dawney, daughter of Thomas and Ann, born Feb. 21, 1730.
Mary Dawney, daughter of John and Lidanus, born Oct. 12, 1732.
Benjamin Gunnery, son of Spry Godfrey Gunnery and Mary his wife,
    born March 3, 1732, and died March 9, 1732.
Jacob Jackson and Frances Dallahide married October 4, 1731.

Page 40

Ann Jackson, daughter of Jacob and Frances, born March 4, 1732.
William Talbott and Mary Roberts married January 30, 1729.
Thomas Pycraft and the widow Sarah Preston married Feb. 5, 1731.
Jane Watson, wife of John, died December 23, 1732/33.
John Watson and Mary Chennerworth, spinster, married May 24, 1733.
John Chennerworth and Mary Smith married November 26, 1730/31.
William Chennerworth, son of John and Mary, born January 8, 1732.
William Noble and Ann Durbin married February 21, 1731.
Elizabeth James, wife of Michael, died August 11, 1732.
Hannah Maccomus, daughter of Alexander and Hannah, born Mar. 25, 1730.
George Pickett, son of Heathcott and Mary, born October 26, 1728.

Page 41

William Pickett, son of Heathcott and Mary, born November 7, 1730.
Mary Bond, wife of William, died October 17, 1732.
William West, living at William Bonds, died March 7, 17--.
Ulick Buck and Mary Leekings married May 14, 1732.
Henry Mitcherll Arnold, servant of Ulick Buck, died Dec. 21, 1732.
Mary Leekings, daughter of Elizabeth Leekings, born May 6, 1729.
Aquila Maccomus, son of Alexander and Hannah, born May 15, 1731.
Nicholas Day Jr., son of Nicholas, died June 18, 1733.
Joseph Ellidge and Mary Rhodes, spinster, daughter of Richard and
    Magdelen, married September 4, 1733.
Philliszana Maxwell, daughter of James Maxwell and Mary his wife,
    he being the eldest son of Coll. James Maxwell, deceased,
    was born March 3, 1723.
Mary Maxwell, daughter of James and Mary, born April 5, 1724.
Elizabeth Maxwell, daughter of James and Mary, born June 3, 1727.

Page 42

Elener Maxwell, daughter of James and Mary, born February 12, 1729.
John Hammond Dorsey and Frances Watkins married February 16, 1743.
John Hammond Dorsey, son of John Hammond Dorsey and Frances Watkins,
    was born February 12, 1744.
John Hammond Dorsey Jr. died May 1, 1748.
Stephen Dorsey, son of John and Frances, born November 29, 1747.

Elizabeth Chenowith, daughter of Thomas and Rachel, born Apr.8, 1768.
Ruxton Chenoweth, son of Thomas and Rachel, born December 12, 1769.
Joseph Smith and Deborah Onion married May 16, 1757, by the Reverend
    Mr. Gilbert Terrent (Lerrent) of Philadelphia.
Ann Price, daughter of William and Mary, born June 25, 1771.
Nicholas Day and Elizabeth Cox married July 14, 1707.
Nicholas Day, son of Nicholas and Elizabeth, born Feb. 25, 1710/11.
Mary Day, daughter of Nicholas and Elizabeth, born Oct. 23, 1713.
John Day, son of Nicholas and Elizabeth, born September 6, 1716.

Page 43

Elizabeth Day, daughter of Nicholas and Elizabeth, born Mar.17, 1719.
Sarah Day, daughter of Nicholas and Elizabeth, born January 29, 1720.
Thomas Day, son of Nicholas and Elizabeth, born July 5, 1723.
Laban Day, son of Nicholas and Elizabeth, born April 2, 1726.
Hanner Day, daughter of Nicholas and Elizabeth, born Dec. 19, 1728.
Samuel Day, son of Nicholas and Elizabeth, born March 1, 1730.
Nicholas Day, son of Nicholas and Elizabeth, died June 18, 1733.
Nicholas Day, second son of Nicholas and Elizabeth, born April 23,
    1734, and died August, 1735.
Betteyer Day, daughter of Nicholas and Elizabeth, born Nov. 21, 1736.
Ruth Samson, daughter of Isaac and Mary, born November 24, 1748.

Page 44

Richard Samson, son of Isaac and Mary, born November 1, 1750.
Mary Allen, wife of James, died August 1, 1755.
Ann Ricketts, daughter of Samuel and Hannah, born September 1, 1754
    and died March 20, 1759.
Edward Ricketts, son of Samuel and Hannah, born March 6, 1756.
Catharine Ricketts, daughter of Samuel and Hannah, born Nov. 6, 1758.
William Slade and Elizabeth Dulany married August 13, 1741.
Margrett Slade, daughter of William and Elizabeth, born Sep. 18, 1742.
Mary Presbury, daughter of Thomas and Ann, born October 18, 1751.
Joshua Buck, son of Jno. and Susannah, born April 5, 1756.
Jno. Desney, son of William and Cathrine, born October, 1756.
Margret Desney, daughter of William and Cathrine, born Mar. 5, 1758.

Ann Woolling, daughter of Major and Frances, born May 7, 1757.
John Woolling, son of Major and Frances, born November 4, 1758.

Page 45

Richard Dunn and Isabellah Dunahue married March 6, 1753.
John Dunn, son of Richard and Isabellah, born March 15, 1755.
William Dunn, son of Richard and Isabellah, born Oct. 21, 1758.
Mary Gardner, daughter of Jno. and Mary, born November 19, 1759.
Mary Gardner, wife of John, died December 3, 1759.
Jno. Kimbrin, son of Mary Ann Kimbrin, born in December, 1759,
    and died the same month.
Susannah Buck, daughter of John and Susannah, born Oct. 31, 1758.
Margrett Cartie, daughter of Brian and Frances, born Jan. 12, 1760.
Henry Wetherall and Mary Ann Osborn married September 25, 1753.
Sarah Wetherall, daughter of Henry and Mary Ann, born Dec. 31, 1754.

Mary Wetherall, daughter of Henry and Mary Ann, born Dec. 5, 1756.
James Wetherall, son of Henry and Mary Ann, born Feb. 15,1759.
Henry Wetherall, son of Henry and Mary Ann, born Jan. 4, 1761.
Cathrine Greer, daughter of Jno. and Elizabeth, born Dec. 26, 1764.

Page 46

Moses Greer, son of Jno. and Elizabeth, born June 21, 1766.
Aquila Greer, son of Jno. and Elizabeth, born July 10, 1768.
Jno. Greer Jr., son of Jno. and Elizabeth, born June 21, 1770.
Salam Poacock, son of Daniel Jr. and Sarah, born March 26, 1753.
Daniel Poacock, son of Daniel and Sarah, born March 24, 1755.
Mary Poacock, daughter of Daniel and Sarah, born April 11, 1757.
James Poacock, son of Daniel and Sarah, born March 15, 1759.
Mary Hunn, daughter of Francis and Margret, born in October, 1756.
Francis Kiteley, son of Francis and Martha, born January 11, 1758.
Sarah Nichols, daughter of James and Drucilla, born Aug. 15, 17--.
William Debruler and Dianah Greenfield married March 23, 1743.
Cordelia Debruler, daughter of William and Dianah, born March 29,
    1744 and died November 7, 1744.
George Debruler, son of William and Dianah, born Dec. 3, 1746.
Cordelia Debruler, second daughter of William and Dianah, born
    November 20, 1748.

Page 47

William Debruler, son of William and Dianah, born Feb. 14, 1750.
Ufaan Debruler, daughter of William and Dianah, born August 26, 1752 and died February 6, 1756.
James Debruler being the first born and Mecajah Debruler they being twins and sons of William and Dianah born Dec. 30, 1755.
Ufaan Debruler, second daughter of that name of William and Dianah, born April 27, 1759.
Josiah Hitchcock and Susannah Garland married July 10, 1755.
Randele Hitchcock, son of Josiah and Susannah, born Aug. 19, 1756.
Henry Hitchcock, son of Josiah and Susannah, born March 22, 1758.
Ann Hitchcock, daughter of Josiah and Susannah, born June 18, 1760.
William Hitchcock, son of Josiah and Susannah, born Oct. 18, 1762.
Jesse Hitchcock, son of Josiah and Susannah, born April 27, 1765, and died in September, 1766.
Mary Tredwell, daughter of Richard Tredwell and Maple Stephenson, his wife, born November 10, 1759.
Leviner Tunis, daughter of Jno. Tunis and Phebe, born Mar. 5, 1760.
Hannah Presbury, daughter of Thomas and Ann, born Sunday, July 15, 1759.

Page 48

Mary Keeth, daughter of David and Sarah, born November 14, 1759.
Benjamin Legoe died in June, 1759.
James Murphey and Phebe Skeerer married September 17, 1753.
Margaret Murphey, daughter of James and Phebe, born Aug. 19, 1756.
Elizabeth Murphey, daughter of James and Phebe, born Apr. 3, 1759.
Martha Tunis, daughter of Jno. and Martha, born May 22, 1760.
Joseph Presbury, son of Joseph and Sarah, born Sept. 5, 1758.
William Dives, son of Francis and Mary, born Feb. 18, 1758.
Sarah Dives, wife of Christopher, died July 25, 1760.
Francis Debruler, son of Benjamin and Semelia, born Oct. 6, 1759.
Thomas Pycraft Presbury, son of Joseph and Sarah, born May 7, 1761.
Elizabeth Robertson, daughter of Edward and Margret, died in May, 1760.
Cassandria Hill, daughter of Elizabeth Hill, born in May, 1760.
Thomas Hill, son of Elizabeth Hill, born September 1, 1754.

Page 49

James Preston Jr. and Mary Bond married May 11, 1756.
Benjamin Preston, son of James and Mary, born Oct. 15, 1758.
Mary Preston, wife of James, died July 11, 1759.
William Williamson, son of George ahd Ketura, born Sept. 28, 1759.
Richard Grimes died in September, 1760.
John Tunis died in December, 1760.
Susannah Woolling, daughter of Major and Frances, born in Oct., 1760.
Cathrine Bain, daughter of Jno. and Mary, born January 7, 1761.
Billingsley Roberts and Bettey Manen married March 2, 1758.
John Roberts, son of Billingsley and Bettey, born Nov. 20, 1759.
Mary Ann Roberts, daughter of Billingsely and Bettey, born
            March 18, 1760.
Mary Sweeting, daughter of Rebecca Sweeting, vorn July 8, 1759.
Isaac Talbee, son of Samuel and Elizabeth, born June 10, 1761.
Thomas Bayley Bayley Jr. and Rachel Towson married Dec. 26, 1758.

Page 50

William Bayley, son of Thomas and Rachel, born Sept. 10, 1759.
Ruth Bayley, daughter of Thomas and Rachel, born March 16, 1761.
Rachel Bayley, daughter of Thomas and Rachel, born Jan. 10, 1763.
Thomas Bayley, son of Thomas and Rachel, born November 7, 1764.
Gilbert Jones, son of William and Elizabeth, born May 13, 1751.
Elizabeth Jones, daughter of William and Elizabeth, born Jan. 17,1754.
Magdelin Jones, daughter of William and Elizabeth, born Apr. 7, 1756.
William Jones, son of William and Elizabeth, born June 6, 1758.
Jacob Jones, son of William and Elizabeth, born June 17, 1760.
Isaac Jones, son of William and Elizabeth, born June 1, 1762.
Cassandra Jones, daughter of William and Elizabeth, born Aug.21,1765.
Stephen Jones, son of William and Elizabeth, born October 28, 1767.
Benjamin George Jones, son of William and Elizabeth, born Nov.10,1769.
William York, son of George and Catherine, born May 4, 1767.
Nicholas York, son of George and Catherine, born April 19, 1769.
Sarah Day, daughter of Jno. Day, son of Edward, and Sarah, his
            wife, was born January 20, 1768.
Alice Legoe, daughter of Spencer and Elizabeth, born June 15, 1769.

Page 51

William Demmett, son of William Demmett and Dorothy Swan, born (although the record shows married) December 14, 1765.

Burch Swan Demmett, son of William and Dorothy, born Sep. 29, 1769.

William Demmett, son of William and Dorothy, born March 25, 1771.

Benjamin Rumsey of Cecil County, Attorney at Law, married to Mary Hall, daughter of Coll. John Hall of Baltimore County, on March 24th,-----.

Hannah Rumsey, daughter of Benjamin and Mary his wife, daughter of Coll. John Hall, born March 31, 1770.

Benjamin Rumsey Jr., son of Benjamin Rumsey, Attorney at Law, and Mary, daughter of Col. John Hall of Baltimore County, was born Friday morning January 27, 1775, about 2 o'clock in the morning.

John Rumsey, son of Benjamin Rumsey and Mary his wife, daughter of Col. John Hall, was born May 3, 1780.

Samuel Scott and Sarah Benton married in June, 1771.

Jno. Scott, son of Samuel and Sarah, born August 14, 1772.

Margaret Ward Poulson born April 6, 1768, being the daughter of Ann Poulson.

Ann Turner, daughter of Thomas and Mary, born April 3, 1773.

Thomas Turner, son of Thomas and Mary, born November 4, 1776.

Joseph Turner, son of Thomas and Mary, born July 26, 1778.

Elizabeth Turner, daughter of Thomas and Mary, born August 3, 1780.

Page 52

Mary Chenoweth, daughter of Thomas and Rachel, born Sept. 8, 1772.

Joshua Merriken, Clerk of Register, 1719.

James Scott, son of Daniel Scott Jr. and Elizabeth, born May 6, 1720.

James Chapman, son of John and Ann, born February 10, 1719.

Sarah Whaylon, daughter of Patrick and Catorine, born Feb. 13, 1720.

James and Charles Ishum, two twins sons of James and Elizabeth, born June 25, 1720.

Henry Armstrong, son of John and Rebeckah, born June 24, 1720.

William York, son of James and Rachell, born August 8, 1720.

Page 53

John Taylor, and Judith his wife, had a son born named Abraham in August, 1720.

James Meed, son of Edward and Darcas, born February 29, 1719.

James Dawney, son of John and Liddiah, born June 20, 1720.
Benjamin Cadle, son of Zachariah and Jane, born Sept. 25, 1720.
Ann Barton, daughter of Thomas and Abigall, born Oct. 28, 1720.
Elizabeth Bond, daughter of William and Mary, born Feb. 16, 1720/1.
Daniel Mecomus, son of William and Hannah, born Feb. 8, 1720/1.
Joseph Ward, son of Joseph and Bridgett, born January 22, 1720/1.
Sarah Day, daughter of Nicholas and Elizabeth, born Jan. 29, 1720/1.
Margrett Hinton, daughter of Mary Hinton, born in August, 1719.
Elizabeth Norris, daughter of Benjamin and Sarah, born Nov. 28, 1720.

Page 54

Hanah Nellson, daughter of John and Frances, born Aug. 10, 1720.
Thomas Ramsey, son of Thomas and Rachell, born Feb. 23, 1720.
John Bull, son of Jacob and Rachell Bull, born November 1, 1719.
Rachell Smithson, daughter of Thomas and Ann, born Oct. 9, 1706.
Rebeckah Smithson, daughter of Thomas and Ann, born April 2, 1707.
Ellinor Smithson, daughter of Thomas and Ann, born May 24, 1704.
Elizabeth Smithson, daughter of Thomas and Ann, born Oct. 10, 1710.
Thomas Smithson, son of Thomas and Ann, born January 30, 1712.
Daniell Smithson, son of Thomas and Ann, born January 2, 1714.
Sarah Smithson, daughter of Thomas and Ann, born January 12, 1718.
Averilla Smithson, daughter of Thomas and Ann, born Dec. 28, 172--.

Page 55

Thomas Amoss, son of William and Ann, born November 23, 1713.
Elizabeth Amoss, daughter of William and Ann, born Oct. 18, 1715.
William Amoss, son of William and Ann, born March 3, 1718.
James Amoss, son of William and Ann, born February 18, 1721.
Thomas Rhodes, son of Richard and Mary, born March 15, 1717/18.
John Rhodes, son of Richard and Mary, born March 28, 1720.
Mary Potee, daughter of James and Elizabeth, born Oct. 19, 1720.
Joshua Bond, son of Thomas and Ann, born October 8, 1718.
Ann Bond, daughter of Thomas and Ann, born May 29, 1720.
Elizabeth Bond, daughter of William and Mary, born Feb. 6, 1719.
Elizabeth Poteete, daughter of John and Elizabeth, born June 20, 1717.
Sarah Preston, daughter of James and Sarah, born December 3, 1711.

Page 56

James Preston, son of James and Sarah, born March 15, 1713.
Daniel Preston, son of James and Sarah, born October 10, 1715.
Elizabeth Preston, daughter of James and Sarah, born Dec. 19, 1720.
Sarah Harper, daughter of John and Jane, born August 3, 1711.
Leana Melton, daughter of Sarah Melton base born and left with
    John Harper. She was born April 10, 1720.
Thomas Crabtree, son of William and Jane, born Oct. 12, 1707.
Grace Crabtree, daughter of William and Jane, born May 29, 1711.
Ann Crabtree, daughter of William and Jane, born Jan. 15, 1714.
James Crabtree, son of William and Jane, born February 20, 1716.
John Crabtree, son of William and Jane, born September 5, 1718.
Elizabeth Crabtree, daughter of William and Jane, born Dec. 20, 1720.
John Hays, son of Edmond and Mary, born April 1, 1708.

Page 57

Edmond Hays, son of Edmond Hays and Mary, born Sept. 9, 1710.
Thomas Hays, son of Edmond and Mary, born October 16, 1712.
Isaack Hays, son of Edmond and Mary, born October 13, 1714.
William Hays, son of Edmond and Mary, born August 26, 1715.
Mary Hays, daughter of Edmond and Mary, born October 2, 1718.
John Miles, son of Thomas and Catherine, born Feb. 9, 1717/18.
Thomas Miles, son of Thomas and Catherine, born August 18, 1719.
Elizabeth Roberson, daughter of Richard and Elizabeth, born
    December 12, 1718.
William Roberson, son of Richard and Elizabeth, born Mar. 7, 1720.
Elizabeth Mecomus, daughter of William and Hanah, born Nov. 4, 1718.

Page 58

Sarah Hanson, daughter of Benjamin and Sarah, born Mar. 29, 1718.
John Hanson, son of Benjamin and Sarah, born November 14, 1720.
Abell Roberson, son of Richard and Elizabeth, born November 15,
    1715, and died in May, 1716.
Charles Roberson, son of Richard and Elizabeth, born March 10,
    1717/18, and died within a month.
Rodea Elliott, daughter of John and Sarah, born March 20, 1720/21.
Comfort Cole, daughter of Elizabeth Cole, born November 8, 1720.

Page 58

Israell Standafar, son of John and Margrett, born Sept. 4, 1720.
John Roberson, son of Jacob and Mary, born May 2, 1715.
Mary Roberson, daughter of Jacob and Mary, born August, 1717.
George Chamberlaine, son of Thomas and Mary, born Dec. 27, 1720.
Benjamin Deson, son of William and Mary, born September, 1719.

Page 59

Edmond Deson, son of William and Mary, born March 31, 1721.
Mary Norrington, daughter of Jno. and Elizabeth, born March, 1711.
Elizabeth Norrington, daughter of Jno. and Elizabeth, born Apr.,1714.
Francis Norington, son of Jno. and Elizabeth, born in June, 1718.
Joseph Taylor, son of Abraham and Dinah, born October 19, 1720.
Samuell Watkins, son of Samuell and Mary, born Nov. 15, 1717.
William Watkins, son of Samuell and Mary, born Dec. 10, 1720.
Martha Watkins, daughter of Samuell and Mary, botn Jan. 15, 1715.
Lewis Demoss, son of Lewis and Catherine, born November 1, 1715.
William Demoss, son of Lewis and Catherine, born Sept. 22, 1716.
Jno. Demoss, son of Lewis and Catherine, born August 9, 1718.
Peter Demoss, son of Lewis and Catherine, born Oct. 25, 1719.

Page 60

Tabitha Johnson, daughter of Thomas and Mary, born Sept. 11, 1720.
Mary Roberson, daughter of William and Elizabeth, born Feb. 1, 1718/9.
Elizabeth Low, daughter of William and Sarah, born June 3, 1721.
John Jones, son of Benjamin and Elizabeth, born April 17, 1721.
Hugh Merriken, son of Joshua and Diana, was born September 17, 1721 "aboute the hour 9 or ten a clock on the Sabbath Day att night."
Peter Miles, son of Thomas and Catherine, born February 28, 1721/2.
Hugh Merriken was baptized the 8th of Aprill in the year of our Lord God Everlasting by Mr. William Tibbs, Minister, and in Gunpowder Church, St. John's Parrish.
John George Bradford, son of William and Elizabeth, was born the 3rd day of September in the yeare of our Lord God 1720 and was baptized Aprill the 8th the yeare aforesaid by the Reverend Mr. William Tibbs. Wm. Bradford, Reg^r.
James Hayes, son of Edmond and Mary, born May 10, 1721.

Page 61

Patrick Whaleland, son of Patrick and Catherine, born Apr. 29, 1722.
Elizabeth Rhodes, daughter of William and Mary, born Aug. 30, 1721.
Elizabeth Elinor Talbot, daughter of Edmund Talbott and Mary, born
    October 30, 1721, and baptized Aprill 8, 1722.
William Dotridge, son of William and Lettice, born Sept. 22, 1721.
William Hougate, son of Jonathan and Elizabeth, born Sept. 16, 1722.
Joseph Rhodous and Ann Polson married in June, 1725.
Sophia Rhodous, daughter of Joseph and Ann, born May 26, 1725.
William Hunter begotten of the daughter of Henry Dunahue was born
    January 29, 1720.
Mary Bradford, daughter of William and Elizabeth, born Sep. 81, 1727.

Page 62

Samuel Baker, son of Samuel and Catherine, born Sept. 19, 1727.
Mary Scott, daughter of Daniel and Elizabeth, born June 16, 1727.
Abraham Tailor, son of Abraham and Dinah, born October 20, 1723.
Isaac Tailor, son of Abraham and Dinah Taylor, born Nov. 25, 1725.
Isaac Bull, son of Jacob and Rachell, born February 3, 1727/8.
Lenitia Sheppard, daughter of William and Margaret, born Oct. 2, 1726.
Hannah Maccomus, daughter of William and Hannah, born April 6, 1723.
Eleanor Maccomus, daughter of William and Hannah, born July 2, 1725.
William Maccomus, son of William and Hannah, born Nov. 24, 1727.
Hannah Presbury, daughter of James and Ann, born August 3, 1726.
Bradford Presbury, son of James and Ann, born October 5, 172-.
Benjamin Amos, son of William and Ann, born February 2, 1724.

Page 63

Joshua Amoss, son of William and Ann, born October 25, 1725.
Mordecai Amoss, son of William and Ann, born February 7, 1727.
Moses Byfoot, son of William and Sarah, born October 12, 1729.
Mary Ward, daughter of Joseph and Bridget, born in July, 1719.
Joseph Ward, son of Joseph and Bridget, born April 1, 1722.
Sarah Ward, daughter of Joseph and Bridget, born September, 1724.
Elizabeth Padget, daughter of James and Mary, born Jan. 6, 1721.
Susanna Padget, daughter of James and Mary, born April 14, 1728.

Agnes Glaron, servant woman of Thomas Hatchman, died in 1726.
Arthur Tayler died at Edward Day's in November, 1728.
Robert Love and Sarah Bond married June 9, 1729.
Thomas Lowe and Thamar Love married in February, 1728/29.

Page 64

Benjamin Greer, son of John and Sarah, born January 6, 1727/28.
Coll. James Maxwell died January 5, 1728.
Thomas Vine, son of Rowland and Elizabeth, born July 11, 1728.
Abraham Wittacre, son of Abraham and Ann, born August 11, 1727.
Hannah Wittacre, daughter of Abraham and Ann, born Mar. 26, 1729.
Thomas Smith, son of Zachary and Margaret, born April 27, 1725.
Zachariag Smith, son of Zachariah and Margaret, born Oct., 1728.
Sarah Byfoot, wife of William, died October 23, 1728.
Edmond Bull, son of Jacob and Rachel, born January 13, 1729/30.
Jemmina Sheppard, daughter of William and Margaret, born Aug. 2, 1729.
William Hicks, son of Nehemiah and Philizanna, born June 14, 1728.
Mary Hicks, daughter of Nehemiah and Philizanna, born Dec. 13, 1726/7.

Page 65

Isaac Hicks, son of Nehemiah and Philizanna, born Jan. 5, 1729/30.
Ann Merrikeen, daughter of Joshua Merrikeen, deceased, and the
        widow Dinah Merrikeen, died May 4, 1730.
Elizabeth Rhodes, daughter of Richard and Magdelen, born July 10,1730.
Ann Hutchings, daughter of John and Elizabeth, born June 7, 1732.
John Stackey of Baltimore County died November 28, 1732.
Sarah Talbott, daughter of William and Mary, born July 7, 1733.
James Talbott, son of William and Mary, born August 20, 1731.
Charles Taylor, son of John and Keziah, born February 4, 1730.
Hannah Taylor, son of John and Keziah, born January 19, 1733/34.
George Armstrong, son of John and Rebekah, born May 5, 1732.
John George Bradford, son of William and Elizabeth, born Sep. 3,1721.

Page 66

Susanna Bradford, daughter of William and Elizabeth, born June 7,1724.
Mary Bradford, second daughter of William and Elizabeth, born
        September 18, 1727.

Martha Bradford, third daughter of William and Elizabeth, born
    April 13, 173-.
Daniel Tredway, son of Thomas and Ann, born November 22, 1724.
Mary Tredway, daughter of Thomas and Ann, born November 8, 1726.
Thomas Tredway, son of Thomas and Ann, born May 20, 1730.
Moses Maccomas, son of William and Hannah, born May 15, 1732.
Edmond Talbott Sr. died November 15, 1731.
Charles Talbott, son of Edmond and Mary, born December 1, 1730.
Anthony Asher, son of Anthony and Susanna, born July 2, 1732.
Joseph Norris, son of Edward and Hannah, born December 5, 1725.
Sarah Norris, daughter of Edward and Hannah, born December 15, 1727.

Page 67

Daniel Norris, son of Edward and Hannah, born December 27, 1728.
Elizabeth Norris, daughter of Edward and Hannah, born March 27, 1732.
John Everit and Rebeca Poteet married October 31, 1728.
Rebecca Everit, daughter of John and Rebecca, born Sept. 29, 1729.
Mary Ellidge, daughter of Joseph and Mary, born June 21, 1734.
James Barton, son of James Barton and Temperence, born October 3,
    1734 and baptized May 18, 1735.
Mordica Durham, son of Samuel and Eliner, born January 1, 1734.
Nathaniel Allen died October 24, 1733.
John Mason and Frances Allen married December 20, 1733.
Ruth Talbott, daughter of Edmond and Mary, born November 16, 1733.
Thomas Talbott, son of Edmond and Mary, born December 8, 1735.
Thomas Amos and Elizabeth Day married December 25, 1735.
Ann Lisby, daughter of Jacob and his wife, born November 3, 1730.
Mary Lisby, daughter of Jacob and his wife, born October 2, 1732.

Page 68

William Caswell, son of Richard and Christian, born Dec. 7, 1726.
Richard Caswell, son of Richard and Christian, born Aug. 3, 1729.
Mary Caswell, daughter of Richard and Christian, born Aug. 1, 1731.
Martin Caswell, son of Richard and Christian, born Feb. 15, 1733.
Hugh Lowe, son of Hugh and Mary, born January 18, 1732/33.
James Barton and Temperance Rollo married October 8, 1730.
Phillis Barton, daughter of James and Temperance, born
    January 5, 1731/32.

William Bond Whitehead, son of Elizabeth Whitehead, born
    March 17, 1732/33.
William Smith, son of Zachariah and Margaret, born July 27, 1732.
Rebecca Smith, daughter of Zachariah and Margaret, born Apr.,1734.
Nicholas Day, son of Nicholas and Elizabeth, born April 23, 1734.
Ann Huggins, daughter of John and Sarah, born October 2, 1725.

Page 69-70

William Huggins, son of John and Sarah, born October 11, 1730.
Daniel Huggins, son of John and Sarah, born August 11, 1733.
Thomas Gadd and Christian Ditto married January 22, 1732.
Margrett Gadd, daughter of Thomas and Christian, born Mar.28, 1731.
Walter Tolley and Mary Garrettson married December 20, 1735.
Elizabeth Tolley, daughter of Walter and Mary, born Nov. 16, 1736.
Isaac Jackson and Mary Hollingsworth married July 17, 1733.
Robert Jackson, son of Isaac and Mary, born August 31, 1735.
Mary Spry Gunrey, daughter of Spry Godfrey Gunrey and Mary his wife,
    born July 21, 1735.
William Amos, son of Thomas and Elizabeth, born December 15, 1736.
John Roberts, son of John and Mary, born June 1, 1708.
Mary Roberts, daughter of John and Mary, born November 24, 1710.
Stephen Roberts, son of John and Mary, born February 24, 171-.
Frances Roberts, daughter of John and Mary, born April 13, 1719.
Lucina Roberts, daughter of John and Mary, born February 18, 1722
    and died October 18, 1723.
Aaron Maccomas, son of William and Hannah, born July 3, 1734.
John Maccomas, son of William and Hannah, born Sept. 15, 1736.
James Richardson, son of Thomas and Sarah, born Jan. 17, 1723.
Thomas Richardson, son of Thomas and Sarah, born May 16, 1726.
John Richardson, son of Thomas and Sarah, born January 15, 1728.
Benjamin Richardson, son of Thomas and Sarah, born Nov. 5, 1730.
Samuel Richardson, son of Thomas and Sarah, born Nov. 2, 1734.
Ann Massey, daughter of Aquila Massey and Sarah, born Feb. 1, 1725.
Mary Massey, daughter of Aquila and Sarah, born March 10, 1727.
Sarah Massey, daughter of Aquila and Sarah, born Feb. 25, 1731.

Page 71

Aquila Massey, son of Aquila and Sarah, born July 27, 1733.
Jonathan Collier Massey, son of Aquila and Sarah, born Apr. 9, 1736.
James Huggins, son of John and Sarah, born July 20, 1736.
Anne Lawson, daughter of John and Frances, born November 9, 1730.
Elizabeth Lawson, daughter of John and Frances, born Sep. 29, 1733.
Mosess Lawson, son of John and Frances, born May 10, 1736.
Sarah Haulaway, daughter of John and Elizabeth, born Nov. 23, 1725.
Elizabeth Haulaway, daughter of John and Elizabeth, born Nov. 26, 1727.
Anne Haulaway, daughter of John and Elizabeth, born Dec. 28, 1729.
Isabella Haulaway, daughter of John and Elizabeth, born Dec. 22, 1731.
Mary Haulaway, daughter of John and Elizabeth, born Nov. 11, 1733.
John Haulaway, son of John and Elizabeth, born September 14, 1735.
Elizabeth Gott, daughter of Robert and Mary, born Dec. 13, 1725.
Mary Gott, daughter of Robert and Mary, born July 19, 1729.
Sarah Gott, daughter of Robert and Mary, born February 19, 1732.

Page 72

Richard Gott, son of Robert and Mary, born June 20, 1734.
Thomas James, son of William and Frances, born August 21, 1724.
Mary James, daughter of William and Frances, born March 5, 1727.
Elizabeth James, daughter of William and Frances, born May 24, 1730.
Sarah James, daughter of William and Frances, born February 13, 1733.
Daniell Darby, son of John and Alice, born August 4, 1734.
James Darby, son of John and Alice, born January 28, 1736.
John Fuller and Ruth Danby married December 10, 1736.
Nehemiah Hicks and Phillisana Hitchcock married June 12, 1725.
Ann Low, daughter of William and Sarah, born February 5, 1735.
Peckett Jones, son of Benjamin and Elizabeth, born June 24, 1721.
Elizabeth Jones, daughter of Benjamin and Elizabeth, born Aug. 31, 1723.
Benjamin Jones, son of Benjamin and Anne, born December 7, 1735,
    "and Anne was born September 21, 1736."
William Talbott, son of William and Mary, born February 10, 1735.

Page 73

Andrew Scott and Anne Smith married April 28, 1737.
William Ingram and Phebe Whitehead married November 6, 1731.
Frances Whitehead Ingram, daughter of William and Phebe, born
    January 3, 1732.

William Ingram, son of William and Phebe, born May 6, 1734.
Eleven Ingram, son of William and Phebe, born November 3, 1735.
Michael James and Constant Sheppard married August 26, 1736.
Michael James, son of Michael and Constant, born April 3, 1737.
Mary Sheppard, daughter of Constant Sheppard, born May 20, 1732.
Sollomon Sheppard, son of Constant Sheppard, born April 20, 1735.
Hannah Norris, daughter of Edward and Hannah, born June 23, 1735.
Elizabeth Norris, daughter of Edward and Hannah, born Apr. 29, 1736.
Samuel Standeford and Anne Rollo married November 30, 1732.

Page 74

Archibald Standeford, son of Samuel and Anne, born May 11, 1733.
Bethiah Standeford, daughter of Samuel and Anne, born Dec. 30, 1735.
George Summons and Jemima Standeford married December 7, 1736.
William Monk and Elizabeth Fuller married December 3, 1736.
William Hitchcock Jr. and Susannah Slade married Nov. 8, 1729.
Isaac Hitchcock, son of William and Susannah, born Nov. 6, 1731.
William Hitchcock, son of William and Susannah, born Dec., 1733,
    and died the same year.
William Hitchcock, second son of William and Susannah, born
    July 26, 1735.
William Andrew and Mary Bond married February 14, 1732.
Joseph Wright Jr. and Jane Wooden married January 8, 1740.
Ann Wright, daughter of said Joseph and Jane, born Nov. 2, 1741.

Page 75

Deborah Smith, wife of Joseph, died September 22, 1767.
Thomas Elliott and Elizabeth Barton married November, 1736.
Thomas Gadd and Christian Ditto married January 21, 1733.
Margrett Gadd, daughter of Thomas and Christian, born Mar. 28, 1734.
John Shoebridge and Mary Morris married September 28, 1732.
John Hicks, son of Nehemiah and Phillissane, born April 8, 1740.
Jacob Hicks, son of Nehemiah and Philliszane, born June 25, 1742.
Joseph Elledge and Mary Rhoades married September 4, 1733.
Abraham Ellidge, son of Joseph and Mary, born February 17, 1736.
Thomas Palmer and Jude Elliott married December 28, 1732.
William Robertson and Alie Thomson married December 26, 1735.

Page 76

Thomas Barton and Elizabeth Ward married February 24, 1733.
Joshua Barton, son of Thomas and Elizabeth, born Nov. 23, 1734.
William York and Elizabeth Debruler married January 1, 1733.
Thomas Norris Jr. and Elizabeth Maccomas married Dec. 26, 1736.
John Norris, son of Thomas and Elizabeth, born Dec. 11, 1737.
Rowland Vine and Sarah_____ married in the year 1727.
Sarah Vine, daughter of Rowland and Sarah, born November 8, 1730
    and died the same year.
Mary Vine, second daughter of Rowland and Sarah, born March 19,
    1732, and died the same year.
John Vine, son of Rowland and Sarah, born May 22, 1733, and died
    the same year.
Sarah Vine, daughter of Rowland and Sarah, born June 11, 1734.

Page 77

John Vine, second son of Rowland and Sarah, born in the year 1735.
James Demmett and Barbaro Broad married March 27, 1723.
Mary Demmett, daughter of James and Barbarie, born Dec. 29, 1734.
Thomas Wright and Christian Enloes married May 5, 1735.
Bloys Wright, son of Thomas and Christian, born November 17, 1735.
Elizabeth Thomas, daughter of David and Elizabeth, born Sep.14,1736.
William Armstrong and Elizabeth Sheppard married in 1735.
Temperance Armstrong, daughter of William and Elizabeth, born
    December 21, 1736.
William Detter and Jane Quine married October 6, 1736.
William Demmitt and Cathrene Wardin Bull married May 13, 1736.
James Demmit, son of William and Cathrine, born March 30, 1737.

Page 78

Humphry Wells Stokes, son of John and Susannah, married Mary Knight,
    daughter of Stephen and Sarah, on December 31, 1730.
William Demmitt, son of William Jr. and Catherine, born Jan.16,1740.
John Demmitt, son of William Jr. and Catherine, born Feb. 7, 1742.
John Dorney, son of James Dorney and Martha Woodland, was married
    December 19, 1771.

Josias Middlemore, son of Josias and Frances, born Oct. 1, 1726.
Edward Middlemore, son of Josias and Frances, born Mar. 23, 1731.
Francis Middlemore, son of Josias and Frances, born Mar. 31, 1733.
David Preston, son of James and Elizabeth, born May 29, 1731.
Luke Preston, son of said Thomas and Elizabeth, born Aug. 7, 1733.
Elizabeth Debruler, daughter of Benjamin and Cemelia, born
    December 14, 1756.
Sabrah York, daughter of George and Catharine, born Dec. 12, 1771.
John Hatten and Sarah Chienie married May 17, 1733.
Thomas Hatten, son of John and Sarah, born October 11, 1735.

Page 79

William Wright, son of William and Elizabeth, born Dec. 3, 1733.
Abraham Wright, son of William and Elizabeth, born Feb. 16, 1735.
Mary Arsmtrong, daughter of John and Rebecca, born Feb. 26, 1735.
John Standeford and Easther Fuller married January 1, 1726.
John Standeford, son of John and Easther, born Nov. 4, 1734.
Edward Day, son of Edward and Avarila, born Feb. 20, 1729.
Michael Day, son of Edward and Avarila, born January 19, 1732.
Avarila Day, second daughter of Edward and Avarila, born July 16,1735.
Jane Day, daughter of Edward and Avarila, born January 30, 1737.
Elizabeth Day, daughter of Edward and Avarila, born April 13, 1742.
Anna Day, daughter of Edward and Avarila, born November 15, 1744.

Page 80

Elizabeth Day, daughter of Edward and Avarrilla, died in Nov., 1746.
Avarilla Bevens, daughter of Joseph and Rebecca, born Nov. 11, 1725.
Phillis Bevens, daughter of Joseph and Rebecca, born March 5, 1731.
Skelton Standeford, son of John and Easther, born August 31, 1734.
William Standeford, son of John and Easther, born Feb. 13, 1736.
Jacob Rockhold, son of John and Elizabeth, born August 27, 1740.
John Rockhold, son of John and Elizabeth, born Feb. 28, 1742.
Mary Rockhold, daughter of John and Elizabeth, born March 1, 1745.
Charles Rockhold, son of John and Elizabeth, born June 17, 1749.
Thomas Rockhold, son of John and Elizabeth, born March 12, 1756.
Elizabeth Rockhold, daughter of John and Elizabeth, born Aug.31,1758.

William Jackson and Mary Griffin married November 12, 1730.
Elizabeth Jackson, daughter of William and Mary, born Feb. 27, 1731.
Mary Jackson, daughter of William and Mary, born Feb. 20, 1732.
Susanah Copland, daughter of John and Mary, born in the year 1731.

Page 81

William Copland, son of John and Mary, born February 7, 1732.
John Copland, son of John and Mary, born February 10, 1735.
Abraham Brusbanks, son of Edward "Sprusbanks" and Jane his wife, born January 5, 1719.
Edward Brusbanks, son of Edward and Jane, born Sept. 27, 1721.
Benjamin Brusbanks, son of Edward and Jane, born Jan. 11, 1722.
Francis Brusbanks, son of Edward and Jane, born Dec. 4, 1725.
Anne Cannock Brusbanks, daughter of Edward and Jane, born Aug. 5, 1733.
Jane Brusbanks, daughter of Edward and Jane, born June 7, 1735.
William Gadd and Mary Standeford married May 29, 1734.
Absolem Gadd, son of William and Mary, born May 9, 1735.
John Dulany, son of Thomas and Sarah, born February 11, 1733.

Page 82

John Bayley died November 6, 1761.
William Bayley, son of John and Ann, born January 28, 1762.
John Jones and Hannah Woolley married December, 1732.
John Jones, son of John and Hannah, born April 9, 1737.
Robert Cutchin and Winiford Brewenton married April 20, 1731.
Beging Cutchin, son of Robert and Weniford, born Jan. 22, 1732.
Greenberrey Cutchin, son of Robert and Weniford, born April 9, 1734, and died the same year in October.
Mary Cutchin, daughter of Robert and Weniford, born Oct. 14, 1735.
Providence Cutchin, daughter of Robert and Weniford, born Feb. 16, 1736.
Daniel Durham, son of Samuel and Elinor, born Jan. 26, 1736.
John Bond and Esabella Robertson married February 21, 1733.
Elizabeth Bond, daughter of John and Esabella, born Dec. 27, 1735.

Page 83

Elizabeth Elliott, daughter of Margaret Elliott, born March, 1756.
Elizabeth Wheatley, daughter of William and Margaret, born Oct., 1760.

Sarah Norris, daughter of Benjamin and Sarah, born May 29, 1725.
Hannah Norris, daughter of Benjamin and Sarah, born July 16, 1727.
Susannah Norris, daughter of Benjamin and Sarah, born Apr. 21, 1730.
Benjamin Norris, son of Benjamin and Sarah, born October 20, 1732.
Joseph Norris, son of Benjamin and Sarah, born January 14, 173-.
William Mitchell and Elizabeth Elliott married Sept. 30, 1736.
Mary Baker, daughter of Samuel and Cathrene, born Oct. 22, 1730.
Bethiah Baker, daughter of Samuel and Cathrene, born Nov. 2, 1732.
Hannah Baker, daughter of Samuel and Cathrene, born March 26, 1734.
John Baker, son of Samuel Cathrene, born October 10, 1736.

Page 84

Thomas Burk and Sarah Sicklemore married April 14, 1737.
Roger Cannan and Anne Gibson married November 18, 1736.
Mary Cannan, daughter of Roger and Anne, born March 18, 1737.
Roger Roberts and Rebecca Crawford married November 2, 1752.
Elizabeth Roberts, daughter of Roger and Rebecca, born Nov. 8, 1753.
Rachael Roberts, daughter of Roger and Rebecca, born May 14, 1755.
Cathrene Warden Bull, daughter of Jacob and Rachell, born Jan.1,1717.
John Bull, son of Jacob and Rachell, born November 1, 1719.
Sarah Bull, daughter of Jacob and Rachell, born January 14, 1721.
Abraham Bull, son of Jacob and Rachell, born January 6, 1723.
Samuel Bull, son of Jacob and Rachell, born December 29, 1725.
Isaac Bull, son of Jacob and Rachell, born January 13, 1729.

Page 85

Jacob Bull, son of Jacob and Rachell, born March 8, 1731.
William Bull, son of Jacob and Rachell, born February 28, 1734.
Rachell Bull, daughter of Jacob and Rachell, born Feb. 28, 1736
   "about seven of the clock in the morning."
Sarah Goldsmith, daughter of Thomas and Lilly, born Mar. 17, 1749.
Ann Goldsmith, daughter of Thomas and Lilly, born August 21, 1751.
William Copeland Goldsmith, son of Thomas and Lilly, born Oct.7,1753.
Thomas Goldsmith, son of Thomas and Lilly, born September 16, 1760.
Stephen Mathews Whealand, son of Ann Whealand and Stephen White
   "as she says was born September 17, 1749."

Peter Fewgate, son of James and Anne, born May 1, 1726.
Edward Fewgate, son of James and Anne, born Sept. 14, 1731.
John Fewgate, son of James and Anne, born March 15, 1732.

Page 86

Easther Fewgate, daughter of James and Anne, born March 15, 1732.
Anne Fewgate, daughter of James and Anne, born April 23, 1735.
William Jones, son of Mary Jones, born March 27, 1735.
Sarah Jones, daughter of Mary Jones, born November 29, 1728.
William Roe and Mary Jones married January 15, 1730.
Sarah Roe, daughter of William and Mary, born February 22, 1731.
Anne Roe, daughter of William and Mary, born March 2, 1733.
William Roe, son of William and Mary, born September 5, 1736.
Edward Phillips and Mary Ledcalf married January 1, 1736.
Elizabeth Norris, daughter of Joseph and Mary, born Dec. 30, 1735.
John Norris, son of Joseph and Mary, born September 10, 1737.
Rebecca Hix, daughter of Nehemiah and Phillis, born April 4, 1731.

Page 87

Elizabeth Hix, daughter of Nehemiah and Phillis, born Nov. 20, 1733.
Nehemiah Hix, son of Nehemiah and Phillis, born September 30, 1735.
Phillisania Hix, daughter of Nehemiah and Phillis, born May 23, 1737.
Francis Ardy and Margertt Mitchell married January 1, 1733.
William Ardy, son of Francis and Margertt, born May 25, 1735.
Thomas Ardy, son of Francis and Margertt, born September 22, 1737,
    and died the same year.
Elizabeth Nearn, daughter of Robert and Anne, born July 18, 1726.
Anne Nearn, daughter of Robert and Anne, born July 4, 1729.
Benjamin Nearn, son of Robert and Anne, born December 22, 1732.
John Nearn, son of Robert and Anne, born November 14, 1736.
Thomas Hallam and Elizabeth Deaton married September 10, 1733.

Page 88

John Hallam, son of Thomas and Elizabeth, born June 1, 1734.
William Sheppard, son of William and Margrett, born March 24, 1736.
John Tuder, son of Joseph and Elizabeth, born September 15, 1756.

Parmelia Nixson, daughter of Thomas and Sarah, born August 1, 1759.
John Bayley, son of John and Ann, born September 25, 1760.
Robert Robison, son of William and Alice, born May 13, 1737.
Lucretia Nicholas, daughter of James and Drucilla, born Sep. 25, 1760.
Mary Nichols died in the month of--------1760.
Jno. Chambers, son of Thomas and Mary, born October 1, 1760.
Thomas Smith, son of Zackary and Margrett, born October 3, 1736.
Benjamin Carroll, son of James and Ann, born August 25, 1760.
Anne Jones, wife of Benjamin, died May 6, 1737.
Lucina Roberts, second daughter of John and Mary, born Mar. 11, 1725.
Daniel Dowley died in the month of June, 1760.

Page 89

William Edwards, son of William and Mary, born September 16, 1760.
Elizabeth Cadle, daughter of Benjamin and Anne, born Jan. 8, 1734.
Isaac Armstrong, son of Henry and Mary, born July 26, 1761, "being the first born of twinns."
Jacob Armstrong, son of Henry and Mary, born July 26, 1761.
Thomas Stephens and Mary Wright married April 28, 1737.
Sarah Stephens, daughter of Thomas and Mary, born June 10, 1738.
Mary Rocketts, wife of Benjamin, died July 10, 1763.
Thomas Lomax and Anne Hakman married January---, 1726.
Thomas Lomax, son of Thomas and Anne, born February 22, 1731.
Theophilas Lomax, son of Thomas and Anne, born December 25, 1737.
William Standeford and Anne Huchens married May 28, 1731.
Huchens Standeford, son of William and Anne, born Sept. 3, 1733.

Page 90

Presilla Standeford, daughter of William and Anne, born Dec. 17, 1735.
Anne Standeford, wife of William, died July-----, 1738.
Samuell Talbee and Elizabeth Hitchcock married December 1, 1736.
Anne Talbee, daughter of Samuell and Elizabeth, born Oct. 6, 1737.
Asaell Talbee, son of Samuell and Elizabeth, born Feb. 10, 1739.
Francis Carty, son of Brian and Frances, born April 14, 1762.

William Metheny and Elizabeth Banberry married January 12, 1735.
Daniell Metheny, son of William and Elizabeth, born Sep. 7, 1737.
Jemima Standiford, daughter of Samuel and Mary Anne, born
    February 20, 1737.
Keziah Standeford, daughter of Samuel and Mary Anne, born
    "the same date above they being twins."
Robert Price and Elizabeth Shepard married December 31, 1734.
Johannah Price, daughter of Robert and Elizabeth, born June 22, 1738.

Page 91

Elizabeth Price died "the 29th day of the said instant."
Elizabeth Isham, wife of James, died in October, 1737, and the
    said Isham and Mrs. Mary Warren married June 1, 1738.
Mary Isham died in August, 1743, and the said Isham and Jane
    Johnstone married October 13, 1743.
Anne Asher, daughter of Anthony and Susannah, born Sept. 21, 1735.
Rachell Asher, daughter of Anthoney and Susannah, born Sep. 20, 1737.
John Pedder and Christian Williams married July 9, 1738.
John Smalley, son of John and Elizabeth, born September, 1734.
Nathan Smalley, son of John and Elizabeth, born January, 1736.
Lemuel Howard and Mrs. Anne Ward married January 11, 1730.
Benjamin Howard, son of Lemuel and Anne, born Sept. 12, 1731.

Page 92

Susannah Howard, daughter of Lemuel and Anne, born Sept. 18, 1735.
Lemuel Howard, son of Lemuel and Anne, born December 28, 1736.
Thomas Durbin and Anne Condry married January, 1737.
Elizabeth Waltham, daughter of Thomas and Elizabeth, born June 24, 1759.
Robert Robertson died in May, 1736.
Martin Taylor died May 4, 1737.
Benjaman Bond and Clemency Taylor married May 28, 1737.
Mary Bond, daughter of Benjaman and Clemency, born July 24, 1737.
John Bond, son of Benjamin and Clemency, born September 15, 1742.
Edmond Hays and Mary Smith married in November, 1731.
Lightwood Somner, son of Edward and Anne, born January 23, 1737.
Anne Hill, daughter of William and Martha, born October 18, 1734.
William Hill, son of William and Martha, born January 3, 1736.

Page 93

Ann Brown, wife of Rateford Brown, died in the year 1749.
Anne Copland, daughter of John and Mary, born May 10, 1737.
Elizabeth Copland, daughter of John and Mary, born May 10, 1742.
Samuell Deason and Mary Johnson married September, 1737.
William Deason, son of Samuel and Mary, born June 20, 1738.
Lanselett Carlile, son of David and Mary, born Nov. 10, 1736.
Elizabeth Meads, daughter of Benjamin and Mary, born Nov. 3, 1765.
Mary Meads, daughter of Benjamin and Mary, born January 27, 1767.
William Meads, son of Benjamin and Mary, born July 24, 1769.
John Meads, son of Benjamin and Mary, born December 30, 1770.
Benjamin Jones and Dinah Merriken married January 5, 1737.
Elishabee Deason, daughter of William and Ann, born Dec., 1743.
Jemima Deason, daughter of Sarah Deason, born March 7, 1744.
William Oakley, son of Thomas and Susannah, born June 16, 1744.
Samuel Day, son of Nicholas and Elizabeth, born March 1, 1730,
   "being the first male child born in the Town of Joppa."
Joseph Meed and Mary Legoe married January 10, 1737.

Page 94

Robert Scott and Ann, daughter Elizabeth, born December, 1730.
Jane Scott, daughter of Robert and Anne, born in 1733.
Robert Scott, son of John Scott and Ann, born in 1735. (Note: The
   record indicates John, but it probably meant Robert.)
Margrett Scott, daughter of Robert and Ann, born in 1737.
Temperrance Rollo, daughter of Rebecca Rollo, born Feb. 10, 1739.
Mary Sheppard, daughter of Mary Sheppard, born January 25, 1743.
Jane Wallix, daughter of John and Elizabeth, born Nov. 28, 1741.
Hannah Wallix, daughter of John and Elizabeth, born July 31, 1744.

Page 95

Dority Rawlings, wife of John, died July 4, 1720.
Dority Groves, wife of William, died July 14, 1720.
Abraham Taylor Sr. died July 20, 1719.
Rebecah Taylor, daughter of John and Judith, died in August, 1719.
Joshua Bond, son of Thomas and Ann, died March 30, 1720.
Ann Bond, daughter of Thomas and Ann, died August 20, 1720.

Elizabeth Bond, daughter of William and Mary, died April 6, 1720.
John Long died at William Bond's on November 15, 1720.
John Poteete died March 5, 1720.

Page 96

John Standafar died April 12, 1720.
William Dawdridge died January 15, 1720/1.
Margrett Durham, wife of James, died in November, 1720.
Martin Taylor died on Good Friday, April 7, 1721.
John Bradshaw died March 14, 1720.
James Cowdrey died in November, 1720.
John Cowdrey died in April, 1721.
Absolem Comoran, son of John Camoran and Sarah, born Sept., 1737.
Elizabeth Sheppard, daughter of John and Margret, born Apr. 7, 1754.
Mary Sheppard, daughter of John and Margret, born Nov. 21, 1756.
John Sheppard, son of John and Margret, born August 9, 1758.

Page 97

Elizabeth Sicklemore, daughter of Sutton and Constant, born
    December 17, 1738.
Margret Sheppard, daughter of John and Margret, born Mar. 17, 1760.
Nathaniel Sheppard, son of John and Margret, born Nov. 20, 1761.
William Dulany and Mary Anderson married in 1736.
Sabarent Dulany, daughter of William and Mary, born Feb. 7, 1737.
Rebecca Dulany, daughter of William and Mary, born Sept. 8, 1742.
William Dulany, son of William and Mary, born January 1, 1744.
Susannah Higginson, son of John and Ann, born February 19, 1730.
Samuel Higginson, second son of John and Ann, born Feb. 23, 1733.

Page 98

Thomas Fuller, son of John Jr. and Susannah, born July 29, 1734.
Jemima Fuller, daughter of John and Susannah, born Oct. 9, 1736.
John Fuller, son of John and Susannah, born January 3, 1738.
Dr. John Dale and Mary Colegate, daughter of Richard Colegate Jr.,
    married April 21, 1767.

Richard Colegate Dale, son of Dr. John and Mary, born July 18, 1770.
Joseph Cox died in 1736.
Sophia Cox, daughter of Joseph and Elizabeth, born Feb. 17, 1736.
Henry Fuller and Elizabeth Cox married August 27, 1738.
Thomas Gadd died December 13, 1738.
Thomas Hutchens and Hannah Seemmons married May 12, 1736.
Keziah Hutchens, daughter of Thomas and Hannah, born Jan. 21, 1737.

Page 99

Elizabeth Scott, daughter of Robert and Ann, born December, 1730.
Jane Scott, daughter of Robert and Ann, born in 1733.
John Scott, son of Robert and Ann, born in 1735.
Margrett Scott, daughter of Robert and Ann, born in 1737.
John Starkey and Ann Greer married July 10, 1738.
Mary Starkey, daughter of John and Ann, born Sept. 10, 1739.
John Starkey, son of John and Ann, born February 12, 1741.
Mary Baker, daughter of Mauris and Christian, born March 4, 1734.
Rhode Baker, daughter of Mauris and Christian, born Mar. 21, 1738.
John Norrinton and Mary Hays married August 1, 1737.
Ann Buchanan, wife of Archibald, died October 29, 1749.
Abraham Enloes and Mary Deason married in 1730.

Page 100

Anthony Enloes, son of Abraham and Mary, born in August, 1731.
Abarillo Enloes, daughter of Abraham and Mary, born in 1734.
Elizabeth Clark, daughter of John and Elizabeth, born Nov., 1761.
Charles Protser and Mary Jarves married November 20, 1738.
John Allen, son of James and Mary, born October 23, 1734.
Ann Allen, daughter of James and Mary, born February 20, 1737,
    and died in 1739.
James Allen, son of James and Mary, born January 8, 1739.
Reubin Allin, son of James and Mary, born March 7, 1743.
Isaac Wright, son of William and Elizabeth, born July 16, 1738.
John Poacocks "first daughter he had by Susannah his wife, was
    born September 10, 1737."
John Braisher, son of John and Sarah, born June 23, 1735.
Elizabeth Hutchens, daughter of John and Elizabeth, born
    September 30, 1734.

Page 101

Major William Dallam died September 22, 1761.
Rachall Horner, daughter of Nicholas and Ann, born June 1, 1727.
Nathan Horner, son of Nicholas and Ann, born March 25, 1729.
Sarah Horner, daughter of Nicholas and Ann, born June 30, 1731.
Reason Horner, son of Nicholas and Ann, born in 1734.
Hugh Meriken died March 9, 1738.
William Mitchell and Elizabeth Elliott married Sept. 30, 1736.
John Mitchell, son of William and Elizabeth, born Nov. 6, 1737.
Aquilla Clark, son of Robert and Elizabeth, born May 24, 1738.
John Wooller and Fanny Brammar married April 3, 1768.
Samuell Willson and Rebecca Smithson married in 1729.
Aquilla Willson, son of Samuell and Rebecca, born March, 1731.

Page 102

Samuell Willson, son of Samuell and Rebecca, born April 13, 1733.
Sarah Willson, daughter of Samuell and Rebecca, born Apr. 14, 1729.
Hannah Willson, daughter of Samuell and Rebecca, born Oct., 1734.
William Richardson, son of Thomas and Sarah, born April 11, 1737.
James Standeford and Martha Watkins married October 6, 1737.
Clorinda Standeford, daughter of James and Martha, born Apr. 23, 1737.
John Jarman, son of Thomas and Mary, born August 19, 1735.
Margrett Carty, daughter of Darby Carty and Susannah, born June 10, 1761.
Benjamin Jones died April 25, 1739.
John Durham, son of Samuell and Eleanor, born February 22, 1738.
Jemima Scimmons died December 25, 1737.
Godfrey Gunner, son of Sprigh Godfrey Gunner and Mary, born Mar. 26, 1739.

Page 103

Rachaell Norris, daughter of Joseph and Mary, born July 21, 1739.
John Ward and Sarah Borrough married December 17, 1737.
William Ward, son of John and Sarah, born March 10, 1738.
Easther Hunter, daughter of John and Margrett, born June 17, 1739.
William Denton Jr. and Rosanna Standton married in 1735.
James Denton, son of William and Rosanna, born February 10, 1735.

John Taylor, son of John and Kissa, born September 24, 1736.
Thomas Taylor, son of John and Kisea, born April 30, 1739.
Bethiah Amoss, daughter of Thomas and Elizabeth, born Feb.22,1738.
William Deele, son of William and Elionor, born March 25, 1739.
William Deason and Ann Sheppard married February 9, 1739.

Page 104

Mary Deason, daughter of William and Ann, born April 8, 1739.
Ann Standeford, wife of William, died in July, 1738.
Joseph Hendon, son of Richard and Sarah, born March 7, 1728.
Sarah Hendon, daughter of Richard and Sarah, born May 27, 1730.
Prudence Hendon, daughter of Richard and Sarah, Oct. 27, 1732.
Richard Hendon, son of Richard and Sarah, born November 30, 1734.
Josias Hendon, son of Richard and Sarah, born June 7, 1739.
John Barton and Ann Hitchcock married May 23, 1738.
John Sherelock and Elizabeth Chesher married November 30, 1737.
Thomas Sherelock, son of John and Elizabeth, born Oct. 27, 1738,
    and died in 1739.
Elizabeth Sherelock, wife of John, died in October, 1739.

Page 105

Thomas Gadd, son of William and Mary, born April 27, 1738.
Sarah Bond, daughter of Peter and Easther, born Dec. 9, 1719.
Ann Bond, daughter of Peter and Easther, born June 18, 1729.
Peter Bond, son of Easther and Peter, born June 10, 1738.
Aquilla Greer, son of John Jr. and wife, born July 29, 1737.
Edmund Talbott, son of William and Mary, born April 20, 1738,
    and died December 10, 1739.
Lucina Talbott, daughter of William and Mary, born June 17, 1743.
John Parker and Elizabeth Danbie married January 1, 1739.
Sarah Parker, daughter of John and Elizabeth, born Feb. 26, 1741.
Martin Parker, son of John and Elizabeth, born January----, 1740,
    "and died the same month."
George Gouldsmith Presbury, son of George and Mary, born May 1, 1737.

Page 106

William Robeson Presbury, son of George and Isabella, born
    September 20, 1742.

Martha Presbury, daughter of George and Isabella, born May 19, 1749.
Abraham Norris, son of Benjamin and Sarah, born July 22, 1739.
George Presbury, son of George and Isabella, born April 22, 1754.
Frances Dives, daughter of Francis and Mary, born April 14, 1760.
Sarah Denton, wife of William Sr., died in November, 1737.
William Denton and Ann Wooden married in March, 1739.
Ann Denton, wife of William, died in March, 1740.
Rachaell Denton, daughter of William Sr., died in February, 1739.
Rachel Bevens, daughter of John Jr., born February 25, 1740.
Charles King and Ann Green married March 29, 1741.
William Jones and Ann Maccubbin married March 30, 1741.
Phebe Jackson, daughter of Jacob and Frances, born May 19, 1734.

Page 107

Cernalia Jackson, daughter of Jacob and Francis, born Apr. 10, 1737.
Anne Jackson, daughter of Jacob and Francis, born in November, 1741.
Robert Jackson, son of Jacob and Francis, born in November, 1741.
Esabela Jackson, daughter of Isaac and Mary, born January 20, 1740.
Elizabeth Bunting, daughter of William Bunting and Drew Andrew his wife, died in 1769.
Hannah Norris, daughter of Edward and Hannah, born Sept. 7, 1738.
Frances Jackson, wife of Jacob, died in November, 1741.
Robert Jackson, son of Jacob and Frances, died in December, 1741.
William Denton, son of William Jr. and Rosana, born Feb. 25, 1740.
Sarah Presbury, daughter of William and Clemency, born Sept. 4, 1758.

Page 108

Anne Meed, daughter of Joseph and Mary, born April 29, 1741.
Elizabeth Mead, daughter of Joseph and Mary, born Jan. 26, 1742.
Hannah Durham, daughter of Samuell and Elioner, born Jan. 26, 1740.
Abraham Green and Ruth Carback married June 25, 1770.
Rachaell Mariarte, daughter of Edward and Sarah, born Mar. 25, 1739.
Thomas Jarman and Mary Rawley married April 29, 1733.
Robert Jarman, son of Thomas and Mary, born February 11, 1734.
John Jarman, son of Thomas and Mary, born September, 1737.
Rachaell Jarman, daughter of Thomas and Mary, born Nov. 15, 1739.
Joseph Bevens, son of Joseph and Rebecca, born December 24, 1739.

Mary Talbott, daughter of Edmund and Mary, born November 29, 1737.
Edmund Talbott, son of Edmund and Mary, born November 3, 1739.

Page 109

Mary White, wife of John, died in January, 1739.
Joshua White, son of John and Mary, born November 4, 1735.
Thomas Shaw, son of Christopher Durbin Shaw and Susanna, was
          born October 1, 1733.
Mary Shaw, daughter of Christopher and Susanna, born Dec. 30, 1735.
Elizabeth Shaw, daughter of Christoper and Susanna, born Aug. 29, 1738.
Rebecca Everett, wife of John, died November 4, 1739.
John Everett and Comford Pearson married in August, 1739.
Kesia Everett, daughter of John and Comford, born Sept. 22, 1740.
Robert Thomas Denboe born August 27, 1735.
Jane Denboe, daughter of Thomas, born February 18, 1738.
Christopher Durbin Shaw died November 24, 1746.
Hannah Hendon, daughter of Josias and Hannah, born Oct. 31, 1727.

Page 110

William Deel, son of William and Elioner, born March 17, 1739.
Frances Poulson, wife of Joseph, died August 20 or 21, 1761.
John Parker and Mary Danbe married January 1, 1739.
Martin Parker, son of John and Elizabeth, born January 9, 1740.
Mary Cadle, daughter of Benjamin and Anne, born March 21, 1738.
Henry Whealand and Rebecca Leagoe married January 27, 1736.
Soll. Whealand, son of Henry and Rebecca, born October 26, 1738.
Peter Carrall and Anne Hitchcock married June 8, 1739.
Eleanor Carroll, daughter of Peter, born March 23, 1739.
Eleanor Carroll, daughter of Peter and Anne, died July 3, 1740.
John Bragg, son of Hannah Bragg, born December 31, 1740.
William Dallam and Elizabeth Johnson married January 10, 1737.
Josias Dallam, son of William and Elizabeth, born August 8, 1739.

Page 111

William Dallam, son of William and Elizabeth, born Jan. 8, 1741.
William Dallam, son of William and Elizabeth, died Oct. 8, 1742.

Richard Dallam, son of William and Elizabeth, born Sept. 24, 1743.
Bezaleel Foster and Mary Meed married December 24, 1734.
Thomas Foster, son of Bezaleel and Mary, born October 6, 1735.
John Foster, son of Bezaleel and Mary, born November 3, 1737.
Benjamin Foster, son of Bezaleel and Mary, born August 23, 1737.
          (The record indicates 1737 although it may be 1739.)
Samuell Standiford, son of Samuel and Anne, born October 20, 1740.
Isaac Elledge, son of Joseph and Mary, born August 20, 1740.
Richard Rhoades and Sarah Whitaker married February 9, 1740.
Mary Norrinton, daughter of John Jr. and Mary, born April 30, 1741.

Page 112

Benjamin Chaeney and Ruth Chaeney married in June, 1719.
Jonathan Hughs and Jane Shepperd married December 10, 1738.
Sarah Hughs, daughter of Jonathan and Jane, born Sept. 14, 1739.
Clemency Hughs, daughter of Jonathan and Jane, born Sept. 25, 1739.
Jemime Scimmons, wife of George, died December 25, 1737.
George Scimmons and Elizabeth Fuller married October 24, 1738.
Hannah Scimmons, daughter of George and Elizabeth, born Oct. 9, 1739.
Francis Dives, son of Christopher and Frances, born November 5, 1739.
Christopher Dives and Sarah Arnell married in August, 1736.
Mary Dives, daughter of Christopher and Sarah, born October 17, 1737.
John Dives, son of Christopher and Sarah, born January 17, 1739.
Jamzim Dives, daughter of Christopher and Sarah, born March 3, 1740.

Page 113

Rozana Ward, daughter of Mary Ward, born January 27, 1740.
Thomas Amoss, son of Thomas and Elizabeth, born August 1, 1740.
Elizabeth Ward, daughter of John and Sarah, born June 21, 1741.
Keturah Dorsey, daughter of Vincent and Sarah, born July 27, 1747.
Keturah Dorsey, daughter of Vincent and Sarah, died Oct. 3, 1747.
Edward Fugate, som of James and Ann, born August 10, 1734.
John Fugate, son of James and Ann, born March 15, 1735.
Easter Fugate, daughter of James and Ann, born March 15, 1736.
Ann Fugate, daughter of James and Ann, born in February, 1738.

George Enzor and Elizabeth Reeves married December 24, 1739.
Rachaell Enzor, daughter of George and Elizabeth, born May 24, 1741.

Page 114

Mary Grimes, daughter of John and Mary, born February 8, 1737.
John Grimes, son of John and Mary, born December 20, 1739.
James Standiford, son of James and Martha, born June 3, 1739.
Israell Standeford, son of James and Martha, born Nov. 13, 1740.
Jishua Legatt, son of John Jr. and Tamer, born December 10, 1740.
Benjamin Enloes, son of Abraham and Mary, born January 19, 1738.
Sarah Enloes, daughter of Abraham and Mary, born Febeuary 16, 1740.
John Worthington, son of Henry and Mary, born August 20, 1741.
William Jenings, son of William and Mary, born April 22, 1738.
Martha Braisher, daughter of John and Sarah, born Nov. 4, 1739.
Margrett Sheppard, daughter of William and Margrett, born Mar.7,1740.

Page 115

Willyahnah, daughter of William Daugh and Ann, born March 7, 1740.
David Scott, son of Andrew and Ann, born December 24, 1738.
Susannah Scott, daughter of David and Ann, born March 10, 1736.
Ann Scott, daughter of Andrew and Ann, born July 19, 1741.
Susannah Westwood, daughter of Mary Westwood, born July 10, 1730.
Elizabeth Ann Demmett, daughter of James and Barbary, born Aug.26,1740.
Elizabeth Wright, daughter of Jacob and Sarah, born January 26, 1739.
Elizabeth Frances, daughter of Charles Prosser and Mary, born
    July 5, 1739.
Sarah Prosser, daughter of Charles and Mary, born April 28, 1741.
John Cross, son of Joseph and Elizabeth, born December 10, 1733.
Ann Cross, daughter of Joseph and Rodia, born May 3, 1739.

Page 116

Rachell Cross, daughter of Joseph and Rodia, born April 25, 1741.
Thomas Haulaway, son of John and Elizabeth, born December 24, 1737.
William Haulaway, son of John and Elizabeth, born May 10, 1740.
Samuell Low, son of William and Sarah, born December 18, 1739.

William Standiford and Stehannah Wright married December 8, 1740.
Aquilla Standeford son of William and Stehannah, born Aug. 24, 1741.
Averilla Standeford, daughter of William and Stehannah, born
    August 24, 1741.
Jacob Johnson, son of Thomas and Mary, born March 15, 1717.
Tabitha Johnson, daughter of Thomas and Mary, born Sept. 9, 1720.
Israell Johnson, son of Thomas and Mary, born December 20,-----.
Benjamin Legoe, Jr. and Judea Bricteon (Buceton) married
    October 25, 1740.
Spencer Legoe, son of Benjamin and Judea, born October 25, 1741.

Page 117

Samuel Warrell and Mary White married May 1, 1742.
Martin Warrell, son of Samuel and Mary, born March 13, 1741.
Elizabeth Whealand, daughter of Henry and Rebecca, born July 19, 1741.
Joseph Yeats and Cathrene Turret married September 14, 1736.
George Gilbert Yeats, son of Cathrine and Joseph, born Apr. 21, 1738.
Joseph Yeats, father of George Gilbert Yeats, died November 9, 1740.
John Shipley, son of Richard and Susannah, born March 25, 1716.
Bezaleel Foster, son of Bezaleel and Mary, born March 6, 1741.
Hannah Meed, daughter of Benjamin and Elizabeth, born April 25, 1725.
Ruth Meed, daughter of Benjamin and Elizabeth, born March 13, 1729.
Elizabeth Meed, wife of Benjamin, died October 6, 1740.
Frederick, son of Roderick Cheyne and Elizabeth "born Monday, Dec. 7,
    1741 and baptized in St. Johns Parrish Church, Messrs.
    William Young and Thomas Gassaway standing God Fathers
    and Mrs. Sarah Gassaway God Mother."
Ruth Meed, daughter of Benjamin and Elizabeth, born in 1731.
Thomas Fuller, son of John and Ruth, born August 14, 1739.

Page 118

Mary Jackson, daughter of Isaac and Mary, born April 3, 1737.
Sarah Taylor, (record indicates son but it should be daughter) of
    John and Anne, born May 10, 1737.
Edward King, son of Charles and Ann, born July 25, 1741.
Mary King, daughter of Charles and Ann, born July 25, 1741.
Mary League, daughter of John and wife, born January 4, 1730.
James League, son of John and wife, born February 14, 1732.
Aquilla League, son of John and wife, born June 23, 1735.

Josiah League, son of John and wife, born October 15, 1737.
Priscilla League, daughter of John and wife, born August 30, 1740.

Page 119

John Ingram, son of John and Susannah, born October 5, 1740.
David Scott, son of Robert and Ann, born November 14, 1740.
James Greer and Elizabeth Wright married May 28, 1741.
Thomas Amoss, son of Thomas and Elizabeth, born August 1, 1740.
John Allen and Ann Rhoades married November 24, 1740.
Richard Allen, son of John and Ann, born November 15, 1741.
Daniel Maccomas and Martha Scott married December 26, 1734.
James Maccomas, son of Daniel and Martha, born Sept. 13, 1735.
Elizabeth Maccomas, daughter of Daniel and Martha, born July 1, 1737.
William Maccomas, son of Daniel and Martha, born May 17, 1739.
John Maccomas, son of Daniel and Martha, born October 20, 1741.

Page 120

Thomas Norris and Avarilla Scott married October 10, 1738.
William Norris, son of Thomas and Avarilla, born December 24, 1739.
Nathaniel Norris, son of Thomas and Avarilla, born Dec. 16, 1741.
William Savory, son of William and Mary, born February 20, 1738.
Batrix Dawney, daughter of Thomas and Ann, born in 1737.
Thomas Dawney, son of Thomas and Ann, born in 1740.
John Chamberlaine and Margarett Gittings married October 31, 1737.
Elizabeth Chamberlaine, daughter of John and Margarett, born October 12, 1738.
Thomas Chamberlaine, son of John and Margarett, born Feb. 19, 1739.
Mary Chamberlain, daughter of John and Margarett, born July 17, 1743.
Margarett Chamberlain, daughter of John and Margarett, born February 23, 1744.
Phillip Chamberlain, son of John and Margarett, born Dec. 12, 1746.
John Denboe, son of Thomas and Elizabeth, born March 16, 1741.

Page 121

Edward Norris, son of Edward and Hannah, born April 8, 1741.
John Standeford, son of Samuel and Ann, born May 26, 1743.

Richard Groome and Margarett Norton married February 13, 1739.
William Groome, son of Richard and Margarett, born May 31, 1741.
William Mitchell and Elizabeth Eliott married Sept. 30, 1737.
John Mitchell, son of William and Elizabeth, born Nov. 5, 1739.
Sarah Mitchell, daughter of William and Elizabeth, born Feb.5,1740.
William Mitchell, son of William and Elizabeth, born July 23, 1742.
Darby Hernly, son of Darby and wife, born May 4, 1733.
Edmund Hernly, son of Darby and wife, born March 20, 1735.
Elizabeth Hernly, daughter of Darby and wife, born July 12, 1737.

Page 122

John Hernly, son of Darby and wife, born July 20, 1739.
William Hernly, son of Darby and wife, born February 2, 1741.
Thomas Price, son of Robert and Elizabeth, born March 6, 1742.
John Denton and Rachell Down married February 3, 1739.
John Denton, son of John and Rachell, born October 31, 1741.
Priscilla Denton, daughter of John and Rachell, born Sept. 4, 1742.
Elizabeth Asher, daughter of Anthony and Susannah, born Dec.31,1742.
Mary Norris, daughter of Joseph and Mary, born June 1, 1742.
Thomas Barton, son of Thomas and Elizabeth, born May 6, 1737.
Ann Barton, daughter of Thomas and Elizabeth, born Jan. 3, 1740.
Elizabeth Barton, daughter of Thomas and Elizabeth, born Jan.3,1741.
Mary Barton, daughter of Thomas and Elizabeth, born March 13, 1742.

Page 123

Peter Golden and Elizabeth Earl married November 15, 1742.
Isaac Risteau, son of John and Cathrine, born November 14, 1724.
Thomas Ensor and Mary Costley married January 27, 1739.
William Ensor, son of Thomas and Mary, born May 7, 1741.
Samuell Smith and Averilla Beek married August 30, 1738.
Mary Smith, daughter of Samuell and Averilla, born Aug. 8, 1740.
Rachell Smith, wife of William, died December 20, 1741.
William Smith died March 20, 1742.
William Smith, son of William and Rachell, born Oct. 28, 1722.
The abovesaid William Smith last mentioned died October 20, 1740.
William Smith, son of Samuell and Avarilla, born Oct. 28, 1742.

Page 124

Robert Bishop and Elizabeth Day married September 22, 1742.
James Baker and Cathrene Smith married September 25, 1742.
John Huggins Jr. and Mary Downs married October 7, 1742.
Charles Summons and Elizabeth Pottet married October 19, 1742.
Edward York and Ann Dorney married October 21, 1742.
Vincent Dorsey and Sarah Day married October 26, 1742.
Isaac Miles and Ann Preston married October 28, 1742.
James Freeman and Margrett Bertram married October 28, 1742.
Joseph Reneher and Elizabeth Wells married October 28, 1742.
William Cole and Mary Stephens married November 16, 1742.
John Cox and Elizabeth Sympson married November 30, 1742.
Benjamin Deason and Tarrisha Sheppard married December 9, 1742.

Page 125

Thomas Wicks and Elizabeth Enlow married December 15, 1742.
Asraell Roberts and Mary Ingram married December 16, 1742.
Joseph Lair and Mary Bishop married January 7, 1742.
Israell Johnson and Sarah Hutchens married January 12, 1742.
John Durbin and Elioner Odean married December 13, 1743.
John Dannock and Mary Palmore married January 16, 1743.
Samuell Whips and Mary Maccomas married January 22, 1742.
John Copas and Manuell Wright married January 24, 1742.
Heathcut Pickett and Elizabeth Wright married January 26, 1742.
Jacob Jones and Rachell Cottrell married February 10, 1742.
Jonathan Eddee and Rebecca York married April 4, 1743.

Page 126

Joseph Jenings and Mary Rider married May 23, 1742.
Daniell Oneall and Susannah Lacy married June 12, 1743.
Edward Brusbanks Jr. and Briggett Baker married June 23, 1743.
Thomas Underwood and Ann Petty married August 1, 1743.
William Hughs and Ann Bellows married June 24, 1743.
Thomas Cotteraell and Frances Milhuse married August 4, 1743.

Page 126-127

Joseph Ward Jr. and Hannah Lee married August 24, 1743.
John Morris and Sarah Gilbert married August 28, 1743.
Richard Green and Elizabeth Henallen married Sept. 2, 1743.
John Beven and Ann Turner married September 6, 1743.
Joshua Starkey and Hannah Meads married September 29, 1743.
John Bradley and Ann Evens married October 2, 1743.
Peircey Potett and Jemima Hitchcock married October 12, 1743.
Joseph Poulson and Frances Allen married in 1739.
Nathaniel Poulson, son of Joseph and Frances, born Apr. 29, 1740, and baptized April 18, 1742.
Robert Price and Elizabeth Miles married September 18, 1739.
Robert Price Jr., son of Robert and Elizabeth, born Nov. 11, 1740.
John Day, son of Edward, and Philliszana Maxwell married July 20, 1742.
Mary Day, daughter of John and Philliszana, born February 5, 1743.
Frederick Cheyne, son of Roderick and Elizabeth, died January 25, "and was buried at St. Johns Church January 28, 1742."
Pamela Cheyne, daughter of Roderick and Elizabeth, born Feb. 6, 1743 "and baptized in St. Johns Church on Trinity Sunday May 20, 1744, Mr. N. Ruxton Gay, Mrs. Christian Deans and Mrs. Christian Caswell standing sureties."
Cloe Cheyne, daughter of Roderick and Elizabeth, born at Baltimore County free school on November 24, 1745.
"1755 Oct 14th day Then was Jno. Day son of John Day son of Edward and Philliszana his wife was born."
Walter Tolley and Mary Garretson married December 20, 1735.

Page 128

Elizabeth Tolley, daughter of Walter and Mary, born Nov. 16, 1736.
Thomas Tolley, son of Walter and Mary, born October 15, 1738.
Mary Tolley, daughter of Walter and Mary, born March 21, 1740.
Sophia Tolley, daughter of Walter and Mary, born March 3, 1742.
Thomas Tolley, son of Walter Tolley, died April 15, 1743.
"All the abovementioned children were baptised in St.John's Church."
Walter Tolley, son of Walter and Mary, born May 10, 1744 "and baptised in Saint John's Church July 6, 1744. James Tolley, Rodrick Chyne Godfathers and Elizabeth Chyne Godmother."
James Tolley, son of Walter and Mary, born June 20, 1746.
"The above child was baptised in St. John's Parrish. Robert Bishop, Richard Garrettson and Elizabeth Bishop sureties."

Thomas Garretson Tolley born June 29, 1748 "and baptised as aforesaid."
Mary Tolley, wife of Walter Tolley, died July 19, 1749.

Page 129

James Baker Sr. died in February, 1743.
James Norris, son of Edward and Hannah, born February 25, 1742.
Thomas Hill, son of William and Martha, born April 10, 1743.
Henry Smith and Elizabeth Druley married June, 1738.
James Smith, son of Henry and Elizabeth, born October 29, 1739.
Elizabeth Smith, daughter of Henry and Elizabeth, born Dec. 27, 1743.
Demuell Baker and Sarah Downs married April 22, 1738.
Mary Baker, daughter of Demuel and Sarah, born June 14, 1741.
Thomas Watkins and Elizabeth Mead married January 19, 1738.
Daniel Watkins Scott born December 5, 1739 and baptised in the
        month of September following, he being the son of Francis
        Watkins and Elizabeth his wife."
Francis Watkins, son of Francis and Elizabeth, born September 27,
        1741 "and baptized in the month of March following."
Jane Watkins, daughter of Francis and Elizabeth, born Nov. 17, 1743
        "and baptized in the month of April following."
Charles Pines and Elizabeth Bays married in August, 1741.
Priscilla Pines, daughter of Charles and Elizabeth, born Feb.7,1742.

Page 130

Abra. Pines, son of Charles and Elizabeth, born April 20, 1738.
Anne Perdue, daughter of Mary Perdue, born May 3, 1741.
William Waaler, son of George and Mary, born in April, 1742.
Mary Copas, daughter of John and Manaby, born December 25, 1743.
John Rutledge and Elizabeth Milhughs married December 10, 1742.
Hannah Rutledge, daughter of John and Elizabeth, born Jan. 10, 1743.
Sebara Milhughs Rutledge, daughter of John and Elizabeth, born
        June 10, 1740.
Zephaniah Talbee, son of Samuel and Elisebeth, born Dec. 29, 1741.
Asael Hitchcock and Sarah Norris married October 8, 1742.
Anne Hitchcock, daughter of Asael and Sarah, born December 11, 1741.
Elizabeth Norris, daughter of Thomas and Elizabeth, born July 11,1741.
John Fitchpatrick, son of Mary Fitchpatrick, born January 16, 1739.

Elizabeth Riddle Dallas, daughter of Walter and Chloe, born
    March 16, 1741.
Sarah Hilton, daughter of John and Sarah, born March 25, 1740.
Mary Hilton, daughter of John and Sarah, born March 13, 1741.
Jemima Elliott, daughter of James and Mary, born Nov. 30, 1738.

Page 131

John Elliott, son of James and Mary, born January 6, 1740.
James Elliott, son of James and Mary, born February 18, 1742.
James Standeford, son of James and Mary, born March 29, 1742.
Thomas Oakley, son of Thomas and Prudence, born April 4, 1742.
Jacob Huggins, son of John Jr. and Mary, born July 20, 1739.
Thomas Whitehead, son of Robert and Elizabeth, born July 15, 1740.
Anne Hutchens, daughter of Thomas and Hannah, born Feb. 6, 1741.
John Marshall, son of Thomas and Sarah, born February 28, 1741.
Job Garretson, son of Paul and Elizabeth, born February 17, 1741.
Rebecca Armstrong, daughter of William and Elizabeth, born
    March 5, 1742.
Rebecca Deason, daughter of Edmund and Elizabeth, born Nov. 23, 1742.
Rebecca Armstrong, daughter of Henry and Mary, born February 4, 1742.
Peter Knowles, son of Peter and Mary, born December 30, 1741.
Temperance Hunt, daughter of William and Elizabeth, born Nov.14,1741.
Elizabeth Bacon, daughter of Martin and Mary, born November 23, 1741.
William Bacon, son of Martin and Mary, born July 19, 1738.
Benjamin Hanbury, son of Dickinson and Phenalopher, born Oct.1,1741.

Page 132

Luke Wyle, son of Luke and Kasiah, born March 29, 1740.
Mathew Wyle, son of Luke and Kasiah, born November 16, 1730.
William Wyle, son of Luke and Kasiah, born January 31, 1731.
Mary Wyle, daughter of Luke and Kasiah, born December 20, 1735.
Athea Wyle, daughter of Luke and Kasiah, born December 31, 1737.
Walter Wyle, son of Luke and Kasiah, born May 8, 1742.
William Anderson, son of Benjamin and Sarah, born March 30, 1730.
Benjamin Anderson, son of Benjamin and Sarah, born Feb. 4, 1732.
Mary Anderson, daughter of Benjamin and Sarah, born Jan. 18, 1736.
John Anderson, son of Benjamin and Sarah, born May 8, 1741.

Sarah Wyle, daughter of John and Hannah, born May 31, 1733.
Benjamin Wyle, son of John and Hannah, born November 25, 1734.
Abel Wyle, son of John and Hannah, born May 15, 1736.
Anne Wyle, daughter of John and Hannah, born in September, 1738.
Margret Wyle, daughter of John and Hannah, born in April, 1742.
John Wyle, son of John and Hannah, born March 22, 1737.
Elioner Bull, daughter of William and Martha, born Jan. 6, 1741.

Page 133

Aquila Scott and Elizabeth Puttee married October 13, 1743.
Asael Hitchcock and Sarah Norris married October 8, 1741.
William Hitchcock, son of Asael and Sarah, born October 30, 1743.
Elisha Beck and Sarah Baker married July 31, 1742.
Averalla Beck, daughter of Elisha and Sarah, born June 30, 1743,
        "and baptized in St. John's Church the same year."
James Hill, son of Elioner Hill, born May 1, 1743.
Sarah Hill, daughter of Elioner Hill, born May 1, 1743.
Thomas King and Elioner Hill married in the year 1744.
Mary Hitchcock, daughter of Asael and Sarah, born Dec. 27, 1746.
Elizabeth Hilton, daughter of John and Sarah, born Aug. 9, 1743.
James Moore Jr. and Hannah Willmott married August 28, 1744.
Elizabeth Moore, daughter of James Jr. and Hannah, born Aug. 9, 1746.
Joshua Starkey died April 22, 1744.
Henry Prosser, son of Charles and Mary, born October 22, 1744.
Emilie Talbee, daughter of Samuel and Elizabeth, born Aug. 26, 1744.
John Taylor and Sarah Ward married June 15, 1742.

Page 134

Joseph Taylor, son of John and Sarah, born October 6, 1744.
Mary Beck died March 19, 1739.
Mathew Beck and Ann Horner married February 10, 1740.
Clemency Beck, daughter of Mathew and Ann, born April, 1742.
James Fraisher, son of James and Elizabeth, born March 17, 1743.
John Hunt, son of William and Elizabeth, born March 27, 1744.
Racheele Edy, daughter of Jonathan and Rebecca, born Dec. 3, 1743.
John Marsh, son of James and Margrett, born June 5, 1744.
Ann Knoles, daughter of Peter and Mary Knowles, born May 12, 1744.

Abraham Frissill, son of Jacob Frissell and Ann, born Aug. 2, 1744.
William Low died April, 1744.
Timothy News and Rebecca Rhodes married March 11, 1741.
Ann Newes, daughter of Timothy and Rebecca, born Jan, 17, 1743.
Mary Demmitt, daughter of James Demmitt, died in January, 1743.
Lewis Lefue and Sarah Low married May 8, 1744.
John Chields and Elizabeth Mead married December 17, 1743.
John Parker, son of John and Elizabeth, born September 2, 1744.
George Childs, son of Benjamin and Martha, born October 1, 1737.

Page 133

Rachel Childs, daughter of Benjamin and Martha, born Aug. 30, 1739.
Mary Childs, daughter of Benjamin and Martha, born March 15, 1742.
Sarah Childs, daughter of Benjamin and Martha, born Oct. 4, 1744.
Thomas Legoe, son of Thomas and Sarah, born in July, 1735.
Hannah Legoe, daughter of Thomas and Sarah, born May 25, 1740.
John Legoe, son of Thomas and Sarah, born in May, 1732, and died
    in June, 1742.
Thomas Legoe died April 20, 1742.
Reubin Legoe, son of Thomas and Sarah, born January 11, 1742.
John White and Sarah Legoe married October 4, 1744.
Elizabeth Cadle, daughter of Ben and Ann, born January 19, 1735.
Cemelie Cadle, daughter of Benjamin and Ann, born May 30, 1740.
Mary Sprigh Gunner, daughter of Godfrey Gunner, born July 21, 1735.
William Childs, son of John and Elizabeth, born September 1, 1744,
    and died the same year.
Edward Mead, son of Edward and Cathrine, born January 26, 1735.
Benjamin Mead, son of Edward and Cathrine, born March 26, 1739.
William Mead, son of Edward and Cathrine, born April 22, 1740.

Page 136

George York and Eliner Meads married in February, 1738.
Ann Dorney, daughter of Daniel Dorney and Hannah, born Oct.29,1732.
Mary Mead, daughter of Edward and Cathrine, born October 22, 1730.
Bethiah Mead, daughter of Edward and Cathrine, born October, 1732,
    and died in August, 1740.
Hannah Mead, daughter of Edward and Cathrine, born March 26, 1733.

John Mead, son of Edward and Cathrine, born October 10, 1736
    and died in August, 1737.
Ann Mead, daughter of Edward and Cathrine, born April 29, 1728
    and died in August the same year.
William Wright, son of Bloice, and Sarah Day married Feb.28,1738.
Elizabeth Wright, daughter of William and Sarah, born Jan.10,1739.
Mary Wright, daughter of William and Sarah, born Dec. 17, 1742.
Benjamin Chainey, son of Ben and Ruth, born June 20, 1722.
Ruth Chainey, daughter of Ben and Ruth, born June 20, 1722.
Sarah Chainey, daughter of Ben and Ruth, born April 25, 1720.
Elizabeth Chainey, daughter of Ben and Ruth, born Dec. 20, 1726.
Richard Chainey, son of Ben and Ruth, born November, 1730.

Page 137

Jacob Chainey, son of Ruth and Benjamin, born in May, 1733.
Elioner Chainey, daughter of Ruth and Benjamin, born Feb. 26, 1738.
Greenberry Chainey, son of Ruth and Benjamin, born in August, 1740.
Thomas Chainey, son of Ruth and Benjamin, born in July, 1743.
Easther Debruler, widow, died December 23, 1742.
William Debruler and Diana Greenfield married March 23, 1743.
Delilah Debruler, daughter of William and Diana, born March 29,
    1744 and died November 7, 1744.
Charles Mathias Bolton and Ann Higginson married in July, 1739.
William Jarman and Sarah Rutledge married February 17, 1739.
Henry Jarman, son of William and Sarah, born May 1, 1741.
Robert Jarman, son of William and Sarah, born May 24, 1743.
Hannah Johnson, wife of Jacob Johnson, died August 26, 1744.
Lemuel Baker and Sophia Mead married March 5, 1739.
Darkes Baker, daughter of Lemuel and Sophia, born June 18, 1740.
James Baker, son of Lemuel and Sophia, born August 25, 1744.
Anne Baker, daughter of Lemuel and Sophia, born August 25, 1744.
David Johnson, son of Thomas and Elizabeth, born December 4, 1744.

Page 138

William Groves died February 18, 1745.
William Norris, son of James and Elizabeth, born February 13, 1745.
Elizabeth Starkey, daughter of John and Ann, born May 8, 1744.

Pages 138-139

Mary Copland, daughter of John and Mary, born November 29, 1744.
Jane Copland, daughter of John and Mary, born November 29, 1744.
Mary Copland, wife of John Copland, died November 30, 1744.
Hugh Scott, son of Robert and Ann, born May 23, 1744.
Andrew Scott, son of Andrew and Ann, born July 18, 1743.
Daniel Scott, Jr., son of James and Ann, born October 29, 1744.
George Childs and Martha Smithson married in November, 1736.
John Childs, son of George and Martha, born in April, 1738.
William Childs, son of George and Martha, born April 5, 1740.
Eliner Childs, daughter of George and Martha, born June 20, 1744.
William Childs died in May, 1744.
Ann James, daughter of William and Frances, born in April, 1737.
William James died in 1738.
Thomas Nichols, son of Thomas and Frances, born Dec. 3, 1742.
Sarah Morris, daughter of Mary Morris, born in November, 1730.
Elizabeth Shewbridge, daughter of John and Mary, born June 2, 1733.
Isabellah Shewbridge, daughter of John and Mary, born Nov. 1, 1737.
Mary Shewbridge, daughter of John and Mary, born January 30, 1735.
John Shewbridge, son of John and Mary, born June 26, 1739.
Billey Drew Andrew, daughter of William and Mary, born July 17, 1738.
William Andrew, son of William and Mary, born September 23, 1744.
Daniel Scott, Sr. died March 20, 1745.
Elizabeth Denboe, daughter of Thomas and Elizabeth, born March 13, 1744.
John Ruff and Mary Freeman married in March, 1744.
Charles Ruff, son of John and Mary, born May 6, 1743.
Hannah Hays, daughter of Edmund Hays Jr. and Elizabeth, born July 22, 1744.
Hannah Norris, daughter of James and Mary, born May 28, 1743.
James Norris, son of James and Mary, born April 18, 1745.
Samuel Smith, son of Samuel and Avarilla, born Sept. 13, 1745.
Frances Shewbridge, daughter of John and Mary, born Sept. 12, 1741.

Page 140

Susannah Shewbridge, daughter of John and Mary, born Mar. 25, 1743.
Charles Shewbridge, son of John and Mary, died in May, 1733.
Hannah Standeford, daughter of James and Martha, born June 6, 1743.
Jacob Jones and Sarah Collett married February 10, 1743.

Alexander Norris, son of Thomas and Elizabeth, born Dec. 9, 1744.
William Ward, son of Mary Ward, born October 9, 1745.
Margaret Hicks, daughter of Nehemiah and Phillisana, born July 22, 1743.
Sarah Hicks, daughter of Nehemiah and Phillisana, born January 8, 1744.
Josias Dallam, son of William and Elizabeth, died Sept. 3, 1744.
Sarah Lusby, daughter of Jacob and Betty, born October 21, 1735.
Robert Lusby, son of Jacob and Betty, born March 6, 1737.
Elizabeth Lusby, daughter of Jacob and Betty, born Feb. 26, 1739.
John Lusby, son of Jacob and Betty, born June 27, 1742.
Joseph Lusby, son of Jacob and Betty, born August 28, 1744.

George Presgrove and Hannah Nicholas married January 1, 1744.
Thomas Wodgworth and Rebecca Pasmore married in January, 1741.

Page 141

Elioner Wodgworth, daughter of Thomas and Rebecca, born Oct.12,1741.
Ann Wordgworth, daughter of Thomas and Rebecca, born May 2, 1743.
John Wodgworth, son of Thomas and Rebecca, born June 22, 1745.
James Everett, son of John and Comfort, born February 5, 1742.
Mary Thomas, daughter of David and Elizabeth, born Dec. 24, 1743.
Thomas Potee and Ann Potee married March 22, 1741.
Lewes Poteet, son of Thomas and Ann, born January 23, 1743.
Mary Poteet, daughter of Thomas and Ann, born July 29, 1744.
Ann Whild, daughter of Jonathan and Sarah, born April 9, 1743.
Benjamin Watkins, son of Francis and Elizabeth, born August 10, 1745 and died October 18, 1745.
Christian Ramsey, daughter of John Jr. and Johannah, born March 29, 1742.
William Ramsey, son of John Jr. and Johannah, born Feb. 18, 1743.
Frances Standeford, daughter of Ephraim and Sarah, born Mar.22,1740.
Jemime Standeford, daughter of Ephraim and Sarah, born Sep. 10,1743.
Ephrim Standeford died December 15, 1742.

Page 142

Tamer Camoron, daughter of John and Easther, born July 16, 1738.
John Martin Camoron, son of John and Easther, born July 16, 1742.
Hannah Rhodes, daughter of Richard Jr. and Sarah, born May 2, 1741.

John Rhodes, son of Richard Jr. and Sarah, born Dec. 20, 1743.
Richard Rhodes, son of Richard Jr. and Sarah, born Nov. 30, 1745.
Alexander Rhodes, son of Richard Jr. and Sarah, born Nov. 30, 1745.
"Memdr. The above 2 male children are twins, Richard being the first born."
James Price, son of Robert and Elizabeth, born July 23, 1745.
Elizabeth Childs, daughter of Benjamin and Martha, born Nov. 1,1745.
George Debruler, son of William and Diana, born December 3, 1745.
Rachael Ward, daughter of James Jr. and Hannah, born Nov. 6, 1745.
Mary Whealand, daughter of William and Martha, born Aug. 30, 1745.
John Rockhold, son of John and Elizabeth Elioner, born Feb.27,1742.
Mary Rockhold, daughter of John and Eliz. Elioner, born Mar.1,1745.
Frenetta Erickson, daughter of Erick and Elizabeth, born June 2,1746.

Page 143

Athaliah Demmett, daughter of James and Barbara, born Feb. 21, 1738.
Mary Demmett, daughter of James and Barbara, born December, 1744.
Samuel Hatfield Warrel, son of Samuel and Mary, born Sept. 24, 1745.
Frenetter Erickson White, daughter of John and Mary, born August 30, 1739.
John White died November 14, 1737.
Elizabeth Jackson, daughter of Isaac and Mary, born Jan, 29, 1745.
Benjamin Cadle died March 30, 1746.
John Buck and Susannah Ingram married February 11, 1742.
Elizabeth Buck, daughter of John and Susannah, born June 30, 1742.
Benjamin Buck, son of John and Susannah, born October 10, 1744.
Frederick Roberts Cammell, son of Asael Roberts Cammel and Mary, born January 5, 1744.
John Bull and Hannah Ruff married February 20, 1739.
Mary Bull, daughter of John and Hannah, born April 30, 1740.
John Bull, son of John and Hannah, born December 6, 1743.

Page 144

Frenetta Erickson died September 17, 1746 about 11 o'clock at night.
Amos Garrett and Frances Drew married August 23, 1744.
Bennett Garrett, son of Amos and Frances, born February 23, 1745.
John Golding, son of Peter and Elizabeth, born October 27, 1744.
Stephen Golding, son of Peter and Elizabeth, born Aug. 10, 1746.

John Howard, son of Richard and Margrett, born Feb. 28, 1738.
Thomas Dulany, son of Thomas and Ann, born June 8, 1743.
Elizabeth Dulany, daughter of Thomas and Ann, born Aug. 17, 1746.
Delilah Richardson, daughter of James and Sophia, born May 12, 1746.
Nancey Standeford, daughter of Samuel and Mary Anne, born Aug. 16, 1745.
Elizabeth Dives, daughter of Chris and Sarah, born May 17, 1743.
Sarah Dives, daughter of Christopher and Sarah, born May 7, 1746.
Annanias Dives, son of Christopher and Sarah, born May 7, 1746.
Charles Scimmons and Elizabeth Poteett married October, 1742.
John Scimons, son of Charles and Elizabeth, born September, 1744.
Charles Scimmons, son of Charles and Elizabeth, born Aug. 3, 1746.

Page 145

Thomas Johnson, son of Israel and Sarah, born February 1, 1745.
John Low, son of John and Susannah, born January 27, 1745.
John Mackenney, son of Samuel and Rebecca, born March 24, 1745.
Elizabeth Deason, daughter of Edmund and Elizabeth, born Nov. 13, 1745.
Ruth Standeford, daughter of Skelton and Elizabeth, born Mar. 13, 1745.
Samuel Hatfield Warrel died October 13, 1746.
Thomas White, son of William, deceased, died October 19, 1746.
Rachel Taylor, daughter of Henry and Sarah, born Dec. 3, 1745.
Richard Savors, son of Nicholas and Elizabeth, born Apr. 17, 1746.
William Bell, son of John and Susannah, born March 2, 1744.
Kezia Rutledge, son of John and Elizabeth, born June 16, 1745.
Allexander Madewell, son of James and Elizabeth, born Mar. 11, 1745.
Solomon Cross, son of Henry and Mary, born May 29, 1745.
Elizabeth White, daughter of John and Jane, born November 3, 1745.
John Enzor, son of George and Elizabeth, born October 29, 1745.
William Fuller, son of Henry and Elizabeth, born Nov. 10, 1745.

Page 146

Patience Mungrum, daughter of Mary Mungrum, born January 1, 1743.
Samuel Deason, son of Samuel and Mary, born November 18, 1746.
Jesclila Bozley, daughter of William and Elizabeth, born June 10, 1745.
Benjamin Watkins, son of James and Mary, born January 11, 1745.

Kezia Arsmtrong, daughter of Solomon and Sarah, born Dec. 9, 1745.
Thomas Hutchens, son of Thomas and Hannah, born December 5, 1745.
Luke Standeford, son of James and Martha, born January 25, 1745.
Anne Megummery, daughter of William and Margret, born Feb.15,1745.
Anne Hutchins, daughter of Nicholas Hutchens and Elizabeth, born
    March 25, 1745.
Edward Corbin, son of Edward and Mary, born April 11, 1746.
Kezie Barton, daughter of John and Anne, born February 3, 1745.
Sarah Frizsell, daughter of Gale and Susannah, born Jan, 25, 1745.
Ruth Boreing, daughter of Thomas and Phillis, born Dec. 15, 1745.

Page 147

Stephen Collett, son of Moses and Elizabeth, born May 4, 1746.
William Edy, son of Jonathan and Rebecca, born August 23, 1745.
Samuel Hines, son of Francis and Frances, born November 15, 1740.
Elizabeth Hines, daughter of Francis and Frances, born Aug. 5, 1742.
Elizabeth Amoss, daughter of Thomas and Elizabeth, born Nov. 14,1745.
Nicholas Amoss, son of Thomas and Elizabeth, born September 19, 1742.
Mary Norris, daughter of Edward and Hannah, born October 23, 1745.
Richard Childs, son of John and Elizabeth, born September 27, 1744.
Daniel Scott and Hannah Butterworth married January 27, 1740.
Elizabeth Scott, daughter of Daniel and Hannah, born Sept. 4, 1743.
William Johnson died March 30, 1747.
Abraham Asher, son of Anthony and Susannah, born February 29, 1744.
John Taylor, son of John and Sarah, born June 22, 1747.
Pressilla Nearn, daughter of Elizabeth Nearn, born Sept. 12, 1745.
James Tolley died October 17, 1744.
Sarah Andrew, daughter of William and Mary, born Sept. 23, 1745.

Page 148

John Dorney, son of James and Mary, born in December, 1744.
John Price, son of Robert and Elizabeth, born December 6, 1747,
    "about two of the clock in the afternoon."
John Paca and Elizabeth Smith married November 2, 1732.
Mary Paca, daughter of John and Elizabeth, born August 5, 1733.
Aquila Paca, son of John and Elizabeth, born June 21, 1738.
William Paca, son of John and Elizabeth, born October 31, 1740.

Elizabeth Paca, daughter of John and Elizabeth, born Sep. 8, 1742.
Martha Paca, daughter of John and Elizabeth, born Feb. 3, 1743.
Ann Holt, daughter of John and Sarah, born June 12, 1744.
Mary Holt, daughter of John and Sarah, born December 12, 1746.
John Pickett, son of Heathcot and Mary, born February 13, 1732.
Ann Pickett, daughter of Heathcot and Mary, born April 2, 1735.
Lueresey Pickett, daughter of Heathcot and Mary, born Oct. 11, 1737.
Avarilla Pickett, daughter of Heathcot and Mary, born Feb. 11, 1739.
Elizabeth Heathcott Pickett, daughter of Heathcot and Mary, born November 15, 1744.
Heathcott Pickett, son of Heathcot and Mary, born March 22, 1746.

Page 149

Vincent Dorsey and Sarah Day married October 26, 1742.
Joshua Starkey, son of John and Ann, born in December, 1746.
Thomas Hays and Mary Norrington married August 11, 1735.
James Hays, son of Thomas and Mary, born October 21, 1738.
Edmund Hays, son of Thomas and Mary, born November 21, 1739.
Elizabeth Hays, daughter of Thomas and Mary, born Feb. 12, 1745.
Richard Ward and Mary Gross married August 15, 1739.
John Ward, son of Richard and Mary, born August 1, 1740.
Mary Gross Ward, daughter of Richard and Mary, born May 17, 1742.
Richard Ward, son of Richard and Mary, born March 28, 1744.
Briggett Ward, daughter of Richard and Mary, born Dec. 18, 1746.
John Ward, son of John and Sarah, born in November, 1742.
Sarah Ward, daughter of John and Sarah, born in the year 1745.
Joseph Ward died in January, 1746.
John Ward died in January, 1746.
William Pinkstone and Ann Inmon married in October, 1743.

Page 150

John Pinkstone, son of William and Ann, born July 24, 1744.
Naomi Pinkstone, daughter of William and Ann, born Dec. 18, 1745.
Greenberry Pinkstone, son of William and Ann, born Apr. 17, 1747.
Edward Day died Jan. 14, 1746 and was buried January 20, 1746.
James Maxwell Day, son of John, son of Edward, and Philliszana, born Oct. 29, 1746, and baptised Feb. 22, 1747.
    Walt. Tolley, Ruxton Gay and Eliz. Maxwell, sureties.

John Buck, son of John and Susannah, born December 12, 1746.
Charles Baker, son of Indemuel and Sarah, born in August, 1746.
Susannah Prosser, daughter of Charles and Mary, born Jan. 23, 1746.
Agnes Carlile, daughter of Robert and Easther, born March 16, 1743.
Jane Carlile, daughter of Robert and Easther, born Feb, 6, 1746.
Shederick Newton, son of Hugh and Elinor, born June 11, 1746.
Michael Martin and Mary Feling married in March, 1736.
Araminta Martin, daughter of Michael and Mary, born March 31, 1738.
Juli Ann Martin, daughter of Michael and Mary, born March 3, 1739.
Samuel Martin, son of Michael and Mary, born August 3, 1742.
Ann Elliott died June 15, 1747.

Page 151

William Costley, son of James and Mary, born June 23, 1745.
Martha Costley, daughter of James and Mary, born Sept. 12, 1747.
Richard Willmott and Mary Gittings married December 22, 1741.
Thomas Willmott, son of Richard and Mary, born December 22, 1742.
Rachel Willmott, daughter of Richard and Mary, born Nov. 15, 1744.
John Willmott, son of Richard and Mary, born February 1, 1746.
Benjamin Ricketts and Eliner Maxwell married October 18, 1746.
James Enzer, son of Thomas and Mary, born August 23, 1746.
Thomas Ensor, son of Thomas and Mary, born May 5, 1745.
    "The above child died in the month of Sept., 1745."
Samuel Smith, son of Samuel and Avarilla, born Sept. 18, 1745,
    and died January 12, 1746.
William Smith, son of Samuel and Avarilla, died Jan. 22, 1746.
Mary Poteet, daughter of John Jr. and Ruth, born April 16, 1747.
Elisacas Erickson, daughter of Erick and Elizabeth, born Oct. 26, 1747.
Mary Bond, daughter of William Jr. and Ann, born Nov. 29, 1745.

Page 152

Robert Price, son of Robert and Elizabeth, born December 6, 1747,
    "about nine of the clock at night."
Merriken Dutton, son of Robert and Mary, born August 7, 1747.
James Carroll and Ann Bond married November 24, 1736.
Elizabeth Carroll, daughter of James and Ann, born May 12, 1738.
James Bond Carroll, son of James and Ann, born Feb. 22, 1739.

Peter Bond Carroll, son of James and Ann, born May 6, 1741.
Mary Carroll, daughter of James and Ann, born April 12, 1745.
Elioner Carroll. daughter of James and Ann, born July 20, 1747.
Coziah Brusbanks, daughter of Edward Jr. and Briggett, born
    November 5, 1743.
Mary Brusbanks, daughter of Edward Jr. and Briggett, born
    February 28, 1746.
Joseph Mead, son of Joseph and Mary, born January 11, 1747.
Martha Whealand, daughter of William and Martha, born Sep. 14, 1747.
Sarah Richardson, daughter of Thomas and Sarah, born January, 1745.
Elizabeth Amoss, daughter of James and Hannah, born Jan. 15, 1743.

Page 153

William Amoss, son of James and Hannah, born August 16, 1745.
James Amoss, son of James and Hannah, born January 8, 1746.
Susannah Childs, daughter of Benjamin and Martha, born Jan. 11, 1747.
Elizabeth Hughs, daughter of Jon. Hughs and Jane, born Aug. 4, 1747.
John Conner and Susannah Burges married in August, 1744.
John Conner, son of John and Susannah, born July 30, 1746.
Clemency Bond, daughter of Benjamin and Clemency, born May 12, 1745.
Josias William Dallam, son of William and Elizabeth, born
    November 5, 1747.
Hannah Bull, daughter of John and Hannah, born February 10, 1747.
Mary Moore, daughter of James Jr., born May 11, 1742.
Rezin Moore, son of James Jr., born August 16, 1744.
Mary Beck, daughter of Elijah Beck and Sarah, born Feb. 18, 1747.
Mary Hays, daughter of Thomas and Mary, born July 15, 1747.
Rachael Wilkinson, daughter of Samuel and Mary, born Dec. 29, 1747.

Page 154

William White, son of John and Sarah, born August 10, 1745.
Thomas Wordgworth, son of Thomas and Rebecca, born March 19, 1747.
Elizabeth Hargisty, daughter of James and Kezia, born Dec.28,1748.
Thomas Marshall, and Sarah Bull, married October 3, 1740.
John Norris, son of Edward and Hannah, born January 26, 1747.
Elizabeth Childs, wife of John Childs, died August 9, 1747.
Ann Bond, daughter of William Jr. and Ann, born May 6, 1748.

Benjamin Clark, son of John and Elizabeth, born in October, 1748.
Rachael Ady, daughter of Jonathan and Rebecca, born December, 1743.
James Maxwell Day, son of John Day, son of Edward, and Philliszana, died January 23, 1747.
Nicholas Day, son of Edward, died January 27, 1748.
Mary Carlile, daughter of Robert and Easther, born October 2, 1748.
Jacob Jackson died May 24, 1747.
Isaac Jackson died January 25, 1748.
Elizabeth Dallam, wife of William, died October 24, 1748.

Page 155

William Standeford and Christiannah Wright married November, 1739.
Aquilla Standeford, son of William and Christiannah, born August 24, 1740.
Averilla Standeford, daughter of William and Christiannah, born August 24, 1740.
William Standeford, son of William and Christiannah, born Nov., 1742.
Abraham Standeford, son of William and Christiannah, born May 18, 1745.
Mary Wordgworth, daughter of Thomas and Rebecca, born Feb. 25, 1748.
Delia William Smith, daughter of Samuel and Avarilla, born June 13, 1748.
"Joseph Smith Gunpd: Died December 17, 1748."
Hannah Childs, daughter of Benjamin and Martha, born Sept. 28, 1748.
Margret Deadman died December 14, 1749.
James Elliott and Mary Weecks married December 29, 1736.
Elisabeth Ady, daughter of Jonathan and Rebecca, born Aug. 13, 1747.
George Grover, son of George and Jane, born November 3, 1730.
John Russel, son of Francis and Jane, born in December, 1737.
Mary Russel, daughter of Francis and Jane, born April 1, 1741.

Page 156

Jane Russel, daughter of Francis and Jane, born August 14, 1745.
Francis Russel died in July, 1748.
Mary Warrel, wife of Samuel Warrel, died December 21, 1748.
John Debruler died April 15, 1749.
Elizabeth Brown, daughter of Ratchford and Ann, born Mar. 21, 1738.
Mary Brown, daughter of Ratchford and Ann, born in February, 1743.
John Brown, son of Ratchford and Ann, born June 6, 1747.

Benjamin Norris, son of Joseph and Mary, born January 17, 1749.
Ezane Denton, daughter of John and Rachael, born August 14, 1748.
William Denton died February 6, 1747.
William Denton Jr. and Elizabeth James married February 2, 1744.
William Denton, son of William and Elizabeth, born March 25, 1749.
John Cowdry, son of Thomas and Ann, born in October, 1736.
Drucilla Durbin, daughter of Thomas and Ann, born October 9, 1738.
Ketura Durbin, daughter of Thomas and Ann, born March 23, 1741.

Page 157

Thomas Durbin, son of Thomas and Ann, born March 8, 1743.
Mary Durbin, daughter of Thomas and Ann. born in November, 1746.
Joseph Poulson, son of Joseph and Frances, born August 2, 1748.
Mary Price, daughter of Robert and Elizabeth, born Dec. 24, 1749.
George Bradford and Margrett Bonfield married December 3, 1746.
William Bradford, son of George and Margrett, born May 20, 1748.
William Yeates died December 6, 1748.
Joseph Yeates died in October, 1748.
John Standerline died in 1749.
Elizabeth Golding, daughter of Peter and Elizabeth, born Aug. 18, 1749.
Elizabeth Ricketts, daughter of Benjamin and Eliner, born Jan. 1, 1747.
Mary Elliott, daughter of James and Mary, born May 24, 1744.
Michael Elliott, son of James and Mary, born October 29, 1747.
Sarah Elliott, daughter of James and Mary, born January 24, 1749.
Jane Brusbanks, daughter of Edward and Briggett, born Aug. 13, 1749.
William Baker, son of Morris and Christian, born February 12, 1749.
John Allender and Lucina Roberts married March 27, 1749.
William Allender, son of John and Lucina, born Sept. 28, 1752.

Page 158

William Allender, son of John and Lucina, died October 6, 1752.
Margrett Allender, daughter of John and Lucina, born Jan. 18, 1753.
Blanch Allinder, daughter of John and Lucina, born December, 1756, and died in 1757.
Sarah Day, daughter of Edward and Ann, born June 20, 1751.
Janet Day, daughter of Edward and Ann, born September 30, 1753.

Anne Day, daughter of Edward and Anne, born October 14, 1755.
Edward Day, son of Edward and Anne, born August 17, 1759.
William Horton, son of John and Prissilla, born March 2, 1743.
Avarilla Day, daughter of John, son of Edward and Philliszana,
    born September 16, 1749.
James Day, second son of John, son of Edward and Philliszana,
    born March 24, 1753, and died March 31, 1753.
John Taylor, son of John Taylor, Joppa, and Sarah Day, was born
    November 21, 1767. (Record indicated he was married
    on this date; obviously a clerical error.)
Ann Taylor, daughter of John and Sarah, born February 2, 1769.

Page 159

Michael Martin died in April, 1749.
John Brown died February 21, 1749.
Ann Wharrington, daughter of Henry and Mary, born Dec. 3, 1743.
Elizabeth Wharrington, daughter of Henry and Mary, born Apr. 3, 1746.
William Edy, son of Jonathan and Rebecca, born August 23, 1745.
Elizabeth Brian, daughter of William and Hannah, born Nov. 10, 1745.
Thomas Savage, son of John and Ann, born May 13, 1747.
Elizabeth Crawford, daughter of Thomas and Martha, born Feb. 16, 1746.
Sarah Lane, daughter of Samuel and Jane, born November 8, 1746.
Wilkinson Lane, son of Samuel and Jane, born April 21, 1743.
Margret Boseman, daughter of Edward and Elizabeth, born Nov. 13, 1744.
John Hitchcock, son of William and Susanna, born October 15, 1746.
Mary Perrigoe, daughter of Henry and Providence, born Oct. 31, 1746.
Charles Scimmons, son of Charles and Elizabeth, born August 3, 1746.
Mary Wicks, daughter of Thomas and Elizabeth, born February 11, 1746.
Thomas Wicks, son of Thomas and Elizabeth, born December 27, 1744.
John Wicks, son of Thomas and Elizabeth, born May 15, 1743.

Page 160

James Demmett, son of James and Barbary, born February 17, 1748.
Joseph Gibbins, son of John and Mary, born July 14, 1749.
John Hogan, son of Jacob and Ann, born August 28, 1749.
Thomas Rhodes, son of Richard and Sarah, born March 1, 1747.
Martha Maccomas, daughter of Daniel and Martha, born June 7, 1749.
John Thurston, son of George and Frances, born May 25, 1749.

John Prosser, son of Charles and Mary, born January 30, 1748.
James Hutchens, son of Thomas and Martha, born March 5, 1747.
Alimessey, daughter of William and Ann, born December 28, 1747.
Ann Jones, daughter of Pickett and Elizabeth, born Feb. 17, 1746.
Elizabeth Christeson, daughter of John and Margrett, born Mar.7,1746.
John Wilkinson, son of Phillip and Rebecca, born April 9, 1745.
Young Wilkinson, son of Phillip and Rebecca, born October 27, 1746.
Elizabeth Wilkinson (Wilkson), daughter of Phillip and Rebecca,
       born September 19, 1748.
William Godigrace, son of John and Rebecca, born January 9, 1738.
Rebecca Godigrace, daughter of John and Rebecca, born Mar. 7, 1740.
John Brown died February 13, 1749.
Ann Brown died in the year 1749.

Page 161

Nathan Scott, son of Daniel and Hannah, born August 14, 1749.
Nathaniel Ricketts, son of Nathaniel and Ann, born January, 1749.
John Nash, son of Elizabeth Nash, born June 2, 1742.
Richard Lynch Lenox, son of James and Mary, born January 8, 1738.
Richardson Lenox, son of James and Mary, born September 21, 1743.
Nathan Lenox, son of James and Mary, born August 31, 1740.
Mary Dutton, daughter of Robert and Mary, born March 20, 1749.
Cloe Denton, daughter of John and Rachel, born January 30, 1749.
Ann Carroll, daughter of James and Ann, born December 17, 1749.
George York, son of Edward and Ann, born in August, 1750.
Fanny Anne Erickson, daughter of Erick and Elizabeth, born
       July 6, 1750.
Jas. (Jos.) Smith Mason died in September, 1749.
Ruth Bozwell died in November, 1750.
Thomas Nixson and Sarah Thompson married July 23, 1741.
William Nixson, son of Thomas and Sarah, born March 27, 1748.
Thomas Nixson, son of Thomas and Sarah, born March 29, 1750.
John Thompson and Sarah Blackwell married December 25, 1740.
Elizabeth Thompson, daughter of John and Sarah, born March, 1741.
Margret Thompson, daughter of John and Sarah, born April 15, 1747.

Page 162

Mary Scott, daughter of Robert and Mary, born in 1749.
James Whealand died August 14, 1750.
William Watson was born July 19, 1738.
Elizabeth Bacon, daughter of Marten and Mary, born Nov. 23, 1741.
John Bacon, son of Marten and Mary, born August 20, 1743.
W. Burk, son of Thomas and Sarah, born January 30, 1740.
Elizabeth Burk, daughter of Thomas and Sarah, born May 5, 1745.
Thomas Burk, son of Thomas and Sarah, born November 17, 1747.
John Barton, son of John and Ann, born February 22, 1749.
John Newton, son of Ann Bewton, born June 26, 1748.
James Sheredine Stephens, son of Maple Stevenson, born Aug. 20, 1749.
Thomas Enzor, son of Thomas and Mary, born November 19, 1749.
Elinor, wife of John Kersey, died in the year 1751.
Lyda Thrift, daughter of John and Sarah, born in June, 1738.
Prudance Thrift, daughter of John and Sarah, born April 7, 1740.
Hickibudd Thrift, daughter of John and Sarah, born May 6, 1743.
Sharlother Thrift, daughter of John and Sarah, born April 5, 1746.
James Thrift, son of John and Sarah, born November 14, 1748.

Page 163

Richard Thrift, son of John and Sarah, born March 25, 1751.
John Thrift died December 13, 1751.
Prudance Thrift died January 11, 1753.
Hannah Kitely, daughter of Francis and Martha, born Feb. 18, 1748.
Mary Kitely, daughter of Francis and Martha, born February 17, 1750.
Elizabeth Dutton, daughter of Robert and Mary, born Nov. 13, 1752.
Hannah Mariter Ricketts, daughter of Benjamin and Eliner, born October 18, 1751.
John Carroll, son of James and Ann, born June 5, 1752.
Betszey Frissele, daughter of Gale Frissell and Susannah, born February 4, 1743.
John Gale Frissell, son of Gale and Susannah, born in July, 1748.
Thomas Frissell, son of Gale and Susannah, born January 12, 1750.
Thomas Cotterrell and Frances Millhughs married August 4, 1743.
Rachaell Cotterrell, daughter of Thomas and Frances, born October 18, 1744.
John Cotterrell, son of Thomas and Frances, born May 14, 1747.

Wealthy Ann Cotterrell, daughter of Thomas and Frances, born
    August 17, 1749.
Mary Wilmott, daughter of Richard and Mary, born Jan. 28, 1753.
Elizabeth York, daughter of Edward and Ann, born April 30, 1753.
William Smith, son of Henry and Cathrine, born March 27, 1752.

Page 164

Josias Hitchcock, son of Assaell Hitchcock and Sarah, born
    June 24, 1753.
Mary Watkins, daughter of Samuel and Margrett, born April, 1753.
Solloman Wright, son of Abraham and Darkes, born March 7, 1747.
Thomas Brereton Sr. died-----------17--.
Ruth Bayly, daughter of Thomas Bayley and Ann, born June 17, 1740.
Rachael Bayley, daughter of Thomas and Ann, born May 21, 1741.
Cathrene Bayley, daughter of Thomas and Ann, born April 24, 1743.
Kezia Bayley, daughter of Thomas and Ann. born November 1, 1745.
Mordicai Meads, son of James, son of Edward and Ann, born
    December 26, 1752 "about sun sett."
James Meads, son of James and Ann, born December 26, 1752
    "about twelve a clock at night."
"The children above mentioned (Mordicai and James) both come at
    a birth."
William Tayman and Ann Nearn married December 25, 1750.
Elizabeth Tayman, daughter of William and Ann, born Feb. 19, 1747.
Benjamin Tayman, daughter of William and Ann, born March 14, 1750.
Jemima Tayman, daughter of William and Ann, born March 13, 1753.
Jemima Johnson, daughter of Jacob and Elizabeth, born "the last
    day of February in the year 1752."

Page 165

Ann Mayes, daughter of James and Mary, born November 26, 1747.
Rachael Moore, daughter of James Jr. and Hannah, born Jan. 8, 1748/9.
James Francis Moore, son of James Jr. and Hannah, born Aug. 12, 1751.
Nicholas Ruxton Moore, son of James Jr. and Hannah, born July 21, 1756.
Eleanor Moore, daughter of James Jr. and Hannah, born May 14, 1759.
John Gay Moore, son of James Jr. and Hannah, born March 8, 1761.
Rachael Bull, daughter of John and Hannah, born November 18, 1753.

James Coffill, son of Pat and Mary, born in December, 1749.
Margarett Coffill, daughter of Pat and Mary, born June 30, 1752.
William Eves, son of Edward and Lucy Ann, born February 23, 1752.
Ann Eves, daughter of Edward and Lucy Ann, born in March, 1754.
Hannah Johnson, daughter of Jacob and Elizabeth, born June 13, 1754.
Michael Duskin, son of Michael and Sarah, born October 27, 1752.
William Hutchens, son of Nicholas and Elizabeth, born Mar. 31, 1754.
John Thomas, son of Martha Thomas, born in February, 1747.

Page 166

William Rowings, son of John and Comfort, born July 20, 1752.
John Rowings, son of John and Comfort, born December 30, 1753.
Mosess Hill, son of William and Martha, born December 4, 1748.
Aron Hill, son of William and Martha, born November 29, 1751.
John Brown died in February, 1749.
Samuel Swan, son of Burch and Margrett, born January 11, 1740.
Muriel Swan, daughter of Burch and Margrett, born Sept. 22, 1742.
Dorothy Swan, daughter of Burch and Margrett, born Aug. 19, 1744.
Bassell Swan, son of Burch and Margrett, born March 31, 1746.
Pencesealah Swan, daughter of Burch and Margrett, born May 16, 1748.
Aquilla Swan, son of Burch and Margrett, born January 29, 1751.
Thomas Burch Swan, son of Burch and Margrett, born August 7, 1753.
Josias Smith, son of Samuel and Avarilla, born June 13, 1754.
Mary Presbury, daughter of Joseph and Sarah, born Oct. 29, 1750.
Eliner Presbury, daughter of Joseph and Sarah, born Nov. 19, 1752.
Joseph Swan, son of Burch and Margret, born September 14, 1756.
Charles Watters, son of John and Providence, born June 8, 1761.
Providence Watters, wife of John Watters, died January 4, 1763.

Page 167

John White, son of Erk. White and Rachel, born February 24, 1762.
Stephen Watters, son of Godfrey and Sarah, born March 15, 1747.
Walter Watters, son of Godfrey and Sarah, born February 8, 1749.
William Watters, son of Godfrey and Sarah, born October 18, 1751.
Godfrey Watters died May 15, 1754.
Isaac Bull, son of Isaac and Betsey Ann, born
        "October 18, 1751 March 25, 1766."

Mary Bull, daughter of Isaac and Betsey Ann, born January 1, 1769.
Stephen Onion died Monday, August 26, 1754.
William Fowler, son of Richard and Mary, born March 26, 1755.
Benjamin Amoss, son of Benjamin and Sarah, born Oct. 11, 1753.
Elizabeth Enzor, daughter of Thomas and Mary, born Nov., 1754.
Rachel Scimmons, daughter of George and Elizabeth, born
    April 8, 1751.
Abigal Scimmons, daughter of George and Elizabeth, born
    September 26, 1753.
Elizabeth Mears, daughter of Abraham and Jane, born Mar. 1, 1753.
Abraham Mears, son of Abraham and Jane, born December 6, 1754.
Sushan Prosser, daughter of Charles and Mary, born Jan. 23, 1746.
Rachael Bull, daughter of Isaac and Hannah, born March 5, 1755.

Page 168

Sarah Carrol, daughter of James and Ann, born December 15, 1754.
Mary Johnson, daughter of Jacob and Elizabeth, born Aug. 31, 1756.
Jacob Bull, son of John and Hannah, born February 24, 1756.
Doctor James McGill died October 20, 1756.
Richard Wilmot and Mary Gittings married December 22, 1741.
Thomas Wilmot, son of Richard and Mary, born Dec. 22, 1742.
Rachael Wilmot, daughter of Richard and Mary, born Nov. 15, 1744.
John Wilmot, son of Richard and Mary, born February 1, 1746.
Elizabeth Wilmot, daughter of Richard and Mary, born Jan. 20, 1748.
Richard Wilmot, son of Richard and Mary, born December 24, 1750.
Mary Wilmot, daughter of Richard and Mary, born January 28, 1753.
John Watters and Mary Horner married "being his second wife"
    February 22, 1767.
Sarah Watters, daughter of John and Mary, born December 29, 1767.
Joshua Brown, son of John and Elizabeth, born November 10, 1755.
    "Departed Nov. 1788."
Jeremiah Chance and Wheatley Ann Milldews married Nov. 25, 1752.
Anne Chance, daughter of Jeremiah Chance and Anne Whealthy,
    born March 21, 1754.

Page 169

Elizabeth Dutton, daughter of Robert and Mary, born Nov. 13, 1752.
Sarah Dutton, daughter of Robert and Mary, born February 16, 1755.

Mary Chance, daughter of Jeremiah Chance and Wealthy Ann,
    born November 25, 1755.
John Hamond Dorsey Jr., son of John and Frances, died May 1, 1748.
Stephen Dorsey, son of John Hamond and Frances, died May 29, 1749.
Mary Hamond Dorsey, daughter of John Hamond and Frances, born
    February 21, 1749.
Rebecca Dorsey, daughter of John Hamond and Frances, born
    March 22, 1752.
John Hamond Dorsey Jr., "the second son of that name" of John
    Hamond and Frances, born February 14, 1754.
Frances Dorsey, daughter of John Hamond and Frances, born
    April 19, 1756.
Elizabeth Chance, daughter of Jeremiah Chance and Whealthy Anne,
    Born March, 1758.
Zelpah Dortridge, daughter of William and Margrett, born
    "February 30, 1750."
Leah Dortridge, daughter of William and Margrett, born Mar. 27, 1758.
Rachael Dortridge, daughter of William and Margrett, Nov. 2, 1757.
Susannah Trigger, daughter of Zebediah Trigger, born July 1, 1755.
Daniel Tredwell, son of Richard and Maple, born April 30, 1754.
John Presbury, son of Thomas and Ann, born February 24, 1755.
Walter Tolley and Martha Hall married December 22, 1751.

Page 170

Edward Carvel Tolley, son of Walter and Martha, born Oct. 14, 1753.
Martha Tolley, daughter of Walter and Martha, born May 21, 1755,
    and died June 3, 1755.
Ann Tolley, daughter of Walter and Martha, born July 7, 1756.
Martha Tolley, daughter of Walter and Martha, born Sep. 17, 1758.
Josias Slade, son of Ezekiel and Ann, born October 12, 1754.
Hannah Armstrong, daughter of Henry and Mary, born Jan. 28, 1744.
John Armstrong, son of Henry and Mary, born February 4, 1746.
Sophia Armstrong, daughter of Henry and Mary, born July 28, 1748.
Elizabeth Armstrong, daughter of Henry and Mary, born in July, 1750.
Tarashar Armstrong, daughter of Henry and Mary, born Mar. 3, 1753.
Henry Armstrong, son of Henry and Mary, born March 3, 1756.
Dixson Stansbury, son of Dixon and Panellipie, born July 22, 1744.
Edmund Stansbury, son of Dixson and Penellipi, born Oct. 6, 1746.
Elizabeth Stansbury, daughter of Dixson and Penellipi, born
    June 7, 1749.

James Stansbury, son of Dixson and Penellipi, born Nov. 7, 1751.

Page 171

Mary Cartee, daughter of Brian and Frances, born in 1751.
John Cartee, son of Brian and Frances, born in 1754.
Thomas Costley, son of James and Mary, born Nov. 6, 1756.
Mary Flanagin, daughter of Batholomas Flanagen and Elizabeth,
    born May 2, 1753.
William Flannagen, son of Batholomew Flannagen and Mary, born
    December 25, 1755.
Henry Flannagen, son of Batholomew and Mary, born May 17, 1757.
Elizabeth Heath, daughter of David and Sarah, born May 27, 1756.
Elinor Ricketts, wife of Benjamin Ricketts, died December 16, 1756.
Guy Litle and Elizabeth Ruff married March 25, 1757.
James Litle, son of Guy and Elizabeth, born January 20, 1752.
Ann Litle, daughter of Guy and Elizabeth, born October 24, 1754.
John Ruff, son of Daniel and Elizabeth, born January 16, 1749.
James Power, son of Nicholas and Elizabeth, born Nov. 24, 1753.
Erick Erickson died 1750.
William Chambers, son of Thomas and Mary, born in 1747.
Elinor Chambers, daughter of Thomas and Mary, born in 1749.
Thomas Chambers, son of Thomas and Mary, born in 1752.
Joseph Chambers, son of Thomas and Mary, born inJanuary, 1755.

Page 172

Mildred Nixson, daughter of Thomas and Sarah, born September 25,
    1755, and died the same year.
William Nixson, son of Thomas and Sarah, died October 14, 1751.
William Nixson, son of Thomas and Sarah, born April 20, 1752.
William Copeland Goldsmith, son of Thomas and Lilley, was born
    "and his left ear growing more from his head then the
    other, the Parents of the said child thought proper to
    request the Clerk of the Register in the parish where
    the said child was born to enter the same on the Register
    aforesaid, be being born with his ear in the form as is
    above expressed, in confirmation of the truth to this
    entry I have hereunto put my hand this 7th day of Oct.,
    1757.   John Roberts, Regr."
Cathender Barton, daughter of Greenberrey and Ann, born Apr. 4, 1768.
Thomas Barton, son of Greenberrey and Ann, born June 4, 1769.

Alice Marsh, daughter of James Jr. and Sarah, born March 5, 1757.
Mordicai Kelley and Mary Hines married January 6, 1757.
John Kelley, son of Mordicai and Mary, born November 19, 1757.
Dilila Kelley, daughter of Mordicai and Mary, born Dec. 14, 1760.
Celia Barton, son of Greenberry and Ann, born November 27, 1771.
Benjamin Smith, son of Samuel and Avarilla, born August 30, 1757.

Page 173

Mary Tunis, daughter of John and Martha, born July 22, 1757.
Mary Buck, daughter of John and Susannah, born March 23, 1762.
Mary White, daughter of Erk. and Rachel, born in March, 1764.
Ann Merredith, daughter of Thomas and Susan, born March 7, 1756.
Henry Merrideth, son of Thomas and Susan, born August 1, 1757.
John Carter, son of William and Mary, born March 8, 1761.
William Chance, son of Jeremiah and Wealththy Ann, born Feb.28,1764.
Edward Norris, son of Joseph Jr. and Mary, born July 29, 1751.
Temperrance Norris, daughter of Joseph Jr. and Mary, born Feb.2,1753.
James Norris, son of Joseph Jr. and Mary, born March 29, 1756.
John Taylor, son of John and Elizabeth, born October 4, 1759.
Benjamin Norris, son of John and Susannah, born August 16, 1745.
John Norris, son of John and Susannah, born June 6, 1747.
William Norris, son of John and Susannah, born March 26, 1749.
Martha Norris, daughter of John and Susannah, born August 16, 1750.
Jacob Norris, son of John and Susannah, born May 10, 1753.
Susannah Norris, daughter of John and Susannah, born May 10, 1753.

Page 174

Thomas Norris, son of John and Susannah, born January 23, 1756.
Sarah Norris, daughter of John and Susannah, born January 23, 1756.
Ann Taylor, daughter of Charles and Elizabeth, born October 3, 1752.
John Taylor, son of Charles and Elizabeth, born in October, 1754.
James Taylor, son of Charles and Elizabeth, born February 17, 1756.
Benjamin Smith, son of Samuel and Avarrilla, born August 30, 1757.
Hannah Carroll, daughter of James and Ann, born August 26, 1757.
John Amoss, son of Benjamin and Sarah, born March 18, 1758.
Walter Pickett, son of John and Amelia, born August 5, 1757.
Hannah Cartie, daughter of Brian and Frances, born Nov. 14, 1757.

John Cartie, son of Darby and Susan, born April 1, 1758.
Cuthbert Greenwell Childs, son of Martha Childs, born Mar. 1, 1760.
Susanna Taylor, daughter of John Taylor son of John and Elizabeth
    born March 23, 1758.
Sarah Bond, daughter of Benjamin and Clemency, born June 13, 1748.
Elizabeth Taylor, daughter of John and Sarah, born Oct. 13, 1758.
William Bain, son of John and Mary, born April 23, 1756.
Mary Bain, daughter of John and Mary, born September 19, 1758.

Page 175

Alexander Norris, son of John Norris son of Benjamin and Susannah
    born May 15, 1759.
Mary Norris, daughter of John Norris son of Benjamin and Susannah
    born May 15, 1759.
Francis Dives, son of Francis Dives and Mary, born Sept, 18, 1765.
Zacheus Onion and Hannah Bond married December 2, 1757.
Elizabeth Onion, daughter of Zacheus and Hannah, born Feb. 2, 1759.
Stephen Onion, son of Zacheus and Hannah, born August 21, 1760,
    and died January 20, 1761.
John Chance, son of Jeremiah and Wealthy Ann, born Nov. 6, 1759
    "about 2 o'clock in the morning."
Sarah Chance, daughter of Jeremiah and Wealthy Ann, born Nov.28,1761.
Stephen Dorsey, son of John Hammond and Frances, born March 7, 1758.
William Campbell, son of Moses and Rebecca, born in September, 1753.
John Campbell, son of Mosses and Rebecca, born in October, 1755.
Mary Campbell, daughter of Mosses and Rebecca, born in Oct., 1757.
John Hill, son of William and Martha, born April 25, 1756.
Mary Wooling, daughter of Richard and Elizabeth, born Sept. 10, 1758.
William Bishop Brown, son of John and Elizabeth, born Oct. 1, 1758.
Godfrey Watters, son of John and Providence, born March 21, 1759.

Page 176

Richard Robertson, son of Edward and Margret, born April 9, 1753.
Elizabeth Robertson, daughter of Edward and Margrett, born
    July 23, 1755.
John Mcfaden, son of John Macfaden and Margret, born May 16, 1743.
Deborah Macfadden, daughter of John and Margret, born June, 1745.
Randell Macfadden, son of John and Margret, born September, 1747.
Mary Mcfadden, daughter of John and Margrett, born in July, 1749.

Thomas Mcfadden, son of John and Margrett, born September, 1757.
John Warrington, son of Henry and Mary, born August 20, 1741.
Ann Warrington, daughter of "said John and Mary" born Dec. 1, 1743.
Elizabeth Warrington, daughter of "said John and Mary" born in
    September, 1745.
Mary Warrington, daughter of "said John and Mary" born Sept., 1747.
William Warrington, son of "said John and Mary" born July 81, 1752.
Henry Warrington, son of "said John and Mary" born March 8, 1754.
Susannah Warrington, daughter of "said John and Mary, born
    April 17, 1756.
(Note: It appears that John Warrington above was also a son of John
and Mary, not Henry and Mary; clerical error by Register. HCP)
Lydia Armstrong, daughter of Henry and Mary, born February 12, 1759.
Joseph Taylor, son of Charles and Elizabeth, born in July, 1758.
Samuel Talbee, son of Samuel and Elizabeth, born November 12, 1758.

Page 177

Mary Whitehead, daughter of William Bond Whitehead and Susannah,
    born February 11, 1754.
William Whitehead, son of William and Susannah, born Jan. 11, 1756.
Christiana Johnson, daughter of Nathaniel and Elizabeth, born
    May 21, 1759.
Cordelia Durbin, daughter of John and Rachael, born Sept. 8, 1757.
David Stevens, son of Giles Jr. and Avarrilla, born Nov. 21, 1756.
William Stevens, son of Giles Jr. and Avarilla, born June 27, 1758.
William Johnson, son of Nathan and Elizabeth, born Feb. 22, 1755.
Mary Johnson, daughter of Nathan and Elizabeth, born Mar. 18, 1757.
Margaret Burk died October 13, 1759.
Christiana Johnson, daughter of Nathan and Elizabeth, born
    March 14, 1760.
John Pocock, son of Daniel and Sarah, born June 20, 1760.
John Stevens, son of Giles Jr. and Avarilla, born Oct. 13, 1760.
Mary Baine, daughter of John and Mary, born May 1, 1766.
James Presbury, son of Joseph and Sarah, born February 10, 1764.
William Presbury, son of Joseph and Sarah, born Dec. 2, 1766.
Robert Dutton and Susannah Howard married February 24, 1757.
Robert Dutton, son of Robert and Susannah, born Dec. 24, 1759.
John Dutton, son of Robert and Susannah, born December 23, 1761.

Page 178

Ann Dutton, daughter of Robert and Susannah, born June 19, 1764.
James Bond Kimberly, son of Mary Kimberly, born July 18, 1761.
John Kimberly, son of Mary Kimberly, born April 27, 1763.
Sarah Kimberly, daughter of Mary Kimberly, born March 13, 1765.
George Gouldsmith Presbury and Elizabeth Tolley married June 10, 1756.
Mary Gouldsmith Presbury, daughter of George Gouldsmith and Elizabeth,
    born July 1, 1758.
George Gouldsmith Presbury, son of George Gouldsmith and Elizabeth,
    born February 21, 1759.
Martha Gouldsmith Presbury, daughter of "said Gouldsmith and Elizabeth"
    born May 7, 1761.
Walter Gouldsmith Presbury, son of "said Gouldsmith and Elizabeth"
    born September 11, 1764.
Philliszana Day, wife of John Day son of Edward and daughter of James
    Maxwell and Mary, died May 21, 1759 "about 11 o'clock in
    the forenoon."
Philliszana Day, daughter of John Day son of Edward and Philliszana,
    born May 21, 1759, and died May 22, 1759 "about 4 o'clock
    in the afternoon."
Thomas Turner and Mary Kimberly married October 26, 1766.

Page 179

Mary Turner, daughter of Thomas and Mary, born January 20, 1771.
William Bond, son of William and Ann, born February 12, 1749.
Sarah Bond, daughter of William and Ann, born June 23, 1752.
Isaac Risteau and Elizabeth Reaven married February 21, 1748.
Sarah Risteau, daughter of Isaac and Elizabeth, born Feb. 18, 1749.
Catherine Risteau, daughter of Isaac and Elizabeth, born May 20, 1750.
Mary Risteau, daughter of Isaac and Elizabeth, born October 27, 1751.
Abraham Risteau, son of Isaac and Elizabeth, born March 4, 1753.
John Talbott Risteau, son of Isaac and Elizabeth, born Nov. 11, 1754.
David Risteau, son of Isaac and Elizabeth, born December 18, 1756.
Joseph Risteau, son of Isaac and Elizabeth, born July 22, 1760.
William Robinson Presbury and Martha Hall, daughter of John Hall
    and Berthiah, married February 23, 1764.
Sophiah Presbury, daughter of William and Martha, born Mar. 13, 1767.
George Presbury, son of William and Martha, born December 27, 1768.
Berthiah Presbury, daughter of William and Martha, born May 6, 1770.
Isabeler Presbury, daughter of William and Martha, born Feb. 26, 1772.

Henry James and Mary Hernly married June 26, 1745.

Page 180

Elizabeth James, daughter of Henry and Mary, born August 3, 1747.
Hilling James, son of Henry and Mary, born November 5, 1749.
Nathan James, son of Henry and Mary, born April 12, 1754.
John James, son of Henry and Mary, born September 30, 1759,
"in the Town of Joppa."
Henry James, son of Henry and Mary, born April 9, 1763,
"in the Town of Joppa."
William Rowing, son of John and Comfort, born 1752.
Pressilla Bennett, daughter of Charles and Martha, born May 27, 1755.
Ann Bennett, daughter of Charles and Martha, born March 3, 1756.
Cathrine Bennett, daughter of Charles and Martha, born Nov. 5, 1758.
Sarah Murphey, wife of James Murphey, died in the year 1750.
Nathan Little, son of Guy and Elizabeth, born June 17, 1757.
George Little, son of Guy and Elizabeth, born October 22, 1759.
Lowraner Greer, daughter of Moses and Mary, born June 7, 1757.
Aquila Greer, son of Moses and Mary, born September 9, 1760.
Stephen Ward, son of Joseph and Mary, born March 17, 1766.
Elizabeth Starkey, daughter of Jonathan and Mary, born May 19, 1758.
William Starkey, son of Jonathan and Mary, born November 21, 1759.

Page 181

Jonathan Starkey, son of Jonathan and Mary, born March 12, 1761.
Wealthy Ann Chance, daughter of Jeremiah and Whealthy, born on
Tuesday, January 14, 1766.
John Scarff, son of Henry and Patty, born October 29, 1759.
Cathrine Poteet, daughter of Thomas Poteet and Ann, born Feb. 8, 1761.
Sarah Ward, daughter of Joseph and Mary, born October 8, 1761.
Elizabeth Ward, daughter of Joseph and Mary, born October 8, 1761.
"They being twins."
Thomas Johnson, son of Nathan and Elizabeth, born July 22, 1762.
Sarah Dortridge, daughter of William and Margaret, died in Mar., 1759.
Lettice Dortridge, daughter of William and Margaret, born Aug.11,1761.
Ann Spencer, daughter of James and Batrix, born April 6, 1759,
"said Ann died 22nd August following."
Nicholas Spencer, son of James and Batrix, born September 30, 1761.
Christopher Dives died November 8, 1766 "about 10 of the clock in
the morning."

William Fell, son of Edward and Ann, born August 29, 1759.
Ann Baine, daughter of John and Mary, born July 3, 1763.
Sarah Davis, daughter of Jacob and Elizabeth, born Oct. 6, 1746.
Elizabeth Davis, daughter of Jacob and Elizabeth, born Mar. 31, 1750.
Mary Davis, daughter of Jacob and Elizabeth, born July 10, 1755.

Page 182

Mary Tuder, daughter of Joseph and Elizabeth, born July 22, 1759.
Elizabeth Tuder, daughter of Joseph and Elizabeth, born June 10, 1761.
William Tuder, son of Joseph and Elizabeth, born August 11, 1763.
William Tuder and Mary Tuder, daughter and son of Joseph and Mary,
    died in the month of March, 1764.
William Norris, son of Joseph son of Edward and Phillice born
    February 1758.
Joseph Norris, son of Joseph son of Edward and Phillice born in
    February, 1761.
Sarah Doubty, daughter of Thomas and Lurauer, born April 17, 1761,
    and died the February following, 1762.
Mary Starkey, daughter of Jonathan and Mary, born August 14, 1762.
Stephen White, son of William and Mary, born February 12, 1770.
Elizabeth Lovies Ridesele, daughter of Tobias Ridsle and Lovies,
    born August 19, 1762 and baptized November 14, 1762.
William Gallaway, son of Moses Galloway and Mary, born Feb. 1, 1751.
John Nicholson Galloway, son of Moses and Mary, born June 4, 1753.
James Galloway, son of Moses and Mary, born March 31, 1755.
Francis Gouldsmith Presbury, son of George and Elizabeth, born
    February 16, 1766.
James Tolley Presbury, son of George and Elizabeth, born Oct. 31, 1772.

Page 183

Esther Horner, daughter of James and Tamer, born February 18, 1761.
Margaret Horner, daughter of James and Tamer, born Dec. 26, 1762.
Absolem Cameron, son of John and Mary Martin, born Oct. 26, 1762.
Joseph Ward, son of Joseph and Mary, born April 8, 1764.
Ann Sevan, daughter of Samuel and Elizabeth, born August 3, 1764.
Henry Presbury, son of Joseph and Sarah, born June 18, 1769.
Stephen Onion, son of Zacheus and Hannah, born November 19, 1761.
Thomas Bond Onion, son of Zacheus and Hannah, born Feb. 1, 1762.
John Onion, son of Zacheus and Hannah, born May 23, 1764.

Zacheus Onion Jr., son of Zacheus and Hannah, born April 12, 1765.
William Francis Heath Onion, son of Zacheus and Hannah, born
    March 29, 1769.
Corbin Onion, son of Zacheus and Hannah, born May 8, 1770.
Sarah Scarff, daughter of Henry and Patty, born June 24, 1761.
John Dives, son of Francis and Mary, born February 4, 1764.
Susanhah Ingram, daughter of Leven and Hannah, born Nov. 1, 1770.
John Shipton and Mary Speer married in October, 1757.
John Shipton, son of John and Mary, born October 13, 1758.

Page 184

Robert Shipton, son of John and Mary, born September 17, 1761.
Phebe Ingram, daughter of Leven and Hannah, born February 16, 1761.
Sarah Ingram, daughter of Leven and Hannah, born October 24, 1762.
Mary Ingram, daughter of Leven and Hannah, born December 29, 1764.
Elizabeth Ingram, daughter of Levin and Hannah, born Dec. 27, 1766.
Hannah Little, daughter of Guy and Elizabeth, born May 4, 1763.
Guy Little died March 20, 1764.
Zerneh Dives, daughter of Christopher and Sarah, born Apr. 9, 1764.
Martha Andrew, daughter of William and Mary, born May 3, 1756.
William Seale, Joppa, died February 5, 1767.
Mary Saunders, daughter of Robert and Elizabeth, born Apr. 13, 1766.
Martha Saunders, daughter of Robert and Elizabeth, born June 30,
    1768 "and departed this life."
Martha Saunders, second daughter of that name of Robert and Elizabeth,
    "born July 26, 1770 in Baltimore County, Maryland in Saint
    Johns Parish and was baptized by the Reverend Mr. Hugh
    Deans, Rector."
Robert Saunders, son of Robert and Elizabeth, born July 12, 1772.
Fergus Lin born June 10, 1769 "being the son of Charles Lin and Ann
    his wife, said Fergus being born in the Town of Joppa."

Page 185

Acquilla McCommass, son of Edward and Mary, born March 30, 1773.
Alexander McComas, son of Edward and Mary, born August 29, 1775.
Solomon Jones, son of John Jr. and Mary, born June 2, 1753.
Mary Jones, daughter of John Jr. and Mary, born July 13, 1755.
Gay Jones, daughter of John Jr. and Mary, born July 5, 1758.
Margaret Jones, daughter of John Jr. and Mary, born Nov. 11, 1764.

Cloe Jones, daughter of John Jr. and Mary, born March 9, 1766.
Comfort Jones, daughter of John Jr. and Mary, born Feb. 10, 1768.
William Horton and Elizabeth Jarrett married October 3, 1769.
William Holland Andrew, son of William and Mary, born Oct. 8, 1760.
Elizabeth Bishop, wife of Robert Bishop, died February 22, 1770.
Asail Hitchcock, son of Josiah and Suzannah, born June 11, 1767.
Josiah Hitchcock, son of Josiah and Susannah, born March 20, 1770.
Ann Toomy, daughter of John and Sarah, born December 6, 1770.
Lilly Gouldsmith Toomy born September 7, 1772.
Mary Waltham, daughter of Thomas and Elizabeth, born Nov. 16, 1761.

Page 186

Thomas Waltham, son of Thomas and Elizabeth, born March 29, 1768.
Philicecanah Waltham, daughter of Thomas and Elizabeth, born August 21, 1771.
Clement Waltham, son of Charlton and Susannah, born Sept. 26, 1779.
Elizabeth Waltham, daughter of Charlton and Susannah, born June 18, 1781.
Thomas Ensor and Mary Talbott married November 22, 1770.
Elinor Ensor, daughter of Thomas and Mary, born January 28, 1772.
Elioner Con, daughter of Robert and Elizabeth, died October 6, 1773.
Daniel Davice, son of John and Ann, born October 15, 1753.
John, lawfull son of Joseph Phipps and Nancy, born June 10, 1778.
Loyd, lawful son of Joseph Phipps and Nancy, born May 9, 1780.
Elizabeth Morsell, lawful daughter of Kidd and Tabitha, born April 17, 1780.
Beal Bosely, lawfull son of Daniel Rowan and Sarah, born Jan. 21, 1780.
Nathan Phipps, son of John and Hannah, born February 17, 1766.
Ann Waltham, daughter of Charlton and Susannah, born March 2, 1783.
Charlton Waltham, son of Charlton and Susannah, born Jan. 26, 1785.

Page 187

John Rumsey, son of William and Sabina Rumsey of Cecil County,
        married Mrs. Martha Giles, eldest daughter of Colonel
        John Hall of Harford County, by the Reverend Andrew
        Landrum, Rector of Saint Georges Parish, Jan. 31, 1771.

Page 187-188

John Beal Howard Esq. and Blanch Hall, daughter of Parker Hall, married by Reverend Andrew Lendrum, April 18, 1765.

Parker Howard, son of John and Blanch, born March 13, 1776, and died September 20, 1766.

Elizabeth Howard, daughter of John and Blanch, born Sept. 7, 1767.

John Beal Howard, son of John and Blanch, born April 3, 1770, "11 clock forenoon."

Edward Aquilla Howard, son of John and Blanch, born Nov. 15, 1775.

Mathias Howard, son of John and Blanch, born December 9, 1777.

Thomas Gassaway Howard Esq. and Frances Holland, daughter of Francis Holland Esq. of Baltimore County, married Feb. 24, 1765, by the Rev. Andrew Lendrum.

Cordelia Howard, daughter of Thomas and Frances, born Feb. 28, 1767.

Elizabeth Howard, daughter of Thomas and Frances, born Mar. 22, 1770.

Frances Holland Howard, daughter of Thomas and Frances, born Sept. 1, 1771.

Thomas Gassaway Howard, son of Thomas and Frances, born August 24, 1773.

Mary Howard, daughter of Thomas and Frances, born August 13, 1775.

Francis Holland Howard, son of Thomas and Frances, born October 10, 1777.

Susannah Howard, daughter of Thomas and Frances, born September 25, 1779.

John Howard, son of Thomas and Frances, born July 31, 1781.

Samuel Standiford, son of Abraham Standeford and Susannah, born January 25, 1771.

Elizabeth Standeford, daughter of Abraham and Susannah, born January 12, 1773.

William Standeford, son of Abraham and Susannah, born Nov. 10, 1774.

Aquila Standeford, a son of Abraham and Susannah, born Nov. 20, 1776.

Mary Standeford, daughter of Abraham and Susannah, born Oct. 28, 1778.

Priscilla Standeford, daughter of Abraham and Susannah, born Dec. 28, 1780.

John Reed and Mary Drew married May 1, 1777.

John Reed Jr., son of John and Mary, born June 21, 1780.

Sarah Drew Reed, daughter of John and Mary, born July 23, 1782.

John Hammond Dorsey and Ann Maxwell, daughter of Capt. James Maxwell, married January 20, 1772.

James Maxwell Dorsey, son of John and Ann, born March 20, 1776.

Page 189

Frances Rebecca Dorsey, daughter of John and Ann, born April 5, 1778.

Marriages

Solomon Stansbury and Hannah Hix married October 27, 1743.
John Parks and Brigett Wilhughs married October 29, 1743.
Jacob Johnson and Hannah Baker married November 23, 1743.
Thomas Cutchin and Mary Gott married December 5, 1743.
John Trevis and Ann Kelsey married December 6, 1743.
James Dorney and Mary Yeats married December 14, 1743.
Samuel Smith and Jane Parrish married December 31, 1743.
Benjamin Ingram and Susannah Coin married January 5, 1743.
Israel Standeford and Cassandra Anderson married January 6, 1743.
Lewes Demorse and Margrett Ramsey married January 6, 1743.
David Keith and Sarah Kitely married January 12, 1743.
Moses Collett and Elizabeth Wyle married January 12, 1743.
Andrew Jenkins and Elizabeth Boyd married January 12, 1743.
John Mullen and Sarah Brown married January 16, 1743.
Daniel Maccomas Jr. and Tabitha Johnson married January 26, 1743.

Page 190

Richard Baskett and Adfire Boyd married January 31, 1743.
John Demorse and Susannah Ramsey married February 2, 1743.
James Steel and Elizabeth Tornley (Tomly) married February 3, 1743.
Israel Parsley and Sarah Cheyrton married February 5, 1743.
Thomas Johnson and Elizabeth Hutchens married February 7, 1743.
Thomas Anderson and Mary Perdue married March 26, 1744.
John Low and Susannah Cox married March 29, 1744..
John Norris and Susannah Bradford married April 3, 1744.
Allexander Hill and Elioner Durbin married May 10, 1744.
John Debruler and Frances Buredy married May 14, 1744.
Henry Morgan and Sarah Pike married May 14, 1744.
David Morgan and Lydia Cooper married May 17, 1744.
Jos. (Jas.) Hawkins and Sarah Macdanile married May 19, 1744.
John Gallaway and Isabella Berm married May 27, 1744.
Thomas Yeats and Elizabeth Martin married June 21, 1744.
William Harman and Sarah Powell married June 24, 1744.
Coleworth Kenhan (Kerrhan) and Mary Tridge married July 7, 1744.

Page 191

William Karson and Elizabeth Johnson married July 29, 1744.
Daniel Tredway and Sarah Norris married August 2, 1744.
Sollomon Armstrong and Sarah Standiford married August 2, 1744.
William Yeats and Ann Thornbury married September 8, 1744.
William Demett and Sarah Smithers married October 3, 1744.
Thomas Durbin and Margrett Stephens married October 4, 1744.
Peter Mason and Mary Davis married October 6, 1744.
Thomas Miles Jr. and Margrett Taylor married October 11, 1744.
John Bourn and Barbara Burke married October 11, 1744.
Addam Hance and Ruth Sutton married October 25, 1744.
Robert Dutton and Mary Merrekin married December 11, 1744.
Thomas Cox and Elizabeth Gaine married December 13, 1744.
John Hely and Sophia Rhodes married December 23, 1744.
William Jones and Cathrine Brokley married December 23, 1744.
John Crockett and Ann Fixson married December 25, 1744.
James Cain and Elizabeth Doyle married December 30, 1744.
James Norris and Elizabeth Davis married January 1, 1744.
Thomas Nichols and Frances James married August 21, 1740.

Page 192

James Cosley and Mary Hill married January 3, 1744.
James Richardson and Sophia Standeford married January 3, 1744.
Thomas Thompson and Sarah Durham married January 15, 1744.
Luke Trotten and Elizabeth Body married January 15, 1744.
Jacob Starkey and Mary Turbel married January 22, 1744.
Elie Dorsey and Mary Crockett married January 24, 1744.
John Wharton and Ann Brown married January 28, 1744.
John Furness and Jane Green married February 10, 1744.
Arnald Holt and Martha Boarding married February 11, 1744.
Peter Whitaker and Emelie Hitchcock married February 12, 1744.
Nathan Hawkins and Ruth Cole married February 14, 1744.
Samuel Sindall and Elizabeth Carter married February 21, 1744.
Joseph Green and Mary Bown married February 25, 1744.
Thomas March and Sophia Carvin married February 26, 1744.
John Timmons and Sarah Copland married April 18, 1745.
Allen Mackenley and Susanna Freziel married April 23, 1745.

William Jones and Ann Huggins married May 2, 1745.
Benjamin Long and Ann Norris married May 7, 1745.
Mordicai Fuller and Mary James married May 6, 1745.

Page 193

Abraham Wright and Darkes Tuder married May 23, 1745.
Henry James and Mary Henly married June 26, 1745.
James Dobson and Jane Mongumry married July 1, 1745.
Erick Erickson and Elizabeth Baker married July 27, 1745.
Robert Carter and Mary Welch married August 8, 1745.
William Carvin and Rachel Wright married August 15, 1745.
John Christian and Margret Hammelton married September 12, 1745.
Henry Taylor and Sarah Armstrong married October 3, 1745.
John Bozwell and Mary Jenings married November 17, 1745.
Benjamin Greer and Rachael Low married January 2, 1745.
Andrew Vannce and Sarah Low married January 4, 1745.
Henry Perigoe and Providence Corbin married January 14, 1745.
William Prigg and Jane Carson married January 27, 1745.
Jacob Davice and Elizabeth Greer married February 6, 1745.
John M. Pike and Mary Poteet married September 1, 1747.
John Willson and Susannah Gittings married September 8, 1747.
Griffin Jones and Mary Smith married September 19, 1747.

Page 194

Jonathan Lyon and Sarah Clark married October 1, 1747.
Daniel Butler and Mary Whitaker married October 4, 1747.
James Steadman and Mary Minson married October 10, 1747.
Joseph Smith and Mary Shepard married October 15, 1747.
Abraham Andrew and Margret Lynch married October 22, 1747.
Cornelias Stewart and Mary Low married November 25, 1747.
Richard Coup and Hannah Stansbury married December 10, 1747.
James Mead, son of Edward, and Ann Forrest married Dec. 21, 1747.
William Hicks and Tabitha Stansbury married December 24, 1747.
John Peacock and Ann Wiggin married December 29, 1747.
Samuel Thornhill and Mary Clybourn married February 4, 1747.
William Perdue and Rebecca Low married February 4, 1747.
Peter Cotterrell and Precilla Gallaway married Feb. 4, 1747.

John Cope and Mary Bush married February 5, 1748.
John Watkins and Elizabeth Jones married February 10, 1747.
Talbert Risteau and Mary Stokes married June 20, 1745.
Samuel Hill and Ann King married February 9, 1745.
Peter Skarabon and Elizabeth Scharf married March 13, 1745.

Page 195

Francis Trew and Kathrine Dennis married April 14, 1746.
Joseph Wharton and Sarah Metheny married April 28, 1746.
William Brian and Hannah Wallis married May 5, 1746.
William Crabtree and Hannah Whitaker married May 27, 1746.
Richard Williams and Ann Nearn married June 12, 1746.
Henry Kersey and Elizabeth Whealand married July 21, 1746.
David Lynn and Elizabeth Copland married August 24, 1746.
Simon Hutchinson and Ann Newman married August 25, 1746.
Robert Green and Unity Corbin married September 25, 1746.
Joshua Hargisty and Kezie Taylor married October 6, 1746.
Robert Cable and Elizabeth Bradfield married November 3, 1746.
Christopher Sutton and Sarah League married October 12, 1746.
William Hendon and Lydie Hendon married November 11, 1746.
Joseph Deason and Ketura Hall married November 27, 1746.
William Grover and Ann Harwood married December 2, 1746.
John Griffith Howard and Elizabeth Bond married Dec. 7, 1746.
James Murphy and Sarah Chainy married December 15, 1746.

Page 196

Pickett Jones and Elizabeth James married December 16, 1746.
Phillip Parks and Hannah Packcow married December 22, 1746.
Joseph Greenway and Elizabeth Tilley married January 25, 1746.
William Low and Ann Davice married January 30, 1746.
Phillip Burgan and Rebecca Green married February 24, 1746.
Patrick Lynch and Averilla Day married April 20, 1747.
John Swinard and Sarah Willson married April 30, 1747.
Isaac Samson and Mary Risteau married April 20, 1747.
John Ristone and Sarah Sinkler married May 21, 1747.
Joseph Brooks and Elizabeth Phillips married June 1, 1747.
James M. Duggle and Eliner Hammond married June 28, 1747.

Thomas Biddeson and Ann Buegain married July 17, 1747.
David Copland and Elizabeth Duglas married August 27, 1747.
John Brown and Comfort White married February 21, 1747.
Richardson Stansbury and Mary Reaven married February 23, 1747.
Thomas Elliott and Ann Robinson married April 14, 1748.
Samuel Wilkinson and Mary Asher married April 14, 1748.
Uriah Bond and Penillipie Coleman married April 23, 1748.
Benjamin Rutledge and Mary Roe married April 28, 1748.

Page 197

William Yeates and Ann Dorney married April 28, 1748.
Joseph Sutton and Ruth Adams married May 1, 1748.
John Wyle and Elizabeth Perdue married May 12, 1748.
John Morris and Sarah Deaver married May 17, 1748.
Samuel Porter and Cathrine Herring married June 6, 1748.
Ambross Leach and Elizabeth Nearn married July 5, 1749.
John Jones and Sarah Poulson married July 14, 1749.
Henry Waters and Ann Beck married July 14, 1748.
John Knowele and Rebecca Blake married July 23, 1748.
Thomas Miller and Sarah Burk married July 24, 1748.
Thomas Chambers and Mary Fox married August 6, 1748.
Richard Robenson Jr. and Jemima Robertson married Sept. 15, 1749.
William Edwards and Jane Broad married September 17, 1748.
James Poteet and Elizabeth Crabtree married September 20, 1748.
Thomas Gibbins and Mary Buckley married September 28, 1748.
Thomas Slade and Hannah Miles married September 29, 1748.
Francis Flannen and Sarah Whealand married October 2, 1748.
Theo. Baker and Elizabeth Beldem married October 6, 1748.
Richard Ellwood and Mary Sinzey married October 9, 1748.
William Miver and Elizabeth Finer married October 10, 1748.
John Hendrixson and Ruth Sing married October 16, 1748.

Page 198

John Mallane and Eddith Cole married November 8, 1748.
Jacob Miles and Hannah Maccomas married November 10, 1748.
John Oggdon and Susannah Harps married November 19, 1748.
Isaac Hicks and Elizabeth Miller married November 24, 1748.

Thomas James and Jane Hicks married November 29, 1748.
William Williams and Sarah Ellwood married December 8, 1748.
George Thyler and Cathrine Graves married January 1, 1748.
William Hicks and Flora Cole married January 12, 1748.
Joseph Wells and Ann Carback married January 30, 1748.
John Long and Blanch Whitaker married January 31, 1748.
Charles Cole and Ruth Samson married February 7, 1748.
Joseph Ward and Mary Perkinson married February 13, 1748.
Mordicai Amoss and Mary Scott married February 16, 1748.
Thomas Hanks and Sarah Hewett married March 9, 1748.
William Lynchfield and Sarah Parks married March 26, 1749.
John Jones and Sarah Morris married March 28, 1749.
Robert Scott and Mary Carlile married March 29, 1749.
James Preston and Clemency Bond married March 30, 1749.
Asael Rockhold and Ann Roe married April 3, 1749.
John Williams and Ruth Rockhold married April 17, 1749.
Stephen Price and Rebecca Hicks married April 20, 1749.
Thomas Owings and Mary Hicks married April 30, 1749.
John Deason and Mary Hall married May 1, 1749.
Abraham Bull and Mary Wyle married June 1, 1749.
James Whiteaker and Mary Saunders married June 29, 1749.
William Scotland and Elizabeth Taylor married July 13, 1749.
Thomas Lawson and Ann Herrington married July 20, 1749.
Daniel Collett and Susanah M'kenly married August 1, 1749.
James Dorney and Ann Cadle married August 9, 1749.
John Barns and Elizabeth Scott married August 10, 1749.
John Hollis and Mary Groom married August 12, 1749.

Page 199

William Kimler (Krinler) and Mary Jackson married August 19, 1749.
Moses Byfoot and Sarah Tayman (Layman) married September 5, 1749.
John Amoss and Elizabeth Stileve married September 17, 1749.
John Beaver and Sarah Hawkins married September 19, 1749.
Samuel Phillips and Solvolitte Bozwell married September 28, 1749.
Thomas Deadman and Sarah Griffith married October 2, 1749.
Thomas Morris and Frances Shaw married October 10, 1749.
Richard Burgis and Sarah Castle married October----,1749.

George Harryman and Sarah Reaven married October 17, 1749.
William Dortridge and Margret Murphy married October 19, 1749.
James Morgan and Mary Green married November 12, 1749.
James Scott and Mary Martin married November 12, 1749.
John Jeffriys and Sarah Williams married November 14, 1749.
Thomas Clark and Cathrine Britain married November 21, 1749.
William Prigg and Martha Morgan married November 22, 1749.
William Clark and Tamer Low married December 7, 1749.
Bazl. Foster and Mary Allender married December 10, 1749.
Aquilla Milhughs and Elizabeth Parkes married December 17, 1749.
Anthony Asher Jr. and Sarah Beven married December 19, 1749.
Peter Ryon and Mary Symson married December 21, 1749.
William Frost and Suhannah Robertson married December 21, 1749.
Edward Garretson and Avarilla Hanson married December 21, 1749.
Richard Griffin and Jane Loyd married December 21, 1749.
David Shadows and Ann Bozwell married December 26, 1749.

Page 200

Barnett Preston and Sarah Ruff married December 28, 1749.
Charles Baker and Elizabeth Cockey married January 9, 1749.
Joseph Presbury and Sarah Pycraft married January 11, 1749.
Aquilla Gilbert and Elizabeth Butler married January 17, 1749.
Isaac Bull and Hannah Robertson married January 23, 1749.
Dennis Dulany and Easter Fugate married January 23, 1749.
Patrick Whealand and Mary Cowdry married January 26, 1749.
William Hudson and Sarah Deason married January 30, 1749.
John Davice and Martha Bull married January 31, 1749.
John Bruff and Ann Allen married January 31, 1749.
Edward Day and Ann Fell married February 8, 1749.
Francis Poulson and Mary Dennock married February 13, 1749.
Emanuel Mallane and Margrett Reeves married February 13, 1749.
Francis Norrington and Mary Everett married February 19, 1749.
Jacob Johnson and Elizabeth Hendon married February 25, 1749.
Samuel Foster and Margrett Gaton married February 26, 1749.
William Bond Whitehead and Suhannah Wood married February 26, 1749.
Isham Hendon and Kezie Johnson married February 27, 1749.

Page 201

Edward Bozman and Rozannah Lyon married February 27, 1749.
John Kersey Jr. and Suhannah Shaw married February 27, 1749.
Nathan Nicholson and Ruth Bond married March 16, 1749.
Mosess Gallaway and Mary Nicholson married April 6, 1750.
Andrew Perrigoe Jr. and Alice Edwards married April 17, 1750.
Thomas Walton and Elizabeth Maxwell married June 21, 1750.
John Watkins and Elizabeth James married June 25, 1750.
William Leggett and Ann Blackett married July 13, 1750.
Thomas Westerman and Mary Tongue married July 14, 1750.
William Standeford and Elizabeth Carlile married July 16, 1750.
John Hows and Penelipy Bond married July 22, 1750.
James Norris, son of Edward, and Philiszana Barton married Aug. 2, 1750.
Francis Rider and Frances Hopham married August 7, 1750.
John Welcher and Unity Coffee married August 7, 1750.
Simon Hutchenson and Pennil Brooker married August 12, 1750.
Joseph Greer and Ann Low married August 18, 1750.
Mordicai Crawford and Suhannah Tucker married September 16, 1750.
John Penman and Margret Bayl married September 20, 1750.

Page 202

Thomas Shannern and Elizabeth Kersey married September 26, 1750.
John Gray and Blansh Cantwell married September 30, 1750.
Thomas Jones and Elizabeth Shaw married October 10, 1750.
Benjamin Gaton and Elizabeth Skinnoni married October 26, 1750.
William Applebee and Mary Jones married November 13, 1750.
William Glede and Jane Russel married November 15, 1750.
Joseph Amoss and Martha Bradford married November 20, 1750.
Peter Youngbloud and Mary Wheals married November 26, 1750.
Mannus Ocain and Elizabeth M'kenly married November 26, 1750.
Mathias Franks and Mary Morris married November 26, 1750.
Thomas Presbury and Ann Woodard married in December, 1749.
William Stevens and Sarah Duke married December 25, 1750.
Charles Taylor and Elizabeth Standeford married December 25, 1750.
William Cammell Tayman and Ann Williams married December 25, 1750.
Stephen White and Hannah Baker married January 1, 1751.
John Gebbs and Hannah Palmer married January 1, 1751.

Brian Cartee and Frances Leshordie married January 2, 1750.
William Jones and Elizabeth Williams married January 22, 1751.

Page 203

William Norris and Elizabeth Horn married January 24, 1751.
John Butler and Ann Allen married January 24, 1751.
John White and Elizabeth Gott married January 29, 1751.
John Rowling and Comfort Brown married February 14, 1751.
John Warren and Elizabeth Keen married February 16, 1751.
George Pickett and Barbary Gorsuch married February 16, 1751.
William Green and Mary Hammond married February 17, 1751.
John Butler and Mary Perryman married February 18, 1751.
John Cammell and Ann Stevens married April 7, 1751.
John Poulson and Elizabeth Stewart married April 8, 1751.
Nathan Frissel and Margaret Deason married April 18, 1751.
Francis Kitely and Mary Thomas married May 12, 1751.
John Rowe and Sarah Wharton married May 29, 1751.
Michael Duskin and Sarah Johnson married June 6, 1751.
Daniel Pocock Jr. and Sarah Jones married June 26, 1751.
David Ervine and Constant Sears married June 30, 1751.
Leven Roberts Cammel and Mary Mainer married August 3, 1751.
Edmund Hays and Mary Bunnell married August 8, 1751.

Page 204

John Sandage and Sarah Grover married September 19, 1751.
James Arnold and Providence Denton married October 2, 1751.
John York and Sarah Horner married October 16, 1752.
Laban Hogg and Ruth Stansbury married October 22, 1751.
Thomas LittleJohn and Margrett Johnson married November 19, 1751.
Thomas Ristien and Margaret Sinkler married November 28, 1751.
William Anderson and Jane Little married December 19, 1751.
Aquilla Maccomas and Sarah Preston married January 2, 1752.
James Archer and Kathrine Mortimer married January 8, 1752.
William Grover and Elizabeth Enloes married January 14, 1752.
William Wheeler and Jane Miller married February 6, 1752.
Charles Newton and Sarah Rice married February 6, 1752.
Charles Harryman and Elizabeth Reaven married February 6, 1752.

William Knight and Sarah Cox married February 7, 1752.
Anthony Gosard and Frances Jones married February 9, 1752.
Benjamin Nearn and Elizabeth Keys married February 11, 1752.
Thomas Brierly and Ann Teat married February 11, 1752.
Edward Eves and Lucy Ann Pine married February 17, 1752.

Page 205

Mosess Long and Margaret Grace Worbleton married March 30, 1752.
Thomas Stubs and Elizabeth Davice married March 31, 1752.
John Kersey and Kathrine Martin married April 18, 1752.
Edward Robertson and Margaret Standeford married April 21, 1752.
William Whealand and Mary Legoe married April 21, 1752.
John Harryman and Elizabeth Clerk married May 19, 1752.
Richard Miller and Elizabeth Hicks married June 4, 1752.
James Robeson and Ann Ashor married June 7, 1752.
William Pike and Mary Crabtree married June 9, 1752.
John Cotterrel and Ann Wood married June 14, 1752.
Richard Tredwell and Maple Stevenson married June 7, 1752.
William Cock and Susanhah Harriott married June 18, 1752.
William Elliott and Karran Johnson married May 17, 1740.
William Watkins and Ann Barkabee married December 9, 1741.
John Thrift and Sarah Dorney married in the year 1732.
Richard Cosley and Elizabeth Rhodes married July 7, 1752.
John Childs and Sarah Groves married July 22, 1752.
Richard Robertson and Mary Hall married August 2, 1752.

Page 206

James Ingram and Cathrine Young married August 25, 1752.
George Groves and Johannah Rigbie married August 26, 1752.
Thomas Buswell and Mary Chamney married August 30, 1752.
William Pollard and Rebecca Hayes married October 2, 1752.
Jacob Bull and Ranrice Bussey married October 17, 1752.
James Stephens and Elizabeth Cadle married November 2, 1752.
Ben. Anderson and Rozanna Litle married November 2, 1752.
Elijah Beck and Martha Greenleefe married November 19, 1752.
John Sharp and Hannah Cook married November 20, 1752.
James Whitington and Levina Marsh married November 21, 1752.

John Smith and Margrett Scarf married December 18, 1752.
Benjamin Amoss and Sarah Lyon married December 19, 1752.
Phillip Elliott and Sarah Wright married December 22, 1752.
Thomas Armstrong and Sarah Dallerhyde married December 28, 1752.
Mary Deason, daughter of John and Mary, born March 7, 1752.
Karanhapage Deason, daughter of John and Mary, born July 17, 1752.
Abraham Mears and Jane Slaughter married December 31, 1752.
Charles Jones and Hannah Nicholes married December 26, 1752.

Page 207

William Wyle and Elizabeth Little married January 1, 1753.
Nicholas Poor and Elizabeth Erickson married January 6, 1753.
Thomas Benson and Esabellah Brown married January 23, 1753.
George Williams and Mary Jarrett married January 25, 1753.
Thomas Elliott Jr. and Rebecca Norris married January 5, 1753.
Thomas Hambleton and Easther Samson married January 30, 1753.
Edmund Deadman and Elizabeth Corbin married January 30, 1753.
Jacob Gladen and Sarah Rice married January 31, 1753.
John Cope and Brigitt Teate married February 5, 1753.
Thomas Scimmons and Pricilla Maccomas married February 6, 1753.
John Almeny and Elizabeth Waddham married February 6, 1753.
William Bennett and Mary Parker married February 6, 1753.
Aquilla Thompson and Cathrine Whiteaker married February 20, 1753.
John Griffin and Ann Harp married March 4, 1753.
Benjamin Richardson and Jemima Standeford married March 5, 1753.
John Green and Ann Hardisty married March 8, 1753.
Daniel Maccomas, son of Elixander Sr., and Hannah Taylor married
    March 15, 1753.
John Ryley and Mary Ruff married April 3, 1753.
David Todd and Cathrine Porter married April 21, 1753.
James Heron and Mary Potter married April 23, 1753.
Andrew Riddle and Jane Venney married April 23, 1753.
William Cross and Alice Cole married April 24, 1753.

Page 208

James Kelley and Mary Beamsley married April 28, 1753.
Mosess Edwards and Ann Pickett married May 1, 1753.
James Elliott and Temperance Armstrong married May 8, 1753.

"Anthony son Degue and Elizabeth Downs were married May 23, 1753."
Charles Green and Mary Colletcon married June 5, 1753.
John Jones and Mary Starkey married June 26, 1753.
Deowald Heldebroad and Mary Pickett married July 8, 1753.
Luke Peacock and Constant Sicklemore married July 26, 1753.
Joseph Hendon and Mary Crudgents married July 31, 1753.
Mosess Greer and Mary Bayley married in January, 1737.
Joseph Boram and Sarah Demmet married August 7, 1753.
John Shepard and Margrett Eliott married August 14, 1753.
John Cross and Philliszana Hicks married August 28, 1753.
Joseph Parrish and Cassandra Talbott married August 28, 1753.
John Bayne and Mary Webber married August 30, 1753.
Charles Bennett and Martha Collins married September 11, 1753.
William Bowen and Elizabeth Moss married September 16, 1753.
Charles Prosser and Margrett Synkins married September 27, 1753.
Salathial Gallaway and Prissilla James married September 28, 1753.

Page 209

William Pollard and Elizabeth Smith married October 13, 1753.
John Brown and Elizabeth Bond married October 17, 1753.
Robert Galaspie and Elizabeth Maxwell married November 6, 1753.
James Skipper and Ann Wareing married November 10, 1753.
Francis Dives and Mary Watters married November 21, 1753.
Benjamin Jerman and Elizabeth Rutledge married November 28, 1753.
Samuel Beck and Mary Groves married December 5, 1753.
Benjamin Giyton and Amelia Scarf married December 13, 1753.
Samuel Rickets and Hannah Mead married December 24, 1753.
James Graham and Mary Vine married December 25, 1753.
Samuel Salter and Mary Pendegrass married December 26, 1753.
Joseph Walton and Mary Gibbins married December 31, 1753.
Ezekiel Slade and Ann Whitaker married January 7, 1754.
Thomas Low and Sarah Mainer married January---, 1754.
Joshua Durham and Sarah Thompson married January 10, 1754.
Joseph Beven and Rachael Asher married January 15, 1754.
Benjamin Cross and Elizabeth Cole married January 20, 1754.
George Armstrong and Mary Grimes married February 4, 1754.
Thomas Downs and Mary Clark married February 5, 1754.
James Hendon and Hannah Norris married February 7, 1754.

Solomon Cross and Mary Keith married February 8, 1754.
Laban Perdue and Sarah Allen married February 11, 1754.
Peter Raynor and Mary Perren married February 14, 1754.
Benjamin Norris, son of Ben, and Mary Devoll married March 7, 1754.
William Oldham and Ruth Talbott married April 1, 1754.
Thomas Legate and Mary Phurmey married April 15, 1754.
Samuel Martin and Eleanor Williams married April 17, 1754.
William Crabtree and Ann Kiley married April 25, 1754.
Benjamin Roberts and Martha Cullinson married May 4, 1754.

Page 210

Thomas Enloes and Sarah James married June 2, 1754.
Corbin Lee and Mrs. Eleanor Thornton married January 31, 1754.
Samuel Groome Osborn, son of Benjamin and Elizabeth, born Dec.13,1752.
Mary Osborn, daughter of James and Jane, born November 12, 1752, and was married September 29, 1774.
Elizabeth Osborn, daughter of Samuel and Mary, born July 17, 1775, and died June 12, 1778.
Benjamin Osborn, son of Samuel and Mary, born March 19, 1777, and died February, 1785.
Charles Christie and Cordelia Stokes married July 21, 1754.
Drew Bond, daughter of William and Ann, born March 12, 1754.
Samuel Groome Osborn, son of Samuel and Mary, born May 9, 1779 "in the morning."
Mary Osborn, daughter of Samuel and Mary, born March 29, 1782.
Sarah Waltham, daughter of John and Margaret, born April 3, 1762.
Thomas Waltham, son of John and Margaret, of Kent County, born January 22, 1770.
Samuel Groome Osborn and Sarah Waltham married January 4, 1784.
James Brian and Mary Reaven married July 4, 1754.
Francis Hunn and Margrett James married July 7, 1754.

Page 211

Richard Richards and Sarah Hooker married July 14, 1754.
Charles Talbott and Elizabeth Young married July 15, 1754.
William Scott and Jane Hughs married August 4, 1754.
John Fulton and Hannah Norris married August 4, 1754.
Isaac Few and Jennet Fell married August 15, 1754.

Abraham Pines and Phillis Beven married September 11, 1754.
Francis Showdy and Louzanna Taylor married September 13, 1754.
Francis Roach and Mary Jarman married September 17, 1754.
John Lane and Avarilla Bozeley married September 18, 1754.
Edward Norris, son of Joseph, and Mary Wyle married Sept. 19, 1754.
William Wood and Ann Watkins married October 3, 1754.
Robert Dew and Easther Reaven married October 3, 1754.
Nathan Butler and Rachael Denbow married October 7, 1754.
William Gynn and Mary Hill married October 10, 1754.
William Criswell and Margret Criswell married October 10, 1754.
John Rhodes and Mary Keen married October 17, 1754.
Edward M'Cullister and Mary Ryley married October 21, 1754.
Henry Barns and Elizabeth Green married October 27, 1754.
George Allen and Elizabeth Dimsdale married November 5, 1754.
Abraham Enloes and Jemima Elliott married November 28, 1754.
Lewis Potee and Sarah Meadows married December 2, 1754.
George Allen and Susannah Wood married December 9, 1754.
Alexander Stevert and Mary M'kinley married December 11, 1754.
Joseph Guyton and Hannah Whitaker married December 12, 1754.
Martin Murphey and Elizabeth Collet married December 15, 1754.
William Huggins and Ann Talbee married December 19, 1754.
Joseph Wells and Rebecca Melloy married.December 24, 1754.
Josias Grover and Mary Anderson married December 25, 1754.
Richard Fowler and Mary Fitch married December 31, 1754.
Reason Rockhold and Elizabeth Sandy married December 31, 1754.
John Webster and Mary Lynch married January 1, 1755.
John Beven and Ruth Jerman married January 2, 1755.
John Fuller and Sarah Gott married January 7, 1755.
Henry Williams and Rachael Williams married January 16, 1755.

Page 212

Thomas Lomax and Sarah Downey married February 11, 1755.
Nathan Johnson and Elizabeth Wright married February 11, 1755.
Christison Monts and Margraretta Miyon married March 30, 1755.
John Symmonds and Elizabeth Powell married March 30, 1755.
John Crabtree and Hannah Butcher married April 22, 1755.
William Brooks and Bethia Stephens married April 28, 1755.

Nicholas Merryman and Avarilla Reaven married May 1, 1755.
William Pollard and Mary Hildebrand married May 19, 1755.
Thomas Merrideth and Susannah Cox married May 22, 1755.
James Yeo and Rebecca Rollo married May 25, 1755.
Jesper Goodbie and Ann Bosell married May 25, 1755.
John Potee and Elizabeth Ryley married June 17, 1755.
James Clark and Annah Meriah Passine married June 22, 1755.
John Rowe and Bridgett Moony married July 22, 1755.
Joseph Maskel and Helen Henderton married August 8, 1755.
John Slater and Roannah Pollard married August 18, 1755.
John Tunis and Martha Hill married August 21, 1755.
William Anderson and Mary Harrard married August 21, 1755.
Richard Horton and Elizabeth Davice married August 21, 1755.
Patrick Murphey and Elizabeth Dunahue married September 2, 1755.
John Evans and Mary Forkner married September 7, 1755.
James Maxwell and Phebe Jackson married September 7, 1755.
John Durbin and Rachel Childs married September 16, 1755.
Hugh Low and Pennellipie Harsh married September 18, 1755.
Benjamin Howard and Sarah Bond married October 7, 1755.
John Treble and Elizabeth Logg married October 21, 1755.
Benjamin Wyle and Elinor Samson married October 30, 1755.
Skelton Standeford Jr. and Elizabeth Pocock married November 4, 1755.
Richardson Roberts and Clorinda Leggatt married November 5, 1755.
David Price and Mary Ann Elliott married November 18, 1755.
William Greenhall and Ruth Harrinton married November 27, 1755.
Samuel Everet and Hannah White married December 9, 1755.
Benjamin Corbin and Sarah Sye married December 9, 1755.

Page 213

Thomas Street and Mary Fox married December 16, 1755.
Edward Rose and Hannah Frost married December 18, 1755.
John Hallam and Isabel Fell married December 18, 1755.
Ralph Rench and Margret Watkins married December 21, 1755.
John Holland and Elizabeth Sicklemore married December 23, 1755.
George Knox and Dinah Detter married December 25, 1755.
James Anger and Mary James married January 1, 1756.

John Maynor and Mary Lawson married January 8, 1756.
Francis Ingram and Sarah White married January 8, 1756.
Josias Reeves and Letitia Reaven married January 11, 1756.
Thomas Meeds and Mary Rowings married January 12, 1756.
Marberril Elliott and Jemima Standeford married January 13, 1756.
William Harrice and Mary Ginn married January 13, 1756.
Joseph Franklin and Elizabeth Oakley married January 15, 1756.
John Knapp and Ann Miller married January 17, 1756.
John Jarman and Mary Russell married January 22, 1756.
John Watters and Providence Baker married February 5, 1756.
Benjamin Debruler and Semele Jackson married February 25, 1756.
Thomas Harryman and Ann Stansbury married March 1, 1756.
Emanuel Cheynard and Sarah Thrift married March 2, 1756.
Charles Franklin and Hannah Harsh married April 19, 1756.
Erick White and Rachael Bevens married April 19, 1756.
John Deaver and Ann Bond married May 11, 1756.
John Maggers and Rebecca Polard married May 26, 1756.
Phillip Leech and Sarah Nearn married June 1, 1756.
Goldsmith Presbury and Elizabeth Tolley married June 10, 1756.
Joseph Tudor and Elizabeth Everrett married June 20, 1756.
John Macgee and Margaret Little married July 15, 1756.
Robert Abertcromby and Ann Hatten married August 6, 1756.
James Marsh and Taylor married August 11, 1756.
Robert Stokes and Rebecca Young married August 15, 1756.
Roger Reeves and Phebe Progdon married September 12, 1756.

Page 214

Francis Darnal and Margaret Hernly married September 12, 1756.
Richard Griffin and Ann White married September 14, 1756.
James Pocock and Jemima Barton married September 20, 1756.
John Pickett and Pemela (Pernela) Dukes married October 3, 1756.
William Allin and Elizabeth Wright married October 5, 1756.
William Warrick and Jennet Thaker married October 17, 1756.
Major Woolling and Frances Johnson married November 5, 1756.
Darby Cartee and Susannah Woolling married November 14, 1756.
Archibald Standeford and Elizabeth Armstrong married June 25, 1754.
Bartholomew Flannagen and Elizabeth Clarage married in Sept., 1750.

William Desney and Cathrine Loge married November 20, 1756.
Joseph Milham and Jane Candle married November 28, 1756.
William Herbert and Elizabeth Inchmore married November 28, 1756.
John Macgall and Jane Martin married December 2, 1756.
Joseph Rogers and Elizabeth Campbell married December 5, 1756.
Thomas Weir and Sarah Puttee married December 7, 1756.
William Denton and Mary Roberts married December 14, 1756.
James Barton and Sarah Everett married December 19, 1756.
William Pickett and Mary Dukes married December 23, 1756.
Henry Dikes and Ann Allexander married December 24, 1756.
Samuel Richardson and Sarah Davice married December 30, 1756.
John Parker and Elizabeth Carback married January 3, 1757.
Giles Stevens Jr. and Avarilla Pickett married January 13, 1757.
William Presbury and Clemency Hughs married January 16, 1757.
Robert Young and Jane Mortimer married January 27, 1757.
Aquila Johns and Hannah Bond married January 27, 1757.
Mosess Johnson and Prissilla Standeford married February 1, 1757.
Beaver Pain and Elizabeth Marshall married February 7, 1757.
John Henry and Mary Copeland married February 10, 1757.

Page 215

Robert Collins and Alice Bonaday married February 12, 1757.
Abraham Isaac Whitaker and Mary Potteet married December 15, 1757.
John Vernun and Susannah Skipton married March 17, 1757.
John Green and Cathrine Todd married March 27, 1757.
Darby Hernly Jr. and Elizabeth Chamberlain married April 12, 1757.
Joseph Crook and Prissilla Gallaway married April 24, 1757.
Robert Gardener and Avarilla Enloes married May 3, 1757.
William Watson and Bethiah Thornberry married May 5, 1757.
William Scott and Mary Smith married May 19, 1757.
Joseph Prickett and Sarah Talbott married May 21, 1757.
Samuell Watkins and Frances Hardesty married June 2, 1757.
Thomas Aspey and Martha Morehead married June 5, 1757.
Thomas Obrian and Amelia Woolling married June 14, 1757.
Jonathan Starkey and Mary Simmons married June 30, 1757.
Lewes Barton and Johannah Simmons married June 30, 1757.
Thomas Wright and Ann Evans married July 5, 1757.
Thomas Jackson and Patience Harryman married July 14, 1757.

Page 216

John Hardy and Hannah Lanardy married August 7, 1757.
Emanuel Jones and Martha Parkew married August 14, 1757.
John Hall and Mary Price married August 14, 1757.
Peter Body and Mary Allinder married August 25, 1757.
William Johnson and Rachael Bull married September 8, 1757.
Thomas Norris and Rebecca Potter married September 11, 1757.
John Cain and Ann White married September 11, 1757.
James Demett and Rachael Sinclare married September 22, 1757.
James Crouch and Hannah Starkey married September 22, 1757.
Groome Bright Bayley and Mary Moore married October 5, 1757.
John Taylor and Elizabeth Norris married October 18, 1757.
William Shepperd and Cathrine Linden married October 18, 1757.
Henry Dulreple and Mary Smith married October 27, 1757.
John Pocock and Ruth Gott married November 3, 1757.
Jacob Fidrack and Elizabeth Blackwalldren married Nov. 14, 1757.
Vachel Worthington and Pressilla Bond married November 17, 1757.
William Keen and Sishannah Copperwhite married November 21, 1757.
Bloyce Wright and Mary Talbott married November 26, 1757.
Henry Watters and Mary Ruff married December 13, 1757.
James Nicholson and Ducella Durbin married December 24, 1757.
John Ward and Elizabeth Potter married December 26, 1757.
James Elliott and Agnes Harris married December 29, 1757.
Edward Fugate and Elizabeth Bacon married January 12, 1758.
John Norris and Mary Blond married January 19, 1758.

Page 217

Alexander Smith and Elizabeth Guyton married January 24, 1758.
William Hughdell and Mary Costley married January 26, 1758.
Thomas Davice and Elizabeth Carback married January 31, 1758.
Richard Woolling and Elizabeth Buchanan married February 5, 1758.
Thomas Tuder and Mary Edwards married February 15, 1758.
Mallakey Popes and Rozina Housten married February 18, 1758.
Henry Fitch and Ruth Bayley married February 28, 1758.
Henry Guyton and Sarah Holt married April 17, 1758.
Mosess Campbell and Rebecca Hughson married in June, 1751.
Benjamin Ricketts and Mary Cutchin married June 2, 1759.

James Condon and Mary Macnamara married April 17, 1765.
John Condon, son of James and Mary, born August 8, 1770,
   "and died the same month and year."
Mary Condon, wife of James Condon, died August 8, 1770.
Michael Moore and Keziah Shipton married April 20, 1758.
Benjamin Barney and Delilah Bozley married April 23, 1758.
Watkins James and Unity Green married May 4, 1758.
Richard Jones and Ann Fraisher married May 25, 1758.
George Williamson and Keturah Durbin married June 15, 1758.
John Gill and Sarah Gorsuch married July 20, 1758.
Richard Mathews and Margret King married August 17, 1758.
James Spencer and Batrix Dorney married August 17, 1758.
William Cullum and Mary Nichols married August 19, 1758.
Henry Dickson and Elizabeth Tate married October 5, 1758.
Daniel Maccomas and Ann Miles married October 10, 1758.
William Row and Ann Wordsworth married October 12, 1758.
Nathaniel Corbin and Sarah James married October 16, 1758.
Absolem Gadd and Elizabeth Cullison married October 19, 1758.
Daniel Thompson and Margaret Clark married October 24, 1758.

Page 218

Aron Johnson and Achseh Merrideth married October 26, 1758.
Luke Swift and Olydia Thrift married October 28, 1758.
Edward Fell and Ann Bond married November 2, 1758.
William Miser and Ruth Meeds married November 4, 1758.
Peter Foreasey and Ann Axter married November 4, 1758.
John Law and Elizabeth Lawson married November 14, 1758.
John Hammilton and Sarah Thrift married December 7, 1758.
Henry Green and Sarah Howard married December 10, 1758.
Richard Samson and Ann Wyle married December 17, 1758.
Richard Towson and Tabitha Rutledge married December 26, 1758.
Robert Rogers and Ruth Williams married December 26, 1758.
Henry Scharf and Patty Hardisty married December 28, 1758.
John Durbin and Elizabeth Smithson married January 2, 1759.
John Standeford and Jemima Robertson married January 11, 1759.
James Richardson and Rachael Stone married January 16, 1759.
Samuel Worthington and Mary Tolley married January 17, 1759.
Abel Wyle and Sarah Samson married January 25, 1759.

William Jameson and Mary Martin married January 25, 1759.
Samuel Wilkinson and Mary Wood married February 12, 1759.
Abraham Wright and Avarilla Harryman married February 20, 1759.
Christopher Hyat and Elizabeth Taylor married February 22, 1759.
John Gardner and Mary Meeds married February 25, 1759.
Samuel Bone and Sarah Harryman married February 25, 1759.
Garrett Hendrixson and Mary Jackson married February 26, 1759.
William Richardson and Mary Davice married March 27, 1759.
James League and Eliner Enloes married May 2, 1759.
William Edy and Sarah Hilton married May 15, 1759.
George Netcomb and Sarah Gregory married June 5, 1759.
Thomas Williams and Susannah Higgs married June 10, 1759.
Enoch James and Temperance Rollo married June 10, 1759.
Thomas Harper and Mary Shields married June 19, 1759.
Henry Cross and Margret Hicks married June 19, 1759.
John Deaver and Susannah Rigbie married July 19, 1759.
William Carter and Mary Day married June 24, 1759.

Page 219

John Demmitt and Frances Waits married August 5, 1759.
Jacob Ruth and Sarah Airs married April 2, 1759.
Edmund Hernly and Lattes Wetherall married September 17, 1759.
William Railey and Margret Rhodes married September 17, 1759.
William Westcomb and Elinor Maskell married September 23, 1759.
John Rich and Ann Massey married October 2, 1759.
William Meale and Sarah Hill married October 7, 1759.
John Hammilton and Elizabeth Dixson married October 8, 1759.
John Bozley and Hannah Bull married October 18, 1759.
Edward Gutterredge and Mary Scarf married October 24, 1759.
John Legatt and Ann James married October 25, 1759.
Daniel Bond and Patience Bozley married November 1, 1759.
Thomas Lawrance and Sarah Briggs married November 1, 1759.
William Fleming and Mary Jane married November 5, 1759.
Robert Clark and Kezia Barton married November 15, 1759.
John Garrett and Margrett Baker married November 22, 1759.
John Doce and Elizabeth Taylor married November 26, 1759.
James Blunder and Sarah Eights married December 1, 1759.
Aquilla Willson and Kezia Everritt married December 4, 1759.

Joseph Lawrance and Ann May married December 5, 1759.
Isaac Whitaker and Elizabeth Hill married December 13, 1759.
John Bayley and Ann Copland married December 23, 1759.
William Tucker and Ann Palmer married December 26, 1759.
John Ween and Elizabeth Godard married January 8, 1760.
William Maccomas and Elizabeth Scott married January 22, 1760.
Nathaniel Murrey and Rachael Bayley married January 24, 1760.
Samuel Higginson and Darkes Baker married January 29, 1760.
William Wheatley and Margaret Elliott married January 30, 1760.
James Cardel and Elizabeth Greaves married February 71, 1760.
John Fulks and Alice Wood married February 18, 1760.
James Tibbett and Rebecca Wordgworth married February 19, 1760.
Robert Thrap and Elizabeth Hilton married February 28, 1760.
James Watters and Lydia Guyton married March 13, 1760.
Aquila Clark and Mary Bull married April 8, 1760.

Page 220

William Edwards and Mary Manes married April 12, 1760.
Thomas Brown and Kezia Phraisher married April 13, 1760.
Blackledge Woodland and Elizabeth Jackson married April 20, 1760.
John Morris and Mary Plummer married May 25, 1760.
Edward Thorp and Mary Green married May 31, 1760.
Roger Mckenley and Mary Kelley married June 1, 1760.
Soloman James and Rachael Corbin married June 18, 1760.
Abraham Stotts and Margret Johnson married June 26, 1760.
Benjamin Gorsuch and Keren Happuck Johnson married July 17, 1760.
Asael Cross and Mary Demmett married August 24, 1760.
George Ward and Mary Oakley married August 24, 1760.
John Miller and Elizabeth Harris married September 9, 1760.
Thomas Holland and Margaret Riley married September 9, 1760.
James Bozley and Rachael Gorsuch married September 18, 1760.
John Beven and Elizabeth Freeman married October 5, 1760.
John Heir and Elizabeth Jones married October 9, 1760.
Ezikiel Bozley and Elizabeth Norris married October 21, 1760.
Charles Billingsley and Ann Barton married October 23, 1760.
Thomas Crabtree and Elizabeth Barton married October 23, 1760.
William Cullum and Margaret Gott married October 30, 1760.
Thomas Doubfty and Luraner Poulson married November 2, 1760.

John Holmoney and Elizabeth Billingsley married October 30, 1760.
John Rooms and Mary Walker married November 12, 1760.
Emanuel Samson and Sarah Rogers married November 11, 1760.
Peter Prynne and Hannah Amoss married November 13, 1760.
Thomas Lane and Elizabeth Prushman married November 16, 1760.
Sollomon Davise and Kesie Tuder married November 20, 1760.
Samuel Sutton and Ann Woodcock married November 20, 1760.
John Taylor and Martha Mayner married November 30, 1760.
James Lattemore and Hannah Bradley married December 7, 1760.
John Roberts Jr. and Mary Jones married December 7, 1760.
Lemuel Howard and Martha Scott married December 7, 1760.
Robert Knight and Ann Limb married December 18, 1760.
William Moore and Martha Mortimer married December 16, 1760.

Page 221

William Grover and Ann Harrod married December 18, 1760.
John Carroll and Cas. Welch married December 24, 1760.
James Horner and Tamer Cameron married December 25, 1760.
Joseph Warrant and Jane James married December 25, 1760.
Rd. Holloway and Elizabeth George married December 26, 1760.
Richard Cross and Tab. Hix married January 1, 1761.
Hugh Stewart and Margaret Coldwell married January 6, 1761.
Aquila Gallaway and Bethiah Stansbury married January 6, 1761.
George Groves and Mary Lax married January 8, 1761.
William Groves and Sarah Dorney married January 15, 1761.
Jonas Jones and Ann Watts married January 15, 1761.
Soll Whealand and Elizabeth Copeland married January 18, 1761.
Thomas Major and Jemima Fuller married January 22, 1761.
Thomas Tredway and Mary Gittings married January 26, 1761.
William Canaday and Mary Stewart married January 27, 1761.
John M'Cubbin and Sarah Holland married January 29, 1761.
Jethro Lynch Wilkinson and Elizabeth Marryman married Jan. 29, 1761.
William Gordon and Johannah Price married January 29, 1761.
William Enloes and Avarilla Beck married February 2, 1761.
Leven Ingram and Hannah Legoe married February 3, 1761.
Edward Bohon and Elizabeth Jones married March 19, 1761.
Thomas Wattson and Fra. Hooper married March 24, 1761.
John Jacob and Mary Lynch married March 29, 1761.

Isaac Burns and_____Duwaull married March 31, 1761.
Samuel Stansbury and Mary Harrod married April 1, 1761.
John James and Avarilla Standeford married April 14, 1761.
John Lofferd and Isabella Ray married April 14, 1761.
Thomas Barton Jr. and Phebe Cammell married April 16, 1761.
Weymouth Shaw and Ann Worthington married April 23, 1761.
James Hix and Mary Mothby married April 23, 1761.
Isaac Wright and Mary Richardson married May 19, 1761.
Paul Shields and Elizabeth Brown married May 21, 1761.
James Bartley and Mary Sheldon married May 25, 1761.

Page 222

Isaac Bull and Betty Ann Slade married May 26, 1761.
James Quinley and Sarah Garritt married May 26, 1761.
Edward Cantwell and Mary Vincent married June 11, 1761.
William Bull and Sarah Billingsley married June 16, 1761.
Thomas Hawkins and Rachael Marsh married June 22, 1761.
John Jarves and Sarah Wright married July 2, 1761.
William Hughdell and Hannah Beck married July 9, 1761.
Thomas M'Cloughon and Deb. King married July 10, 1761.
Devans Scotter and Mary Porrord married July 19, 1761.
Thomas Norris, son of Ben, and Ann Buckingham married July 20, 1761.
Thomas Faurnan and Sarah Chapman married August 4, 1761.
Morgan Conway and Hannah Ruse married August 12, 1761.
Edward Manby and Mary Rice married August 30, 1761.
George Palmer and Mary Tipper married August 30, 1761.
Edward Parker and Elizabeth Westcomb married September 3, 1761.
Laban Welch and Leah Corbin married September 3, 1761.
Samuel Yearks and Sarah Mortimer married September 3, 1761.
James Fitzsimmons and Mary Conner married September 10, 1761.
Jas. (Jos.) Frost and Mary Baker married October 2, 1761.
William Bane and Lydia Johnson married October 14, 1761.
Thomas Gallyhamton and Ann Mary Moore married October 22, 1761.
Nicholas Day Amoss and Christian Ditto married October 29, 1761.
John Parks and Lezia Rutledge married November 3, 1761.
Isaac Lowe and Sarah Mitchell married November 5, 1761.
John Owen and Permelie Cheyne married November 12, 1761.
Daniel Nuservonden and Sarah Asher married November 14, 1761.

James Maccomas and Elizabeth Hillin married November 15, 1761.
Robert Parks and Mary Fuller married November 19, 1761.
Edward Fairchild and Margarey Bringingham married Dec. 6, 1761.
William Kelsey and Ann Hutchins married December 8, 1761.
John Cameron and Mary Brown married December 8, 1761.
John Row and Deb. Jones married December 17, 1761.
Thomas Gibson and Katherine Demorce married December 22, 1761.
John Elliott and Elizabeth Wright married December 23, 1761.

Page 223

John Gardner and Mary York married December 23, 1761.
Thomas Poteet and Elizabeth Taylor married December 24, 1761.
John Jarvis and Mary Freeman married December 29, 1761.
Daniel Scott Watkins and Elizabeth Hatten married Dec. 29, 1761.
William Cuninggam and Margarett Brierly------no date given in this record, but it probably was Dec. 29, 30 or 31, 1761.
Chainey Hatten and Kez. Bayley married December 31, 1761.
John Heirs and Ann Welmoth married January 7, 1762.
William Wood and Elizabeth Davice married January 7, 1762.
John Berrey and Elizabeth Berry married January 14, 1762.
Luke White and Deborah Simmons married January 17, 1762.
Benjamin Merryman and Mary Bell married February 2, 1762.
William Tucker and Clement Beck married February 9, 1762.
George Prickett and Mary Johnson married February 11, 1762.
Francis Wilkins and Frances Carback married February 18, 1762.
Henry Fuller and Elizabeth Greer married February 18, 1762.
Robert Garrett and Mary Dunstone married February 20, 1762.
Thomas Lucas and Mary Chamberlaine married March 2, 1762.
Edward Edwards and Cas. Beard married April 1, 1762.
John Poteet and Ann M'Comas married April 20, 1762.
Thomas Grundy and Elizabeth Price married May 2, 1762.
John Wright and Jemima Hendon married May 4, 1762.
Thomas Norris and Hannah Norrington married May 4, 1762.
Benjamin Mead, son of Benjamin, and Mary Brannan married May 6, 1762.
James Preston Jr. and Ann Lusby married May 13, 1762.
Adam Ramage and Susannah Horner married May 27, 1762.
Chris. Dives and Sarah Nixion married June 24, 1762.
Rd. Woolling and Mary Mulling married July 8, 1762.

Luke Bond and Frances Webster married July 18, 1762.
Sutton Sicklemore and Prudence Hindon married July 29, 1762.
Underwood Guyton and Prissilla Jackson married August 12, 1762.
John Gillitt and Sarah Walton married August 22, 1762.
John Helm and Cueler Bozley married September 2, 1762.
Phill. Lock Ellcott and Sarah Sparks married September 3, 1762.
John Hail and Hannah Poteet married September 14, 1762.

Page 224

William Wright and Sarah Childs married September 28, 1762.
Daniel Norris and Sarah Beaver married September 28, 1762.
Seaborn Tuckin and Elizabeth Hitchcock married November 9, 1762.
Abraham Ristone and Elianor Farlow married November 11, 1762.
Spencer Legoe and Elizabeth Jackson married November 16, 1762.
James Lynch and Comfort Burton married November 18, 1762.
Robert Parker and Mary Capas married November 29, 1762.
Abraham Norris and Rebecca Kitely married December 4, 1762.
James North and Margaret Richardson married December 5, 1762.
Charles Baker Jr. and Elizabeth Wheeler married December 16, 1762.
Thomas Baker and Ann Pocock married December 20, 1762.
Walter James and Cordelia Legoe married December 23, 1762.
James Hill and Camilia Cadle married December 23, 1762.
John Fuller Jr. and Avarilla Barton married December 24, 1762.
Nicholas Hutchins Jr. and Mary Standeford married January 4, 1763.
Thomas Wantland and Susana Cullisson married January 20, 1763.
Laban Haddinton and Ann James married January 27, 1763.
William Hannah and Martha Meers married February 3, 1763.
John Ash and Sabre Milhughs married February 8, 1763.
Thomas Nichols and Prissella Back married February 10, 1763.
Abraham Anderson and Ruth Merrideth married February 10, 1763.
Benjamin Buck and Darkes Sutton married February 10, 1763.
Thomas Merrideth and Hannah Hutchens married February 13, 1763.
William Burton and Sarah Legatt married February 17, 1763.
John Cotterel and Sarah Reaven married March 10, 1763.
Rd. Menson and Mary Ward married March 24, 1762.
William Davice and Sarah Andrews married March 27, 1763.
Michael Clebedints and Cathrine Rozomister married March 27, 1763.
John Marsh and Mary Rockhold married April 7, 1763.

Edward Talbott and Margaret Slade married April 7, 1763.
Thomas Kitten and Mary Bood married April 7, 1763.
Jacob Hendrixson and Ann Low married April 7, 1763.
Sutton Legatt and Hannah Green married April 7, 1763.

Page 225

Samuel Taylor and Patience Tipton married April 12, 1763.
Daniel Shaw and Prudence Bozley married April 14, 1763.
John Jones and Mary Airs married April 17, 1763.
Benjamin Hendrixson and Cathrine Hanndrix married April 28, 1763.
Henry Enloes and Mary Ellcott married May 26, 1763.
William Miser and Hannah Berry married June 7, 1763.
John Buchanan and Mary Ramsey married July 5, 1763.
Thomas Knight and _____ Burns married July 18, 1763.
Zepheniah Talbee and Mary Woolling married July 21, 1763.
Hezekiah Carman and Elinor Talbott married July 24, 1763.
John Stevenson and Anther Wyle married August 11, 1763.
James Whitaker and Cathrine Potee married August 25, 1763.
Thomas Green and Mary Wright married August 25, 1763.
John Breen and Elizabeth Barton married August 25, 1763.
John Baton and Rebecca Armstrong married September 1, 1763.
"Rd. sister Poess and Johannah Thomas married September 4, 1763."
John Hognar and Artelier Lowen married September 6, 1763.
Elias Majors and Diana Bozley married September 8, 1763.
Benjamin Scarff and Ann Bayley married September 13, 1763.
Benjamin Coats and Mary Bellance married October 13, 1763.
George Grove and Bethia Pines married October 17, 1763.
John Cornel Gash and Elizabeth Rogen married October 17, 1763.
John Thomas and Sharlote Thrift married November 6, 1763.
Samuel Swan and Elizabeth Demmett married October 25, 1763.
Thomas Egle and Mary Bay married November 6, 1763.
Benjamin Ansell and Elizabeth Johnson married November 7, 1763.
John Willion and Rachael Rigbee married November 10, 1763.
Joseph Winks and Mary Palmer married November 27, 1763.
Joseph Rockhold and Elizabeth Rutledge married December 8, 1763.
Aquila Paca and Elizabeth Franklin married December 8, 1763.
William Hannah and Ann Blood married December 13, 1763.
Thomas Vaughn and Mary Poteet married December 15, 1763.
John Hall and Elizabeth Williamson married December 22, 1763.

Page 226

Thomas Hill and Christian Meek married December 25, 1763.
Angel Barterstin Elder and Mary Shelvey married December 26, 1763.
Walter Wyle and Susannah Norris married December 29, 1763.
Thomas Mibbs and Latitia York married January 5, 1764.
Josiah Prickett and Mary Elliott married January 10, 1764.
John Huxson and Ann Wood married January 26, 1764.
George Harryman and Sarah Merryman married January 31, 1764.
John Christopher and Susan Saddon married January 31, 1764.
Henry Dixson and Sarah Dallerhyde married February 6, 1764.
William Debruler and Sarah Watters married February 9, 1764.
William Bradford and Sarah M'Comas married February 16, 1764.
Nathaniel Harrington and Temperance Merryman married Feb. 16, 1764.
Joseph Whitemore and Hannah Hammelton married February 26, 1764.
John Holland and Mary Wicks married March 4, 1764.
Charles Baker, son of Morris, and Elizabeth Ditto married Mar. 6, 1764.
Anthony Stewart and Jane Dick married March 15, 1764.
Rd. Lenox and Prissilla Carter married April 15, 1764.
Robert Hawkins and Martha Davice married April 23, 1764.
John Welcher and Ann Foreasjute married April 24, 1764.
Nathaniel Horner and Jane Wiggfield married April 26, 1764.
Samuel Webb and Margaret Tuder married May 13, 1764.
Abraham Simmons and Mary Garrett married June 3, 1764.
Rd. Jones and Sarah Wright married June 7, 1764.
Isaac Hitchcock and Nancy Horne married July 5, 1764.
Edmund Parks and Elizabeth Sinkler married July 9, 1764.
Hen. Whealand and Isbell Willson married July 21, 1764.
John Horne and Eleanor Ryley married July 24, 1764.
James Graves and Tab. Reevs married July 26, 1764.
Benjamin Egleston and Sarah Dallas married August 18, 1764.
John Clark and Elizabeth Grates married August 26, 1764.
John Smith and Elizabeth Daws married September 3, 1764.
James Cooper and Keziah Leach married September 6, 1764.
Mos. Long and Ann Brown married September 13, 1764.

Page 227

Thomas Egleston and Cloe Dallas married September 15, 1764.
Richard Hopkins and Elizabeth Gellard married October 14, 1764.
Edward Hammelton and Margaret Smith married October 18, 1764.

Alexander Smith and Elizabeth Smith married November 6, 1764.
W. Burke and Mary Lemmon married November 8, 1764.
Samuel Calwill and Ann Richardson married November 13, 1764.
Joseph Bond and Ann Watters married November 13, 1764.
John Lawson and Sarah Harratt married November 15, 1764.
Aron Hughs and Elizabeth Taylor married November 22, 1764.
Levin Mathews and Mary Day married November 29, 1764.
Thomas James and Elizabeth Clark married December 4, 1764.
Thomas Chamberlaine and Elizabeth Wilkinson married Dec. 9, 1764.
William Demmett and Dorthy Swan married December 13, 1764.
Timothy New and Sarah Beaver married December 13, 1764.
Adam M'Clong and Letitia Richardson married December 24, 1764.
William Everrett and Sarah Bord married December 25, 1764.
Aquila Standeford and Sarah Clark married December 27, 1764.
Absolem Camoran and Sarah Beamer married December 30, 1764.
John Day, son of Edward, and Sarah York married December 30, 1764.
John Walker and Easther Lyon married January 6, 1765.
John Demmett and Rhoda Sinkler married January 10, 1765.
James Groombridge and Sarah Wyle married January 15, 1765.
John Whicks and Mary Petetow married January 24, 1765.
Thomas Bond 3rd and Cathrine Fell married February 3, 1765.
William Harding and Mary Wuskitt married February 5, 1765.
Mansfield Hattfield and Hannah Armstrong married February 7, 1765.
Ephraim Rutledge and Ann Dallas married February 7, 1765.
David Judy and Elizabeth Masters married February 7, 1765.
John Benkin and Mary Fell married February 9, 1765.
David Chalson and Mary York married February 14, 1765.
Richard Mainard and Ann Wright married February 19, 1765.
John Mercer and Rebecca Judy married February 28, 1765.
William Thomas and Ichabard Thrift married April 8, 1765.
Samuel Young and Rebecca Stokes married April 9, 1765.

Page 228

Anthony Alleycock and Elizabeth Fish married April 10, 1765.
James Cooper and Ann Price married April 14, 1765.
John Denton and Sarah Starkey married April 15, 1765.
Robert Johnson and Mary Fleming married April 20, 1765.
Charles Stansbury and Elizabeth Buck married April 25, 1765.

Robert Saunders and Elizabeth Andrew married April 28, 1765.
Richard Dallam and Frances Paca married May 16, 1765.
Thomas Tomkins and Esther Burch married May 19, 1765.
Thomas Ruby and Charity Marsh married May 27, 1765.
Robert Lusby and Elizabeth Hughs married May 30, 1765.
Nicholas Wood and Mary Parker married June 30, 1765.
Samuel Palmer and Sarah Fields married July 14, 1765.
Owen Williams and Mary White married July 21, 1765.
Peter Crow and Elizabeth Brown married July 27, 1765.
Jno. Webster and Sarah Stevenson married July 27, 1765.
Thomas Combs and Ann Nowland married July 31, 1765.
Jacob Wright and Prissilla Ingram married August 4, 1765.
Luke Reaven and Ann Rigbie married August 20, 1765.
Richard Coleman and Mary Hatten married August 22, 1765.
David Armstrong and Isabella Brierly married September 5, 1765.
Jno. Hooper and Sarah Jernes married September 19, 1765.
Benjamin Guyton and Cathrine Adams married September 26, 1765.
James Badwell and Ann White married October 6, 1765.
David West and Hannah Thomson married October 10, 1765.
William Tipton and Mary Miller married October 26, 1765.
Robert Lyon and Susan Rhodes married October 31, 1765.
William Johnson and Cathrine Desney married November 3, 1765.
Henry Oram and Sarah Dives married November 7, 1765.
Jacob Allam and Sarah Run married November 12, 1765.
David Durham and Sarah Smithson married November 14, 1765.
Jno. Hatten and Unity Welcher married November 16, 1765.
James Norris and Mary Norris married December 5, 1765.
Michael Rutledge and Elinor Deason married December 17, 1765.
Robert Amoss and Martha McComas married December 22, 1765.

Page 229

Jos. Hindon and Hannah Starkey married January 9, 1766.
Thomas Jones and Jane Russel married January 14, 1765.
Thomas Gillis and Jane Ross married January 16, 1766.
Edward Owing and Ruth Carlile married January 20, 1766.
Thomas Talbott and Belander Slade married January 21, 1766.
Eprm. Rutledge and Susan Poccock married February 6, 1766.
Benjamin Samson and Jemoma Standeford married February 11, 1766.

Luke Legoe and Cloe Denton married February 18, 1766.
Soll. Whealand and Elizabeth Ward married February 22, 1766.
Wm. Bond Whitehead and Sarah Ingram married March 10, 1766.
Jno. Ledgley and Susan Foreacher married March 13, 1766.
George Cozens and Margaret Whitely married March 13, 1766.
William Mairer and Mary Armstrong married April 1, 1766.
Henry Jackson and Mary Bond married April 3, 1766.
Jno. Jacob Summers and Araminta Roberts married April 27, 1766.
Jos. Legatt and Elizabeth Burk married May 6, 1766.
Jno. Little and Elizabeth Little married May 19, 1766.
Samuel Thompson and Isbel Barns married May 29, 1766.
George Wright and Sarah Scoles married June 8, 1766.
Jno. Dives and Mary Greer married June 10, 1766.
Thomas Fowler and Jane Taylor married June 19, 1766.
Henry Gooding and Murrun Swan married June 15, 1766.
Benjamin Howard and Mary Dutton married December 4, 1766.
Robert Barns and Morra Brian marroed July 21, 1766.
Thomas Lax and Mary Groves married July 27, 1766.
Jas. White and Jane Watkins married August 7, 1766.
William Enzoe and Martha Costley married September 4, 1766.
Thomas Chinwoth and Rachel Moore married September 14, 1766.
William Door and Bathsheba Green married September 21, 1766.
George Sunk and Elizabeth Pennenton or Pennington married
            September 23, 1766.
Peter Carroll and Elizabeth Kitely married October 2, 1766.
Jno. Ward and Elizabeth Sharp married October 6, 1766.
Henry Wood and Susannah_____married November 3, 1766.
William Smithson and Elizabeth Scott married November 11, 1766.

Page 230

Thomas Whicks and Terriner Wilford married November 20, 1766.
Jos. Norris and Christian Price married November 20, 1766.
George York and Cathrine Gardner married November 30, 1766.
Abraham Corbin and Rachael Marshall married December 4, 1766.
Thomas Holland and Ann Vitean married December 21, 1766.
Jeremiah Coney and Mary Coleman married December 23, 1766.
Alexander Smith and Martha Chalk married December 25, 1766.
Jno. Lattamore and Ann Wright married December 25, 1766.

William Meed and Sarah York married January 10, 1767.
James Trevis and Ann Hutchins married January 15, 1767.
Richard Hatchens and Philliszaner Standeford married
    January 20, 1767.
Thomas Smithson, Jr. and Sarah Bond married January 22, 1767.
Bazl. Billingsley and Ruth Smithson married January 29, 1767.
Thomas Hatlin and Cathrine Bayley married January 29, 1767.
William Wright and Mary Heathcut Pickett married Feb. 3, 1767.
Charles Jones and Mary Clark married February 6, 1767.
James Hill and Hannah Wright married February 12, 1767.
Nathaniel Yearly and Rachel Edy married February 12, 1767.
Nicholas Fuller and Elizabeth Brian married February 17, 1767.
Jno. Hughs Jr. and Sarah Day Wright married February 19, 1767.
Jno. Watters and Mary Horner married February 22, 1767.
Jacob Hicks and Ann Hitchcock married March 2, 1767.
William Baker and Elizabeth Nichols married May 3, 1767.
Jno. Mattucks and Mary Parwell married May 17, 1767.
William Standeford Jr. and Reb. Deason married May 27, 1767.
Zachariah Murrey and Margaret Simmons married May 27, 1767.
James Brown and Reba. Wood married May 31, 1767.
Jas. Billinsgley and Ruth Gilbert married June 16, 1767.
James Phillips and Martha Paca married June 25, 1767.
William Johnstone and Mary Griffin married June 28, 1767.
Robert James and Sarah Jones married July 2, 1767.
Robert Hopkins and Elizabeth Talbott married July 16, 1767.
Thomas Whealand and Martha Dorney married July 21, 1767.
Robert Crawford and Alice Sattle married July 27, 1767.

Page 231

Pat. Whealand and Phebe Tunis married August 6, 1767.
Jno. Gorsuch and Mary Wright married August 6, 1767.
Lambert Wilmer and Hannah Rickitts married October 8, 1767.
Jas. Hill and Sarah Alms married October 15, 1767.
Thomas Logdin and Ann Conner married November 22, 1767.
David Clark and Salley Lewes married November 23, 1767.
Jas. Sinkler and Jane Macmar married December 1, 1767.
Stephen Airs and Elizabeth Watson married December 29, 1767.

Simon Prine and Hannah Miles married January 3, 1768.
William Robeson Jr. and Cathrine Miles married Jan. 21, 1768.
Luke Pinder Gist and Rachel Simmons married January 26, 1768.
Eprm. Stevens and Temperance Green married January 28, 1768.
Benjamin Rutledge and Elizabeth Rockhold married Feb. 2, 1768.
Jas. Scott and Ann Amoss married February 9, 1768.
Thomas Bond (son Barnet) and Sarah Bond married in Feb., 1768.
Jeremiah Airs and Sarah Deason married February 11, 1768.
Nicholas Cleggett and Reba. Young married February 11, 1768.
William Chambers and Mary Jewel married February 11, 1768.
Lewes Jenkins and Elizabeth Harris married February 14, 1768.
George Carrothers and Jane Mitchell married February 18, 1768.
Jno. Morris (son Edward) and Mary Beaver married February 25, 1768.
Archibald Buchanan and Sarah Lee married March 10, 1768.
David Tate and Elizabeth Sinklar married March 15, 1768.
David Friley and Elizabeth Armstrong married March 17, 1768.
Jas. Greer and Eliner Hughs married March 24, 1768.
George Garretson and Martha Presbury married March 24, 1768.
Benjamin Norris and Elizabeth Richardson married April 3, 1768.
John Woaler and Frances Brannan married April 4, 1768.
Samuel Gallion and Sarah Mitchell married April 27, 1768.
Edward Perrey and Frances Saunders married May 10, 1768.
William Cantwell and Mary Baxton married May 23, 1768.
Jas. Hope and Eliner Demorce married May 24, 1768.
Spencer Legoe and Elizabeth Hicks married May 26, 1768.

Page 232

Cha. Lin and Ann Howard married May 26, 1768.
Geo. Crutchinton and Ann Baker married June 16, 1768.
Wm. Cromwell and Elizabeth Risteau married June 16, 1768.
Phillip Henderson and Elizabeth Smith married June 30, 1768.
Thomas Miles and Mary Coeing married August 7, 1768.
George Long and Susannah Pollard married August 9, 1768.
Jno. Philber and Eliner Wordgworth married August 11, 1768.
Thomas Wordgworth and Mary Wyle married August 18, 1768.
Archibald Barkley and Martha Sheldon married August 25, 1768.
Benjamin Vanhorne and Martha Tunis married August 29, 1768.
John Toomy and Sarah Gouldsmith married November 10, 1768.

Daniel Rowan and Sarah Bosely, daughter of Captain James Bosely
    of Baltimore County, married February 18, 1779.
Kidd Morsel and Tabitha Clayton married July 1, 1779.

"The days of the month of the year when people of St. John's
Parrish departed this life."

Rebecka Scott, daughter of Daniell Scott Jr. and Elizabeth,
    died April 2, 1720.

Page 233

"The Test. I do declare that I do believe that there is not any transubstantiation in the Sacrament of the Lord's Supper or in the elements of bread and wine at or after the consecration thereof by any person whatsoever.

James Maxwell	Richard_____
Archibald Rollo	Joshua_____
Henry Wetherall	John_____
James Presbury	George Presbury
James Isham	Benjamin Bond
John Roberts	William Bradford
Thomas Hatchman	Walter Tolley
Edward Day	Thomas Franklin
Thomas Miles	Jos. Nevins
William Bradford	William Wright
Charles P. Simmons	Benjamin Jones
(his mark)	William Standeford
	("M" his mark)

Page 234

William Bradford	1746, Mar. 31	Jno. Chamberlain, Vestryman
Walter Tolley	1746, Mar. 31	Erick Erickson, Vestryman
William Savory	1746, June 3	Benjamin Bond, Church Warden
Henry Ogle	1746, June 3	Vincent Dorsey, Church Warden
Darby Hernly		
Benjamin Norris	1747, May 5	Jo. Hamon Dorsey, Vestryman
John Taylor		John Holt, Church Warden
John Lloyd		Jonathan Starkey, Ditto
William Dallam		Heathcoat Pickett, Vestryman
George Brown		Jno. Day (son Edward) Ditto
William Dallam		
James Maxwell	1748, Apr. 11	W. Young, Church Warden
Thomas Gittings		Ruxton Gay, Ditto
("T" his mark)		William Dallam, Vestryman
W. Young		Thomas Gittings, Ditto
Thomas Gassaway		Jno. Paca, Ditto
James Maxwell	1749, May 2	William Savory
W. Bond		Roderick Cheyne
Luke Wyle		Richard Willmott
Daniel Maccomas	1749, June 6	George Presbury, Inspector

1743, Juley 5th
   Joshua Starkey
   Walter Tolley
April 3d 1744
Walter Tolley, Vestryman
Ruxton Gay, Church Warden
Thomas Gittings, Vestryman

Edward Norris, Church Warden
Ruxton Gay, Vestryman
George Presbury
J. Chamberlain, Church Warden
Erick Erickson, Do.
James Scott. Vestryman

June 6th 1749
Walter Tolley, Inspector, Joppa
William Bradford, Inspector
Benjamin Norris, Inspector

1749 Sept. 5th
Walter Tolley, Vestryman

Page 235

August 7, 1750
    Daniel Maccomas, Inspector
    Jno. Smith, Church Warden
    Richard Willmott, Vestryman
    Daniel Maccomas, Jr., Church Warden

June 4, 1751
    Robert Boyce, Vestryman
    Benjamin Norris, Do.
    John Day son of Edward, Do.

September 3, 1751
    William Davice (his mark), Church Warden

April 7, 1752
    Godfrey Watters, Church Warden
    Thomas Bailey
    Jno. Chamberlain
    John Howard, Church Warden
    George Symons, Church Warden
    Thomas Waltham
    Jno. Paca

April 27, 1754
    Roderick Cheyne

May 7, 1754
    Thomas Gittings, Jr.
    W. Young
    John Howard
    Henry James

May 6, 1755
    Beale Bordley, Church Warden
    Chas. Christee, Do.

July 1, 1755
    Robert Adair, Vestryman

June 1, 1756
    William Scott, Church Warden
    Jacob Johnson, Do.
    Beale Bordley, Vestryman

August 7, 1757
    Jno. Merryman, Vestryman

August 2, 1757
    Robert Bishopp, Church Warden

Page 236

August 3, 1757
    Ben Norris, Vestryman
    John Day son of Edward, Vestryman
    Joseph Crook, Vestryman

May 2, 1758
    John Watters, Church Warden
    Thomas Meridith, Church Warden

June 6, 1759
    Robert Bishopp, Vestryman
    Edward Day, Church Warden
    Thomas Franklin, Vestryman
    David McCulloch, Vestryman
    James Gittings, Church Warden
    William Debruler, Vestryman

June 3, 1760
    George Presbury, Vestryman
    Jno. Chamberlain, Vestryman

July 15, 1760
    Geo. Gould Presbury, Church Warden
    Asael Gittings, Church Warden

April 7, 1761
    James Preston, Jr., Warden

May 5, 1761
    Walter Tolley, Vestryman
    J. G. Howard Warner (should be Warden)

May 4, 1762
    William Presbury, Church Warden
    James Preston, Jr., Vestryman
    J. G. Howard, Vestryman
    Jo. Hamon Dorsey, Vestryman

May 3, 1763
    Archibald Buchanan, Warden
    Joseph Lewis, Warden
    Jas. Gittings, Vestryman
    Asl. Gittings, Do.
    Nathn. Nicholson, Do.

June 6, 1764
    Benjamin Rickitts, Vetsyrman
    William Bradford, Do.
    Beale Howard, Warden

April 8, 1765
    Robert Bishopp, Warden

Page 237

May 21, 1766
    William Robert Presbuty, Vestryman
    Thomas Gassaway Howard, Vestryman

August 5, 1767
    Geo. Gould. Presbury, Vestryman
    James Gittings, Vestryman
September 1, 1767
    Walter Tolley, Jr., Warden
September 6, 1768
    John Watters
    Jno. Day son of Edward, Vestryman
October 4, 1768
    Thomas Franklin, Vestryman
    Thomas Talbott, Warden
October 25, 1768
    Samuel Young, Vestryman
April 18, 1769
    Walter Tolley, Vestryman
    John Watters, Vestryman
    John Beale Howard, a Vestryman
    John Browne, Church Warden
April 16, 1770
    Henry Wetherall
May 1, 1771
    John Howard, Warden
    W. Young, Vestryman
    Thomas Talbott, Vestryman
    Thomas Franklin, Church Warden
September 1, 1772
    John Howard, Church Warden
    J. Beale Howard, Vestryman
October, 1772
    Samuel Young, Vestryman
    Edward Day, Vestryman
    Robert Bishopp, Church Warden
1772
    Thomas Franklin, Vestryman
    Benjamin Rumsey, Vestryman
    Alexander Cowan, Do.
    Jos. Slade
April 17, 1775
    Walter Tolley, Vestryman
    John Howard, Vestryman
    Benjamin Rogers, Do.
January 18, 1776
    J. Beale Howard, Vestryman
    Benjamin Boyce, Vestryman
June 4, 1776
    Thomas G. Howard, Vestryman
    Walter Tolley, Jr.

Page 238

"The Test. I A.B. do declare that I do believe that there is not Transubstantiation in the Sacrament of the Lord's Supper or in the Elements of Bread and Wine at or after the Consecration thereof by any person whatsoever.

                                           Jas. M'Comas
                                           John Dorsey

BOOK OF PUBLICATIONS, ST. JOHN'S PARISH, 1742
Small book on the inside of cover: "Joppa 1742"

August 6th (times) James Hunt 1.2.3 and Mary Murrin both of this parish.
August 29. John Hugins 1.2.3 and Mary Downes married, both of this parish.
Sept. 26. Edward York and Anne Dorney married, both of this parish 1.2.3. October 21.
October 10. James Freeman and Margaret Butram, both of this parish, married October 28th 1.2.3.
           Peter Golden and Eliz. Earl both of this parish married. 1.2.3. times
November 21. William Cole and Mary Stevens, both of this parish married 1.2.3.
Eod. Die. Benjamin Deason and_____Shepard, both of this parish, married 1.2.3.
December 5. John Dunnikc and Mary Pasmore, both of this parish married 1.2.3. Joppa 1742.
Eod. Die. James Mead, times 1.2.3. and Elizabeth James, both of this parish.
Eod. Die. Ashell Roberts 1.2.3. and Mary Ingrim, married, both of this parish.

(NOTE: To conserve space, the words "both of this parish" and the "times 1.2.3." are omitted; only exceptions will be noted.)

December 12, 1742. Thomas Weekes and Elizabeth Enlowe married.
December 19, 1742. Joseph Lare and Mary Bishop, married.
December 26, 1742. Uriah Bond and Anne Moon, married.
Jan. 16, 1742/43. John Copass and Manerlin Wright, married.
Jan. 16, 1742/43. Sabret Tayrman and Jemima Hitchcock, married.
March 27, 1743. Jonathan Ady and Rebeccah York, married.
April 24, 1743. Joseph Lennings and Mary Rider, married.
June 19, 1743. Edward Brusbanks and Bridget Baker, married.
July 17, 1743. John Bevan and Anne Turner, married.
July 31, 1743. Thomas Underwood and Anne Petty, married.
Eod. Die. Thomas Cottrall and Frances Williams, married.
July 31, 1743. John Morris and Sarah Gilbert, married.
Eod. Die. Richard Green and Elizabeth Feluallen, married.

Page 239

August 7, 1743. Joseph Ward and Hannah Lee, married.
September 4, 1743. John Parks and Bridget Milhews, married September 11, 1743.
September 4, 1743. John Bradley and Anne Evans, married.
October 23, 1743. Thomas King and Elianor Hill, married.
November 20, 1743. James Dawney and Mary Yeats, married.
November 27, 1743. John Travis and Anne Kelsey, married.
       Thomas Gudgins and Mary Gott, married.
December 4, 1743. John Childs and Elizabeth Meads, married.
December 18, 1743. Samuel Smith and Jean Parish, married.
December 25, 1743. David Keith and Sarah Kitely, married.
Eod. Die. Henry Jenkins and Elizabeth Boyd, married.
January 1, 1744. Lewis Demors of Opecan, and Margaret Ramsey of this Parish, married.
Eod. Die. John Demors of Opecan, and Susanna Ramsey of this Parish, married.
January 15, 1744. John Moulins and Sarah Brown, married.
January 22, 1744. Israel Pasley and Sarah Cheverton, married.
January 29, 1744. Joseph Steel and Elizabeth Tomlin, married.
Eod. Die. Richard Basket and Adfia Boyd, married.
March 18, 1744. Thomas Anderson and Mary Perdue, married.
March 26, 1744. John Low and Susannah Cox, married.
June 17, 1744. Thomas Yeats and Elizabeth Martin, married.
Eod. Die. William Harmon and Sarah Powel, married.
August 5, 1744. William Yeats and Anne Thornbury, married.
September 23, 1744. John White and Sarah Legoe, married.
       Adam Hendress and Ruth Sutton, married.
October 21, 1744. Abraham Hays and Fanny Lyttle, married.
December 13, 1744. Jacob Cox and Elizabeth Gain, married.
December 23, 1744. John Hely and Sophia Rhodes, married.
       William Jones and Katharine Brokley, married.
December 25, 1744. John Crokat and Anne Hickson, married.

Page 240

December 25, 1744. James Cain and Elizabeth Doyle, married.
       James Costly and Mary Hill, married.
January 28, 1745. John Wharton and Anne Brown, married.
February 10, 1745. Peter Whitaker and Amelia Hitchcock, married.
       John Furness and Jane Green, married.
       Thomas Marsh and Sophia Corbin, married.

February 10, 1745. Arnold Holt and Martha Boarding, married.
February 24, 1745. Joseph Green and Mary Bowen, married "1.2.&".
April 14, 1745. Abraham Wright and Dorcas Toder, married.
Eod. Die. William Jones and Anne Huggins, married.
April 28, 1745. Mordecai Fuller and Mary James, married.
June 23, 1745. James Dobson and Jane Montgomery, married.
　　　　　Will Reeves and Mary Got "stopt for Bigamy, 1++".
August 11, 1745. William Corbin and Rachel Wright, married.
September 22, 1745. Edward Barnaby and Elisabeth Farmer, married.
November 17, 1745. John Boswell and Mary Jennings, married "1.2.X".
November 24, 1745. Henry Perigoe and Providence Corbin, married.
January 26, 1746. William Prigg and Jean Carsan, married "1.2.+".
February 9, 1746. Samuel Hall and Anne King, married.
March 23, 1746. Joseph Walton and Sarah Matheny, married.
　　　　　Robert Robell and Elizabeth Bradfield, married.
April 13, 1746. William Bryan and Hannah Wallace, married.
June 12, 1746. Richard Williams and Anne Nairne, married.
July, 1746. Thomas Hinkes and Sarah Hewitt "at Jacob Bull."
　　　　　Henry Carey and Elizabeth Waller, married.
August 24, 1746. Simon Hutcheson, and Anne Newman, married.
September 21, 1746. Robert Green and Unity Corbin, married.
October 5, 1746. Joshua Hardesty and Keziah Taylor, married.
November 9, 1746. James Murphey and Sarah Cheyne, married.
November 23, 1746. John Lee and Margaret Howard, married.
　　　　　Joseph Deason and Keturah Hall, married.
　　　　　William Grover and Anne Harrod, married.
December 14, 1746. Picket Jones and Elizabeth James, married.

Page 241

December 14, 1746. Philip Parks and Hannah Peckon, married.
April 12, 1747. John Surnard and Sarah Wilson, married.
April 17, 1747. Isaac Sampson and Mary Ristone, married.
May 10, 1747. Nathaniel Richardson and Elizabeth Gott, married.
　　　　　John Peacocke and Anne Higgins, married.
May 17, 1747. John Ristone and Sarah Sinclair, married.
May 28, 1747. Joseph Brooks and Elizabeth Phillips, married.
July 5, 1747. Joseph Smith and Mary Shepard, married.
July 12, 1747. Samuel Porter and Katherine Herring, married.

August 23, 1747. Daniel Butler and Mary Whitaker, married.
Eod. Die. James Steedman and Mary Munson, married.
October 20, 1747. James Latimore and Sarah Thompson, married.
1750. Charles Borewell and Mary Hammond "forbid".
    Joseph Wright and Margaret James, married.
    John Boulson and Elizabeth Steward, married.
    William Camel Tayman and Anne Williams, married.
1751. Stephen White and Hannah Baker, married "1.2.+"
    John Gibbs and Hannah Palmer, married.
    John White and Betty Gott, married "1.2.X"
    John Warren and Elizabeth Cane, married.
    John Mackness and Elizabeth Morris, married.
    John Rownes and Comfort Brown, married.
    Francis Kitely and Martha Thomas, married.
    John Campbell and Anne Stevens, married.
    Nathan Frizell and Margaret Deason, married.
August 25, 1751. John Sandige and Sarah Grover, married.
November, 1751. William Whaland and Mary Legoe, married.
    Thomas Ryston and Margaret Sinclair, married.
    Anthony Guyshard and Frances Jones, married.
December, 1751. William Smith and Anne Peacock, married.
May, 1752. Thomas Boswell and Mary Chanley, married.
    John Childs and Mary Groves, married.
    John Cotrall and Anne Wood, married.
November, 1752. John Cope and Bridget Tafe or Tate, married.

Page 242

1752. Thomas Benson and Isabell Brown, married.
    Charles Jones and Hannah Nichols, married.
    Thomas Armstrong and Sarah Dellerhide, married.
1753. Philip Cordsman and Anne Brooks, married.
    Edmund Deadman and Eliza Corben, married.
    Thomas Elliot and Rebecca Norris, married.
    William Bennett and Mary Parker, married.
    John Almaney and Eliza Warhorn, married.
    Joseph Barham and Sarah Demmett, married.
    James Clarke and Margaret Plant, married.
    Charles Prosser and Margaret Simkins, married.
    William Bowing and Elizabeth Moss, married.

1753. Charles Bennet and Martha Collins, married.
William Pollet and Elizabeth Hill, married.
James Pring and Rachel Riset, married.
Isaac Ward and Anne Fields, married.
Joseph Beaven and Rachel Ashen, married.
Benjamin Terman (Jerman?) and Elizabeth Rutledge, married.
James Skipen and Anne Warring, married.
November. James Graham and Mary Vine, married.
Samuel Beck and Mary Groves, married.
Thomas Low and Sarah Mainer, married.
1747. James Poor and Sarah Elliot, married.
Cornelius Steward and Mary Lowe, married.
December 6, 1747. Richard Coop and Hannah Stansbury, married.
James Meads and Anne Forrest, married.
William Hicks and Tabitha Stansbury, married.
January 3, 1748. Samuel Wilkinson and Mary Asher, married.
January 31, 1748. John Lake and Mary Smith, married.
Samuel Thornhill and Mary Clyburn, married.
William Perdue and Rebecca Lowe, married.
John Cope and Mary Bush, married.
John Brown and Comfort White, married.
Edward Felin and Mary Linsey, married.

Page 243

April 3, 1748. Benjamin Rutldge and Mary Row, married.
Thomas Niel and Mary Wagstar, married.
John Wiley and Elizabeth Perdue, married.
April 24, 1748. William Yates and Anne Dorney, married.
July 7, 1748. Ambrose Leech and Elizabeth Nairn, married.
John Jones and Sarah Poulson, married.
John Thompson and Anne Petty, married.
Theophilus Miller and Sarah Burk, married.
Thomas Chambers and Mary Cox, married.
September 4, 1748. William Miver and Isabell Fara, married.
William Edwards and Jane Broad, married.
Francis Flannel and Sarah Whaland, married.
October 9, 1748. Richard Ellwood and Mary Lindsay, married.
October 23, 1748. John Oakdin and Susannah Harps, married.
November 6, 1748. Jacob Miles and Hannah Maccomas, married.

November 6, 1748. John Mallance and Ediff Cole, married.
                   George Thayer and Katherine Graves, married.
December, 1748.   William Williams and Sarah Ellwood, married.
                   Francis Polson and Mary Dennick, married.
                   Joseph Wells and Anne Carback, married.
February 3, 1749. William Lynch and Margaret Lynch, married.
                   Joseph Ward and Mary Parkinson, married "1.2.+"
March 26, 1749.   William Lunchfield and Sarah Parks, married.
                   Asall Rockhold and Anne Row this Court married.
                   John Jones and Sarah Morris this Court married.
                   John White and Mary Horton, married.
                   Hugh Cuninghame and Mary Acre, married.
                   John Deason and Mary Hall, married.
                   John Williams and Ruth Rockhold, married.
May 14, 1749.   Daniel Collett and Susanna McKenly, married.
                   James Dorney and Anne Caddle, married.
May 28, 1749.   John Jeffrey and Sarah Williams, married.
July 2, 1749.   William Scott and Elizabeth Tayler, married.
                   John Handland and Mary Cantwell, married.

Page 244

July 30, 1749.   John Hollis and Mary Groom, married.
                   William Kimber and Mary Jackson, married.
August 20, 1749.   Richard Burgess and Sarah Caswell, married.
August 27, 1749.   Moses Byfoot and Sarah Tayman, married.
September 3, 1749. William Dawdrege and Margaret Murphey, married.
                   John Emes and Elizabeth Stiles, married.
September 24, 1749. Thomas Deadman and Sarah Griffin, married.
                   James Morgan and Mary Green, married.
                   Thomas Morris and Frances Shaw, married.
                   James Scott and Mary Martin, married.
                   Thomas Clerk and Kathrine Breton, married.
November 26, 1749. Anthony Asher and Sarah Bevan, married.
                   Richard Griffin and Jean Lord, married.
December 17, 1749. Aquila Milhuse and Elizabeth Parks, married.
                   William Frost and Susannah Roberson, married,
                                                              "1.2.+"
                   John Bruff and Anne Allen, married.
                   William Hudson and Sarah Deason, married.

December 17, 1749. William Bond Whitehead and Susannah Wood, married.
       Thomas Arnstrong and Mary Carter, married.
       David Shadows and Anne Boswell, married.
       Patrick Whealand and Mary Candry, married.
February 11, 1750. Emanuel Mallance and Margaret Reeves, married
                     "1.2.+"
       Francis Norrington and Mary Everitt, married,
                     "1.2.+"
       Samuel Foster and Margaret Guiton, married "1.2.+"
       Edward Bosman and Rose Lyon, married.
       William Legat and Martha Bracket, married.
       John House and Penelope Bond, married.
August, 1750. Simon Hutchison and Penelope Brooke, married.

Page 245

1747. James Lennox Dr.
     To cash paid Mr. Dallam, 14 sh. 7 d.
     To cash at two times, 9 sh. 6 d.
     To Tob. paid I. Risteau, 478.
     To Ditto to Mr. McCulloch, 303.
     To 3 Ells Osnabrigs, 2/9.
     To Talbot Risteau, 7.
     To 1½ Bush Salt from Mr. Lawson, 9.
     To S. Peacock's Levie, 174.
             Ł 2..0..1. 955 Tob.
1748. To Cash, 4..6.
Oct. 18th. To Do., 5.
    To 55 Lebe Tob, c@d. 9..2.
July 22, 1749. To cash paid him in full, 8..3.
              Ł 3..07..1.

   William Gleed and Jean Russel

    James Lennox Cr.
  By Ploughing, 15s.
  By Rolling 6 hhds., 15s.
  By Cow, Tob. 800.
  By a Lamb, 100.
  By a Lamb formerly, 10.
        Ł 2..0.0 Tob. 900.
   By Ball.   1   55
   Dec. 21, 1747 2..0.1   955

1748. By bringing Home the negroe, 10s.
   By going after him again, 14.6.
   By cutting pigs, 2.6
         Tob. 900 3..7..1
   By 55 lbs.

Page 246

1750	Jacob Davies Dr.	Currency Sterl.
Aug. 18	To Ball of Jo. Grierr marriage fee	Ł 2..6
	To 6½ pds. Sugar	4s.
	To 10½ pds. Bacon	3..6
Sept. 7	To Cash	5s.
Dec. 1	To Cash to buy Corn	1..5
Dec. 7	To Ditto	..10
	To Ditto 2 pieces of Eight	9
Dec. 22	To Cash 3 pieces of Eight	13.6
1751		
Feb. 5	To Cash given you	Ł 10 1..15
April 4	To Cash paid the Sheriff	11.8
	To Mr. Tolley	4.1.5
May 24	To Cash given you	2.0.0
	To Credit Mr. Thomas Gittings	3.0
Aug. 7	To Cash given you	1.0
	To Credit Mr. McCulloch	1.9.6
Aug. 26	To Credit Mr. Dallam	7.6.9
		22..16..10
Nov. 11	To Ł 2..16..10 currency charged sterl.	1..15
		3..10
		Currency
1752	The above Jacob Davis Dr.	Ł s d
	To Credit Mr. McCulloch	1..18..3
May 9	To Cash given you	10..0
July 14	To 13 Ells Ozambregs bed	19..6
	To 2 Bottles of Rum	4
		Sterl.
1750	Jacob Davies Cr.	Ł s d
November	By Building a Corn House	3..10---
1751		
April 4	By Sundry Jobs as per his Acctt.	2..2..0
Nov. 11	By Sundries Garden Inclosed	17..18.0
		Ł 20..0..0
	By Sterl. Ł1.15 charged	2.16.10
		22.16.10
	By Building a Stable	Ł4..10.0

Page 247

Joppa, January 2, 1744, for Glebe Plantation, Thomas Lawson, Overseer, to have full share of Tob, Corn, Oats, Cyder, etc. (Wheat only excepted) I pay his Levy.

Dennis Dun to have 2000 Tobo. three pounds Currency, one pair shoes and one hat. I pay his Levy.

Daniel Sullivan

. Anne Barclay
gett for them   4 Broad Hoes, 5 Narrow Hoes, 2 Grubbing Hoes, 4 Wood Axes, 1 Broad Do., 1 Drawing Knife, 2 Plough Horses, 1 Plough of Browns kind, 1 Cart and Cart Saddle, 1 Collar and Heams for Do., 2 Collars and Heams for plough, 3 pairs of braces 2 for plough and 1 for cart, 2 Milch Cows, 8 Breeding Sows, 10 or 12 Sheep, Cask, a Grinding Stone, Scythe and Sickles, 1 Spade,

a small Pot, a frying Pan, a sifter, a Brown Mug.

For the House Repairs, Plank, Shells for Lime, Bricks and Brick Layn, Joists for flooring, Chimneys built, House moved and covered, Orchard enclosed, Ditto pruned, Fodder bought, Corn bought, Cyder Mill bought, Wheat enclosed, Kitchen mended up, Ruggs & Blankets, Build a 30 foot Tobacco House, House of 20 foot of old one.

Page 248

1748 Isaac Risteau   Dr. To his Note of Hand Tobco. for 5120.

October 1749 Memorandum   Have agreed to take corn for ballance of the above accompt at rate of 50 pd. Tob. a Barrel.   Hugh Deane

1749 Isaac Risteau   Cr.
By Paid his Brother Talbot my note of Hand to Robert Bishop
                                                            1000
By paid Ditto my note of hand to Thomas Day   2000
By paid Ditto Costs of Suit

November 24, 1749   By corn from Mill   1 half bar.
December   By Do.   2 bar.
December 21   By Do. No. 3   1 bar.
                    By Do. No. 4   1 bar.
January 4, 1750   By Do. No. 5   1 bar., 1 half bar.
January 13, 1750   By Do. No. 6   1 bar., 1 half bar.
January 20, 1750   By Do. No. 7   1 bar.

Page 249

February 3, 1750   By Do. No. 8   1 bar.
February 12, 1750   By Do. No. 9   1 bar, 1 half bar.
February 13, 1750   By Do. No. 10   1 bar, 1 half bar.
March 3, 1750   By Do. No. 11   1 bar, 1 half bar.
March 9, 1750   By Do. meal   1 bar.

Married

Summer 1742   William Watkins and Anne Blackaby on W. Carbels Land.
              Mrs. Lawson, Mrs. Giddins, present.

              Darymple and Sarah Braser in the forest.
              William Reaves and Martha Stevens Quart.

              Witnesses of Watkins marriage
              William Shepard and his wife
              Eulick Burck and wife
              John Somner and wife
              Henry Perigue and wife
              David Carlisle
              John Bosworth and Mary Jennings
                   Stop Bigamy

1744   Debitors   £   sh.
          Joseph Renshaw   1   0
          Sam. Whips   1   0
          Mrs. Lowe etc.   2   0
          Mrs. Paca   3   0

Debitors	£	sh.
_____Starkeys	2	0
Piercy Petit	-	10
R. K. Chey.	2	0

Creditors
  Mr. Onion   Mr. Roberts
  Mr. England   Mr. Culvert

Page 250

  Messrs. Ayton   Mr. Richard
  Mr. Dallam   Mr. Williams
  Jo. Hollaway   Mr. Allen
  Wm. Kitely   Mr. Barber
  Geo. Debrula   Servant
    Cyder & Corn   Mr. Tolley
  Charlton Waltham   Starkey
  Tho. Gassaway   Bastard
  Mr. Ja. Dick
  Mr. C. Johnston
  Mr. Jo. Wardrop
  Mr. Danl. Campbell
  Mr. Andrew Miller
  Mr. Tho. Brierwood
  Captain Bird
  Coll. White
  Benjamin Caddle
  Dr. Middlemore

Pasted on the inside of cover

Revd Sir
    Your & Mistr's Dean's Company is Desired at the funeral of Doctor Josias Midlemore next Thursday being the 20th Instant. It is to hold at St. George's Church.
    If you will be so good as to give notice to your Congregation that those who are Inclined to Come may know the day & that there will be a Sermon will very much olige yours.
                                               Andrew Lendrum
by order from Mists. Midlemore
  Saturday 15th, 1755

Page 251

On Thursday the 27th of February died at his House in Baltimore County, after two Days Illness, supposed of the Gout, in his Head and Stomach, Doctor Josias Middlemore in the 73d year of his, who came from England in the year 1720, since which Time he hath been a Resident in this County and one who without Fraud and without Guile was more solicitous to be a Christian in deed with a becoming Fortitude and Constancy, the Distemper which after many violent and severe Fits at last carried him off, was in him, neither the Effect of Indolence nor Intemperance, but of Constitution, as he was of all men the most temperate or rather abstenious than appear to be so

without Guile and without Hypocrisy he had an Inocency and
inoffensiveness of Life that was exemplary and a simplicity
of manners truly primitive, his Spirit and Temper were Christian
meek and quiet and peaceable adorned with an Humility, Moderation
and Temperance that was singular as the Benevolence of his Heart
made him a friend to all he was loved and esteemed and one whouse
all men spoke well of, the Disorder that carried him off was in
him the Effect of Constitution not of Indolence and Intermperance,
as he was temperate or rather abstenious and was also a Man of
Action and Industry, he acquired himself a pretty good Estate by
fair and Lawfull means his grand Policy was Honesty and his Religion
not Roman but true and Catholick, a Conscience void of Offence, very
patient he bore with great Patience and Resignation the severe and
heavy trials Divine Providence exercised him with as appeared about

Page 252

3 years ago on the Death of his son and only Child in his 19th year
a virtuous youth and gave promising Hopes as he had set the Lord
always before him and lived the Life of the Righteous, his Latter
End was like his full of Immortality.
His patience met with another tryal in the Loss of a Considerable
Part of his Fortune by the Bankruptcy of a late Merchant in London,
this he also bore with becoming Fortitude and Constancy, in many
Instances more particularly as appeared a few years since, on the
death of his only son Francis in his 19th year, a very promising
and virtuous youth.
His funeral Rites were solemized on the 20th Instant and a Sermon
preached from these words 2 Chron. 3. and all Judah and Jerusalem
mourned for Josiah.

                        The Revd. Hugh Dean

                    By his Excellency
                    Horatio Sharpe, Esqr.
        Governor and Commander in Chief in and
           over the Providence of Maryland

Whereas, Application hath been made to me, by John Marcer and
Rebecca Judah to be joined in Holy Matrimony; These are therefore
to License and Authorize you to solemnize the said Marriage, between
the said Persons, according to Law; there appearing no lawful Lett
or Impediment by Reason of any Pre-Contract, Consanguinity, Affinity
or any just Cause whatsoever, to hinder the same.
Given under my Hand and Seal this 18th Day of February in the Year
of our Lord 1765.
To the Reverend Mr. Hugh Deans Rector of St. John's Parish in
Baltimore County.   Recd. 25, for this Licence, R. Gay.

Horatio Sharpe   L S

Page 253

1774 (No heading, but it appears these were marriages.)

February 1.	James Scot	Letitia Lewis
February 13.	James Brooks	Mary Kinnedy
February 20.	Thomas Travers	Hannah Hutchins
February 20.	William Galloway	Mary Pocock
March 13.	Philip Hodge	Jane Sutten
March 28.	Joseph Read	Agnes Miller
May 29.	Thomas Gray	Mary Legget
June 5.	Jacob Marshal	Mary Sandeford
June 9.	Peter Griffin	Sarah Scarf
June 12	Peter Finley	Eleanor Murphy

The Reverend Mr. Hugh Dean

Sir
    I should be much obliged to you if you would please to call at M. Andrews before you leave town this afternoon as a young man & young   are there waiting for you in great need of your assistance.
        I am sir
                Your most obt.
                hble. Servt.
Sunday   Robt. Saunders
April 28, 1765

Page 254

Publish the Bans of Marriage between John Bickerton and Ann Peaifers. Not in this Parish and forbid by Aquila Hall. Bixerton his Servant.

Sir   Please to publish the Bains of Marridge betwixt Henry Wood and Susanah Ramsey boath of this parrish
                and youl oblidge your
July 20th 1766.   H. Servt.
                Henrey Wood

September 15th 1771

Revd Sir   Pleas to publish the Bans Matrymony between Edward Read and Susannah Shelly.

Revd Sir.
    Being at Present without Marriage Licences, and not in my power just now to supply my old frience, Mr. Skinner with out, I beg you will do the needfull and I will give you a Lycence in a few days. I am   Revd. Sir
                      Your mo: Obt. St.
                      J. Beale Howard
To the Revd. Mr. Deans   May 27th 1776.

Sir
    Please to Publish the Bannes of Mattrimony between Robert Howlet and Elizebeth Boone, Both of the Parish of St. John's. I begg the favor to lett them be asked once to morrow and twice next Sunday.

Page 255

Reverd. Sir
    Be pleas'd to publish the Banns of Matermoney between James Clark and Rachel Rock and you will oblidge yr. Humble Servt.

                                                James Clarke
To the Revd. Mr. Dean.

                        July 27th 1771
Reverend Sir
    It is requested that you will Publish the Banns of Marriage between William Henderside and Mary Williams to know if there is any just cause or impediment why they should not be joined together.
                                        his
                        William M   Henderside
                                 mark
                                        her
                        Mary   X   Williams
                                 mark

Please to publish the Banns of Matrimony between Joshua Legett and Elizabeth Burk both of Baltimore County on Sunday next.

To Request Mr. Hudson if you pleas to publish the bains of marrige between Asel Rockhold & Mary Rutledge bouth of this Parrish and in so doing you will oblige them bouth.
                                                her
                A Rockhold   Mary   X   Rutledge
                                            mark

Reverand Sr. be pleas'd to publish in your Church William Curle and Elizabeth Ward for three Sundays - but you may Call us twice the second Sunday.   This 10th day of August 1775.
Page 256
Please to Publish the Banes of Matrimony Between Malcom Macfee and Elizabeth Franklin Both of This Parish.
                                                Hugh Dean.

Page 257
                St. John's Joppa Harford Co. Register
                Births, Marriages & Deaths 1769-1849.

(Note: The heading indicates the register began in 1769; however, the first entries are without dates, but it appears they were made for September through December of 1768 since they are in order.)

        17   Williams Smith and_____.
        17   Robert Shafford and Catherine_____.

```
           21  Dunham Cowan and Mary Taylor
           29  Jacob Standiford and Elizabeth Robinson
            6  William Williams and Mary Rynoo
               John Lane and Rebeca Dorsey
           11  Joseph Sadlers and Ann Roberts
           13  Joseph Burton and Constant Legatt
           25  John Rhodes and Sarah Standiford
           27  Hankeah James Balch and Martha McKinley
November   10  John Toomy and Salley Gouldsmith
           13  Thomas Mooles and Mary Drake
           17  Juron Henderson and Martha Wood
           20  Vincent Trapnell and Marth Bozley
December    1  John Willson and Deliah Smith
           15  Elisha Dorsey and Mary Slade

1769
January    2  James Mitchel and Mary Hardwick
           3  Peter Burnett and Elisabeth Solomon
           5  Patrick Cavindire and Mary Potee
          12  James Green and Elizabeth Stevens
          22  William Anderson and Mary Hooper
          24  Vincent Wyle and Sarah Sutton
          29  George Townsend and Mary Burnet
          30  Andrew Sheldon and Mary Fields
          31  William Standiford and Elinor Carlile
February   2  William Hichcock and Cordelia Robison
           5  William Hughs and Ann Beck
           7  Robert Hodday and Mary Byde
          16  William White and Mary Whitehead
          16  Andrew Hall and Jane Kelley
          16  Hen. Househoulder and Mary Jonas
```

Page 258

1769
February 21 Richard Willis and Hannah Bu_____.
         23 Hennery Thomas and Elizabeth Piles
         26 John Ross and Sarah Smith
March   2 William Worthington and Sarah Ristow
          2 Gist Vaugham and Rachael Norris
          2 William Sinkler and Mary Norris
          6 Thomas Beal and Sarah Prisley
          9 James Elliot and Mary Atkins
         15 Thomas Pennick and Ann Almon
         16 James Mock and Hannah Holebrook
         16 James Johnson and Elisabeth Hall

March 17 John Cammall and Margret Msds.
      19 Joseph Kimber and Salley Willmot
      23 Edward Bond and Ruth Sampson
      23 John Benet and Eliz. Anderson
      23 William Hadmington and Eliz. Bozley
April 6   James Hughs and Elizabeth Weeks
      11 Nathaniel Wright and Sophia Rutlege
      16 Richard Rodes and Susan Prosper
      20 William Cole and Elizabeth Hadisty
May 14   Nathaniel Sheppard Armstrong and Hannah Norris Lee
     14   James Monday and Elisabeth Little
     25   Thomas Huet and Ann Wyle
     28   James Clarke and Rachael Rock
     30   John Murry and Wealthy Ann Cotteral
     30   David Can and Mary Steel
     30   Thomas Dickin and Mary Perdue
June 4   John Cain and Cathern Gibson
     11   John Cunningham and Elizabeth Young
     13   Charles Upsal and Rylaid Wheatly
     13   James Bevan and Mary Ricket
     13   _____iggan and Mary Gordin
     20   George Elliot and Theresa Anderson
     22   Joseph Hilton and Mary Troit

Page 259

June 29   Abraham Cox and Elizabeth Merrydeth
     29   Elisha Bozley and Elizabeth Merryman
July 2   John Whey and Salley Taylor
      2   John Johnston and Elizabeth Easton
      2   Andrew Wilb and Mary Matthews
     13   John Anderson and Isbell Carr
     23   John Williams and Ann Renshaw
August 11 Patrick Brannan and Elizabeth Johnston
       29 Azel Barton and Ann Holt
September 14 Valentine Corback and Rachael Colls
          17 Enoch Dawson and Elizabeth Legat
          25 Francis Watkins and Elizabeth Pines
          27 John Oram and Rachael Wantland
October 5 Thomas Bradley and Elizabeth Harwood

October   8 Abraham Standiford and Susan Chaberlane
          19 Vissey Price and Sim. Barton
          28 Phillip Dushan and Elizabeth Mallett
November   5 John Palmer and Sidie (Lidie?) Collins
           9 Richard Cook and Rebeca Murrey
          23 John Edward and Unity Legatt
          24 Isaac Farnell and Rebeca Sweeting
          28 Thomas McBride and Mary Scotty
December   2 John Logan and Elizabeth Pristlay (Pustlay?)
           4 Richard Bennet and Elizabeth Jarom
           5 William Ditto and Leah Legoe
           7 William Wells and Elizabeth Wattson
          26 Phillip Johnson and Sophia Wathusd
          28 Lawrence Craft and Mary Lymes

1770
January   4 Thomas Hughs and Margret Talbott
          16 William Slade and Elizabeth Stansbury
          16 Aquilla Scott and Mary Preston
          25 Joseph Norris and Elizabeth Cole
          27 Thomas Gullam and Mary Green
February   4 John Allin and Jemima Stansbury

Page 260

February   6 John Almoney and Mary Watson
          13 Jarvis Bidison and Ruthe Robison
          20 Joseph Legoe and Nancy Wilcher
          22 William Ducke and Jane Thompson
          22 Benn Biddle and Katheran Happuck Barton
          27 Edward Willion and Sally Green
March   8 William Shea and Elizabeth Willson
          27 William Thomas and Ann Colegate
April   3 Thomas Colegate and Elizabeth Clarke
           4 Thomas Gulliver and Jane Clinerown
          10 Aquila Wyle and Pine Sparks
          15 James Scott and Casandera Bond
          15 James Price and Elinor Carrol
          17 Buckley Bond and Charity Bond

May	1	Richard Croxal and Hannah Jennings
	3	Danial Watkins and Sosia Biddeston
	13	Benn Trasey and Tempy Edwards
	16	Benn Carter and Martha Garison
June	3	Mouldin Amos and Rachael Bull
	4	Joseph Stone and Elizabeth Mitchell
	5	William Thine and Sarah Davinne
	7	Josia Pitts and Sarah Barton
	7	Thomas Ruvis and Mary Connelly
	9	Richard Wood and Mary Kun
	10	John Cromwell and Mary Dorsey
	25	Abraham Green and Ruthe Curbeck
July	12	Joseph Parish and Charity Bosley
	22	John Willson and Margret Edy
	22	John Golding and Rachael Demmit
	29	John Scarff and Hannah Talbott
August	5	William Bosick and Mary Philpot
	7	Benadick Legoe and Sally Hick
	20	William Jennings and Hannah Rutlidge
September	16	James Bosley and Temperance March

Page 261

September	27	John Leach and Mary Johnson
October	7	Peter Carrol and Martha Clarke
	14	John Holland and Ann Baker
	17	John Slowin and Elizabeth Smith
	28	Artura Conelly and Elizabeth Parker
November	6	Thomas Rooke and Mary Flanngin
	8	Jacob Householder and Eliza White
	13	Sutton Grudgings and Mary McGrevey
	22	William Edye and Cloe Standiford
	22	Thomas Ensor and Mary Talbott
	25	Martin Preston and Rebecca Scott
	27	James Ingram and Mary Holt
December	2	Robert Jackman and Sarah Whitaker
November	29	Nerson Hugs and Margret Little
December	4	Arthur Carty and Mary Murphey
	4	Robert Clarke and Elizabeth Rigdon

December   6 Benjamin Thornhill and Ann Scott
          13 Thomas Bosley and Mary Richards
          17 Abell Green and Lydie Palmer
          18 John Dorcey and Marth Woodland
          20 John Barton and Ruthe Gorsuch

1771
January   6 Vincent Richardson and Martha Norris
          20 James Lyder and Ann Meedes
          20 Michael Byle and Margret Gohon
          22 John Ward and Sally Danton
          27 William How and Margret Jackman
          31 Michael Mallaney and Elizabeth Collison
February   5 Richard Hill and Martha Chapman
          10 John McGuire and Mary Tipton
          10 Joseph Morton and Molley Shelby
          14 Williams Stephens and Margret Smith
March   3 Thomas Hobeard and Dinah Marel
          19 Robert Taylor and Isabel Smith
          24 John Huff and Elizabeth Ferguson

Page 262

March   28 Vincent Bozley and Wheelamina Norris
          28 James Dail and Ann McGaberon
          31 Ribulon Hedington and Elizabeth Lemmon
April   4 Vincent Standiford and Prissilla Nearn
           9 George Chalke and Elizabeth Hughs
          11 William Jones and Hannah Hynes
          14 William Harkin and Christian Holland
          23 John Woodlow and Ruth Tower
          25 Robert Davity and Margret Ellison
          28 Charles Baker and Dinah Hendon
          28 Phillip Hooper and Elizabeth Palmer
          30 William Edwards and Susan Airs
May   2 Alexander Cowan and Elinora Boyce
           5 John Everat and Elizabeth Jackman
           7 John Bill and Mary Edwards
          16 James Thrift and Ann Wilson
          19 William Price and Mary Noland

May 23   John Hughs and Tabitha Haryman
June 2   Henry James and Mary Smith
     4   James Harris and Cassandera James
     22   George Jackman and Elizabeth Giles
     27   John Wane and Margret Allinder
July 5   John Morton and Sarah Harlins
     7   John Gordon and Catherine Hunt
     14   John Rockhold and Jemima Deeson
     18   Zachius Sank and Jemima Wicks
August 10 Henry Forsett and Margret Beally
       15 Hugh Brown and Ruth Barney
       18 William Handerside and Mary Williams
       22 Robert Evins and Ann Bartinn
       25 John Bacon and Temperance Hunt
       27 John Petticoat and Rebeca Boring
September 3 William Presbury and Cordelia Debruler
         10 Daniel Wheeks and Nancy Lueester

Page 263
1771
September 10 Thomas Davinn and Ann Harmpmann
          19 Edward Day and Rebecca Claggled (Claggett?)
          22 James Rumpley and Sarah Gibson
          24 Arthur Brownly and Nancy Norris
October 3 William Stanley and Margret Backhouse
         14 Giles Baker and Elizabeth Clarke
         24 Samuel Chamberlane and Elizabeth Pakt.
         24 Jeremiah Dannely and Elizabeth York
         31 Simon Hunt and Mary Noland
November 7 William Andss and Sarah Morris
         14 Markum McFeel and Elizabeth Franklin
         14 John Rocker and Esabel Brown
         16 William Bond and Sarah Wrongs
         21 Edward Norris and Elizabeth Amoss
         21 William Prine and Sophia Colebeck
         21 Thomas Bond and Ruth Morrow
         23 John May and Elizabeth Buckley
         29 Samuel Heath and Susan Lewis
         29 Elizth. (?) Leemon and Rachel Stansbury
December 1 Thomas Cooly and Sarah Collins

```
December  10  John Hughston and Hannah Waltham
          10  Thomas Miles and Hannah Thompson
          10  John Dunnock and Casandra Sutton
          12  George Bogan and Elizabeth Amoss
          15  John Standiford and Ruthe Rutlidge
          19  Thomas Bond and Reneckah Stansbury
          24  John Gillcoat and Providence Ensor
          25  John Soullavin and Kitty Grooves
          26  John Willard and Mary Jones
          29  John Towson and Prunelfry Buck
          31  Abraham Whitaker and Elizabeth Wheeler
1772
January    9  Gidion Bosley and Sarah Cole
           9  John Marrer and Rebecka Coligate
          16  William Purere and Elizabeth Perdere
```

Page 264

```
January   19  Mathew Coligan and Sarah Neale
          20  John Hammon Dorsey and Ann Maxwell
          26  John Page and Deep Rose
February   2  James Armstrong and Martha H_____.
          13  Walter Billinsley and Ruth Clarke
          16  Sylvanus Hocraft and Mary Goff
          25  Peter Bond and Elizabeth Scott
          27  John Shoats and Mary Kug
          27  Calib Bozley and Elizabeth Wheeler
March      3  Humphrey Chilcoat and Sarah Ensor
          10  Alexander Hill and Elizabeth Kelley
          22  Francis Gurnill and Judith Carthy
          28  Thomas Albudd and Dinah Parker
April     21  Joseph Cullison and Sarah Walker
          23  Robert Thesbord and Catheran Floud
          27  Peter Stafford and Jane Lewis
May       10  Richard Wiat and Dinah Corbin
          17  Edward Hart and Mary Gaffin
          17  James Hall and Sarah Burk
          19  Jonas Tipton and Elizabeth Ford
          19  Robert Hawlines and Arebella Mitchel
          28  Thomas Durbin and Frances Carty
```

May 28   Daniel Dreston and Ann Rigdon
    31   Abraham Airs and Billey Drue Andrew
June 2   William Baker and Roxannah Whiley
     5   William Jones and Elizabeth King
     7   Sollomon Hughs and Sophia Wright
    11   Thomas Price and Mary Gatt
    21   Thomas Burk and Deliah Peacock
    23   Robert Bradin and Elizabeth Wilkinson
    25   James Leggot and Elizabeth Baker
    27   Daniel McClogan and Eliner Price
    30   Jessey Lecester and Constantine Morioke
July 2   John Ensor and Dorcas Gorsich

Page 265

1772
July 7   Thomas Street and Sarah James
     7   Joseph Woodland and Cassandra Masscey
    30   Jonathan Procter and Gorinth Prington
August 6 Abraham Rhodes and Roxa. Standiford
      18 John Thompson and Elizabeth Rumsey
September 3 Michael Taylor and Salley Hall
          3 John Brown and Margret O'Donil
          3 Robert Howard and Susan Holland
          6 William Cole and Roxana Hilton
         10 James Butlin and Sarah Brock
October 6 Robert Crookshanks and Ann Day
        6 John Buckley and Ann Gouldsmith
       11 William Thomas and Mary Pardon
       11 Thomas Amoss and Mary Miles
November 5 Skelton Standiford and Mary Richardson
        12 John Norris and Marth Long
        17 Joseph Aldrutt and Jemima Says
        19 Henry Young and Delila Harryman
        26 William Smith and Rebecca Whelar
December 3 David Evans and Elizabeth Chance
         8 Richard Green and Ann Jones
        27 William Radford and Jane Jones
1773
January 1 James Braham and Ellis Cooke
        7 Moses Legoe and Catherine Hutton

1773
January 7 Charles Mulner and Casander Chamberlane
        14 Thomas Parson and Mary Perdue
        20 James Buck and Cloe Crooke
        21 William Richardson and Elizabeth Norton
February 2 Vincent Talbott and Elizabeth Bozley
         4 John Rutlidge and Ruth Standiford
         4 Donnole Ashew and Elizabeth Holt
        11 Peter Puttee and Elizabeth Hughes
        18 James Francis Moore and Ann Standiford
        22 James Hawkins and Susannah Atlar

Page 266

March 11 Thomas Hutchins and Jemima Johnson
      22 James Roose and Margret Hitely
      25 Edward Bosman and Frances Saunders
April 9 Lidius Drivett and Ann Webster
      13 Cornelius Stewart and Ann Studart
May   4 William Todd and Presella Harryman
       5 Gabrial Holland and Sarah Harryman
      20 James Prine and Mary Stewart
      20 Isaac Phillips and Prudence Sickelmore
      21 Garrett Murphey and Catherine Small
      31 Thomas Smith and Dinah Blackburn
June   1 James Amoss and Catherna Ristau
July   4 Garret Patteson and Cloe Dean
August 1 Anthony Nelman and Mary McCall
       1 James Cunningham and Pathiah Standiford
       1 Charles Vershon and O'Statis Oram
       8 Henry Hendon and Mary Westfield
       8 Charles Divine and Tamer Horner
John Day and Mary Gouldsmith Presbury were married Nov. 30, 1775.
John Day, son of Edward, and Sarah York was married about four
   o'clock in the afternoon, December 30, 1764.

1780
December 12 Henry Hart and Mart Cartwright
May 21 William Wallis and Hannah Cartwright

1783
January 21 Abraham Cartwright and Mary Hart

James Carrol, Esq. of Arundel County, was married to Sophie Gough daughter of Harry Dorsey Gough, Esq. of Perry Hall, Dec. 18, 1787, by L. Heath, Minister of Saint John's Parish, Joppa.

John Day to Miss Sarah Allender, Friday, February 29, 1788, by L. Heath.

Page 267

By virtue of a Licence granted the tenth Day of April Eighteen hundred and four by William Gibson Clark of Baltimore County & counter signed Thomas Harwood directed to the Reverend Mr. Coleman or any other Person so qualified by Law to celebrate the Marriage in the State of Maryland Isaac Hollingsworth of Baltimore County in St. John's Parish now of Harford County in the Parish aforesaid and Cassandra Divers Daughter of Annanias Divers of same Parish & Baltimore County on the seventeenth Day of April in the same month and year were joined in Holy Matrimony and the Rights of Marriage solemnized between them in St. John's Parish by the Revd. John Coleman.

Baptised by the Reverend John Coleman, Gassaway West who is said by them Son of Luke and Sarah West who is said by them to be two years old the 18th of April 1804, and two black children as by Certificate from him.

Marriages, Births, Deaths, during the Revd. Mr. James Jones Wilmer's Pastroship 23rd May 1800. Baptized 7 children, 4 whites to wit Elizabeth, Eleanor, Sarah and Mary Rogers, and 3 black children.

July 28, 1800 Baptised 2 children viz. Levy Alexander McCubbin and Lloyd McCubbin, Sons of McCubbin at the little Falls Gunpowder.

September 11th 1800 Henry Hale was married to Susan Hall, Daughter of Col. Aquila Hall of Baltimore County.

October 7 10 & 12 three sic Infants were baptised to wit Joseph Corbin Turner, Sarah Ellinder and Celia White.

Page 268

Jan. 4, 1801. Lambert Willmer was buried.

January   Was baptised James Lambert Maxwell, son of Moses Maxwell.

Jan. 6, 1801. Walter Tolley Hall was married to Charlotte White Hall daughter of Benedict Edward Hall, Esq., of Havre de Grace.

Jan. 8, 1801. Thomas Doughty was married to Providence Cravins, both of Baltimore County.

Jan. 11, 1801. Edward Day was married to Mary Brown.

Clement Waltham of Harford County was married to Alisanna Webster of same county on the 29th January 1801.

Dr. Day was buried on the 1 Feby. 1801. 4 Infants and two adults baptised, names not known.

Margarett Cord, Daughter of John Cord, baptised 1 March 1801.

George Young was buried 22 March 1804.

James Shields was married to Elizabeth Thomas the 23 March 1801.

June 14, 1801. Mary Louisa Howard the Daughter of Edward Howard and Charlotte Howard was baptised about 6 months old.

July 5. an Infant was baptised.

Benjamin Tinecum was married to Elizabeth Scaulty both of Harford County July 5, 1801.

July 12, 1801. John Onion and Lloyd Onion, sons of William Onion were baptised.

26. Two children were baptised names not returned by Mr. Wilmer.

Page 269

30th Aug. 1801. Mary Ann Day, Daughter of John Day, was baptised.

Oct. 8th, 1801. Isaac Daws was baptised.

Oct. 8th, 1801. Richard Thrift and Mary Daws was married.

Oct. 15, 1801. Alexander Rogers, Esq., and Delia Christie, Daughter of Gabriel Christie, Esq., were married together, both of Havre de Grace.

Nov. 12, 1801. Thomas Turner and Phoebe Morris were married together both of Harford County. 4 Infants baptised names unknown.

November 15th. William Chambers was married to Sarah York alias Strong.

1 January 1802. Miss Mary Bond Daughter of Jacob Bond was baptised.

5 January 1802. Miss Mary Bond buried.

24 January 1802. Old Mr. Graves buried.

February 7, 1802. Benjamin Daws was married to Elizabeth Norris.

Feb. 7th. Two children of J. Norris were baptised. Henrietta Baker and Mary Norris, also Elizabeth Baker.

Sophia Nowland Daughter of Perefrine Nowland was baptised 10 Feb 1802.

Miss Cofield buried 17 Feb 1804 at Havre de Grace.

Andrew Gray was married to Miss Rebecca Rogers, Havre de Grace, February 23, 1802.

Stephen Waters was married to Mary Ann Brown, both of St. John's Parish, April 1, 1802.

Page 270

Thomas A. Hays of Harford was married to Elizabeth Jones April the 8th, 1802.

James Lee Morgan was married to Sophia Monks of Abingdon, daughter of John Monks, 8th April 1802.

John St. Clair of Baltimore County was married to Charity Saunders of Harford, April the 18th 1802.

Roger McNeal was married to Cassandra Lynch both of Havre de Grace, May 1802.

Mary Ann Hall, daughter of Walter Tolley Hall of Havre de Grace in May 1802. (Note: This probably was a baptism.)

William David Thompson, son of J. Thompson of Havre de Grace, was baptised in May 1802.

Thomas Knight, son of Mr. Knight of Havre de Grace, was baptised in May 1802.

William Brook was married to Ann Walker 27 May 1802.

Martha McCloskey, daughter of Mr. McCloskey, was baptised 27 May 1802.

1802 May 30. A sick infant of John Days was baptised.

Sarah Row, daughter of Mr. Row. was baptised 6 June 1802.

Ann Dorsey was buried May 9th 1802.

June 27th 1802 Theodore, son of John Beale Howard, was baptised.

Mrs. Seal was buried aged 85. July 4, 1802.

Page 271

July 6th 1802 Michael McKennar was married to Martha Garrett both of Harford County.

John Rumsay Howard, son of Edward Aquila Howard and Charlotte his wife, was baptised 25 July 1802.

Thomas Durham was buried in August 1802.

Elizabeth Tootle the wife of Dr. Tootle of the City of Annapolis was buried 22 August 1802.

Ruth Wright and her two daughters Rachael and Frances were baptised September 19, 1802.

Philip Coffman & Hiccabud Thrift were married Oct. 17th 1802 by Licence.

Hannah Carroll, Rachel Whitaker and Mary William Richardson were baptised 17th October 1802.

Ephraim Hopkins and Mary Morgan were married 21 October 1802.

George York buried 7 November 1802.

Ephraim Cox and Elizabeth Wilson were married 2 December 1802.

1802   End of Mr. Wilmer's account and the following are from the Revd. Mr. Coleman.

James Haley, son of George and Sarah Haley, was born 12 Oct. 1798.

John Haley, son of the above parents, born Dec. 10, 1800, and both were baptised March 2, 1802.

Page 272

Baptisms. Marriages & Funerals returned according to Law by the Revd. Mr. Allen, Rector of St. George's Parish, Harford County, to the Register of St. John's Church of said County.

Temperance, the daughter of Samuel Fuller and Elizabeth his wife was born on the 16 day of January 1800 & baptised 12 March 1800.

Elizabeth, daughter of William & Catherine Bishop, was born February 1, 1800 and baptised June 30th in the same year.

Edward, son of Thomas Tredway and Christina his wife, was born December 15, 1783 and baptised October 17th in the year 1800.

Sarah, daughter of the same parents, was born November 26, 1776 and baptised 17th Oct. 1800.

Christina, daughter of Edward Sanders and Christina his wife, was born May 27, 1782 and baptised Oct. 17, 1800.

Mary, daughter of Thomas Tredaway and Christina his wife, was born March 6, 1786, baptised Oct. 17, 1800.

Thomas Doughty, son of Thomas Doughty and Christina his wife, was born November 8, 1781 and baptised Oct. 17, 1800.

Ann Doughty, daughter of the same parents, was born May 12, 1792 and baptised Oct. 17, 1800.

John Norris was born February 26, 1796 and baptised Oct. 17, 1800.

Sarah, daughter of Conrad Row and Mary his wife, was born Feb. 14, 1800 and baptised November 10, 1800.

Page 273

Mary Ann, daughter of Joseph and Elizabeth Cox, was born May 7, 1799 and baptised November 10, 1800.

Susanna, daughter of William and Mary Robertson, was born Nov. 2, 1799 and baptised November 10, 1800.

Richard Touchstone and Sarah Touchstone were married Jan. 7, 1800.

George Stolinger and Ann Deaver married January 23, 1800.

Benjamin Wilmer and Margarett Crawford married May 29, 1800.

Andrew McClean and Esther Israel married December 2, 1800.

Catherine Wilmer was buried on January 7, 1800.

Thomas Bond was buried on September 5, 1800.

William, son of William and Catherine Truss, was born April 9, 1790 & baptised April 26, 1800.

Harriott, daughter of William and Mary Truss, was born May 11, 1796 & baptised April 26, 1801.

Catherine, daughter of the same parents, was born December 22, 1799 and baptised April 26, 1801.

Thomas, son of John and Mary Howard, was born April 12, 1801 and baptised April 26, 1801.

Page 274

James Woodland, son of James and Sophia Dawney, was born Dec. 20, 1787 and baptised September 9, 1801.

William Wilson and Margarett Winstondey (or Winstandley) were married March 26, 1801.

Isaac Kelly and Drusilla Durbin Nichols married April 2, 1801.

James Wood and Elizabeth Maxwell married April 9, 1801.

Gilbert York and Mary Chilson married April 26, 1801.

George Bradford and Susanna McComas married May 26, 1801.

Thomas Hill and Martha Browning married June 8, 1801.

Thomas Spencer and Mary Nabb married June 11, 1801.

Edward Day of John, and Hannah Wilmer married August 6, 1801.

Daniel Ruff and Hannah Maffitt married December 31, 1801.

Marriages made and celebrated by the Revd. William Coleman and returned by him to the Register of St. John's Parish.

John Grayham and Mary McGowley married August 31, 1787, they being both of Harford County.

Page 275

Bond James Kimbley and Mary Mills both of Harford County were married on September 11, 1787.

Edmund Standiford and Hannah Gray both of Harford County were married October 13, 1787.

John Holt Guyton and Sarah Watkins of Baltimore County were married October 30, 1787.

Godfrey Waters and Martha Bradford both of Harford were married on November 13, 1787.

Dennis McLaughlin and Rachel Norris of Baltimore County were married December 18, 1787.

Thomas Chinworth and Rachel both of Harford County were married January 1, 1788.

Michael Craws and Sarah Hauson of Harford County were married February 28, 1788.

Peter Holding and Sarah Hair both of Harford County were married May 4, 1788.

Thomas Worrall and Mary Conden of Baltimore County were married May 12, 1788.

John Green and Cassandra Smithson of Harford County were married July 1, 1788.

Peter Bowles and Rachel Coon of Harford County married July 17, 1788.

Page 276

Benjamin Downs and Blanch Hampton of Harford County were married October 2, 1788.

Abraham Jones and Mary Gittings of Baltimore County were married October 28, 1788.

Samuel Hickerson of Baltimore County and Mary Throp of Harford County were married November 13, 1788.

Martin Renshaw of Baltimore County and Magdalen Jones of Harford County were married November 19, 1788.

John Burnett and Hannah Spencer of Harford County were married November 23, 1788.

Thomas Nash and Lucretia Wicks of Harford County were married December 25, 1788.

Thomas Dunstan and Ann Leget of Baltimore married January 1, 1789.

William Lee and Margarett Day of Harford County were married on January 4, 1789.

Nathan Phips and Rebecca Davies of Harford County were married January 29, 1789.

Richard Taylor and Clemency Thompson of Harford County were married February 2, 1789.

Emanuel Reed and Ann Hunt of Harford County were married February 8, 1789.

James Steward and Eleanor Dynes of Harford County were married February 22, 1789.

Page 277

John Neal and Mary Scofield of Baltimore County were married April 14, 1789.

Charles Hipkins and Elizabeth Mires of Baltimore County were married May 10, 1789.

James Montgomery and Susanna Whitaker of Harford County were married June 7, 1789.

James Mulley and Sarah Wicks of Harford County were married August 10, 1789.

John Norton and Sarah Jones of Harford County were married September 24, 1789.

Robert Peak and Elizabeth Murray of Harford County were married September 27, 1789.

Abraham Hilton and Elizabeth Grimes of Baltimore County were married October 20, 1789.

Frederick McComas and Susanna Onion of Harford County were married November 17, 1789.

Isaac Guyton and Margarett Hilhorn of Harford County were married November 21, 1789.

Lucas Gillam and Temperance Corbin of Harford County were married December 24, 1789.

John Rockhold and Martha Waters of Harford County were married February 2, 1790.

Henry Norris and Margarett Gordon of Harford County were married April 3, 1790.

Page 278

Thomas Corbin and Nancy Turner of Harford County were married May 11, 1790.

Daniel Rawley and Mary Robb of Harford County were married May 18, 1790.

John Hambleton and Phebe Maxwell of Harford County were married May 20, 1790.

Robert Alexander and Rebecca Hayes of Harford County were married June 27, 1790.

James Galloway and Mary Chine of Baltimore County were married September 5, 1790.

Nathaniel Nicholas and Elizabeth Harris of Harford County were married October 21, 1790.

William Grant and Catharine Holland of Harford County were married November 18, 1790.

William Magness and Sarah Waters of Harford County were married December 23, 1790.

George Collins and Sarah Bailey of Baltimore County were married December 26, 1790.

Thomas Crouch and Elizabeth McGowan of Harford County were married December 27, 1790.

James Fullerton and Sarah Bradford of Harford County were married January 13, 1791.

Benjamin Vanhorn and Charity Sanders of Harford County were married February 15, 1791.

Page 279

Thomas Durham and Rachel Shondy (Shoudy) of Harford County were married March 15, 1791.

Charles Coleman and Lydia Forwood of Harford County were married March 17, 1791.

Thomas Wright and Ann Green of Harford County were married March 17, 1791.

Ephraim Donavan and Charlotte Taylor of Harford County were married March 28, 1791.

Leonard Cowen and Mary Fowler of Harford County were married May 15, 1791.

Thomas Rock and Rebecca Reed of Harford County were married May 29, 1791.

John Branian and Sarah George both of Harford County were married June 23, 1791.

George Debrular and Arminta Nutterville of Harford County were married July 12, 1791.

Kidd Lynch and Sarah Sumarts of Harford County were married August 21, 1791.

John Wright and Rebecca Otherson of Harford County were married August 21, 1791.

Peter Long and Margarett Carr of Harford County were married August 30, 1791.

James Wear and Charity Key of Harford County were married September 11, 1791.

Page 280

David Asquith and Frances Nichols of Baltimore County were married October 2, 1791.

John McCubbin and Polley Tudor of Baltimore County were married December 27, 1791.

Asael Barton and Susanna Millikin of Baltimore County were
married December 27, 1791.

Arthur Langden and Mary Lewis of Harford County were married
January 25, 1792.

Enoch Churchman and Martha Norris of Harford County married
February 2, 1792.

George Ellinder and Sarah Grimes of Baltimore County married
February 12, 1792.

Henry Bateman Goe and Susanna Gittings of Baltimore County
married February 16, 1792.

Henry Waters and Grace Wilson of Harford County were married
February 21, 1792.

Benjamin Parish and Nancy Hunter of Baltimore County married
March 1, 1792.

Aquila Galloway and Ann Barton of Baltimore County were married
April 4, 1792.

Zacharias Durham and Lucia Husband of Harford County married
March 11, 1792.

Maurice Maulsby and Eleanor Maulsby of Harford County married
March 22, 1792.

Peter John Roberts and Maria Sanderson of Harford County were
married April 23, 1792.

Henry Patrick Finnagan and Aransa Demaker of Harford County
married June 17, 1792.

Thomas Johnson of Harford County and Elizabeth Cord of Baltimore
County were married June 17, 1792.

Samuel McMath and Mary Curry of Harford County married June 18, 1792.

Anthony Lynch and Mary Barton of Baltimore County md. June 21, 1792.

Jesse Mathews and Ann Conn of Harford County married Aug. 1, 1792.

Arnold Rush and Janett Conn of Harford County md. Aug. 27, 1792.

Joshua Tudor & Susanna McCubbins of Baltimore Co.md. Oct. 9, 1792.

Francis Carty & Magdalen Juel of Harford County md. Oct. 1, 1792.

John Addison & Sarah Lietch of Baltimore County md. Oct. 11, 1792.

Joshua Ady of Harford and Mary Ford of Baltimore County married
November 6, 1792.

Page 282

Lambert Smith and Elizabeth Gittings of Baltimore County married
November 6, 1792.

William Wilkinson Waits and Susanna Stansbury of Baltimore County
married December 4, 1792.

William McMath and Sarah Moores of Harford County were married
December 11, 1792.

Jacob Fulks and Priscilla Perkins of Baltimore County married December 13, 1792.

James Woodland and Sarah Collins of Harford County married December 25, 1792.

Benjamin Carrol and Mills Proctor of Harford County married December 25, 1792.

Moses Taylor and Nancy Durban of Harford County were married December 27, 1792.

Daniel Moores and Sarah Budd of Harford County md. Jan. 1, 1793.

William Roach and Elizabeth Hambleton of Harford County married January 27, 1793.

John Lucas and Sarah Divers of Baltimore County md. Feb. 7, 1793.

Thomas Gassaway Howard and Martha Susanna Tolley of Baltimore County were married April 2, 1793.

John Hambleton and Peggy Bond of Harford County md. June 17, 1793.

Page 283

John Strickland and Alice Perry of Harford County md. June 30, 1793.

Charles Hopkins of Harford and Ann Jenkins of Baltimore County were married July 23, 1793.

Thomas Brown and Hannah Murrey of Baltimore County were married July 29, 1793.

John Middleton and Mary Cowan of Harford County md. Sept. 15, 1793.

John Bowers and Hannah Bronnell of Harford County md. Nov. 3, 1793.

Thomas Sadler and Elizabeth Howard of Baltimore County were married November 7, 1793.

Andrew Stevenson and Isabella Smith of Harford County were married November 30, 1793.

Moses Maxwell and Sally Charity Bond of Harford County were married December 10, 1793.

Isaac Leadley and Nancy McCubbins of Baltimore County were married December 26, 1793.

Edward Daws and Ann Grunden of Harford County md. Dec. 29, 1793.

Peter Delivett and Ann Jones of Baltimore County md. Feb. 16, 1794.

Thomas Johnson and Ann Giles of Baltimore County md. May 22, 1794.

Page 284

James McComas and Sarah Howard of Harford County md. Mar. 29, 1794.

John March and Hannah Onion of Harford County md. June 5, 1794.

John Little and Elizabeth Adams of Harford County md. July 20, 1794.

Nicholas Day McComas and Elizabeth Onion of Harford County married July 24, 1794.

Paul Aime Fleury and Clara Young of Baltimore County were married October 28, 1794.

John Clark and Cassandra Anderson of Harford County were married November 15, 1794.

Henry Dorsey (of Edward) and Elisabeth Smithson of Harford County were married February 5, 1795.

William Ellenor and Barbara Bemer of Baltimore County were married February 19, 1795.

Joseph Scott of Baltimore County and Hannah Norris of Harford County were married March 5, 1795.

William Everitt and Sarah Cooper of Harford County were married March 29, 1795.

Henry Wilson and Sarah Worthington of Baltimore County were married April 9, 1795.

Thomas Waltham and Martha Greenfield of Harford County were married May 21, 1795.

George Spear and Catharine Birmer of Baltimore County were married May 24, 1795.

John Lawrence and Rebecca Yarley were married July 5, 1795.

Page 285

William Askew of Baltimore and Sarah Calwell of Harford County were married December 10, 1794.

Richard Gott and Ruth Bailey of Baltimore County were married December 17, 1795.

Ralph Yarley and Ruth Barton of Baltimore County were married December 24, 1795.

Robert Whitfoed and McCarman were married February 2, 1796.

Daniel McComas and Elizabeth Scott of Harford County were married February 18, 1796.

John Watkins and Ruth Guyton of Baltimore County were married June 2, 1796.

Thomas Johnson and Elizabeth Taylor of Harford County were married November 17, 1796.

John Hambleton and Aley Gafford of Harford County were married January 26, 1797.

Thomas Sheredine and Ann Neil of Harford County were married March 9, 1797.

Page 286

Daniel Scott and Margarett Short of Harford County married April 6, 1797.

Francis Holland and Sybell West of Baltimore County married May 25, 1797.

William Godman and Delilah White of Harford County married July 22, 1797.

Henry O'Henry and Ann Price of Harford County married July 27, 1797.

John Moore and Mary Scarbrough of Harford County married Aug. 3, 1797.

Richard Tydings and Susanna Chamberlain of Baltimore County married August 8, 1797.

James Smith and Sarah Haley of Harford County married Sept. 21, 1797.

William Witherall and Mary Presbury of Harford County were married September 21, 1797.

Parker Gilbert and Martha McComas of Harford County were married September 21, 1797.

Daniel Cunningham and Ann Amos of Harford County married Oct. 19, 1797.

William Neill and Mary Sheredine of Harford County were married November 2, 1797.

Ruthan Garrison and Mary Gallion of Harford County were married November 23, 1797.

Page 287

William Linam and Sarah Pinox of Harford County married Dec. 17, 1797.

Thomas Birkhead and Elizabeth Waters of Harford County were married December 7, 1797.

Thomas Stocksdale and Sarah Baxter of Harford County were married December 18, 1797.

Morgan Jones and Cordelia Baker of Harford County were married January 25, 1798.

Charles Kinzell and Ann Johnson of Harford County were married February 8, 1798.

Samuel Vance and Mary Walters of Harford County married Oct. 9, 1798.

Edward Aquila Howard of Baltimore and Charlotte Rumsey of Harford County were married December 11, 1798.

Philip Moore and Delia Hall of Baltimore County married Apr. 30, 1799.

Nathan Horner and Delia Carroll of Harford County married May 2, 1799.

Page 288

Marriages made and celebrated by the Revd. Mr. Allen and by him returned to the Register of St. John's Parish.

Jonas Stevenson and Rachel Hughes were married May 12, 1799 by virtue of a license granted the 10th of same month.

Alexander Hillen and Susanna Durham were married May 16, 1799 by virtue of a license same date.

James Walter Tolley and Susanna Howard were married May 21, 1799 license dated 18th.

Greenberry Debrular and Rachel Henley were married May 23, 1799 by license same date.

Walter Chilsom and Hannah Martin were married June 10, 1799 by license dated 4th.

John Magnes and Martha Morris were married August 1, 1799 by license dated July 20, 1799.

Thomas Wells and Elizabeth Flanagan were married September 5, 1799 by license date 4 same month.

Henry Dawney and Martha Hill were married September 12, 1799 by license dated 10th of said month.

John Powell and Isabella Nasbitt were married October 24, 1799 by license dated 15th same month.

Patrick Dargay and Polly McComas were married October 24, 1799 by license of 23 same month.

Page 289

Richard Touchstone and Sarah Touchstone married January 7, 1800.
George Stolinger and Ann Doover were married January 23, 1800.
Benjamin Wilmer and Margarett Crawford married May 29, 1800.
Andrew McClean and Esther Israel were married December 2, 1800.
William Wilson and Margarett Winstandry married March 24, 1801.
Isaac Kelley and Drusilla Durbin Nichols married April 2, 1801.
James Wood and Elizabeth Maxwell were married April 9, 1801.
Gilbert York and Mary Chilson were married April 26, 1801.
George Bradford and Susanna McComas married May 26, 1801.
Thomas Hill and Martha Browning were married June 8, 1801.
Thomas Spencer and Mary Nabb were married June 11, 1801.
Edward Day (of John) and Hannah Wilmer married August 6, 1801.

Page 290

Daniel Ruff and Hannah Maffitt married December 31, 1801.

Baptism returned by the Revd. Mr. John Coleman to be registered according to Act of Assembly in such case made and provided.

Charles Ridgely, son of the Revd. John and Pleasance Coleman, was born April 17, 1786.
Rebecca Ridgely, daughter of same parents, born August 8, 1787.
John Ridgely, son of same parents, was born December 15, 1788.
Samuel Jarrett Ridgely, son of same parents, born June 1, 1791.
Samuel Williamson Ridgely, son of same, born February 9, 1793.
Cuthbert William Ridgely, son of same, born September 8, 1794.
Lusby, son of John and Sarah Thompson, born September 24, 1787.
Ann, daughter of Alexander Thompson, born September 4, 1787.
John, son of John Carroll, born May 27, 1787.
Alexander, son of William and Eleanor Martin, born April 25, 1785.

John Taylor, son of Daniel and Susanna Smithson, born June, 1786.
Colegate, child of Nathan and Mary Scott, was born June 4, 1787.

Page 291

Mary Ford, an adult, born October 13, 1767, daughter of Joseph and Mary Ford. Joseph Ford, an adult about 49 years old (1738).
Ann, daughter of Samuel and Martha Howard, born in August, 1769.
Cassandra Divers was born August 24, 1785, daughter of Annanias Divers and Cassandra his wife.
Sarah Divers, daughter of Annanias Divers and Cassandra his wife, was born December 10, 1787.
Salathiel Divers----------.
William Byford born January 20, 1790, son of Henry and Mary Byford.
John Barton, son of James and Margarett Barton, born June 16, 1785.
Mille Barton, daughter of James and Margarett, born Sept. 28, 1787.
Rachel Whitaker, daughter of John and Rachel, born May 11, 1789.
Ruth Bull, daughter of Walter and Sarah Bull, born March 25, 1788.
Walter Billingsley Bull, son of Walter and Sarah, born Nov. 5, 1789.
Pamela Galloway, daughter of Thomas Galloway and Catharine Read Dallas, born August 21, 1784. (Thomas married Catharine on May 13, 1781.)

Page 292

Thomas Galloway, son of Thomas and Catharine Galloway, born Nov. 11, 1787.
Harriott Bond, daughter of Dennis and Mary Bond, born March 17, 1778.
Benjamin Guyton, son of John and Frances Guyton, born June 3, 1788.
Mary Greenfield, daughter of William and Elizabeth, born May 19, 1783.
Elizabeth Greenfield, daughter of same parents, born February 25,____.
Sarah Greenfield, daughter of same parents, born June 11, 1798.
Mary Turnpace, daughter of John and Hannah, born October 28, 1788.
Cassandra Turk, daughter of Esan and Catharine, born March 1, 1784.
John Turk, son of Esan and Catharine Turk, born January 11, 1779.
Elisabeth Turk, daughter of same parents, born August 3, 1782.
James Turk, son of same parents, born June 29, 1786.
Martha Turk, daughter of same parents, born April 24, 1789.
Abraham Risteau, son of John and Elisabeth, born May 16, 1789.
Abraham Biddeson, son of Mesheck and Kerenhappuck Biddison, born March 22, 1789.
George Lytle, son of George and Elizabeth, born October 5, 1785.
Thomas Lytle, son of same parents, born February 27, 1788.

Page 293

Elisabeth Harrington, daughter of _____, born Dec. 27, 1789.
John and Joshua Macather, twin sons of Thomas Macather, born May 3, 1789.
Josias Hendon, son of Benjamin and Sophia Hendon, born May 25, 1790.
James Marsh, son of James and Prudence Enlow, born April 20, 1790.
Walter Robinson, son of Charles and M. Robinson, born May 24, 1790.
Aquila Robinson, son of same parents, born July 3, 1788.
James Richardson, son of John and Sarah, born June 27, 1787.
Benjamin Richardson, son of same parents, born June 21, 1790.
Nancy Hilton, daughter of Abraham and Elisabeth, born August 1, 1790.
Samuel Chamberlain, son of John and Elisabeth Chamberlain, was 6 years and 3 months old on the Day of Baptism. (Sep. 11, 1790)

Page 294

Philip Chamberlain, 4 years old on said Day, of same parents.
William Chamberlain, son of same, 3 years old same Day.
Thomas Chamberlain, son of same, 10 months old same Day, and the above 4 were baptised September 11, 1790.
Benjamin Green, son of John and Cassandra, born September 24, 1789.
John Green, son of John and Cassandra Green, born November 12, 1790.
Alexander McComas Lytle, son of George and Elisabeth, born May 2, 1790.
John Hilton, son of John and Lydia Hilton, was born May 3, 1791.
Elisabeth Hamilton, daughter of William and Rebecca, born July 6, 1790.
Phebe Maxwell, daughter of John and Phebe Hamilton, born Mar. 13, 1791.
Juliet Day, daughter of Edward and Mary Day, was born February 14, 1790 and baptised July 12, 1791.
Salem, son of Mesheck and Kerenhappuck Biddison, born March 30, 1791.
John Phipps, son of Nathaniel and Rebecca Phipps, born June 7, 1791.
Amos McComas, son of James and Ann McComas, born August 13, 1785.

Page 295

Sarah McComas, daughter of same parents, born December 28, 1787.
Clemency McComas, of same parents, was born October 12, 1790.
Sarah Weeks, daughter of John and Ann Weeks, born August 9, 1791.
Jacob Demmitt, son of William and Dorothea, born July 12, 1791.
Sarah McComas, daughter of John and Mary, born January 21, 1781.
Elisabeth McComas, daughter of said parents, born July 25, 1790.
Jane Bond, daughter of Dennis and Mary Bond, born October 25, 1789.
Joshua Johnson Whitaker, son of John and Rachell, born Aug. 5, 1791.

Chloe Buck, daughter of Joshua and Sarah, born December 1, 1790.

Thomas Parry Hall, son of Jacob and Mary Hall, born December 21, 1789 and baptised November 30, 1791.

Mary Bull, daughter of Jacob and Sarah, born October 9, 1780.

Margarett Bull of said parents was born March 14, 1791.

Eleanor Guyton, daughter of John and Frances Guyton, was born May 9, 1792 and baptised October 14, 1792.

Catharine Johnson McGowen, daughter of John and Mary McGowen, was born June 23, 1792.

William Sligh, son of Edward and Elizabeth Flanagan, was born April 1, 1779.

Page 296

Sophia Flanagan, daughter of said parents, born January 7, 1786.

Marion Flanagan of said parents was born June 8, 1789.

Maria Rumsey, daughter of Henry and Hannah, born June 7, 1790.

Amelia Rumsey of said parents was born April 14, 1792.

Pamala Day, daughter of William Fell and Letitia Day, was born March 20, 1792.

Cassandra Fulton Day of same parents was born May 28, 1793.

Mary Flincham, daughter of Edward and Sarah, born Nov. 17, 1791.

Bazil Sewell, son of John and Elizabeth, was born February 26, 1792.

Priscilla Galloway and Elizabeth Divers, January 25, 1793.

Ishmael Day, son of Edward and Mary Day, was born March 20, 1792.

Patty Hilton, daughter of Abraham and Elizabeth, born Jan, 13, 1793.

Margarett Wooden, daughter of Asael and Susanna Barton, was born March 4, 1793.

Abraham, son of John and Lydia Hilton, was born June 11, 1793.

Mary, daughter of Thomas and Leah Hartly, born September 9, 1792.

George Turk, son of Esan and Catharine, born September 15, 1793.

Nicholas Grimes Ellinder, son of George and Sarah Ellinder, was born April 20, 1793.

Polly Grimes, daughter of John and Elizabeth Grimes, was born November 17, 1792.

Page 297

Daniel Biddeson, son of Mesheck and Karenhappock Biddison, was born November 26, 1793.

William Henry Hall, son of Aquila and Ann Hall, was born November 11, 1793 and baptised May 22, 1794.

Ann Divers, daughter of Annanias and Cassandra Divers, was born February, 1794, and baptised April 13, 1794.

Rebecca Young Day, daughter of John and Agness Day, was born August 7, 1794, and baptised January 2, 1794 (1795).

John Hilton, son of Abraham and Elisabeth, born October 13, 1794.
Benjamin Colegate Scott, son of Nathan and Mary, born Feb. 23, 1794.
William Monks, son of John and Mary Monks, born January 6, 1787.
Anne Belle Monks of same parents born September 12, 1789.
Louisa Monks of same parents born March 1, 1793.
Mary Ann Monks of same parents born February 12, 1791.
Elican Monks of same parents born January 25, 1795.
Mary Hall, daughter of Jacob and Mary, born October 3, 1793.
Harry Page Osborn, son of William Osborn, born April 1, 1794.
Elizabeth Galloway, daughter of Absolem and Rebecca Galloway, was born October 23, 1794.
Berthia Galloway of same parents was born in 1790.
Mary Ann Green, daughter of John and Cassandra, born Jan. 16, 1793.
Thomas Smithson Green of same parents was born February 20, 1794.
John Holliday Flanagan, son of Edward and Elisabeth Flanagan, was born July 22, 1792. Nesah Holliday Flanagan, twin, born same time.

Page 298

Mary Galloway Divers, daughter of Annanias and Cassandra Divers, was born May 28, 1795.
Rebecca Weston Onion, daughter of William and Elizabeth Onion, was born in 1796.
Benjamin Buck, son of Christopher and Heziah Buck, was born December 18, 1795.
Caty Maria Collins, daughter of George and Sarah Collins, was born March 19, 1796.
Joshua Ellinder, son of George and Sarah, born April 26, 1795.
Aquila Hall, son of Aquila and Ann Hall, was born May 27, 1795.
Frances Cordelia Howard, daughter of Thomas Gassoway Howard, was born November 18, 1795.
John Wana Allinder, son of William and Sophia, born May 5, 1796.
Catharine Reed Dallas, daughter of Walter and Catherine Dallas, was born August 26, 1796.
Benjamin Merriman Buck, son of John and Catherine Buck, was born June 18, 1797.
Edward Carvill Hall, son of Aquila and Ann, born Nov. 23, 1797.
Eliza Helen Grindal, daughter of Joseph and Elisabeth Ann, was born March 10, 1798.
Shadrick Biddison, son of Mesheck and Kanenhappuck Biddison, was born March 11, 1795.
Maria Clark, daughter of George and Nancy, born March 23, 1797.
Keturah Hilton, daughter of John and Lydia Hilton, was born December 27, 1797.

Page 299

Charles Henry Rumsey, son of Henry and Hannah, born Aug. 14, 1796.
William Hilton, son of Abraham and Elizabeth, born April 13, 1798.
Elizabeth Ellinder, daughter of George and Sarah, born July 9, 1798.
John Lytle, son of John and Elizabeth Lytle, was born September 30, 1798 and baptised March 31, 1791.
William James, son of Eliakins and Pamela James, born October 6, 1798 and baptised May 14, 1799.
James Buck, son of Joshua and Sarah, was born November 17, 1793.
John N. Grimes, son of John and Elisabeth Grimes, was born March 30, 1798 and baptised August, 1799.
James Edward Stansbury, son of Abraham and Elizabeth Stansbury, was born February 26, 1799 and baptised September 25, 1799.
John Sterrett Gittings, son of James and Harriott Gittings, was born May 22, 1798 and baptised November 15, 1799.
Edward Augustua Day, son of John and Agness, born Sept. 3, 1796.
William Young Day, son of same parents, was born March 7, 1799.
Henrietta Jane Howard, daughter of Edward Aquila and Charlotte Howard, was born October 25, 1799 and baptised December 1, 1799.
"Many more baptised but the names not given in to me and some given in without mentioning the Parish the boundaries of which are not known by many who have children baptised so says the Revd. John Coleman."

Page 300

Baptisms returned by the Revd. Mr. Allen according to Act of Assembly.

Thomas Gazzoway, son of Thomas Gassoway Howard, was baptised May 21, 1799, also son of Martha Susanna Howard, wife of the said Thomas Gassoway Howard, born December 2, 1798.
Emiline Cordelia, daughter of William and Elizabeth Hughes, was born April 21, 1799 and baptised May 21, 1799.
William, son of Jesse and Mary Taylor, was born March 10, 1799 and baptised September 12, 1799.
Sarah, daughter of James and Dorothy Hudson, was born March 31, 1799 and baptised September 12, 1799.
Ann Sophie, daughter of Greenberry and Sophia Dorsey, was born about the year 1780 and baptised October 13, 1799.
Micah Gilbert McComas, child of Aaron and Martha McComas, was born November 18, 1798 and baptised November 10, 1799.

Buriels returned by the Revd. Mr. Coleman according to Act of Assembly in such case made and provided.

October, 1791, Mrs. Bailey, wife of Thomas Bailey, Esq., aged 60.
Walter Perdue aged about 86, Harford County, November 3, 1792.
James Buck, aged 5 months, Baltimore County.

Sarah Flindam, 4 years old, Harford County, December 9, 1792.
John Wana (Joppa), aged 50 years, December 16, 1792.

Page 301 (Burials continued)

Aquila Hall, son of Aquila Hall, Esq., 4 years old, Feb. 19, 1793.
John Bond (Joppa), 27 years old, March 10, 1793.
Sarah Davis, a widow of Joppa, age unknown, May 5, 1793.
Mary Baxter, aged 40 years, July 14, 1793.
Margarett Robinson of St. John's Parish, 60 years old, Aug. 1, 1793.
Sarah Richardson, aged 8 years, August 21, 1793.
John Buck, aged 72 years, Baltimore County, October 8, 1793.
Mrs. Buck, relict of John Buck, aged 70 years, October 30, 1793.
Rebecca Wright of Joppa, aged 35 years, November 3, 1793.
James Ward, aged 60 years, November 4, 1793.
_____ McComas, 19 years, Harford, November 16, 1793.
John Griffith, a child 3 months old, Baltimore County, Nov. 17, 1793.
Mrs. Baker, wife of James Baker, Harford County, and at the same time a child interred in the same grave with the mother, Nov. 18, 1793.
William Bradford, aged 55 years, of Harford County, Feb. 12, 1794.
Thomas Durham, aged 66 years, February 13, 1794.
Hannah Kemp, St. John's, aged 70 years, February 19, 1794.
John Thomas Brown, aged 22 years, March 2, 1794.
Mrs. Mathers, aged 76 years, March 3, 1794.
Moses McComas, aged 53 years, March 24, 1794.
John Griffin, Sr., aged 65 years, May 11, 1794.
Abraham Norris, aged 4 years and 8 months, June 22, 1794.
Aquila Howard, aged about 6 years, and Nancy Howard, aged about 7 or 8 years, 1794, June 22.
Damiel McComas, aged 74 years on the 18th February, 1794.
William Wilson, aged 3 years, February 20, 1794.
Thomas Bond, Middle River Neck, about 56 years, March 30, 1794.
Hannah Taylor, 25 years old, June 11, 1795.

Page 302

Leah Hartley, aged about 30 years, September 10, 1795.
Thomas Smithson, Sr., aged 83 years, October 3, 1795.
Sall, child of James Gittings, Jr., aged about 3 years (1795).
Sally Amos, aged 3 years, November 25, 1795.
Elizabeth Robinett, Joppa, age not given, February 14, 1796.

(Burials continued)

Edward Flanagan, aged 45 years, April 25, 1796.
May 6, 1796, a child of Harry Green, aged 8 months.
May 14, 1796, Harry Wright of Thomas and Ann Wright, aged 3 years.
August 26, 1796, Mrs. Day of St. John's Parish, aged 60 years.
November 21, 1796, Mary Chambers aged 56 years.
March 29, 1797, Mrs. Grayham, aged about 55 years.
March 30, 1797, Aquila Hall, aged about 2 years, son of Aquila Hall, Esqr.
June 7, 1797, Joshua Ellinor, aged about 18 months.
Solomon Ellinor about 2 months old.
August 13, 1797, John Whittaker, aged 4 years.
September 4, 1797, Doctor Aquila Durham, aged about 25 years.
October 17, 1797, Ann Durham, aged about 57 years.
John Day, son of Dr. Day, aged 2 years.
John Buck, aged 15 years, March 10, 1798.
March 31, 1798, Joshua Green, aged 18 months.
June 17, 1798, Widow Jarvis, aged about 65 years.
In the Fall 1798, Samuel Day, aged about 70 years.
January 20, 1799, Benjamin Rumsey, Jr.
January 30, 1799, Elisabeth Smith, aged 7 months.
August 20, 1799, Catherine Buck, aged 30 years.
Samuel Jarrett Coleman died 17 Augt. 1791. 2 months.
Samuel Williamson Coleman died 24 Octr. 1793.
Cuthbert William Coleman died 5 Octr. 1794.
Charles Ridgely Coleman died 5 Aug. 1795.
John Coleman, son of John, died 8 Augt. 1795.

Page 303

Funerals returned by Mr. Allen agreeable to Act of Assembly in such case made and provided.
John Rumsey, 30th June 1799.
John Beale Howard, 17th July 1799.
Catherine Wilmer, buried 7th Jan. 1800.
Thomas Bond was buried 3 Sept. 1800.

A List of Marriages returned by the Revd. Mr. John Allen, Rector of St. George's Church, Harford, by him celebrated in St. John's Parish in said County according to Act of Assembly in such case made and provided.

Benjamin Hill and Sarah Roberts by license of same date were married March 3, 1803.

John Winstandly and Cassandra Baker were married by license dated 15th of same month, August 18, 1803.

October 26, 1803, Robert Porter and Mary Cowan were married by license of the same date.

January 5, 1804, David Swift and Martha Roberts were married by license dated 7 December 1803.

March 1, 1804, William Webster and Mary Hollis were married by licence dated 29 February 1804.

March 27, 1804, Samuel Taylor and Julia Welsley were married by licence dated 26th same month.

April 26, 1804, Aquila Hughes and Ann Statia Gafford were married by licence dated the 21 of same month.

June 28, 1804, John Howlett and Betsy Smith were married by licence dated 21st of the same month.

July 30th, 1804, Elisah Osborn and Hannah Birkhead were married by licence dated the same day.

Page 304

James Maxwell Day and Rebecca Nabb were married by licence dated the 3rd of December on the 6th day of December 1804.

February 25, 1805, John Monks and Sarah Rebecca Lewis were married by licence dated on the same day.

March 5, 1805, Andrew Thompson and Frances Day were married by licence dated the same day.

July 25, 1805, William Brazier and Elisabeth Saunders were married on July 25th 1805 by virtue of a licence granted said day.

January 30, 1806, Thomas William Bond and Sarah York Scott were married by licence dated the 27th of the same month.

February 7, 1806, Gabriel Sostater and Julian Waskey were married by licence dated the 4th of the same month.

April 1, 1806, Francis Delmas and Mary Walters were married by licence dated the same day.

April 1, 1806, William Partridge and Rosanna Wilmer were married by licence dated 29th March 1806.

April 3, 1806, Benjamin Legs and Elizabeth York were married by licence dated the 2nd day of April 1806.

May 1, 1806, John Yellott and Rebecca Ridgely Coleman were married by licence dated the same day.

November 27, 1806, Ephraim Swarts and Susanna Jones were married by licence dated the 25th of same month.

Ford Barns and Elizabeth Dutton were married 25th Dec. 1806 by licence dated 22nd of same month.

A List of Baptisms returned by the said Revd. John Allen (and Births).

Robert Thomas Allen, son of William Allen and Howard his wife born the first day of November 1901 was baptized Oct. 28, 1804.

Ebenezer Nun Allen, born of same parents the 2nd day of August 1803 was baptised October 28, 1804.

Page 305

March 29, 1805, Mary Ann, born of Samuel Taylor and Juliet his wife 4th February 1805, was baptised.

George Washington, born of John Walmsley and Rebecca his wife about May 1795, was baptised March 29, 1804.

Rebecca, born of Joseph Cox and Elizabeth his wife on the 25 February 1802, was baptised April 12, 1805.

William, born of same parents on the 7th of December 1804, was baptised on the same day.

William Young, born of John Young Day and Agness his wife on the 3rd March 1800, was baptised July 20, 1805.

John Young, born of same parents on the 7th day of February 1803 was baptised same day.

Anne Maria, daughter of John Shields and Sarah his wife born 11th July 1803 was baptised July 20th 1805.

Naddy Bar, born of Barnett Mitchell and Milcah his wife on the 7th of February 1805 was baptised 20th July 1805.

Parker, born of John Mitchell and Martha his wife on the 18th June 1805 baptised on the said 20 July 1805.

Ellen, born of William Sheerswood and Hannah his wife 8th March 1805 and was baptised 25th July same year.

Caleb, son of Charles Hipkins and Elisabeth his wife, was born the 18th day of January 1801 and baptised the 1st June 1806.

Jarrett, born of said parents on the 28th September 1802 and baptised same day.

Eliza, daughter of said parents born 28th August 1805, baptised 1 June 1806.

Witness: B. Rumsey, Regr.

Page 306

Deaths, Births, Marriages given in by the Revd. Mr. Coleman, Rector of St. James Parish in St. John's Parish in the vacancy of a Pastor.

William Wilmer and Anne Ford married February 21, 1804.

Isaac Hollingsworth and Cassandra Divers married April 1, 1805.

John Sheredine and Ann Allen living in St. George's but married in St. John's Parish, April 1, 1805.

Thomas Raine and Charlotta Craven married July 25, 1805.

William Ewing and Elizabeth Norrington married November 21, 1805.

Charles Worthington and Hannah Yellott married in April, 1806.

John Yellott and Rebecca Ridgely married May 1, 1806, celebrated by the Revd. Mr. John Allen.

Baptisms returned by Mr. Coleman.

James Edwards, son of Abraham and Elizabeth Stansbury, born February 26, 1799 was baptized September 23 same year.

Eleanor, daughter of Robert and Mary Williams, born June 24, 1802.

Mary Ann, daughter of Thomas and Elizabeth Johnson, was born October 4, 1802, baptized November 25 following.

Gassaway West, son of Luke and Sarah West, born April 12, 1792, baptised April 18, 1804.

        Witness: Benjamin Rumsey, Regr.

Charles Edward, son of Charles G. Ridgley and Ruth Ingram Ridgley was born July 10 and was baptised September 3, 1804.

Page 307

Ann Yellott, daughter of Robert and Mary Williams, was born August 23, 1804 and baptised December 26, 1804.

Luther Thomas, son of Nancy Standiford, was born July 15, 1804 and baptised December 26, 1804.

Joseph Ashton, son of John and Susanna Ashton, born September 6, 1801, baptised 1805.

Hannah Ashton, daughter of John and Susanna Ashton, born Nov. 23, 1802, baptised in 1805.

John Ashton, born November 21, 1804, was baptised in 1805. Son of John and Susanna.

Chloe Ady, daughter of John and Rebecca Preston, born Sept. 16, 1805.

Anna Maria, daughter of John and Elisabeth Jackson, born Feb. 4, 1806.

Hannah Yellott, daughter of Robert and Mary Williams, born Oct. 13, 1806.

    Witness: Benjamin Rumsey, Regr. of St. John's Parish, Harford Co.

A List of Buriels by the Revd. Mr. Coleman.

Benjamin Rumsey Jr. was buried Jan. 20, 1799, aged about 24 years.

Elizabeth G. Smith, aged about 7 months, buried January 30, 1799.

Catherine Buck, aged about 30, was buried August 26, 1799.

Elizabeth Tolley, aged about 14, was buried December 2, 1800.

Blanch Howard was buried January 15, 1800, aged about 58 years.

Page 308

Martha Tolley, aged about 82 years, was buried September 1, 1801.

Eliakim James, aged about 35, was buried October 28, 1801.

Thomas Gassoway Howard, aged about 60, was buried in 1803.

Hannah Fulton, aged about 71, was buried May 6, 1804.

John Howard, aged about 96, was buried March 20, 1805.
William Dimmitt, aged about 60, was buried May 2, 1805.
Priscilla Fulton, aged about 40, was buried March 3, 1806.
   Witness: Benjamin Rumsey, Regr. of St. John's Parish, Harford Co.

The Revd. John R. Keech was ordained January 24, 1819 and took charge of St. John's Parish February 21, 1819.

Official Acts: Marriages.
Stephen W. Falls and Henrietta Jane Howard, December 14, 1819.
Barney Bond and Ann Maria Gallop, August 22, 1820.
Charles H. Rumsay and Caroline B. Howard, December 19, 1820.
John King and Henrietta Day, January 25, 1822.
Ishmael Day and Charity Johnson, March 21, 1822.
Capt. John B. Bayliss and Eliza Day, April 2, 1822.
John Fuller and Margaret Webb, December 10, 1822.

Page 309

George Madrin and Jane Barr, May 16, 1822.
John Onion and Mary Ann Baker, December 5, 1822.
Daniel McConn and Emily Kenly, November 26, 1822.
Henry Denmead and Hannah Gartside, July 10, 1822.
Dr. David S. Gitting and Julian W. Howard, July 29, 1822.
Dr. Joshua Wilson and Rebecca Lee, April 24, 1824.
Samuel Ricketts and Elizabeth Watters, November 11, 1824.
John Wood and Anne McCowen, August 25, 1825.
Richard Kinley and Mary Ann Gallop, September, 1825.
James Starr and Ann Tudor, November 17, 1825.
Charles Duer and Elizabeth Ann Norris, February 2, 1826.
John B. Bayless and Elizabeth H. Hall, July 30, 1826.
Hezekiah B. Small and Harriot McNeal, August 3, 1826.
John G.(or Y.) Day to Maria Hughes, December 12, 1826.
Stephen Bridge and Margaret McClennel, December 30, 1827.
In St. James Parish, Henry Gustavus Maynadier to Elisabeth Yellott, February 11, 1828.
John H. Fuller to Elisabeth Mott, March 18, 1828.
Daniel Jones to Sarah Allender, April 10, 1828.
Thomas Gorsuch to Hannah Onion, May 29, 1828.
Upton March to Mary Jane Norris, October 13, 1828.
John Lewis to Rebecca Guyton, January 29, 1829.
Jacob Stover to Rebecca Williams, February 26, 1829.

Oliver H. Amoss to Elizabeth Ann King, March 18, 1829.
Chancy Haskins to Mary Cassandra Hollingsworth, May 14, 1829.
Mr. George Torrence of Baltimore to Miss Elenor Fulford of
    St. George Parish, Harford Co., June 30, 1829.
Dr. William Sappington and Miss Amelia J. Rumsay, Aug. 12, 1830.
William Ashtown and Sarah Summon, October 5, 1830.
James Bevard to Alisanna Brannan, May 20, 1832.
Mr. William H. Hughes to Mrs. Mary Thompson, June 30, 1833.
Alexander Kennard to Miss Anna M. Onion, November 14, 1833.
Francis Ashbury Foock to Mary Eliza Canoles, May 6, 1834.

Page 310

Major Charles W. Howard of St. John's Parish to Miss Amanda T.
    Slade of St. James Parish, September 23, 1834.
A colored man of Mr. Inloes named Elijah to a woman of Thomas
    Hanway's named Eliza, October 2, 1834.
William T. Lewis of New Orleans to Mary Minerva Monk of Abingdon,
    October 29, 1834.
Gabriel A. McComas to Miss R. S. Bradford, November 12, 1834.
Robert S. Wilson to Frances H. Sadler, November 25, 1834.
John Poll to Emily Carroll, April 9, 1835.
Dr. Samuel Chew to Henrietta S. Scott of Baltimore, Apr. 29, 1835.
William Turner to Amelia Standiford, September 9, 1835.
Francis Grupy to Mrs. Sarah Grupy, October 6, 1836.
James Murray Lloyd to Elizabeth Campbell McBlair, Nov. 1, 1836.
Israel Atkinson to Mary Ann Lewis, January 19, 1837.
Robert Cocknan to Mary Rown, September 21, 1837.
Washington M. Slade to Mary McComas, February 6, 1838.
John W. Wane to Mary Harvard, May 17, 1838.
Thomas W. Hall to Caroline A. Howard, January 14, 1840.
Thomas B. Amoss to Sarah Ann Maulsby, September 20, 1841.
Joseph Gwinn Burton to Cassandra Foard, October 28, 1841.
Married a colored man of John Baldwin's named Henry to a colored
    woman named Harriet, January 15, 1842.
A colored man of Isaac Ford's named James to a woman of Silas
    Baldwin's named Delia, February 12, 1842.
Isaiah Watkins to Elizabeth D. England, May 10, 1842.
Married a colored man of Henry Guyton to Sarah Jane Cohen,
    August 30, 1843.
Daniel Shaffer to Sarah Guyton, September 20, 1843.
George M. Rea to Julia Ann Gyton, 1844.

Jacob H. Munnukkhyam to Charlotte Howard, December 18, 1844.
Elijah S. Goodin to Elizabeth A. Lee, December 25, 1845.
Charles J. Bullus to Mary J. Rumsey, November 19, 1846.

Page 311

Married Charles & Fanny a colored couple belong to Mrs. Reynolds, February 10, 1847.
John W. Hollis to Emeline Eliza Anderson, colored, Oct. 27, 1848.
George Wood to Chloe Amelia Ady, November 30, 1848.
Married John a colored man of Dr. Gittings to Elizabeth Williams, colored, December 25, 1848.
George W. Lee to Eliza Jackson, colored, January 25, 1848.
William Hill and Maria Kell, colored, December 28, 1848.
Joseph Force to Ann Holland, December 11, 1851.
George W. League of Baltimore to Elizabeth A. Gorsuch of Baltimore County, December 16, 1851.

Baptisms by Revd. J. R. Keech.

July, 1819, for Mr. John Norris by his brother Oliver, names not given.
    Miss Elizabeth Scott.
February 24, 1820, for Joseph McCubbin & wife in private.
March 31, 1820, Mrs. Barr and daughter, adults.
May 14, 1820, Hannah Maria and Hannah Juliet Onion.
    Columbus Franklin Gilder.
May 26, 1820, for John and Mary Barr, Douglass A., Robert C., Elizabeth Ann, Mary Ann, John and Susan, 6.
July 23, 1820, Bapd. John Rumsay, born 31st May 1816, and James Oscar born Dec. 9th 1817 Gittings, children of Mr. Archabald and Martha Patty Gittings.
August 23, 1820, bapd. a colored child at Taylors Mount.
September 4, 1820, bapd. a colored child Pine Grove.
September 5, 1820, bapd. Martha Pyles, adult on sick bed.
October 29, 1820, bapd. for Col. Ed. A. and Agness Ann Howard, Caroline Ann.
November 3, 1820, bapd. a colored child at Mr. Rumsay's.
November 14, 1820, bapd. at Mrs. Sattler's. Elenor & Sophia, col. ch.
Mar.18, 1821, bapd. Mrs. Emily N. Hughs and Miss Anna Maria Hughs.
March 29, 1821, William Henry Hughes, son of William & Emily Hughs.
February 5, 1822, bapd. for Charles H. Rumsay and Caroline his wife Mary Jane, born October 16, 1821.
July 9, 1822, bapd. for Joseph R. Ford & wife, Edward Septemus and Joseph Octavus.

Page 312

February 7, 1823, for Mr. & Mrs. McCubbin their daughter Susan.
June 16, 1823, bap. Capt. Gilder.
August 31, 1823, At Mrs. Sadler's, John & Selena, colored children.
April 11, 1824, bap. John Beal Onion.
June 7, 1824, a child named Benson.
August 24, 1824, bap. Oliver Henry Buck, born Feb. 16, 1820, Elizabeth Divers Buck, born March 19, 1824, children of Benjamin Buck and wife.
    Bapt. 5 colored children, Emeline, Ann Lemon, Mary Johns, Henry Carrol, and Frances.
November 5, 1824, bapt. Mary Ann and William Janison.
November 21, 1824, bapt. Frances Henry Grupy, son of Jacob Grupy.
December 27, 1824, bap. John B. H. Rumsay, son of Ch. H. and C. B. Rumsay, born September 27, 1823.
1825, bapt. for Dr. D. S. and Julian his wife, Beale Howard Gittings born December 18, 1824.
September 27, 1825, at Mrs. Sadler's, 2 colored children named Sidney and William.
November 20, 1825, bap. Edward Presbury Day, son of Ishmael and Charity Day, born November 8, 1824.
January 29, 1826, bap. for Jacob and Eliza Grupy, Susan Grupy born June 24, 1825.
1826, bapd. for Abner and Martha Ruvit, Elizabeth born August 30, 1822, James born April 20, 1824 and John born Jan. 17, 1826.
August 13, 1826, bapd. in St. James Parish for Benjamin and Matilda Hudson, their daughter Lucretia Harriet, born Jan. 20, 1826.
March 6, 1827, bapd. for Dr. D. S. and Julian Gittings, their daughter Mary Sterret, born September 2, 1826.
    Bap. Margaret West Rumsay, daughter of Ch. T. H. and Caroline B. Rumsay, born October 20, 1825.

Page 313

December 30, 1827, bap. at Mrs. Sadler's colored child named James.
    At church, a child named Robert Bruce McClennan.
1829, bap. at Mrs. Sadler's 3 colored children, Harriot born July, 1828, Burke born Feb. 9, 1829, and Owen born Mar. 1, 1829.
    Bap. for Benjamin Buck and wife, Augusta born Oct. 26, 1826, Cassandra Olivia, born September 29, 1828, and 2 colored children named Charlotte and Peter.
June 28, 1829, bapd. for Dr. D. S. and Julian Gittings, their daughter Margaret West, born July 29, 1828.
September 23, 1829, bapd. in her sick bed Miss Anna Maria Amoss.
    At Mrs. Sadler's, a colored child named Frances.

January 12, 1831, bapd. for Dr. D. S. and Juliana Gittings, their son Richard James, born May 22, 1830.

February 14, 1831, for Thomas and Hannah Gorsouch, their Charles William, born March 23, 1839.

April 11, 1831, for Walter and Jane Cuningham, their son Walter born June 1, 1820, Daniel born August 23, 1826, and Elizabeth born August 19, 1828.

January 20, 1832, Bapd. on his sick bed John Baker, an adult.

July 22, 1832, Bapd. for William Y. and Charlotte Day, their daughter Agness Ann, born November 17, 1832.

October 14, 1832, Bapd. for Ishmael and Charity Day, Silas Johnson born April 3, 1826, Mary Eliza born October 8, 1827, Louisa born February 28, 1830, and Edward William born Nov. 29, 1831.

October 11, 1832, Bapd. for Dr. D. S. and Juliana Gittings, their daughter Louisa born July 7, 1832.

August 16, 1832, Bapd. at Mrs. Sadler's a child for Charlotte named Augustus.

October, 1835, Bapd. for William Y. and Charlotte Day, Edward Augustus born December 1, 1833 and Mary born June 19, 1835.

June, 1835, Bapd. for Dr. D. S. and Juliana Gittings, their son David Sterret born March 20, 1835.

April 25, 1837, Bapd. for Dr. D. S. and Julian Gittings, their son John Beale Howard born April 1, 1837.

Page 314

May 27, 1838, bapd. for Robert and Frances Wilson, their son Stephen Haven born April 24, 1838.

May 21, 1838, bapd. for William Y. and Charlotte Day, their son John Osso born November 25, 1837.

March 24, 1839, bapd. for Ishmael and Charity Day, their daughter Amelia Emily born April 6, 1838.

April 6, 1840, bapd. for Henry Conly and Lavinia his wife, Margaret Elizabeth born December 15, 1839.

January 17, 1841, bapt. for Thomas W. and Caroline Ann Hall, their daughter Agness Sophia born October 18, 1840.

March, 1841, bapt. Sarah Kigeran on her death bed.

February 23, 1842, bapt. for James and Ann McNeil, their daughter Mary Ann born July 1, 1840.

September 13, 1842, bapd. for Thomas and Hannah Gorsuch, their son William Harrison born July 3, 1840.

July 27, 1842, bapd. for Dr. John Carvil and Marianna Howard, John Beale born April 3, 1842.

March 1, 1843, bapd. for Thomas W. Hall and Caroline A. his wife, Charlotte Elizabeth born October 29, 1842.

December 7, 1830, for Jacob and Sally Grupy, Charles born Feb. 11, 1827, Jacob born September 2, 1828, Julian born November 2, 1832, Anna Virginia born March 11, 1834.

For Ishmael and Charity Day, Adeline born November 9, 1834.

February 1, 1835, for Thomas and Hannah Gorsuch, Elizabeth Ann born September 30, 1831, Thomas Bosley born April 24, 1834.

1844, bapd. for Edward and Annah Whannah Guyton, their daughter Sarah Ann born July 11, 1843.

Bapd. for Thomas and Ann Clarke, their son Augustus born October 15, 1845.

Bapt. on death bed, Julian Rea.

September 19, 1844, bapd. for Thomas W. and Caroline A. Hall his wife, Edward A. H. Hall born April 4, 1844.

Page 315

September 24, 1844, bapd. for Thomas and Julia Gittings, Erskins their son aged 4 years and 5 months.

Bapd. at Sherwood, a colored child named Hannah Ann Dering, born October 20, 1844.

January 1, 1846, bapd. Robert Stephen Wilson, an adult, in sick chamber, a convert from the Presbyterians.

February 12, 1844, bapd. for Thomas T. and Mary Cornelia Evans, their child Mary C. born November 6, 1845.

Bapd. for George Pierce and wife, their son Harrison, born September 20, 1840.

Bapd. for Thomas W. and Caroline A. Hall, their daughter Martha White born February 28, 1846.

Bapd. for Dr. John C. Howard and Mary his wife, Carvil Charles born May 21, 1845.

May 29, 1848, bapd. for Thomas W. and Caroline A. Hall, their son William George born November 17, 1847.

July 17, 1849, bapd. at Mrs. Reynolds, Baltimore County, named Mary Elizabeth born July, 1847.

August 8, 1849, bapd. on death bed, Mr. Philip Pierce, adult, born October 8, 1878 (Obvious mistake in the year of birth).

September 13, 1850, Mary Jane, daughter of Amoss and Hannah Anderson, born August 17, 1849.

February 28, 1850, for Thomas W. and Caroline H. Hall, their daughter Isabella Bethia born December 5, 1849.

April 24, 1850, for Richard and Jerush Sneed, their son Edward Harwood Sneed born December 28, 1849.

July 4, 1850, for David S. and Arabella Gittings, William Bose Gittings born March 6, 1850.

August 28, 1850, bapd. for Thomas and Julia Gittings, their children Julia Evans born_____and_____born_____.

The Rev. John R. Keech died December 23, 1861. S.W.Falls, Register.

Page 316

Communicants

Mr. John Rumsay, deceased.
Mrs. Margaret Howard, deceased.
Mrs. Sadler, deceased.
Colonel Edward A. Howard
Mrs. Susan Tolley, deceased.
Mrs. Martha Gittings, withdrawn.
Miss Mary Ann Sadler
Mrs. Elizabeth Hughes
Miss Emmeline Hughes, deceased.
Miss Anna B. Courtney, withdrawn.
Miss Harriet Rumsey, deceased.
Miss Mary Rumsey, deceased.
Miss Amelia S. Rumsey, removed.
Mrs. Caroline B. Rumsey, deceased.
Mrs. Agness A. Howard, deceased.
Mrs. Julian Gittings, deceased.
Mrs. Courtney, deceased.
Mrs. Henrietta S. Falls
Mrs. Sarah Buck, deceased.
Mrs. Roun, removed.
Mr. William Dimvutt, deceased.
Mrs. Anna M. Day
Miss Nancy Treadway, withdrawn.
Mr. Francis Grupy, deceased.
Mr. Stephen W. Falls, withdrawn.
Miss Anna M. Hall, deceased.
Mrs. Ann Kennard, withdrawn.
Mr. James Buck, removed.
Mrs. Frances Wilson
Miss Stearns, removed.
Mrs. Hannah Gorsuch
Miss Margaretta Howard
Mrs. Byass, deceased.

Page 317

Miss Emily Howard, removed.
Miss Mary Rumsay
Miss Mary J. Rumsey
Miss Charlotte Hall, withdrawn.
Miss Sophia Hall, withdrawn.
Mr. Isaac I. Martin, withdrawn.
Mrs. Julia Martin, withdrawn.
Mr. Thomas W. Hall joined St. Mary's Con.
Francis H. Grupy, Jr., withdrawn.
Mrs. Caroline A. Hall joined St. Mary's.
Mr. Robert S. Wilson deceased.
Mrs. Charlotte Day
Mrs. Charity Day, deceased.
Mrs. Ann Reynolds
Miss Harriot Reynolds
Miss Anna Rebecca Reynolds
Mrs. Arabella Gittings
Mrs. Dr. Lenox Birckhead
Miss Jane M. Birckhead
Miss Louisa Birckhead

Mrs. Serusha Sneed, deceased.
Miss Rachel Cairnes
Miss Susan H. Birckhead
Mr. Raymond Anselmo Robinson
Mr. John H. Birckhead

Funerals

Mr. James Gittings, March 12, 1820
Dr. John Scott, July 30, 1820
Mr. William Wilson's child, Sept. 11, 1820
Miss Martha Pyle, September 22, 1820
Mrs. St. Clair, October 23, 1820
Mr. John Howard, November 11, 1820
A son of Mr. Joseph R. Ford's, 1822

Page 318

Mrs. Rusey, 1823
A son of Mr. J. Rouse, 1824
Miss Nancy Lowery, August, 1824
A child at the Factory, August, 1824
Mary T. Norris, August 27, 1824
Miss Emeline Hughes, September 20, 1824
Andrew Ullman, November 5, 1824
A daughter of Mr. Benjamin Bucks, Nov. 15, 1824
A daughter of Ishmael Day, January, 1825
Mr. Knight, May 13, 1825
Oliver Buck, son of Benjamin, May 13, 1825
Prudence G. Carroll, daughter of Harry Carroll, July 25, 1825
John Beale Howard, son of Dr. D. S. & Julian Gittings, November 17, 1825
Lloyd Ludley, December 15, 1825
Samuel Swann, March 6, 1826
Ann Jemeson, aged 11 years, June 26, 1826
A child of Harry & Eliza Carroll, August 2, 1826
Miss Elizabeth Scott, August 2, 1826
Miss Nancy Miligan, September 12, 1826
Mrs. Miller, October 2, 1826
Mrs. Thompson, December 31, 1826
Mr. James Dimmitt, May 25, 1827
Mr. Williams, at Trinity, September 9, 1827
Captain McCurdy, November 15, 1827
Ishmael Day's child, December 19, 1827
Dr. Moore's child, 1828
Mr. John Rumsey, March 18, 1828
A funeral at church, October 19, 1828
Ch. H. Rumsey, May 5, 1829
Mr. Richard Gittings, February 1, 1830
Mrs. Eliza Grupy, October 3, 1830
Mr. John Baker, July 17, 1832
Mr. Benjamin Buck, July 24, 1832
Sophia Ludley, child of Isaac, August 15, 1832

Funerals (continued)

Mr. John Roun, December 17, 1832
Thomas Gorsuch's child, September 22, 1833
Miss Charlotte Swann, March 1, 1834
Mrs. Sarah Monk, March 21, 1834
Mrs. Carr, "Long Green", November 14, 1834
  (Mrs. Hetty Carr, widow of Peter of Albemarle, Va.)
Jacob Grupy, 1835
Col. John Beale Howard, December 27, 1835
Ishmael Day's child, October 2, 1836
Mr. Abram King, December 13, 1836
Mrs. Mary Chew, Havre de Grace, April, 1837
Miss Mary Rumsey, June 2, 1838
Mrs. Mary M. Lewis and child, of New Orleans,
  at Spesutia, June 2, 1838
Miss Harriot Rumsey, October 21, 1839
Mrs. Sarah Grupy's daughter, April, 1839
Mrs. Onion, May 5, 1839
Lloyd J. Foard, July 4, 1839
Ananias Buck, June 11, 1840
Mrs. Johnson, March 13, 1841
Mr. Whistler, March 18, 1841
Sarah Kern, April 18, 1841
John Onion's child, August, 1841
Isaac I. Martin's child, September, 1841
Mr. Cary's child, 1842 (Virginia Randolph, daughter
  of Colonel Wilson Miles Cary)
Charles Risteau, April 8, 1842
William Harrison Gorsuch, infant, September 9, 1842
John Guyton, August 4, 1843
Julian Rea, June 12, 1844
Mrs. Margaret Howard, relict of Col. J. B. Howard,
  daughter of Revd. West, September 29, 1844
Dr. John Carvil Howard, December 14, 1844
Charles Grupy, November 9, 1845
Agnes A. Day, daughter of William and Charlotte Day,
  December 9, 1845
Mrs. Agnes A. Howard, wife of Col. E. A. Howard,
  December 30, 1845

Mr. Robert T. Wilson, January 12, 1846
A child of Thomas and Cornelia Evans, Feb. 14, 1846
Mr. William Dimmitt, May 5, 1846
Mrs. Caroline B. Rumsay, June 5, 1846
Mrs. Risteau, January 7, 1847
Mrs. Julian Gittings, January 18, 1847
Mrs. Elizabeth Sadler, January 28, 1847
Mr. Charity Day wife (?), April 28, 1847
Mr. John Watkins, aged 90, May 3, 1847
Mrs. Guyton, a convert from M., July 23, 1847
Mr. Gibson Reynolds of Baltimore, December 11, 1847
A child of James and Emily Baxter, June 13, 1848
Old Mrs. Swann, June 19, 1848
Mary Anotony, July 19, 1848
Francis Grupy, an aged man, September 27, 1848
Philip Pierce, an aged man, December 30, 1849
Charles Rullus, January 19, 1850

Miss Charlotte Baldwin, May 13, 1850
Mrs. Harriot Foard, March 14, 1851
Miss Rebecca Demmitt, January 19, 1852

Persons confirmed by Bps. Doane of New Jersey,
February 11, 1839
Miss Margaretta Howard
Miss Charlotte Howard
Miss Emily Howard
Miss Mary Jane Rumsey

Page 321

Families belonging to the Church

Mrs. Margaret Howard
Col. Edward A. Howard
Mrs. Elizabeth Sadler
Mr. William Dimmitt
Mrs. Caroline B. Rumsey
Mr. John Young Day
Mr. William Young Day
Mr. Ishmael Day
Doctor David S. Gittings
Dr. Tolly Allender
Mr. Francis Grupy
Mr. Stephen W. Falls
Mr. Thomas W. Hall
Col. Henry Hall
Mr. Thomas Gittings
Mrs. Thomas Gorsuch & children
Dr. John C. Howard

Elizabeth Maxwell Day, daughter of John Day, Jr. and Mary his wife, born September 10, 1776.

James Maxwell Day, son of the above, born September 20, 1779.

Sarah Day, daughter of John Day, son of Edward and Sarah, born January 20, 1768.

Charlotte Day, daughter of anove, born July 17, 1770.

Nicholas Day, son of above, born March 14, 1773.

Edward Day, son of above, born November 7, 1776.

Rachel Monk, daughter of Richard and Jane Monk, born Jan, 20, 1769.

Page 322

Martha Monk, daughter of above, born February 15, 1773.

Susannah Monk, daughter of above, born March 20, 1778.

The Issue of Daniel McComas, son of William, and Mary his wife:
William McComas, born April 24, 1778
Charles McComas, born October 9, 1779
Solomon McComas, born August 23, 1781

Hannah McComas, born July 16, 1784.
John McComas, born June 14, 1786.

Registered on the 18th day of June in the year of our Lord Seventeen hundred and ninety four by the Subscribers Vestryman at the request of the said Daniel McComas as witness our hands (having no register).
            Benjamin Rumsey
      James Crook
      Daniel Maccomas

Page 323

St. George's Parish, Harford Co.
Register 1795-1814 & 1846-1851
Also St. John's Parish 1795-1814

Registry of Baptisms in Saint George's Parish, Harford County, Maryland during the incumbency of the Revd. John Allen, commencing in the year 1795.

March 19, 1795
 John Hanson Osborne, son of James and Amelia Osborne
 Susanna Brown (born Jan. 30, 1795) of John & Susanna Brown
 Chauncey Webster, of Joseph and Martha Webster
 Amos Hollis, of Amos and Elizabeth Hollis
March 20, 1795
 John Gray, of James and Elizabeth Gray
May 24, 1795
 William Montjar (born Apr. 16, 1795) of William & Mary Montjar
July 13, 1795
 James Kimble, of Stephen and Hannah Kimble
 Maria Kimble, of Stephen and Hannah Kimble
July 26, 1795
 John Henson, of Jacob and Ann Henson
August 13, 1795
 Jesse Magnus (born Apr. 29, 1793) of Moses & Rachel Magnus
 Rebecca Baxter (born Jan. 23, 1784) of William & Sarah Baxter
 Ann Vance (born Jan 24, 1788) of Samuel & Elizabeth Vance
 Sarah Vance (born Sept. 27, 1791) of Samuel & Elizabeth Vance
September 16, 1795
 Richard Ruff (born Sept. 10, 1779) of Richard Ruff & Mary Ross
September 17, 1795
 Sarah Bradley (born Aug. 16, 1793) of John and Mary Bradley
 Mary Bradley (born Sept. 9, 1795) of John and Mary Bradley
 Frances Martha Lee (born Apr. 16, 1793) of Parker Hall Lee
               and Elizabeth Lee.
 Margaret Middleditch (born June 4, 1789) of Michael Middleditch
               and Mary.
 Mary Ann Palmer (born Apr. 30, 1794) of William & Sarah Palmer
 Elizabeth Dagg (born Oct. 12, 1794) of James and Ann Dagg
 Thomas Dagg (born Aug. 23, 1793) of James and Ann Dagg
October 6, 1795
 John Backwood (born Feb. 12, 1788) of Samuel and Mary Backwood
 James Backwood (born Sept. 14, 1790) of Samuel & Mary Backwood
 Delpha Dale (born May 29, 1793) of John and Mary Dale
 Sarah Dale (born June 1, 1795) of John and Mary Dale

Mary (conditionally), born April 25, 1788, of John Dale and
Margaret, his late wife; baptized October 6, 1795.

Page 324   Baptisms (continued)

October 11, 1795
Jane Elinor Donnel, born July 3, 1795, of Patrick and Mary Donnel
Richard Crosby, born Aug. 21, 1795, of William & Cassandra Crosby
October 18, 1795
Edward Jackson, born May 24, 1794, of Samuel & Elizabeth Jackson
James Jackson, born Dec. 7, 1792, of Samuel & Elizabeth Jackson
James Gallion Copeland, born Sept. 14, 1792, of John & Margaret
William Pitt Copeland, born June 6, 1795, of John and Margaret
October 24, 1795
Joshua Allender, born Mar. 11, 1788, of Nicholas & Elizabeth Allender
Mary Allender, born April 1, 1786, of Nicholas & Elizabeth Allender
Elizabeth Morris, born February 1783, of John and Elizabeth Morris
Phebe Morris, born January, 1780, of John and Elizabeth Morris
November 3, 1795
John Sydney Hall, born Oct. 15, 1795, of Benedict Edward Hall
and Milcah his wife.
November 8, 1795
George Griffith, born Apr. 28, 1793, of Samuel & Elizabeth Griffith
Mary Goldsmith Griffith, born Sept. 19, 1794, of same parents
Elizabeth Holley, born June 20, 1795, of William and Sarah Holley
December 15, 1795
Joseph Johnson, born Oct. 10, 1792, of Josiah and Martha Johnson
John Johnson, born June 16, 1793, of same parents
December 17, 1795
Samuel Prigg, born Dec. 29, 1793, of John and Mary Prigg
December 22, 1795
William Brown, born Feb. 6, 1791, of John and Susanna Brown
Aquila Brown, born Apr. 12, 1792, of same parents
December 30, 1795
Julia Ann Morgan, born Aug. 20, 1793, of Robert & Martha Morgan
William Jewells, born Oct. 23, 1792, of Richard & Elizabeth Jewells
Sarah Jewells, born June 8, 1790, of same parents
Agnes Jewells, born January 1, 1788, of same parents
George Jewells, born July 22, 1785, of same parents
Blanche Jewells, born July 3, 1788, of same parents
Frances Jewells, born March 26, 1795, of same parents
William Smith, born Oct. 1, 1794, of Samuel Smith & Elizabeth Arnold
Edward Lee, born Sept. 23, 1793, of John and Martha Lee
David Lee, born Sept. 13, 1795, of same parents
David Dick, born October 13, 1791, of David and Mary Dick
Robert Dick, born May 10 or 11, 1786, of same parents
Elizabeth Dick, born Sept. 5, 1784, of same parents

Page 325
January 15, 1796
Mary Jefferies, born May 6, 1794, of Thomas Jefferies & D. Knight
January 28, 1796
William Dawson, born Mar. 3, 1771, of Isaac and Elizabeth Dawson

Baptisms (continued)

February 7, 1796
Mary Henderson, born Sept. 2, 1795, of Nathanael & Elizabeth
Samuel Prichett, of James and Sarah Prichett
James Prichett, of same parents
Mary Prichett, of same parents

March 17, 1796
Peter Montjar, born Mar. 12, 1793, of William and Mary Montjar
Mary Barnes, born Oct. 29, 1795, of Nehemiah and Margaret Barnes
Robert Dobbins, born in Fall of 1788, to James & Sarah Dobbins
William Thomas Hoggins, born Feb. 13, 1781, of James & Elizabeth

March 18, 1796
John Morris, born July 26, 1795, of William and Hannah Morris
William Morris, born Nov. 9, 1793, of same parents
Isaac Morris, born Sept. 3, 1788, of same parents

March 20, 1796
Elizabeth Baylaff, born Aug. 10, 1755, of Thomas & Ann Baylaff
Mary Dawson, born Mar. 15, 1778, of Jesse and Elizabeth Dawson

March 27, 1796
John Allen, born Feb. 18, 1796, of John and Brasseya Allen

April 3, 1796
Hugh Boil, born Mar. 11, 1796, of Hugh and Ann Boil

April 11, 1796
Elizabeth Dawson, of William and Mary Dawson

May 28, 1796
Mary Hambleton, born May 5, 1796, of John and Margaret Hambleton

June 12, 1796
John McLaughlin, born Aug. 25, 1795, of Daniel & Cassandra
Charlotte Caulfield, born July 9, 1795, of Thomas and Martha
Pincen Steel, born Oct. 21, 1795, of Joseph and Margaret Steel

June 19, 1796
Mary Sophia Hall Gilbert, born Jan. 23, 1795, of Michael & Betsy
John Saunders, born March 27, 1796, of Joseph and Sarah Saunders

July 10, 1796
John Rodenheizer, born Jan. 14, 1796, of Peter and Margaret

July 17, 1796
Elizabeth Parker, born July 13, 1781, of John and Mary Parker
Ann Knight, born Mar. 27, 1796, of Isaac and Tabitha Knight
Charlotte Day, born June 10, 1795, of Joshua and Sarah Day
Sianna Day, born Sept. 5, 1793, of same parents

July 28, 1796
Hannah Ritter Gallion Brazier, born Nov. 27, 1780, of Robert & Frances
Susanna Hargrove, born Apr. 23, 1790, of Richard Hargrove and Rachel Armstrong

August 9, 1796
Elizabeth Thompson, born Oct. 16, 1795, of James and Hannah Thompson
James Thompson, born July 14, 1793, of same parents

Page 326

August 21, 1796
John McComas, born Feb. 9, 1739, of Alexander and Deborah McComas

Baptisms (continued)

September 11, 1796
Jarrett Donovan, born Jan. 11, 1795, of John and Frances Donovan
Elizabeth Bartley, born Oct. 20, 1795, of Bernard and Elizabeth
Catharine Root, born Apr. 27, 1796, of Samuel and Mary Magdalen Root
John Root, born Feb. 7, 1794, of Samuel and Mary Magdalen Root
Leah Sinclair, born Feb. 9, 1796, of John and Margaret Sinclair

September 16, 1796
Henry Bare, born Sept. 12, 1796, of John and Barbary Bare

September 18, 1796
Ann McNab, born March 13, 1796, of Isaac and Jane McNab
Margaret Robinson, born May 27, 1792, of James and Mary Robinson
Jane Robinson, born January 14, 1790, of same parents
John Robinson, born April 11, 1787, of same parents

September 25, 1796
Margaret Moore, born May 8, 1796, of William and Martha Moore
George Carton, born July 12, 1794, of Joseph and Elizabeth Carton
Jane Carton, born July 4, 1796 of same parents

October 11, 1796
Jesse Bell Johnson, born Sept. 24, 1796, of John Johnson & Lethe Bell

October 23, 1796
Unity Donnel, of Patrick and Mary Donnel
Mary Ann Goddin, of Aaron and Elizabeth Goddin

December 4, 1796
Mary Garrett, born Feb. 21, 1796, of Alexander and Martha Garrett

January 22, 1797
Cassandra Horner, born Jan. 24, 1796, of Crispin and Elizabeth Horner

February 9, 2797
John Chauncey, born Oct. 22, 1790, of John and Elizabeth Chauncey
Nestor Chauncey, born March 21, 1793, of same parents

March 2, 1797
Elizabeth Vansicle, born Nov. 12, 1792, of Henry and Elizabeth

March 3, 1797
Jacob Forwood Matthews, born Aug. 20, 1794, of Josiah and Jane
John Matthews, born October 15, 1792, of same parents
Constance Eliza Matthews, born July 6, 1796, of same parents
Benedict Charles Hall, born Feb. 10, 1797, of Benedict Edward Hall
and Milcah his wife.

April 4, 1797
Harriot Osborne, born Dec. 7, 1796, of Cyrus and Martha Osborne
Sarah Webster, born Dec. 26, 1796, of Joseph and Mary Webster

April 9, 1797
Mary Hagarty, of Daniel and Elizabeth Hagarty

April 18, 1797
William Prigg Johns, born June 3, 1794, of Henry and Sarah Johns
Mary Johns, born November 2, 1796, of same parents

April 20, 1797
Carvel Prigg, born July 19, 1796, of William and Susanna Prigg
Elizabeth Way, of John and Sarah Way

Page 327 Baptisms (continued)

April 20, 1797
James Way, of John and Sarah Way
Leveridge Way, of John and Sarah Way

April 30, 1797
Garret Vansicle Nelson, born about August 14, 1796,
    of Aquila and Frances Nelson

May 7, 1797
Mary Hall, born Sept. 12, 1796, of James White Hall and Sarah.

May 14, 1797
John Bravat Cunningham, born Sept. 21, 1796, of George & Kezia.

May 25, 1797
Peggy Fielding Knight, born Nov. 15, 1795, of Aquila & Elizabeth.

June 1, 1797
Anna Kitty Dunn Tomkins, born Oct. 27, 1793, of Thomas Tomkins
                        and Elizabeth Stallings.

June 4, 1797
Ann Montgomery Smith, born Dec. 6, 1776, of William and Margaret.

June 6, 1797
John Farmer, born November 22, 1796, of William and Sarah Farmer
Mordecai Orr, born May 12, 1795, of Robert and Ruth Orr
Sarah Orr, born April 30, 1797, of Robert and Ruth Orr
William Rees, born October 13, 1793, of William and Jane Rees
Jane Rees, born May 18, 1795, of same parents
Alexander Rees, born May 12, 1797, of same parents
Samuel Scarborough, born April 23, 1793, of James and Hannah.
Thomas Gilbert Smith, born Dec. 15, 1796, of Samuel and Mary.
James Scarborough, born May 11, 1794, of William and Mary.
Charlotte Jones, born Dec. 20, 1797, of Charles and Mary Ann.
Charles Jones, born Oct. 19, 1771, of Benjamin and Sarah.
Rebecca Jones, born June 14, 1776, of same parents
Elizabeth Ellis, born May 7, 1784, of Henry and Ann Ellis.
William Scarborough, born Feb. 8, 1796, of James and Hannah.

June 9, 1797
James Wilson, born March 26, 1797, of Samuel and Fanny Wilson.

June 20, 1797
John Osborne, born November 9, 1796, of Amos and Elizabeth Osborne.
Edwin Bayley, born May 20, 1797, of Benedict and Mary Bayley.
Jarrett Edwards, born Feb. 21, 1797, of Thomas and Elizabeth.
Mary Scarborough, born Sept. 25, 1777, of Joseph and Sarah.

June 29, 1797
Daniel Ellot, born July 15, 1793, of Thomas and Susan Ellot.
George Ellot, born March 17, 1795, of same parents
Jane McCreary, born October 1, 1796, of Ralph and Jane McCreary.
William Stroud, born June 29, 1797, of Thomas and Mary Stroud.
Elizabeth Rigdon, born Sept. 25, 1787, of Alexander and Ann Rigdon.

August 17, 1797
Harriot Johnson, born May 20, 1796, of Joseph and Rebecca Johnson.

Page 328

August 20, 1797
George Thomas Gilbert, born Feb. 28, 1797, of Michael and Betsy.

Baptisms (continued)

September 7, 1797
Philip Chamberlain, born Jan. 25, 1797, of Philip and Elizabeth.
Nancy Kindle, born June 11, 1797, of John Kindle & Margaret Myers.

November 2, 1797
John Mooberry, born Sept. 15, 1796, of William & Elizabeth Mooberry.

December 10, 1797
Catharine Sally Hambleton, born Mar. 10, 1794, of John and Peggy.
Araminta Elizabeth Gibson, born Oct. 12, 1792, of Thomas & Betsy.
Emily Catharine Gibson, born about Sept. 15, 1790, of same parents.

December 17, 1797
Harriot Armstrong, born Jan. 15, 1797, of Solomon and Cassandra.

January 7, 1798
Richard Nun Allen, born Dec. 11, 1797, of John and Brasseya Allen.
John Carvel Matthews, born April 16, 1797, of Carvel and Ann.

January 8, 1798
George Gray, born Dec. 15, 1797, of James and Elizabeth Gray.

February 4, 1798
James Brookes Monk, born Nov. 4, 1797, of William & Elizabeth Monk.

March 14, 1798
James Shields, of John Shields and his wife.

April 8, 1798
Benjamin Hollis, born May 25, 1797, of Amos and Elizabeth Hollis.

April 9, 1798
James McKelvey Cartwright, born Jan. 3, 1798, of John Cartwright and Sarah Hamme.

April 10, 1798
Charlotte Nowland, born Jan. 17, 1798, of Peregrine and Rebecca.
Edward Albert, born Jan. 15, 1798, of Philip and Rachel Albert.

April 29, 1798
John Donnel, born Mar. 23, 1798, of Patrick and Margaret Donnel.
Benjamin Wells, born July 16, 1797, of James and Ruth Wells.

May 20, 1798
Edward Crayton, born May 6, 1797, of Patrick & Elizabeth Crayton.
Elizabeth Crayton, born Dec. 11, 1795, of same parents.
Joseph Crayton (conditionally), born Apr. 6, 1789, of same parents.

May 27, 1798
William Stallings, born in Aug., 1796, of William & Rebecca.
Samuel Stallings, born about July 1, 1795, of same parents.
Samuel Montjar, born Sept. 12, 1797, of William & Mary Montjar.

June 3, 1798
Ann Prichett, of James and Sarah Prichett.

July 1, 1798
John Lisbey Barnes, born Dec. 17, 1797, of Hoshea and Mary Barnes.
John Wood, born March 17, 1798, of Joshua and Ann Wood.

July 3, 1798
Samuel Briscoe, born April 16, 1797, of Joseph and Ann Briscoe.

July 12, 1798
Richard Webb, born July 9, 1798, of_____Webb.

July 28, 1798
Ann Eliza Maxwell, born May 12, 1798, of Moses and Ann Maxwell.
George Chauncey, born April 27, 1798, of George & Frances Rebecca.

July 28, 1798
Henry Lambert Wilmer, born Mar. 30, 1798, of William and Kitty.

Page 329 Baptisms (continued)

September 16, 1798
Elizabeth McKee, born July 25, 1797, of Thomas and Ann McKee.

October 21, 1798
Caroline Webster, born April 23, 1798, of Joseph and Martha.

November 8, 1798
William Carver, born June 24, 1798, of Henry and Elizabeth Carver.

November 11, 1798
Frances Susanna Hall, of Benedict Edward Hall and Milcah his wife.
John Turner, born March 31, 1798, of Noble and Ann Turner.

November 22, 1798
Nathaniel Smith, born April 9, 1779, of William and Margaret.
Alexander Smith, born July 31, 1782, of same parents.
William Smith Devlin, born Feb. 9, 1796, of William Devlin and
John Devlin, born May 16, 1794, of same parents. Mary Adamson.
Robert Stein Devlin, born May 3, 1798, of same parents.

November 24, 1798
Charlotte Knight, born Aug. 3, 1798, of William and Sarah Knight.

December 26, 1798
Robert White, born Dec. 10, 1798, of Robert and Mary Ann White.

January 13, 1799
Mary Ann Holmes, born Dec. 4, 1797, of William and Jane Holmes.
Samuel Cromwell, born Dec. 27, 1794, of Jesse and Letitia Cromwell.

March 10, 1799
John Henderson, born Aug. 22, 1797, of Nathaniel and Elizabeth.

April 21, 1799
Henry Nelson, born Oct. 15, 1798, of Aquila and Frances Nelson.

May 5, 1799
Rachel Blake, born about Fall 1780, of Isaac Blake and Margaret.
William Goldsmith Burke, born May 19, 1798, of John and Susanna.
Henrietta Knight, born Oct. 15, 1798, of Abraham and Ann Knight.

May 6, 1799
Elizabeth Bartley, born April 26, 1799, of Barney and Elizabeth.

May 14, 1799
Thomas Scarborough, born July 13, 1798, of Thomas and Margaret.
Anne Smith, born August 20, 1798, of James and Sarah Smith.
Priscilla Elizabeth Lee, born June 5, 1796, of Parker Hall Lee and
Richard Dallam Lee, born Apr. 18, 1799 of same parents. Elizabeth.

May 25, 1799
Joseph Prigg, born May 16, 1798, of John and Mary Prigg.

May 26, 1799
John Carvil Cranberry Hall, born May 6, 1795, of Josias & Martha.
Adeline Berthia Hall, born April 19, 1797, of same parents.

June 16, 1799
Henry Everet Michael, born Feb. 9, 1798, of Jacob and Mary Michael.
John Courtney, born Feb. 8, 1796, of Hollis and Elinor Courtney.
Hollis Hanson Courtney, born July 21, 1797, of same parents.

July 10, 1799
Gideon Gilbert, born June 26, 1798, of Parker and Martha Gilbert.

July 12, 1799
Maria Chamberlain, born May 24, 1799, of Philip and Elizabeth.

July 13, 1799
Margaret Wareham, born Sept. 19, 1793, of John and Rachel Wareham.

Page 330   Baptisms (continued)

July 13, 1799
John Wareham, born Sept. 14, 1795, of John and Rachel Wareham.
Henry Wareham, born Aug. 19, 1798, of same parents.
Abraham Steel McLaughlin, born Nov. 13, 1798, of Daniel & Cassandra.
James O'Neil, born March 14, 1798, of John and Mary O'Neil.
Jacob Suter, born July 25, 1791, of Nicholas and Mary Suter.
Mary Suter, born August 19, 1793, of same parents.
Ann Suter (conditionally), born Jan. 27, 1796, of same parents.
Gabriel Suter, born March 22, 1798, of same parents.

July 28, 1799
Cassandra Steel, born July 4, 1797, of John and Mary Steel.

August 15, 1799
Martha Culver, born Dec. 2, 1798, of Levi and Elizabeth Culver.

September 29, 1799
Matilda Wood, born June 23, 1799, of Joshua and Ann Wood.

September 30, 1799
Paca Smith Donovan, born Jan. 21, 1799, of John and Fanny Donovan.

October 20, 1799
Elizabeth Gover, born Dec. 28, 1798, of Robert and Martha Gover.
George Ray, born June 10, 1799, of Robert and Sarah Ray.

October 28, 1799
Sophia Elizabeth McComas, born Jan. 7, 1797, of Daniel & Elizabeth.

November 10, 1799
Isaac Periman Henderson, born Oct. 8, 1799, of Nathaniel & Elizabeth.

November 24, 1799
Robert Price, born in July 1787, of Robert and Hannah Price.
John Price, of same parents.
Joseph Price, of same parents.
Charles Price, of same parents.

December 19, 1799
John Touchstone, born Oct. 29, 1792, of Benjamin and Esther.
Nancy Touchstone, born Dec. 11, 1797, of same parents.
Amos Anderson, born Oct. 18, 1793, of Daniel and Rachel Anderson.
Susanna Anderson, born Oct. 6, 1795, of same parents.

December 25, 1799
Thomas Decran (?), born Sept. 12, 1799, of John and Deborah Decran.

December 27, 1799
Elizabeth Webb, born Sept. 28, 1799, of George and Margaret Webb.
Erwin Lewis McLaughlin, born Nov. 27, 1799, of Patrick and Ann.

January 20, 1800
Mary Osborne, born April 7, 1799, of Cyrus and Martha Osborne.
Kendel Powell, born Nov. 7, 1799, of William and Avarilla Powell.
William Wright, born Oct. 1, 1799, of James and Ruth Wright.

January 24, 1800
James Hall, born Oct. 14, 1798, of James White Hall and Sarah.
Harriott Barnes, born Oct. 27, 1799, of Myer and Margaret Barnes.

Page 331 Baptisms (continued)

January 26, 1800
James Montjar, born Dec. 9, 1799, of William and Mary Montjar.
Samuel Wilson, born Nov. 9, 1798, of Samuel and Frances Wilson.

February 6, 1800
William Taylor, born July 22, 1799, of James Taylor & Sarah Aitken.

February 10, 1800
Hannah Cole, born March 4, 1799, of John Beagle Cole and Priscilla.

April 13, 1800
William Greenly, born Nov. 18, 1795, of Samuel and Rachel Greenly.
Gilbert Greenly, born March 3, 1797, of same parents.
Greenberry Greenly, born Jan. 12, 1800, of James Greenly & Mary Redman.

April 26, 1800
William Smith, born March 23, 1800, of James and Sarah Smith.

April 27, 1800
Garret Brown, born June 11, 1794, of Thomas and Elinor Brown.
Avarilla Brown, born Sept. 9, 1796, of same parents.
William Brown, born April 26, 1798, of same parents.

May 4, 1800
Mary Rebecca Matthews, born June 7, 1798, of Joseph & Jane Matthews.
Milcah Lusby Matthews, born Feb. 28, 1799, of Carvil & Ann Matthews.

Jun 10, 1800
Stephen Chesolm, born Feb. 18, 1800, of John Chesolm & Sarah Dawney.

May 11, 1800
William Grey, born April 4, 1800, of James and Elizabeth Grey.

June 15, 1800
Elizabeth Sophia Mitchell, born Dec. 4, 1798, of Richard & Priscilla.
Cassey Bennet, born January 26, 1798, of Philip and Sarah Bennet.

June 19, 1800
Chauncey Hollis, born March 29, 1800, of Amos and Elizabeth Hollis.

July 6, 1800
Moses Scott McComas, born Dec. 5, 1799, of Daniel & Elizabeth McComas.

July 20, 1800
Cassandra White, born March 17, 1800, of Robert and Mary Ann White.

July 21, 1800
Robert Brooks, born July 13, 1791, of John and Margaret Brooks.
Sarah Brooks, born April 25, 1785, of same parents.
Martha Brooks, born December 27, 1786, of same parents.
John Brooks, born June 12, 1799, of Thomas and Sarah Brooks.
James Grace, born May 19, 1800, of Bowyer and Mary Grace.

August 1, 1800
Matthew Johnson Allen, born July 16, 1800, of John & Brasseya Allen.

August 6, 1800
Isaac Spencer, born Sept. 28, 1799, of Richard and Martha Spencer.

August 12, 1800
Letitia Harward, born Aug. 26, 1799, of John and Margaret Harward.
Jane McKee, born May 16, 1800, of Thomas and Ann McKee.

August 14, 1800
Jemima Kimble (conditionally), born Feb. 22, 1800, of Zachariah and
    Frances Kimble.
Elizabeth Treadaway, born about 1782, of Thomas & Christiana Treadaway.
Aquila Treadaway, born April 8, 1789, of Thomas & Christiana Treadaway.

September 7, 1800
Elizabeth Martin, born Sept. 20, 1799, of John and Sarah Martin.

Page 332 Baptisms (continued)

September 7, 1800
Joseph Bare, born June 18, 1790, of John and Barbara Ann Bare.
Elizabeth Bare, born December 31, 1785, of same parents.
Samuel Bare, born November 18, 1787, of same parents.
Nicholas Suter, born May 3, 1800, of Bicholas and Mary Suter.
John O'Neal, born March 27, 1800, of John and Mary O'Neal.

September 8, 1800
Mary Chauncey, born Nov. 18, 1793, of Benjamin & Elizabeth Chauncey.
Benjamin Chauncey, born April 3, 1797, of same parents.
Ann Eliza Chauncey, born August 15, 1799, of same parents.

October 2, 1800
Polly Hughes, born May 26, 1798, of John and Charlotte Hughes.
John Hall Hughes, born May 29, 1800, of same parents.
James Botts Hughes, born Sept. 8, 1794, of Everett and Nancy Hughes.
John Hall Hughes, born March 24, 1796, of same parents.
Everett Scott Hughes, born April 22, 1798, of same parents.

October 27, 1800
John Henderson Steel, born July 13, 1798, of Joseph and Margaret Steel.

December 26, 1800
Mary Ann Bartley, born Sept. 28, 1800, of Barnabas and Nancy Bartley.
Ann Michael, born August 15, 1800, of William and Ann Michael.
Martha Michael, born December 18, 1798, of same parents.

January 9, 1801
Charlotte Taylor, born Oct. 26, 1799, of Ashbury Taylor and Frances
Sylvester Taylor, born Jan. 24, 1798, of same parents.   Shody.
Otho Taylor, born July 2, 1796, of same parents.
Susanna Taylor, born March 18, 1795, of same parents.

January 14, 1801
Nathan Hughes, born Nov. 19, 1800, of Nathan Hughes and Elizabeth
Benedict Hughes, born May 23, 1798, of same parents.   McClain.

February 5, 1801
Benedict Edward Mitchell, born July 4, 1799, of Aquila & Susanna.

March 19, 1801
Isabella Boyd, born Aug. 15, 1798, of John and Avarilla Boyd.
Anna Boyd, born January 29, 1800, of same parents.
Eliza Mitchell, born Oct. 13, 1798, of William and Sarah Mitchell.
Martha Mitchell, born January 18, 1800, of same parents.

March 31, 1801
Ashbury Kimble, born Aug. 10, 1800, of Stephen and Anna Kimble.
George Washington Kimble, born October 8, 1797, of same parents.
John Kimble, born February 27, 1799, of same parents.
James Gray, born March 17, 1801, of James and Elizabeth Gray.

May 22, 1801
Elizabeth Evertt, born Dec. 21, 1800, of Joseph and Clara Everett.

Page 333 Baptisms (continued)

May 22, 1801
Jacob Greenfield, born Sept. 7, 1799, of Jacob and Elizabeth.

June 19, 1801
Polly Kimble, born March 24, 1801, of Elijah and Mary Kimble.
William Henry Dorsey, born July 1, 1799, of Frisby & Ann Dorsey.

June 21, 1801
Sarah Prichett (an adult), born about 1784, of James and Sarah.
Thomas Doolsacus, born April 19, 1793, of Lewis & Mary Doolsacus.

June 26, 1801
James Skidmore Dunnings, born Sept. 18, 1800, of John and Lydia.

July 2, 1801
Sarah Barnes, born Jan. 24, 1796, of Ford Barnes and Mary Gilbert.
Judith Boland, born in January 1793, of Peter and Rachel Boland.

July 30, 1801
Hugh McGowan, born Dec. 29, 1790, of Michael and Margaret McGowan.

August 9, 1801
Francis Cunningham, born Dec. 10, 1798, of Crispin and Rachel.
Crispin Cunningham, born April 19, 1801, of same parents.
Sarah Bean, born August 11, 1799, of Edmond and Elizabeth Bean.

August 10, 1801
Cassandra Lynch (adult), born Aug. 4, 1781, of John & Sarah Lynch.
Andrew Lynch (adult), born June 24, 1775, of John and Rosanna Lynch.
Jackson Yokely, born Oct. 11, 1795, of John and Sarah Yokely.

August 23, 1801
John Dorsey Chancey, born Feb. 5, 1801, of George & Frances Rebecca.

August 30, 1801
Joshua Wood Barnes, born May 1, 1801, of Hoshea and Mary Barnes.

September 5, 1801
Rebecca McIntire, of James and Rachel McIntire.

September 5, 1801
Mary McIntire, of James and Rachel McIntire.

September 6, 1801
Thomas Martin, born April 17, 1800, of Andrew & Elizabeth Martin.
Jane Martin, born April 17, 1800 (same day) of same parents.
Anne Amos Bevard, born Nov. 11, 1799, of William and Rebecca.
James Ezekiel Donnel, born Sept. 27, 1800, of Patrick & Margaret.
Cassandra Prigg Gover, born July 22, 1801, of Robert and Martha.
Peggy Lee, born June 22, 1801, of Marshall and Rachel Lee.
William Carton, born in October 1798, of Joseph and Elizabeth.
Mary Carton, born September 5, 1800, of same parents.

September 13, 1801
John Mackibbin, born June 19, 1801, of William and Elizabeth.
Thomas Hagerty, born June 12, 1799, of Daniel and Elizabeth.

November 15, 1801
Loyd Kelly, born Oct. 29, 1801, of Isaac Kelly and Drusilla Durbin.

December 17, 1801
Henry Mitchell, born Oct. 5, 1801, of Richard & Priscilla Mitchell.
Gideon McComas, born Dec. 19, 1800, of Charles and Mary McComas.
Ann Martha Gilbert, born Oct. 4, 1801, of Parker and Martha Gilbert.

Page 334 Baptisms (continued)

December 21, 1801
James Thomas, born Nov. 26, 1801, of Moses and Nancy Thomas.

January 15, 1802
John Wade, born Jan. 6, 1802, of John and Jane Wade.

February 17, 1802
Thomas Lynch, born about 1791, of John and Sarah Lynch.
Elizabeth Lynch, born about 1793, of same parents.

March 19, 1802
William Henry Herbert, born Dec. 21, 1801, of Benjamin & Sarah.
Mary Ann Herbert, born February 23, 1797, of same parents.
Hiram Herbert, born April 6, 1799, of James and Anna Herbert.
Anna Maria Herbert, born Oct. 29, 1801, of same parents.
Jane Herbert (adult), born July 24, 1785, of Richard and Jane.

March 21, 1802
William Wood, born January 6, 1802, of Joshua and Ann Wood.

April 11, 1802
Benedict Finicum, born Dec. 5, 1801, of Benjamin Finicum and Polly
                                                            Combess.
Charlotte Osborne, born Feb. 22, 1802, of William Osborne and Polly
                                                             Horner.
April 25, 1802
Elizabeth Austin Greenfield, born Sept. 26, 1801, of Jacob and
                                                          Elizabeth.
Anna Maria Michael, born Dec. 26, 1801, of Jacob and Mary Michael.
Ethan Michael, born October 20, 1799, of same parents.

April 26, 1802
John Knight, born March 7, 1802, of William and Sarah Knight.
Hannah Robison, born March 2, 1774, of Jacob Robison & Mary Knight.
Elizabeth Robison, born May 5, 1787, of Abraham & Elizabeth Robison.
William Robison, born December 26, 1790, of same parents.
Andrew McLaughlin, born Jan. 25, 1802, of Patrick & Ann McLaughlin.

May 19, 1802
Mary Brisland, born April 2, 1802, of Dennis and Ann Brisland.

June 6, 1802
John Magaw, born Feb. 12, 1802, of John Magaw and Priscilla Crawford.

June 28, 1802
Anna Elizabeth Turner, born April 5, 1802, of Daniel & Anna Elizabeth.

July 4, 1802
Elizabeth Rogers, born April 18, 1801, of Alexander Rogers and Mary Williams.

July 8, 1802
Richard Deeran, born Nov. 13, 1801, of John and Deborah Deeran.

August 8, 1802
Sophia Stansberry Hall, born Dec. 3, 1799, of Josias & Martha Hall.
George Josias Ontario Hall, born March 29, 1802, of same parents.

August 9, 1802
Eliza Bean, born in April 1802, of Edmond and Elizabeth Bean.
Harriott Bartol, born May 12, 1802, of Barney and Nancy Bartol.
Charles Chamberlaine, born May 20, 1802, of Philip and Elizabeth.
Clarissa Coffield, born Jan, 10, 1802, of Thomas and Martha Coffield.
Jacob Wareham, born April 17, 1801, of John and Rachel Wareham.

Page 335 Baptisms (continued)

August 22, 1802
Elizabeth Rigden, born September 2, 1758
Charles Rigden, born September 5, 1792   (Note in margin
Rachel Rigden, born April 22, 1795   indicates this
Jane Rigden, born December 21, 1796   was family of
Henry Rigden, born August 26, 1799   Charles Rigden's)

August 29, 1802
Mary Ann Nelson, born Dec. 22, 1801, of John and Rebecca Ann Nelson.

September 5, 1802
Sally Elizabeth Munjar, born March 20, 1802, of William and Mary.

September 12, 1802
George William Hall, born April 2, 1798, of William & Sophia Hall.
Thomas White Hall, born May 7, 1800, of same parents.

October 10, 1802
Elizabeth Price, born Aug. 29, 1802, of James and Isabella Price.

October 24, 1802
Ann Steel, born October 14, 1801, of John and Mary Steel.

November 4, 1802
Daniel Mitchell, born May 4, 1802, of Aquila and Susanna Mitchell.

December 12, 1802
John Federal William Carlile, born Jan. 4, 1802, of John & Elizabeth.

December 26, 1802
Jane Adeline Allen, born Nov. 30, 1802, of John and Brasseya Allen.

January 2, 1803
George Nelson, born Oct. 4, 1801, of Aquila and Frances Nelson.

February 1, 1803
Joseph Cole, born Sept. 4, 1801, of John Beagle Cole and Priscilla.

March 1, 1803
Ann Hughes, born April 7, 1784, of John Hall Hughes and Ann.

April 6, 1803
Margaret Harward, born Aug. 9, 1802, of John and Margaret Harward.

May 7, 1803
Catharine Jellett, born April 29, 1803, of Morgan and Anna Jellett.

May 8, 1803
Lewis Griffith, born March 24, 1796, of Samuel and Elizabeth Griffith.
Eliza Griffith, born May 1, 1799, of same parents.
Samuel Griffith, born November 21, 1800, of same parents.
Edward Griffith, born March 10, 1802, of same parents.

July 3, 1803
Alexander Cowan, born Jan. 21, 1803, of Roger Boyce Cowan and Sarah.

August 14, 1803
Harriott Harwood, born Aug. 31, 1802, of James and Sarah Harwood.
Samuel Griffith Smith, born Dec. 25, 1794, of Alexander Lawson Smith
Maria Matilda Smith, born July 1, 1799, of same.   and Martha.
Francinia Frenetta Smith, born Nov. 10, 1797, of same.

August 15, 1803
William Fleetwood, born about Oct. 20, 1801, of Benjamin and Elinor.
John Fleetwood, born February 20, 1803, of same parents.
Margaret Gay, born May 18, 1803, of Henry and Mary Gay.

September 18, 1803
Hannah Brisland, born Aug. 23, 1803, of Dennis and Ann Brisland.

Page 336 Baptisms (continued)

September 18, 1803
George Warren, born July 7, 1803, of Bayley and Sarah Warren.
Bayley Warren, born April 14, 1775, of William and Margaret Warren.

September 26, 1803
John James Burke, born March 10, 1803, of John and Susan Burke.

November 9, 1803
Jane Burton Culver, born Dec. 26, 1801, of Levi and Elizabeth Culver.
Hannah Culver, born June 4, 1803, of same parents.

No date or name of child for Jacob Washington Giles & Martha, wife.

January 18, 1804
Elizabeth Broom, born Aug. 28, 1803, of James and Ann Broom.

January 19, 1804
Mary Ann Andrews, born June 29, 1802, of Abraham and Mary Andrews.
Abraham Andrews, born January 5, 1795, of same parents.
Caterina Andrews, born June 4, 1788, of same parents.
John Hanson Andrews, born Sept. 19, 1789, of same parents.
Sarah Andrews, born January 1, 1784, of same parents.
Eliza Williams, born Dec. 19, 1803, of William Williams and Lina Andrews.
Charles Bailey, born Jan. 7, 1797, of Josias and Avarilla Bailey.
Mary Bailey, born Dec. 26, 1798, of same parents.
Ezra Bailey, born Nov. 11, 1803, of Benedict and Mary Bailey.

February 2, 1804
Clarke Hollis, born Dec. 1, 1803, of Clarke and Cymelia Hollis.
Levina Wright, born July 22, 1803, of James and Ruth Wright.

April 28, 1804
John Sidney Hall, born Dec. 5, 1803, of Walter Tolley Hall and Charlotte White.
William Henry Watkins, born April 8, 1804, of Tobias & Mary Watkins.
James Anderson, born Sept. 19, 1803, of James and Betsy Anderson.

May 20, 1804
Thomas McKibbin, born Dec. 25, 1803, of William and Elizabeth.

June 24, 1804
John Harvey McFaddon, born Jan. 22, 1801, of Benjamin and Sarah.
Charles Gilbert McFaddon, born March 18, 1803, of same parents.
Mortimer Cunningham, born Feb. 20, 1803, of Crispin & Elizabeth.

July 21, 1804
Hannah Price, born March 6, 1804, of James and Isabella Price.

July 25, 1804
Mary Elizabeth Matthews, born Apr. 28, 1801, of Carvil and Ann.
William Levin Matthews, born April 19, 1804, of same parents.

August 12, 1804
James Taylor, born Oct. 4, 1802, of Ashbury and Frances Taylor.

September 9, 1804
Sophia Hall, born July 23, 1795, of Thomas and Isabella Hall.
Isabella Hall, born January 1, 1799, of same parents.
John Thomas Hall, born March 17, 1801, of same parents.
Edward Benedict Hall, born March 1, 1803, of same parents.

Page 337 Baptisms (continued)

September 14, 1804
Eliza Hughes, born Feb. 11, 1804, of Nathan Hughes and Elizabeth McClain.

October 14, 1804
Thomas Suter, born Dec. 21, 1802, of Nicholas and Mary Suter.
William Webb, born Dec. 28, 1802, of George and Margaret Webb.

October 14, 1804
Anna Maria Webb, born March 24, 1804, of George and Margaret Webb.

November 5, 1804
William McLaughlin, born Dec. 30, 1803, of Patrick and Ann.
Amelia Carman (adult), born March 3, 1777, of Israel and Amelia.
Jane O'Neil, born June 2, 1802, of John and Mary O'Neil.
Mary Chamberlaine, born Nov. 2, 1804, of Philip and Elizabeth.

November 25, 1804
Patty Scott Hughes, of James and Hannah Hughes.

December 27, 1804
Barnet Mitchell, born Sept. 2, 1804, of Richard and Priscilla.

Registry of Baptisms in Saint George's
Parish Commencing January 1, 1805

January 8, 1805
James Hagarty, of Daniel and Elizabeth Hagarty.

January 10, 1805
Emeline Cordelia Hall, born Jan. 18, 1804, of Josias and Martha.

January 11, 1805
Charlotte, born about July 1804, "William & Sarah Neg. Mrs. Griffith".
Amy, born about October 1797, "David & Prina Neg. Mrs. Griffith".
Fanny, born in December 1800, "Bill Rodes & Prina Neg. Mrs. Griffith".
Kitty, born in August 1800, of same parents.

January 20, 1805
Charles Pinkney, born Feb. 4, 1797, of William and Ann Pinkney.
Charlotte Pinkney, born October 4, 1798, of same parents.
Caroline Pinkney, born September 14, 1800, of same parents.
Edward Coote Pinkney, born October 1, 1802, of same parents.
Frederic Pinkney, born October 14, 1804, of same parents.

February 18, 1805
Susanna, born Sept. 17, 1803, "Sam & Hagar Estate Thos. Hall Dec'd."
Welton, born about Fall 1797, "Sam & Ann Estate Thos. Hall Dec'd."
Robert, born Dec. 25, 1800, "Bob & Ann Estate Thos, Hall Dec'd."

February 20, 1805
Isaac, born Nov. 23, 1804, "Isaac & Bet Neg. Mr. Paca Smith."

March 5, 1805
Eliza Ann Giles (Adult), born Dec. 23, 1792, of Thomas & Rebecca.

April 9, 1805
Henry, born about Sept. 1, 1802, "Sampson & Vinetta Neg. Jacob W. Giles"
Jenny, born March 1, 1803, "Jack & Avarilla Neg. Sarah Scovall"

April 11, 1805
Naomi Louisa Combess, born Dec. 14, 1803, of Utey Combess and Milla Collins.

Page 338 Baptisms (continued)

April 28, 1805
Louisa Garretson Nelson, born Dec. 9, 1803, of Aquila and Frances.

May 11, 1805
Charles, born January 1800, "Mensis & Nancy Neg. John Adlin."
Elinor, born November 1804, of same parents.

March 27, 1805
Hannah West, born Nov. 23, 1797, of Thomas and Elizabeth West.
Washington West, born December 15, 1799, of Thomas and Elizabeth.
Jesse West, born March 26, 1803, of same parents.

July 12, 1805
Elizabeth Dawney, born Feb. 26, 1790, of James and Sophia Dawney.
Thomas Dawney, born March 21, 1797, of same parents.
William Collins Dawney, born April 14, 1799, of same parents.
John Dawney, born April 2, 1804, of same parents.
Mary Ann, born July 7, 1804, "Thomas and Hannah Neg. D. Elrai."
Martha Ann Elizabeth Hall, born February 3, 1805, of Thomas Hall, Dec'd. and Isabella.
Bill, born in October 1795, "Emanuel & Dina Neg. Estate Thos, Hall Dec'd."
Jacob, born June 1, 1799, of same parents.
Diana, born August 10, 1804, of same parents.

July 28, 1805
Martha Phillips Giles, born Dec. 24, 1804, of Jacob Washington Giles and Martha.
Henrietta Richards, born June 9, 1805, "Sampson & Violette Neg. J.W. Giles Esqr."

August 4, 1805
Elinor Evans, born May 17, 1792, of Amos and Sarah Evans.
Margaret Evans, born June 15, 1798, of same parents.
Amos Evans, born December 17, 1800, of same parents.
Francis Evans, born November 30, 1804, of same parents.

August 15, 1805
Mary Collins, born March 15, 1791, of Jacob and Hannah Collins.
Hannah Collins, born May 17, 1802, of same parents.
Harriot Collins, born March 19, 1804, of same parents.

August 21, 1805
Sarah Price, born July 29, 1805, of James and Isabella Price.

August 25, 1805
John Sears Dutton, born June 5, 1803, of John and Amelia Dutton.
James Dutton, born May 16, 1801, of same parents.
William Dutton, born March 4, 1805, of same parents.

September 1, 1805
Cordelia Phillips Archer, born May 5, 1805, of Thomas & Elizabeth.
Harriot Pinion, born Dec. 23, 1804 of "Joe & Hetty Pinion Free Black."
James Rice, born Jan. 31, 1804, "Saml. Rice & Milcah Neg. Mrs. Martha Phillips."

September 15, 1805
John Magroth, born April 12, 1805, of William and Caroline Magroth.
Eliza, born Feb. 25, 1802, "William Bowzer & Sylina Neg. Mrs. Mary Johns."

Page 339 Baptisms (continued)

September 1, 1805
Richard, born October 8, 1804, of same parents.

August 18, 1805
Ezekiel Bayley, born March 12, 1799, of Benedict and Mary Bayley.
William Morgan Bayley, born May 25, 1801, of same parents.
Harriot Barns, born Dec. 24, 1796, of Gregory and Elizabeth Barns.
Richard Barns, born March 26, 1799, of same parents.
Ford Barns, born August 4, 1801, of same parents.
William Barns, born March 24, 1804, of same parents.
Thomas Harley Mitchell, born Mar. 9, 1803, of William & Sarah.
Richard Mitchell, born October 18, 1804, of same parents.
Mary Ann Osborne, born March 4, 1802, of Amos and Elizabeth.

October 4, 1805
Eliza McGill, born Nov. 11, 1803, of William and Mary McGill.

October 6, 1805
John Cowan, born Oct. 20, 1804, of Roger Boyce Cowan and Sarah.

October 24, 1805
John Swan Everett, born Nov. 26, 1803, of John and Clare Everett.
Jane Elizabeth Madden, born Jan. 26, 1804, of James and Comfort.

October 29, 1805
Isaac Wilson, born July 21, 1805, of Isaac Wilson & Charlotte Aikers.

December 26, 1805
Charlotte, born March 1805, "Simon and Mary Neg. Dr. Elijah Davis."
Nancy, born December 1804, "Jacob and Jane Neg. Dr. Elijah Davis."
Harry Pinckney, born April 1805, "Richard Harris and Maria Neg. Do."
Mary Ann, born Nov. 2, 1802, of Thomas and Elinor Brown.
Aquila Dawes, born March 28, 1802, of Benjamin and Elizabeth Dawes.

December 27, 1805
Roger Matthews, of Josiah and Jane Matthews.

February 22, 1806
Barney Bell Bartoland, born Sept. 18, 1805 of Barney and Nancy.

February 23, 1806
Prina, born about August 1801, "David and Hannah Neg. Edward Griffith."
Susanna, born May 20, 1804, of same parents.

March 22, 1806
Anna Huber Walkins, born Nov. 25, 1805, of Tobias and Mary Walkins.

March 27, 1806
William Allen Small. born Dec. 10, 1805, of David and Mary Small.

April 1, 1806
John Jefferson Johnson, born July 21, 1803, of Richard and Mary.

April 24, 1806
Nancy Everist, born Nov. 26, 1803, of Thomas and Avarilla Everist.
Benjamin Everist, born February 3, 1806, of same parents.

May 4, 1806
Thomas Charles Gorsuch Knight, born March 17, 1804, of Isaac and
                                                    Tabitha Knight.

June 18, 1806
Susan More, born April 16, 1804, of John and Ruth More.
William More, born January 23, 1806, of same parents.

Page 340 Baptisms (continued)

June 18, 1806
Barbara Kingsley, born April 17, 1797, of Samuel and Barbara.
William Kingsley, born July 30, 1802, of same parents.
Susan Kingsley, born February 14, 1806, of same parents.

July 26, 1806
Clarissa Everist, born Febeuary 5, 1806, of Joseph and Clare.

September 11, 1806
Cassandra Dawes, born August 17, 1806, of Benjamin and Elizabeth.

September 18, 1806
William Griffith, born December 19, 1805, of John Griffith and
                                                    Susan Calmody.
September 30, 1806
Thomas Greenlee, born March 1, 1806, of James and Mary Greenlee.
William Johnson, born June 3, 1805, of Asam and Hannah Johnson.

October 25, 1806
Anna Maria Knight, born December 8, 1804, of William and Sarah.

October 26, 1806
Hannahretta Gallion, born May 6, 1804, of James and Philizana.
Mary Ann Knight, born December 15, 1805, of Thomas and Sally.

November 3, 1806
James Phillips Archer, born October 29, 1806, of Thomas & Elizabeth.

November 13, 1806
Jane Knight, born December 25, 1802, of Aquila and Elizabeth Knight.
John Knight, born November 15, 1805, of same parents.

November 16, 1806
Margaret Knight, born February 15, 1793, of Thomas and Ann Knight.
Michael Knight, born June 6, 1795, of same parents.
Aquila Knight, born May 14, 1797, of same parents.
Robert Knight, born October 5, 1799, of same parents.
Hannah Knight, born March 14, 1802, of same parents.
Cassandra Knight, born March 9, 1805, of same parents.
James Lynch, born in May, 1798, of John and Sarah Lynch.
Sarah Porter, adult, born June 11, 1791, of John and Catharine.
Eliza Porter, adult, born August 1, 1793, of same parents.
Roxana Dorset, adult, born January 2, 1786, of Jonathan & Martha.
Martha Dorset, adult, born February 14, 1788, of same parents.
George Webb, born May 5, 1806, of George and Margaret Webb.
Charles O'Neil, born July 30, 1806, of John and Mary O'Neil.

November 3, 1806
Elizabeth Boyd, born Jan. 16, 1803, of John and Avarilla Boyd.
Sarah Boyd, born February 16, 1805, of same parents.
Harriot Mycos born March 3, 1802, of John Kentle Mycos & Margaret.
Alexander Mycos, born February 24, 1804, of same parents.

November 8, 1806
William Osborne, born June 27, 1802, of Aquila and Martha.
Elizabeth Osborne, born September 14, 1803, of same parents.

Page 341 Baptisms (continued)
November 8, 1806
Sarah Osborne, born January 15, 1805, of Aquila and Martha.

December 7, 1806
Matilda Frances Nowland, born Sept. 15, 1803, of Peregrine & Rebecca.
Edward William Benjamin Nowland, born Mar. 14, 1806, of same parents.

January 2, 1807
William Smith, born June 14, 1804, of Winston and Cassandra Smith.

January 3, 1807
Frances Smith, born Feb. 14, 1801, of Winston and Cassandra Smith.
Elizabeth Giles Smith, born October 14, 1802, of same parents.

February 19, 1807
Catharine Hollis, born May 9, 1806, of Clarke and Cymelia Hollis.

February 27, 1807
William McComas, born Oct. 24, 1801, of Aaron and Martha McComas.
Jacob McComas, born August 27, 1802, of same parents.
Solomon McComas, born January 23, 1804, of same parents.

March 31, 1807
Sarah Ashby Jones, born Sept. 29, 1794, of Robert and Mary Jones.

May 17, 1807
Mary Montjar, born Nov. 21, 1804, of William and Mary Montjar.
Joseph Montjar, born March 30, 1807, of same parents.
Sarah Hagarty, born May 13, 1805, of Daniel and Elizabeth.

May 31, 1807
Mary Hall, born in October 1796, of Parker Hall & Catharine McClean.
William Thomas, born Feb. 26, 1802, of William and Catharine Thomas.
Martha Thomas, born September 26, 1804, of same parents.
John Thomas, born January 1, 1807, of same parents.
Maryanna Taylor, born March 19, 1807, of Ashbury and Frances Taylor.

June 10, 1807
Mary Wood, born March 23, 1804, of Joshua and Ann Wood.
Susanna Robison Wood, born April 1, 1806, of same parents.

June 14, 1807
Harriot Amanda Boyer, born Jan. 16, 1807, of David and Sarah Boyer.
Bennet Nelson, born March 8, 1806, of Aquila and Frances Nelson.

July 5, 1807
Susanna Smith, born Dec. 25, 1803, of James and Sarah Smith.
Mary Smith, born October 3, 1805, of same parents.

August 9, 1807
Delia More Hall, born August 31, 1805, of Walter Tolley Hall
                                    and Charlotte White.
September 6, 1807
Eloiza Johnson, born Oct. 26, 1804, of William and Mary Johnson.
Ileland Casine Johnson, born March 11, 1807, of same parents.
Mary Smith, born Sept. 6, 1794, of Henry and Mary Smith.
Araminta Smith, born (not given), of same parents.
James McLaughlin, born June 14, 1804, of John and Elizabeth.
Ann Flaherty, born May 29, 1806, of Joshua and Mary Flaherty.
James Lemmon, born January 12, 1805, of John and Ann Lemmon.
Ann Perry Lemmon, born December 19, 1806, of same parents.

Page 342   Baptisms (continued)

October 1, 1807
Mary Ann Cunningham, born April 9, 1805, of Crispin & Elizabeth.
Mahela Mitchell, born April 20, 1804, of Aquila (dec'd.) & Susanna.
John Hawkins Barns, born Nov. 19, 1806, of Gregory and Elizabeth.

November 23, 1807
Edward Magaw, born Sept. 29, 1806, of William (dec'd.) & Caroline.

November 29, 1807
Sarah Collins, born about Sept., 1806, of Mahlon and Mary Collins.

January 10, 1808
William Jolley Gilbert, born Sept. 1, 1807, of Parker & Elizabeth.
Elizabeth Mary Twiford, born Nov. 13, 1807. of James and Mary Ann.

January 25, 1808
John Holley, born Sept. 28, 1807, of William and Sarah Holley.
Rebedee Oliver, born in Sept. 1806, of James Oliver & Elizabeth Madden.

February 1, 1808
Louisa Ann Griffith, born Jan. 3, 1805, of James and Sarah Griffith.
William Harman Cox Griffith, born November 11, 1806, of same parents.

February 15, 1808
Stephen Kimble, born in April 1802, of Stephen (dec'd.) and Hannah.
Miranda Kimble, born in January 1803, of same parents.
Henry Kimble, born June 8, 1806, of same parents.

March 3, 1808
George Knight (no birth date given), of William and Sarah Knight.

March 10, 1808
Matilda Knight, born Feb. 11, 1807, of Thomas and Ann Knight.
James Knight, born Feb. 8, 1808, of Aquila and Elizabeth Knight.
Micajah Tilman Thomson, born March 25, 1803, of Micajah and Sarah.
Rachel Thomson, born October 28, 1807, of same parents.

March 27, 1808
Elizabeth Cowan, adult, born Feb. 26, 1791, of Thomas Cowan and
                                    Sarah, his late wife.
Mary Cowan, born in March 1799, of same parents.
Martha Cowan, born February 3, 1804, of same parents.
Thomas Cowan, born April 11, 1806, of same parents.

197

March 27, 1808
Morgan Thomas, born Feb. 14, 1807, of James and Arabella Thomas.
Clemence Mitchell, born Dec. 13, 1801, of William and Sarah.
Anna Mitchell, born May 26, 1807, of same parents.

June 5, 1808
John Moore, born Sept. 23, 1807, of John and Ruth Moore.

June 12, 1808
Avarilla Frances Griffith, born May 18, 1808, of James & Sarah.

June 23, 1808
Mary Leitle Chauncey, born Sept. 17, 1804, of George & Frances Rebecca.
James Maxwell Chauncey, born January 30, 1808, of same parents.
Susanna Faithful Matthews, born Nov. 26, 1807, of Josiah and Jane.

June 28, 1808
Abraham Steel, born Dec. 16, 1806, of Theophilus Steel & Ann Robinson.

June 29, 1808
Mary Sophia Small, born Nov. 23, 1807, of David and Mary Small.

Page 343 Baptisms (continued)

James Smith, born August 23, 1807, of James and Sarah Smith.
Samuel Ellott, born Nov. 14, 1807, of William and Faithful Ellot.
Cassandra Ellott, born March 26, 1806, of same parents.

July 6, 1808
Robert Price, born Nov. 14, 1807, of James and Isabella Price.

August 9, 1808
Elizabeth Hughes, born Aug. 24, 1804, of Scott and Martha Hughes.
Berthia Clemency Hughes, born September 21, 1806, of same parents.

September 4, 1806
Samuel Curry, born July 16, 1808, of Samuel and Catharine Curry.
Mary Ann Mitchell, born Jan. 19, 1807, of John and Hannah Mitchell.
Elizabeth Curry, born in April 1795, of John and Mary Curry.
Thomas Curry, born in April 1796, of same parents.
Sarah Curry, born April 11, 1799, of same parents.

September 11, 1808
Bennet Armstrong, born March 2, 1807, of Robert Armstrong and
                                                    Elizabeth Shay.
September 12, 1808
Sophia Dawney, born July 31, 1808, of Lloyd and Phebe Dawney.

October 22, 1808
James White Knight, born July 28, 1807, of Isaac and Tabitha.
Philip McGonegal, born Sept. 29, 1808, of Daniel and Mary, his
                                                    late wife.
Elisia Elizabeth Burke, born August 25, 1805, of John and Susanna.
Edward Burke, born August 25, 1808 (same date), of same parents.
Thomas Burke, born April 1, 1808, of same parents.

October 29, 1808
Elizabeth Brookes, born Dec. 11, 1805, of Thomas and Sarah.

October 29, 1808
Isaac Brookes, born Sept. 8, 1808, of Thomas and Sarah Brookes.
William Bowyer, born Aug. 8, 1808, of David and Sarah Bowyer.

November 18, 1808
John Hopkins, of John and Mary Hopkins.
Elizabeth Hopkins, of same parents.
William Hopkins, of same parents.
Henry Hopkins, of same parents.
George Morris, born Jan. 12, 1803, of John and Elizabeth Morris.
Mary Ann Morris, born Sept. 15, 1805, of same parents.
Eliza Morris, born March 15, 1808, of same parents.

November 20, 1808
William Godwin Chauncey, born June 21, 1806, of George & Rebecca
                                                              Frances.
December 2, 1808
Joseph Thomas, born May 30, 1807, of Moses and Nancy Thomas.

December 4, 1808
Elinor Everist, born November 19, 1806, of Samuel and Mary Everist.

December 30, 1808
Sally Rider, born October 14, 1806, of Noble and Artridge Rider.

January 17, 1809
Jacob Brown, born January 20, 1770, of Thomas and Mary Brown.

Page 344 Baptisms (continued)

January 17, 1809
Miranda Chauncey, born March 11, 1802, of Benjamin and Elizabeth.

January 20, 1809
Mary Ann Dougherty, born Sept. 14, 1805, of Patrick and Sarah.

January 26, 1809
Amos Knight, born Oct. 12, 1807, of Thomas and Sarah Knight.

January 27, 1809
James Lawder, born Nov. 7, 1801, of William and Rachel Lawder.
Frances Lawder, born May 19, 1804, of same parents.
Samuel Lawder, born March 6, 1808, of same parents.

February 11, 1809
Charity Amanda Cole, born Sept. 26, 1808, of John Beagle Cole and
                                                           Priscilla.
April 10, 1809
Jesse Harman Mitchell, born October 24, 1808, of Thomas Mitchell,
                                           of William, and Elinor.
April 11, 1809
John Johnson Crane, born Aug. 5, 1808, of John and Ann Crane.

April 17, 1809
Bennett Oliver,   born Jan. 10, 1802, of Nathaniel and Priscilla.

June 1, 1809
John Bonaparte McFaddon, born Jan. 10, 1802, of William & Margaret.

June 9, 1809
John Hanson Hollis, born Jan. 13, 1808, of Clarke and Cymelia.

June 25, 1808
Mary Ann Sunderland, born Jan. 20, 1806, of Benjamin & Elizabeth.
John Sunderland, born August 3, 1807, of same parents.
James Sunderland, born June 14, 1809, of same parents.

October 26, 1809
Joseph Johnson, born Sept. 11, 1809, of Frances Johnson - father not disclosed.
Jacob Collins, born Jan. 12, 1809, of Mahlon and Mary Collins.
Samuel Thomas, born May 6, 1806, of Joseph and Pamela Thomas.

October 28, 1809
Catharine Taylor, born Oct. 4, 1808, of Ashbury and Frances Taylor.

December 27, 1809
Betsy Knight, born Oct. 26, 1809, of William and Sarah Knight.

January 9, 1810
Mortimer Michael, born Jan. 2, 1808, of Daniel and Martha Michael.
Melville Michael, born Jan. 2, 1808 (same date), of same parents.
Matilda Michael, born July 3, 1809, of same parents.

March 3, 1810
Fanton Mercer Brown, born Dec. 24, 1809, of Jacob & Mary Brown.

March 8, 1810
Benedict Henry Hanson, born Dec. 23, 1809, of Benedict Hollis Hanson and Ann.

March 26, 1810
Margaret Miller, adult, born Sept. 8, 1780, of Joseph and Susanna.

April 5, 1810
Gregory Farmer Barnes, born Feb. 1, 1809, of Gregory and Elizabeth.
Elizabeth Barnes, born March 5, 1810, of same parents.

April 6, 1810
Susan Ann Hollis, adult, born Feb. 13, 1794, of William Hollis and Mary Combest.
Louisa Ann Greenlee, born March 6, 1810, of James and Mary Greenlee.

May 6, 1810
John Archer, born April 19, 1810, of Thomas and Elizabeth Archer.
James Phillips Archer, born same day, of same parents.

June 27, 1810
Peter Body, born Nov. 25, 1794, of Benjamin and Jane Body.

Page 345 Baptisms (continued)

June 27, 1810
Anne Body, born April 23, 1798, of Benjamin and Jane Body.

July 28, 1810
Frances Ann Armstrong, born July 11, 1810, of Robert and Hannah.

August 12, 1810
Mary Flaharty, born March 5, 1809, of Joshua and Mary Flaherty.
Coozine Johnson, born April 13, 1810, of William and Mary Johnson.

September 16, 1810
John Barnes Knight, born September 29, 1809, of Thomas Knight, of
William, and Sally.

October 8, 1810
Elizabeth Morgan, born Nov. 1, 1772, of William & Cassandra Morgan.
Cassandra Morgan Chew, born Nov. 12, 1796, of Thomas Sheredine Chew
and Elizabeth.
William Morgan Chew, born July 14, 1791, of same parents.

November 18, 1810
Winston Gorril, born July 7, 1782, of John and Avarilla Gorril.
Sophia Gorril, born Feb. 3, 1805, of Winston Gorril and Elizabeth
Mitchell.

January 8, 1811
Elinor Riely, born in December 1793, of Terence and Elinor Riely.

January 13, 1811
Sarah Ellet, born Sept. 28, 1809, of William and Faithful Ellet.
Jane Ellet, born April 11, 1804, of same parents.
Elizabeth, born in September 1801, Father not disclosed, mother
Priscilla.

January 20, 1811
Ann Weeks, born March 25, 1788, of Daniel and Mary Weeks.
Mary Weeks, born November 22, 1790, of same parents.
Daniel Weeks, born June 13, 1792, of same parents.
John Weeks, born September 2, 1794, of same parents.
Catharine Weeks, born November 6, 1796, of same parents.
Ezekiel Weeks, born March 17, 1799, of same parents.
James Weeks, born March 25, 1801, of same parents.
Sarah Weeks, born April 27, 1803, of same parents.
Martha Weeks, born September 3, 1806, of same parents.
Rachel Weeks, born May 30, 1809, of same parents.
Susanna Weeks, born September 30, 1810, of same parents.

January 25, 1811
Margaret Catherine Adlur(?), born May 27, 1810, of John & Margaret.

February 10, 1811
Belinda Slades, born April 6, 1803, of Josias and Lurena Slades.
Martha Slades, born January 12, 1805, of same parents.
Caroline Slades, born October 12, 1806, of same parents.
Elizabeth Slades, born July 28, 1808, of same parents.
Edwards Slades, born June 14, 1810, of same parents.

February 16, 1811
John Henry Chauncey, born No.v 1, 1809, of Garrett and Elizabeth.

March 24, 1811
Sarah Smith, born July 3, 1809, of James and Sarah Smith.

Page 346 Baptisms (continued)

March 24, 1811
Eliza Smith, born Dec. 3, 1810, of Richard and Mary Smith.
Rachel Jones, born Jan. 15, 1808, of Joseph and Mary Jones.

March 24, 1811
Elizabeth Jones, born May 3, 1810, of Joseph and Mary Jones.
George Ditto, born April 5, 1809, of Callender and Ann Ditto.

April 28, 1811
Sarah McClaskey, born Nov. 10, 1806, of David and Ann McClaskey.
William Henry McClaskey, born March 1, 1808, of same parents.
Mary McClaskey, born December 5, 1809, of same parents.

May 8, 1811
Catharine Regan, born March 19, 1806, of James and Mary Regan.

June 14, 1811
John James Madison Griffith, born Aug. 13, 1810, of James & Sarah.

June 27, 1811
Priscilla Ann Henderson, born June 13, 1811, of George and Charity.

July 14, 1811
Evan Evans, adult, born May 5, 1795, of Amos and Sarah Evans.

August 29, 1811
Thomas Brown, born Feb. 1, 1811, of Jacob and Mary Brown.

September 11, 1811
Jane Watts, born June 15, 1811, of Allen and Anna Watts.

September 26, 1811
John Armstrong Price, born May 13, 1810, of James and Isabella.

January 19, 1812
James Martha Phillips, born Sept. 29, 1809, of James and Sarah.

January 25, 1812
Ann Elizabeth Chauncey, born March 17, 1811, of George & Frances Rebecca.

February 2, 1812
James Osborne, born April 3, 1810, of William and Harriott Osborne.
Mary Susanna Osborne, born October 16, 1811, of same parents.

June 7, 1812
George Gould Patterson, born March 3, 1811, of William Presbury Patterson & Frances.

June 14, 1812
Susan Brown, born May 13, 1812, of Jacob Brown & Mary his late wife.
Carvil Osborne Hollis, born February 23, 1807, of James Hollis (dec'd) & Sarah lately his wife.
James William Hollis, born March 3, 1812, of same parents.
Garrett Knight, born Feb. 1, 1811, of Thomas and Sally Knight.
Rebecca Knight, born April 11, 1812, of same parents.

July 18, 1812
Sarah Brewer, born October 7, 1800, of James and Margaret Brewer.
Aquila Henry Michael, born March 5, 1811, of Daniel and Martha.

September 5, 1812
Juliet Ann Slaids, born March 8, 1812, of Josias and Lurena Slaids.

September 6, 1812
Eliza Johnson, born April 3, 1810, of Thomas and Elizabeth Johnson.

September 6, 1812
Elijah Johnson, born April 3, 1810, of Thomas & Elizabeth Johnson.
Joseph Frazer, born February 9, 1799, of Samuel & Penelope Frazer.
Elihu Frazer, born February 13, 1801, of same parents.
Margaret Frazer, born May 14, 1802, of same parents.
Priscilla Frazer, born May 14, 1802, of same parents.

Page 347   Baptisms (continued)

September 6, 1812
Moses Frazer, born June 17, 1804, of Samuel and Penelope Frazer.
Julia Ann Frazer, born June 13, 1808, of same parents.
Sarah Jane Frazer, born April 12, 1812, of same parents.
November 16, 1812
Mary Ann Price, born Sept. 27, 1812, of James and Isabella Price.
November 26, 1812
Mary Gay, born October 16, 1805, of Henry and Mary Gay.
January 31, 1813
Evelina McClaskey, born Dec. 5, 1809, of David and Ann McClaskey.
February 14, 1813
Harriott Susan Arnold, born Feb. 19, 1796, of William and Susan.
Sally Sutton, born January 2, 1799, of Jonathan and Sally.
Mary Loney, born February 24, 1788, of William and Mary.
Thomas Peregrine Frisby Forwood, born Feb. 23, 1811, of John & Mary.
William Loney Forwood, born February 10, 1805, of same parents.
April 3, 1813
Ann Maria Adlum, born March 29, 1813, of John and Margaret.
April 5, 1813
William Knight, born April 1, 1813, of William and Sarah.
May 9, 1813
Garrett Chauncey, born July 12, 1812, of Garrett and Elizabeth.
September 9, 1813
James Geary, born April 11, 1813, of Everett & Mary his late wife.
October 13, 1813
Mary Elizabeth Kelly, born June 19, 1812, of James and Elizabeth.
November 6, 1813
Jesse Dawson Small, born Sept. 10, 1813, of David Small and
                                                Elizabeth Dawson.
November 26, 1813
Avarilla Hollis, born June 1, 1810, of Clarke and Milla Hollis.
Martha Osborne Hollis, born January 19, 1813, of same parents.
January 31, 1814
Ashbury Cord Taylor, born Feb. 25, 1811, of Ashbury and Frances.
February 5, 1814
Theodore Edward Chauncey, born Dec. 18, 1813, of George and Frances
February 15, 1814   Rebecca.
Mary Hawkins, born November 14, 1801, of Mathew and Sarah Hawkins.
William Alfred Patterson, born August 13, 1812, of William Presbury
                                                Patterson and Frances.

April 22, 1814
William Carvil Cunningham, born Dec. 4, 1807, of Crispin & Elizabeth.
John Archy Beatty Cunningham, born Oct. 24, 1810, of same parents.

March 18, 1814
Mary Ann Michael, born January 13, 1814, of Daniel and Martha.

June 19, 1814
Robert Thomas Allen, born Sept. 26, 1813, of Richard and Sarah.

September 3, 1814
Walter Harward, born January 26, 1814, of Charles and Mary.

October 11, 1814
Archibald Armstrong, born Dec. 8, 1812, of Robert and Hannah.

October 25, 1814
Hannah Price, born June 2, 1811, of Robert and Mary his late wife.
Daniel Price, born January 17, 1813, of same parents.

December 29, 1814
Jane Turk, born about Spring, 1792, of Esan and Catharine.
James Madison Cunningham, born July 10, 1809, of Walter Cunningham and Cassandra his late wife.

Page 348 Baptisms (continued)

December 29, 1814
William Washington Cunningham, born February 22, 1812, of Walter Cunningham & Cassandra his late wife.
George Petit Cunningham, born November 11, 1813, of same parents.

February 16, 1815
Catharine Fulford, born Dec. 24, 1814, of William and Mary Fulford.
James Hervey Osborne, Adult, born Oct. 18, 1795, of John & Elizabeth.
Ann Osborne, Adult, born June 30, 1799, of same parents.
Henry Fielding Arnold, Adult, born Aug. 27, 1797, of Wm. & Susanna.
Mary Arnold, Adult, born August 7, 1799, of same parents.
Sophia Western Arnold, Adult, born April 22, 1801, of same parents.
Delia Arnold, born August 11, 1808, of same parents.

July 6, 1815
James William Kelly, born Jan. 19, 1814, of James and Elizabeth.

August 1, 1815
David Bowyer, born Sept. 8, 1813, of David and Sarah.
Mary Ann Bowyer, born March 12, 1815, of same parents.

September 28, 1815
Martha Elizabeth Day, born August 3, 1806, of Joshua and Sarah.
Mary Ann Day, born October 16, 1807, of same parents.
Belinda Day, born February 26, 1810. of same parents.
Joshua James Day, born March 1, 1814, of same parents.
Hannah Price, born February 2, 1815, of James and Isabella.

October 2, 1815
Ann Miller (no date of birth given), of Joseph Miller.
Elizabeth Chew (no birthdate), of Thomas Sheridine Chew & Elizabeth.
Margaret Chew (no birthdate), of same parents.
Elizabeth Louisa Shields, born Mar. 22, 1810, of John and Sarah.
Cassandra Fulford Ashton, born Apr. 9, 1813, of John and Susanna.
Catharine Bull Ashton, born August 26, 1815, of same parents.

August 30, 1816
Sarah Martha Chauncey, born Apr. 15, 1815, of George & Frances Rebecca.

Page 349   Registry of Marriages in Saint George's
            Parish, Harford County, Maryland, during
            the Ministry of the Revd. John Allen,
            commencing in the year 1795

"Days of Marriage" / "Names of Persons Married"	"Authority"
March 19, 1795, David Crane and Susanna Osborne	License
May 29, 1795, James Jones and Mary Stockdale	License
August 13, 1795, George Davis and Elizabeth Scott	License
November 12, 1795, Jacob Michael and Mary Everett	License
November 26, 1795, Cyrus Osborne and Martha Warfield	License
December 29, 1795, Richard Brooke and Cassandra Prigg	License
January 28, 1796, Carvil Matthews and Ann Matthews	License
January 28, 1796, Thomas Chesholm and Sarah Rigdon	License
March 17, 1796, Daniel Hagerty and Elizabeth Jones	License
March 22, 1796, John Otley and Lydia Dean	License
March 22, 1796, John Hanna and Ann Rogers	License
July 28, 1796, William Shidle and Mary McGill	License
September 1, 1796, Laurence Harp and Mary Delany	License
September 18, 1796, Samuel Wilson and Frances Jones	Asked
November 10, 1796, John McGill and Martha Brazier	License
December 7, 1796, William Holmes and Jane Cook	License
December 22, 1796, William Mitchell and Sarah Mitchell	License
January 22, 1797, Skipwith Cole and Elizabeth Gilbert	License
February 14, 1797, William McComas and Mary McComas	License
March 30, 1797, John Stricker and Catharine Wilson	License
April 4, 1797, James Cole and Catharine Holles	License
April 18, 1797, Robert Gover and Martha Wheeler	License
April 20, 1797, John Jolley and Elizabeth Dallam	License
April 20, 1797, John Wilson and Norry Brady	Asked
May 4, 1797, Joshua Wood and Ann Osborne	License
May 23, 1797, Edward Bean and Elizabeth Wood	License
May 25, 1797, John Burke and Susanna Templeton	License
June 1, 1797, Levi Culver and Elizabeth Stallings	License
June 15, 1797, George Duncan and Sarah Evans	License
June 19, 1797, Nicholas Allender and Sarah Bradford	License

Page 350

July 6, 1797, William Smith and Elizabeth Mahon	License
July 9, 1797, William Michael and Ann Judd	License
July 20, 1797, Robert Hawkins and Ann Mitchell	License
August 10, 1797, Reason Dorsey and Frances Cromwell	License

"Days of Marriage"	"Names of Persons Married"	"Authority"
August 15, 1797, William Fox and Mary Carrol		License
August 17, 1797, Adam Johnson and Johanna Gilbert		License
August 31, 1797, James Brewer and Margaret Young		Asked
September 7, 1797, Thomas Annis and Mary Dunn		License
September 14, 1797, James Billingslea and Elizabeth Matthews		License
October 1, 1797, William Knight and Sarah Robison		License
November 2, 1797, Nathan Gordon and Delia Stevenson		License
December 3, 1797, Roger Boyce and Hannah Day		License
January 23, 1798, Amos Cord and Elizabeth Swaine		License
February 4, 1798, Thomas Zara and Elizabeth Dulany		Asked
February 4, 1798, James Bevard and Amelia Chance		License
February 11, 1798, Isaac Whitaker and Margaret Everett		License
February 13, 1798, John Prosser and Sarah Hall		License
February 13, 1798, Joshua Hartley and Ann Bayne		License
February 15, 1798, Richard Mitchell and Priscilla Gilbert		License
March 1, 1798, Nathanael Moreton and Sarah Copeland		License
March 5, 1798, Peter Night and Sarah Cline		Asked
April 8, 1798, James Holles and Sarah Osborne		License
April 12, 1798, James More and Rebecca Crabson		Asked
April 26, 1798, Bowyer Grace and Mary Brooks		License
May 31, 1798, Richard Graves and Charlotte Dorsey		License
June 3, 1798, Owen Roberts and Jane Vansick		License
June 17, 1798, "Martha Molton and Sarah Boyd"		Asked
July 17, 1798, Thomas Brooks and Sarah Blake		License
September 6, 1798, John Mitchell and Martha Matticks		Asked
September 18, 1798, John Deeran and Deborah Dormer		Asked
November 8, 1798, Patrick McLaughlin and Ann Chandley		License
November 8, 1798, George Webb and Margaret Baughman		License
November 8, 1798, Joseph Adlum and Ann McPhail		License

Page 351

(Last six entries on page 350 were repeated on page 351)

November 29, 1798, Jervis Gilbert and Sophia Cole		License
December 20, 1798, Nicholas York and Margaret Sutton		License
January 13, 1799, Marshall Lee and Rachel Blake		License
February 6, 1799, Charles McLaughlin and Margaret Armstrong		License
February 7, 1799, John Cozens and Elizabeth Jackson		License
February 7, 1799, Paca Smith and Sarah Phillips		License
February 21, 1799, Elijah Small and Rebecca Jemmison		License

"Days of Marriage"	"Names of Persons Married"	"Authority"
February 28, 1799,	Ralph Higginbotham & Isabella Presbury	License
March 12, 1799,	John Harvey and Hannah Johnson	License
March 28, 1799,	Richard Dallam and Priscilla Paca	License
April 7, 1799,	Thomas Adlum and Sarah McCaskey	License
May 5, 1799,	Thomas Rand and Mary Burns	Asked
July 24, 1799,	Andrew Martin and Elizabeth Evett	License
August 15, 1799,	William Perry and Mary Griffith	License
October 23, 1799,	Richard Johnson and Mary Herbert	License
October 29, 1799,	Joseph Thomas and Hannah Carty	License
November 7, 1799,	William Chambers and Elizabeth Doyle	License
November 16, 1799,	Jesse Cromwell and Margaret Paca	License
November 19, 1799,	William Lester and Elizabeth Fawcet	License
November 21, 1799,	John Dunning and Lydia Wilson	License
December 19, 1799,	John St. Clair and Temperance West	License
December 29, 1799,	Moses Thomas and Nancy McClain	Asked
January 14, 1800,	James Curry and Nancy Thompson	Asked
January 16, 1800,	James Hamby and Ann Williams	License
February 6, 1800,	James Taylor and Sarah Aitken	License
February 25, 1800,	James Lee and Elizabeth Lee	License
March 20, 1800,	William Rodgers and Mary Hanna	License

Page 352

April 3, 1800,	John Dougherty and Ann Chauncey	License
April 13, 1800,	James Greenly and Mary Redman	License
April 20, 1800,	Robert Ingham and Lydia Yorke	License
April 27, 1800,	Thomas Greenly and Mary Howard	License
June 15, 1800,	Charles McComas and Mary Gilbert	License
June 19, 1800,	George Henderson and Charity Cole	License
June 26, 1800,	John Dutton and Amelia Carman	License
August 7, 1800,	Mark Cummin and Mary McDole	Asked
August 12, 1800,	Hugh Haughey and Susan Harwood	License
August 14, 1800,	William Hamby and Susanna Cowan	License
August 14, 1800,	Peter Ross and Arabella Cantler	Asked
September 21, 1800,	Joseph Degeon and Margaret Gorril	Asked
September 23, 1800,	John Nelson and Rebecca Ann Munroe	License
September 29, 1800,	George Foster and Mary McPhail	License
October 2, 1800,	Parker Gilbert, Jr. and Martha Hughes	License
October 2, 1800,	Jonas Stephenson and Mary Dunsheath	License

"Days of Marriage"	"Names of Persons Married"	"Authority"
October 16, 1800,	Roger Matthews and Constant Forwood	License
November 27, 1800,	William Mahon and Anne Jones	License
December 24, 1800,	Isaac Allen and Mary Herring	License
December 25, 1800,	Richard Taylor and Eleanor Courtney	License
December 25, 1800,	Nicholas Lewis and Mary Mackie	License
January 15, 1801,	Edward Stiles and Mary Angell	License
January 31, 1801,	Israel Bowman and Elizabeth Day	License
February 1, 1801,	Micajah Debruler and Sarah York Howard	License
February 5, 1801,	John Henson and Matilda Courtney	License
February 5, 1801,	Joseph Prigg and Mary Cox	License
February 19, 1801,	William Tomson and Margaret Williams	Asked
March 1, 1801,	Frederic Mitchell and Pamelia Trago	License
March 5, 1801,	James West and Sarah Murphey	License
March 8, 1801,	William McKibbin and Elizabeth Dormer	License
March 19, 1801,	John Courtney and Clemency Mitchell	License
March 26, 1801,	Edward Miller and Sarah Miller	License
April 3, 1801,	Philip Fulton and Sarah Hanna	License

Page 353

May 12, 1801,	William Thomas and Catharine McClain	Asked
July 2, 1801,	John Magaw and Phebe Gilbert	License
July 8, 1801,	Dennis Brisland and Nancy Ronay	License
July 30, 1801,	George Kenney and Mary Daugherty	License
September 24, 1801,	William Fields and Betsey Truelove	Asked
October 29, 1801,	Nathan Swain and Nancy Nowland	License
November 17, 1801,	James Price and Isabella Armstrong	License
November 19, 1801,	Aquila Osborne and Patty Michael	License
December 3, 1801,	Benjamin Hobbs and Rachel Thomson	License
December 15, 1801,	James Madder and Comfort Rigdon	License
December 17, 1801,	James Hughes and Hannah Gilbert	License
December 24, 1801,	William Bradley and Rebecca Stallions	License
December 31, 1801,	James Chamberlaine and Margaret Lucas	License
January 2, 1802,	Joseph Steele and Susanna Wood	License
January 28, 1802,	John Nowland and Ann Garaway	License
February 2, 1802,	John Pogue and Ann Greenland	License
February 4, 1802,	James Brown and Ann Baldwin	License
March 4, 1802,	Thomas Lotton and Sarah Wilson	License
March 4, 1802,	Ashbury Taylor and Frances Shody	License

"Days of Marriage"	"Names of Persons Married"	"Authority"
March 16, 1802,	James Johnson and Sarah Mason	License
March 16, 1802,	Morris Malsby and Mary Lee	License
March 19, 1802,	Gideon Herbert and Mary Curley	License
April 1, 1802,	Henry Gay and Mary Lanagan	License
April 6, 1802,	Roger Boyce Cowan and Sarah Chauncey	License
April 8, 1802,	William Rogers and Jane Rogers	License
April 11, 1802,	James Jackson and Priscilla Johnson	Asked
April 20, 1802,	Josias Slade and Lurana Morgan	License
August 10, 1802,	William Frost and Sarah Stollcup	License
September 9, 1802,	Abraham Johnson and Polly Donovan	License
September 23, 1802,	Timothy Kean and Harriott Baylis	License
November 4, 1802,	John Dunn and Milcah Courtney	License
November 7, 1802,	Jesse Mahone and Susanna Brown	License
December 9, 1802,	Micajah All and Rachel Cannon	License

Page 354

December 30, 1802,	Jacob Washington Giles & Martha Phillips	License
January 13, 1803,	Clark Hollis and Cymelia Lancaster	License
March 1, 1803,	James Botts and Ann Hughes	License
March 24, 1803,	William Shearswood and Hannah Brazier	License
April 14, 1803,	William Divers and Elizabeth Hannah	License
May 12, 1803,	John Courtney and Sarah Deaver	License
June 9, 1803,	Thomas Archer and Elizabeth Phillips	License
August 11, 1803,	James Griffith and Sarah Cox	License
August 18, 1803,	James Fulton and Susanna Trago	License
September 25, 1803,	James Harris and Ann McNiece	License
November 5, 1803,	John Corse and Susanna Coale	License
November 24, 1803,	Samuel Winchester and Eliza Gover	License
December 8, 1803,	John Forwood and Mary Loney	License
December 15, 1803,	Parker Gilbert and Elizabeth Henderson	License
January 19, 1804,	William Williams and Lina Andrews	License
January 19, 1804,	Amos Gilbert and Sarah Bailey	License
January 22, 1804,	Thomas Knight and Sarah Barns	License
January 29, 1804,	Jeremiah Rogers and Priscilla Miller	License
February 2, 1804,	Henry Vansicle and Cordelia Chauncey	License
February 9, 1804,	James Taylor and Susanna Kimble	License
February 9, 1804,	Reuben Sutton and Ann Armstrong	License
March 15, 1804,	John Vanzant and Ann Pennington	License
April 19, 1804,	William Magaw and Caroline Cannon	License

"Days of Marriage"	"Names of Persons Married"	"Authority"
May 16, 1804,	David Bowyer and Sally Williams	License
June 18, 1804,	William Fulford and Mary Frances Patterson	License
June 24, 1804,	Scott Hughes and Mary Gilbert Gilbert	License
July 18, 1804,	Barnet Harper and Milcah Dawes	License
August 12, 1804,	Richard Everist and Sarah Michael	License
September 6, 1804,	David Cantler and Mary Lee	Asked
September 27, 1804,	Zaccheus O. Bond and Mary Ann Lee	License
December 24, 1804,	James Kirk and Isabella Wiley	License
December 27, 1804,	Andrew Thompson and Mary Cunningham	License

Page 355   Registry of Marriages for Saint George's Parish
Commencing January 1st, 1805

January 10, 1805,	Isaiah Taylor and Cath. Kimble	License
January 10, 1805,	Edward Griffith and Cordelia Hall	License
January 31, 1805,	Peter Murray and Elizabeth Bare	License
March 28, 1805,	Arthur Curry and Sarah Cain	License
April 11, 1805,	Mahlon Collins and Mary Greenlee	License
August 15, 1805,	Joseph Thomas and Pamelia Collins	License
August 24, 1805,	William Middleditch & Nancy Gib Townsley	Asked
September 5, 1805,	William Smithson and Margaret Lee	License
September 5, 1805,	David Small and Mary Dawson	License
October 17, 1805,	Daniel Pogue and Alice Crapson	License
October 17, 1805,	Joshua Green and Elizabeth Myers	License
October 24, 1805,	Samuel Everist and Mary Rigdon	License
December 5, 1805,	Robert Cantler and Margaret Middleditch	License
December 24, 1805,	Cyrus Osborne and Sarah Nelson	License
December 26, 1805,	Jesse Nowland and Elizabeth Crabson	Asked
December 26, 1805,	Thomas Lee and Fanny Andrews	License
January 16, 1806,	John Mitchell and Hannah Davis	License
January 30, 1806,	George Taylor and Florella Kimble	License
February 1, 1806,	Hampton Gilbert and Henrietta Miller	"Alleged consent of mdsters."
March 27, 1806,	Matthew Thompson and Mary Ellis	License
March 27, 1806,	William Gackett and Sally Jamison	License
April 10, 1806,	Amos Cord and Sarah Howard	License
April 24, 1806,	William Cronin and Margaret Whitaker	License
May 22, 1806,	Bennett Taylor and Mary Deaver	License
May 22, 1806,	Reuben Leigh and Nancy Williams	License
June 18, 1806,	William Russell and Margaret Kinsley	License
June 29, 1806,	Patrick Lockery and Mary Kenny	Asked

"Days of Marriage"   "Names of Persons Married"   "Authority"
May 29, 1806, Thomas H. Gray and Julian Crow   License
August 10, 1806, James McGaw and Sarah Bennet   License
September 29, 1806, Nicholas Allender and Elizabeth Morris   License

Page 356

September 30, 1806, John Murphy and Martha Greenlee   License
October 2, 1806, James Taylor and Hester Saunders   License
October 21, 1806, John Rodgers and Minerva Dennison   License
November 4, 1806, John Day Lewis and Sophia White Hall   License
November 13, 1806, Thomas Miller and Elizabeth Robinson   License
November 25, 1806, Asbury Cord and Ann Rigdon   License
February 5, 1807, Bennet Vansicle and Susanna Chauncey   License
February 19, 1807, George Lytle and Mary Cole   License
March 31, 1807, Archibald Dorsey and Mary Patterson Luckey   License
May 31, 1807, Thomas Brooks and Elizabeth Sprucebanks   License
August 27, 1807, Joshua Deaver and Martha Kimble   License
September 17, 1807, William Wilson and Susanna Webster   License
September 22, 1807, Nathan Hughes and Elizabeth Maclain   License
October 1, 1807, Amos Osborne and Susanna Mitchell   License
November 17, 1807, Isaac Wilson and Mary Brookes   License
December 10, 1807, William Stump and Margaret Miller   License
December 27, 1807, Benedict Hanson and Ann Matthews   License
December 29, 1807, Evan Mitchell and Elizabeth Webster   License
March 10, 1808, Joseph Mitchell and Mary Lynch   License
May 12, 1808, William Worthington and Rebecca Richardson   License
June 14, 1808, Cornelius Cole and Martha Osborne   License
June 23, 1808, William Paca and Harriott Matthews   License
June 28, 1808, William Brookes Stokes and
          Henrietta Maria Chamberlaine Hughes   License
August 18, 1808, James Phillips and Sarah Phillips Wilmer   License
September 22, 1808, John Hays and Elizabeth Sampson   License
October 6, 1808, Basil Moxley and Rachel Greenlee   License
December 1, 1808, John Kimble and Nancy Foard   License
December 22, 1808, Levi Howard and Ezana Gallion   License
December 29, 1808, Jacob Michael and Susanna Crane   License
December 29, 1808, Noble Rider and Artridge Cannon   License
January 8, 1809, Hoshea Barnes and Elizabeth Lester   License
January 17, 1809, Jacob Brown and Mary Brown   License

Page 357

"Days of Marriage"	"Names of Persons Married"	"Authority"
January 19, 1809,	George Herbert and Levina Kennedy	License
January 26, 1809,	Garrett Chauncey and Elizabeth Garretson Vansicle	License
February 2, 1809,	Robert Tragor and Sarah Gallion	License
March 19, 1809,	Isaac Montgomery and Charlotte Aikers	Asked
April 17, 1809,	Nathaniel Oliver and Priscilla Crawford	Asked
May 4, 1809,	James Taylor and Charlotte Dulany	License
June 1, 1809,	John Hopkins and Sarah Wilson	License
June 1, 1809,	George Norris and Margaret Riely	License
June 6, 1809,	William Osborn and Harriott Barnes	License
June 8, 1809,	William Bolster and Frances Hollis	License
August 15, 1809,	Simon Brown and Sarah Jones	License
October 10, 1809,	George Cornacle and Ann McFadden	License
October 26, 1809,	Elias Nowland and Charlotte Collins	License
October 28, 1809,	Robert Armstrong and Hannah Kimble	License
November 2, 1809,	James Kelly and Elizabeth Lyons	License
December 21, 1809,	Hudson Wood and Frances Matthews	License
January 18, 1810,	Jamces Paca and Ann Rieley	License
January 28, 1810,	William Allender and Mary Foster	License
February 20, 1810,	William Presbury Patterson and Frances Gould	License
March 1, 1810,	Thomas Shay and Clarissa Everist	License
March 8, 1810,	Thomas Turner and Mary Price	License
April 5, 1810,	James Riggin and Mary Parsons	License
May 17, 1810,	Robert Price and Mary Gubbin	License
May 24, 1810,	Samuel Taylor and Sarah Stricklen	License
June 7, 1810,	James Strong and Susan Combess	License
August 30, 1810,	James Morris Magnus and Jane Smith Reed	License
February 19, 1811,	James Lee Morgan and Susan Wheeler	License
June 27, 1811,	William Bradford and Susan Drew	License
August 29, 1811,	Thomas Peregrine Frisby and Susanna Mahon	License
September 26, 1811,	John Price and Nancy Kean	License
November 28, 1811,	Joseph Hopkins and Sarah Cox	License
December 3, 1811,	Charles Vincent and Cassandra Webster	License

Page 358

December 26, 1811,	Bennett Stewart and Rebecca McGay	License
January 2, 1812,	John Johnson and Mary Hayward	License
January 23, 1812,	Aquila Drew and Martha Nelson	License

"Days of Marriage"	"Names of Persons Married"	"Authority"
February 18, 1812,	Thomas Clarke and Hannah Evans	License
March 12, 1812,	Everit Gairy and Mary Hall	License
March 19, 1812,	John Barnes and Elizabeth Barnes	License
March 26, 1812,	Hosea Barnes and Mary Garretson	License
May 31, 1812,	John Kirk and Hannah Beatty	License
October 8, 1812,	William Trigger and Sarah Meeks	License
November 26, 1812,	Charles Harward and Mary Brown	License
January 7, 1813,	Nathan Hughes and Frances Taylor	License
January 10, 1813,	Joshua Wood and Hannah Bradford	License
February 7, 1813,	George Veasey and Rebecca Barnes	License
March 4, 1813,	William Dulen Reason and Sarah Jones	License
October 10, 1813,	William Fletcher and Phebe Gallion	License
St. John's, Oct. 19, 1813,	James McCormick & Elizabeth Henderson	Lic.
St. John's, Oct. 21, 1813,	Richard Frisby Hollis and Catharine Theresa Norris	License
November 18, 1813,	George Griffith and Emily Periman	License
November 25, 1813,	James Reason Rockhold and Martha Hollis	License
December 16, 1813,	James Chamberlaine Hughes and Anna Maria Lee	Lic.
January 30, 1814,	Jesse Nowland and Susan Taylor	Asked
February 17, 1814,	William Morgan Chew and Anne Webster Richardson	Lic.
March 3, 1814,	John Ruff and Elizabeth Nelson	License
April 10, 1814,	James Taylor and Mary Cannon	License
May 12, 1814,	Richard Cummins Stockton and Eliza Potts Hughes	Lic.
June 16, 1814,	Thomas William Jackson and Hester Touchstone	Lic.
July 14, 1814,	John Cannon and Rebecca Yokely	License
October 11, 1814,	James Dennison and Mary Cunningham	License
December 22, 1814,	Ephraim Arnold and Sophia Barnes	License
December 29, 1814,	Walter Cunningham and Jane Turk	License
February 16, 1815,	Benjamin Cole and Elizabeth Arnold	License
March 2, 1815,	John Clark and Rebecca Smith	License
April 6, 1815,	Ignatius Gibson and Mary Sutton	License
July 27, 1815,	Matthew Hawkins and Martha Perryman	License

Page 359   Registry of Funerals in Saint George's Parish Harford County, Maryland, during the Ministry of the Revd. John Allen, commencing in the year 1795

"Days of Funeral"	"Names of Persons Buried"
July 20, 1795	Livingston
August 14, 1795	Francis Holland
April 1, 1796	Jane Hollis
April 8, 1796	John Brown
April 9, 1796	Ann Everett

"Days of Funeral"	"Names of Persons Buried"
October 2, 1796	George Gallion
October 9, 1796	_____Nowland
October 28, 1796	Elizabeth Dormer
November 4, 1796	Harriot Carlile
December , 1796	_____Garrett
April 24, 1797	Hannah Rumsey
May 21, 1797	Benjamin Chauncy
May 27, 1797	_____Jones
May 28, 1797	Richard Wilmott
June 6, 1797	Cassandra Brooke
November 6, 1797	Betsy Gilbert
November 7, 1797	Susanna Scott
November 22, 1797	Mary Gazzoway
February 2, 1798	_____Geale
February 4, 1798	Mary Prichett
February 4, 1798	James Adams
February 19, 1798	William Osborne
March 5, 1798	_____Matthews
July 3, 1798	Mary Chauncey
July 12, 1798	Richard Webb
September 9, 1798	John Brown
September 12, 1798	Charlotte Nowland
October 29, 1798	Thomas Giles
November 13, 1798	Rebecca Stevenson

Page 360

December 6, 1798	Elizabeth Allender
December 25, 1798	Thomas Savin
February 7, 1799	Jesse Dawson
March 7, 1799	John Hanson
May 5, 1799	Sarah Morris
May 23, 1799	Catharine Nelson
May 25, 1799	Joseph West
June 2, 1799	Henry Austin Everett
(no date given)	Alexander Garrett
September 3, 1799	John Sydney Hall
September 26, 1799	Gideon Dennison
October 13, 1799	Frances Susanna Hall
October 20, 1799	Ann West
October 28, 1799	Martha Gilbert
December 10, 1799	Elizabeth Wells
January 13, 1800	Martha Webster
January 20, 1800	Avarilla Powell
January 31, 1800	James Hall
March 9, 1800	Joseph Webster
May 19, 1800	George Bradford
July 20, 1800	Sarah Prichett
September 8, 1800	John Barney Hayward
September 9, 1800	Ford Barns
October 15, 1800	Mary Monks
November 13, 1800	_____Ruff
November 19, 1800	Mary Osborne
February 13, 1801	Henry Hayward
March 7, 1801	Martha Brown
March 15, 1801	Jonas Stevenson
April 16, 1801	William Beatty
May 4, 1801	Mitchell Stewart

"Days of Funeral"	"Names of Persons Buried"
July 25, 1801	Harriott Coffield
September 13, 1801	Edward Hall

Page 361

September 16, 1801	Henry Vansicle
November 8, 1801	Conna Matthews
November 19, 1801	_____Dallam
November 28, 1801	Frisby Dorsey
November 29, 1801	Benjamin Chauncey
December 15, 1801	Fanton Brown
December 31, 1801	George Chauncey
January 18, 1802	Benjamin Osborne
January 26, 1802	Alexander Lawson Smith
February 4, 1802	Elizabeth Carlile
February 7, 1802	John Hall Hughes
April 28, 1802	Mary Brown
June 19, 1802	Jacob Greenfield
July 9, 1802	Richard Deeran
September 29, 1802	John Phillips
October 1, 1802	John Sears
December 22, 1802	John Carlile
January 7, 1803	Elizabeth Greenfield
January 8, 1803	Samuel Griffith
January 23, 1803	Michael Gilbert
March 31, 1803	Mary Michael
April 4, 1803	John Frisby
April 11, 1803	North Meeks
June 19, 1803	Alexander Flanagan
February 16, 1804	John Hall
June 26, 1804	Martha Hall
June 29, 1804	Sophia Morgan
August 10, 1804	Thomas Hall
November 25, 1804	_____Magaw
December 6, 1804	Aquila Michael

Page 362

March 4, 1805	Joanna Giles
April 9, 1805	Sarah Hawkins
May 10, 1805	John Hughes
October 28, 1805	Cordelia Griffith
December 8, 1805	Jacob Collins
December 15, 1805	James Osborne
December 27, 1805	Carvel Matthews
January 14, 1806	Nicholas Gazzoway
June 22, 1806	Joseph Everist
August 3, 1806	Bennett Matthews
August 26, 1806	Bathera Patterson
September 22, 1806	Susanna Risteau
November 25, 1806	John Michael
December 10, 1806	Frances Garretson
January 2, 1807	John Brown
January 18, 1807	Thomas Johnson
March 17, 1807	Elinor Brown
April 5, 1807	Garret Brown
July 9, 1807	Mary Willmott
August 5, 1807	William Loney

"Days of Funeral"	"Names of Persons Buried"
August 18, 1807	Thomas Hall
November 27, 1807	Stephen Kimble
December 3, 1807	Martha Griffith
December 30, 1807	Elizabeth Allen
February 7, 1808	Ann Cox
February 28, 1808	Thomas Brown
March 12, 1808	James White Hall
March 13, 1808	George Patterson
March 27, 1808	Gregory Barnes
April 2, 1808	Gabriel Christie
September 20, 1808	John Rodgers

Page 363

April 18, 1809	Joseph Greenfield
September 14, 1809	John Day Lewis
October 11, 1809	John Chauncey
December 24, 1809	Avarilla Frances Griffith
December 28, 1809	Jacob Forwood
January 5, 1810	James Garretson
February 22, 1810	Roger Mathews
February 27, 1810	Elizabeth Stewart
March 22, 1810	Elizabeth Barnes
April 12, 1810	Susanna Brown
October 22, 1810	Peregrine Nowland
October 28, 1810	Milcah Hall
November 8, 1810	Harriott Paca
November 11, 1810	James Osborne
November 16, 1810	Mary Everist
January 18, 1811	Robert Magaw
February 15, 1811	John Osborne
February 17, 1811	Reuben Leigh
April 7, 1811	Sarah McCandless
May 4, 1811	William Frisby
June 15, 1811	James Michael
June 28, 1811	Susanna McDaniel
July 7, 1811	Thomas Lyons
August 13, 1811	Ann Wood
August 16, 1811	John Matthews
October 3, 1811	Albert Nowland
November 2, 1811	John Allen - service performed by the Revd. George D. S. Handy
December 27, 1811	Dorothy Allen (as above)
December 29, 1811	James McDaniel
February 13, 1812	James Phillips
March 7, 1812	James Grey
May 9, 1812	Jacob Hall
June 14, 1812	Mary Brown

Page 364

January 12, 1813	Edward Giles
February 26, 1813	Ann Monks
May 20, 1813	Nestor Chauncey
June 20, 1813	Mary Geary
July 16, 1813	Garrett Chauncey
August 4, 1813	Rebecca Ann Nelson

216

"Days of Funeral"	"Names of Persons Buried"
October 31, 1813	Kerenhapuck Elliott
October 31, 1813	Samuel Webb
November 3, 1813	Ann McLaughlin
November 9, 1813	Matthew Snody
November 29, 1813	Matthew Hawkins
December 4, 1813	Harriott Hall
April 18, 1814	Josias Michael
June 19, 1814	William Knight
October 13, 1814	Catharine Stark
December 24, 1814	Thomas Peregrine Frisby
February 17, 1815	Henry Vansicle
February 20, 1815	Archibald Beatty
March 26, 1815	Sarah Barnes
April 4, 1815	John Hall Griffith
April 10, 1815	Alexander C. Griffith
April 13, 1815	Mary Goldsmith Davis
May 9, 1815	John Forwood
May 23, 1815	Jacob Giles
June 14, 1815	Ann Lawder
September 22, 1815	Samuel Stokes
September 25, 1815	Catharine Fulford

Page 365 Baptisms (Queen Caroline Anne Arundel)

June 12, 1805
Rachel Boston, born Feb., 1805, of Chas. and Nan. Boston
                                         "Neg. Rd. G. Stockett"
Sophia Cooke, born Feb., 1805, of Chas. and Nelly Cooke
                                         "Free Black"
July 28, 1798
Ann Eliza Maxwell, born May 12, 1798 of Moses and Ann.
George Chauncey, born April 27, 1798, of George and Frances
                                         Rebecca.
Henry Lambert Wilmer, born March 30, 1798, of William and
                                         Kitty.
May 21, 1799
Thomas Gassoway, born Dec. 2, 1798, of Thomas Gassoway
                               Howard and Martha Susanna.
May 27, 1799
Emiline Carelia Hughes, born Apr. 21, 1799 of Wm. & Elizth.
September 12, 1799
William Taylor, born Mar. 10, 1799, of Jesse and Mary.
Sarah Hudson, born Mar. 31, 1799, of James and Dorothy.
October 13, 1799
Ann Sophia Dorsey, born about 1780, of Greenberry & Sophia.
November 10, 1799
Micah Gilbert McComas, born Nov, 18, 1798, of Aaron and
                                         Martha.
March, 1800
Temperance Fuller, born Jan. 16, 1800, of Samuel & Elizth.
June 30, 1800
Elizabeth Bishop, born Feb. 1, 1800, of Wm. and Catharine.

October 17, 1800
Edward Treadaway, born Dec. 15, 1783, of Thomas and Christina.
Sarah Treadaway, born November 26, 1776, of same parents.
Christina Saunders, born May 27, 1752, of Edward and Christina.
Mary Treadaway, born March 6, 1786, of Thomas and Christina.
Thomas Treadaway, born November 8, 1781, of same parents.
Ann Treadaway, born May 12, 1792, of same parents.
John Norris Treadaway, born February 26, 1796, of same parents.

November 10, 1800
Sarah Row, born February 14, 1800, of Conrad and Mary.
Mary Ann Cox, born May 7, 1799, of Joseph and Elizabeth.
Susanna Robertson, born Nov. 2, 1799, of William and Mary.

April 26, 1801
William Truss, born Apr. 9, 1790, of Wm. and Catharine his late wife.
Harriott Truss, born May 11, 1796, of William and Mary.
Catharine Truss, born Dec. 22, 1799, of William and Mary.
Thomas Howard, born April 12, 1801, of John and Mary.
James Woodland Downey, born Dec. 20, 1787, of James and Sophia.

March 19, 1802
Lambert Wilmer Bond, born Aug. 29, 1795, of James and Martha.

December 15, 1802
George Spears, born Nov. 25, 1802, of Samuel and Rosanna.

Page 366 Baptisms (continued)

December, 1802
Elizabeth Fuller, born Aug. 27, 1802, of Samuel and Elizabeth.
Peter Everett Whitaker, born Mar. 3, 1803, of Isaac and Margaret.
_____Day Lewis, born Aug. 27, 1780, of Clement and Mary Lewis.
_____, born Nov. 23, 1803, of William Harrison Sewell and
                                                        Rebecca Bowers.
_____, born 1804, of Benedict and Sarah Hill.

October 28, 1804
Robert Thomas Allen, born Nov. 1, 1801, of William and Hannah.
Ebenezer Nun Allen, born August 2, 1803, of same parents.
"The last two baptisms retunred to Benjamin Rumsey, Regr. of
St. John's Parish, August 3, 1807."

       Registry of Baptisms performed in St. John's Parish
       Harford County by the Revd. John Allen, Rector of Saint
       George's Parish in said county, commencing Jan. 1, 1805

March 29, 1805
Mary Ann Taylor, born Feb. 4, 1805, of Samuel and Juliet Taylor.
George Washington Walmsley, born about May 1795, of John & Reb.

April 12, 1805
Rebecca Cox, born Feb. 25, 1802, of Joseph and Elizabeth.
William Cox, born December 7, 1804, of same parents.

July 20, 1805
William Young Day, born March 3, 1800, of John Young Day and Agness.
John Young Day, born February 7, 1803, of same parents.
Anna Maria Shields, born July 11, 1805, of John and Sarah Shields.

July 20, 1805
Neddy Bar Mitchell, born Feb. 7, 1805, of Barnet and Milcah.
Parker Mitchell, born June 18, 1802, of John and Martha.
July 25, 1805
Ellen Sheerswood, born March 8, 1805, of William and Hannah.
Stephen, born about July 1804, of Wm. & Fanny, "Neg. Jas. Lee Morgan."
January 1, 1806
Caleb Hipkins, born Jan. 15, 1801, of Charles and Elizaneth Hipkins.
Jarrett Hipkins, born Sept. 28, 1802, of same parents.
Eliza Hipkins, born August 28, 1805, of same parents.
Spencer Harris, born Oct. 31, 1805, of Curtis Harris and Fanny
"Neg. Mrs. Agnes Day"
Febeuary 10, 1807
James Kirchen, born Jan. 12, 1805, of Samuel and Elizabeth Kirchen.

Page 367

July 16, 1807
Peggy Bond Allen, born Aug. 15, 1805, of William and Hannah.
William Fell Allen, born July 8, 1807, of same parents.
Mary Frances Matthews, born June 19, 1806, of Carvil, dec'd. & Ann.
August 2, 1807
Mary Yellott, born April 13, 1807, of John Yellott and Rebecca Ridgely.
November 25, 1808
Mary Ann Turner, born Sept. 20, 1805, of Thomas and Phebe Turner.
Thomas Turner, born October 26, 1806, of same parents.
June 25, 1809
Hannah Ann Allen, born Jan. 5, 1809, of William and Hannah.
August 29, 1809
Sarah Ann Lewis, born Sept. 20, 1807, of John Day Lewis & Sophia White.
"1807, Aug. 3rd. A copy of the above to the end of the year 1806 sent to Benj. Rumsey, Register of St. John's Parish by me John Allen Rector of St. George's Parish."

Baptisms in St. John's Parish

August 29, 1809
William Young Lewis, born Jan. 20, 1809, of John Day Lewis
and Sophia White.
February 17, 1810
Margaretta Norris, born March 31, 1807, of Henry Davis Norris
and Margaretta.
April 9, 1810
John Norris, born February 1801, of James and Jane Norris.
James Norris, born Feb. 26, 1808, of same parents.
Cassandra Renshaw, born in 1804, of Joseph Renshaw & Mary Feeson.
October 5, 1812
Anna Maria Allen, born May 13, 1810, of William and Hannah Allen.
Ellen Elizabeth Bond, born June 15, 1807, of Thomas William Bond
and Sarah York.
Emily Achsa Bond, born November 17, 1810, of same parents.
March 12, 1815
George Smith Sewall, born July 30, 1814, of Charles Smith Sewall
and Anne Catharine.

March 12, 1815
Jacob Smith Sewall, born May 27, 1813, of Charles Smith Sewall
and Anne Catharine.
October 2, 1815
Sarah Elizabeth Allen, born Feb. 19, 1813, of William and Hannah.

Page 368   "Baptisms Havre de Grace Parish"

September 10, 1809
Susanna Osborne, born June 4, 1808, of Amos and Susanna Osborne.
March 22, 1811
Elizabeth Brewer, born June 10, 1806, of James and Margaret Brewer.
Mary Ann Brewer, born June 18, 1808, of same parents.
Rachel Brewer, born October 18, 1810, of same parents.
May 4, 1811
Charles Henry Rhoades, born Aug. 8, 1808, of Andrew and Susanna.
William Barnes, born Oct. 25, 1808, of Richard and Susanna.
John Loyd Mitchell, born July 16, 1810, of Joseph and Mary.
July 27, 1811
Mary Ann McLaughlin, born Feb. 3, 1806, of Patrick and Ann.
Ketitia McLaughlin, born July 18, 1808, of same parents.
May 20, 1812
Amos Osborne, born Nov. 2, 1810, of Amos and Susanna Osborne.
January 20, 1813
Samuel Hughes Stokes, born Jan. 7, 1813, of William Brooke Stokes
and Henrietta Maria Chamberlaine.
July 11, 1813
Mary Ann Barns, born Dec. 15, 1812, of Gregory and Elizabeth Barns.

"St. Paul's Parish Baltimore County Baptisms"

January 26, 1814
Philip Robert Gover, born Jan. 12, 1801, of Jarrett and Sarah.
Margaretta Carroll Gover, born Oct. 4, 1798, of same parents.

"St. Thomas' Parish Baltimore County Baptisms"

June 8, 1813
Samuel Walters Crooks, born Dec. 9, 1809, of Henry and Catharine.
William Corbin Clarke, born Aug. 25, 1812, of William and Catharine.
November 13, 1814
Mary Collins Mull, born Sept. 22, 1814, of Jacob and Rosanna Mull.
August 13, 1815
Ebenezer Nun Allen, born May 22, 1815, of Richard and Sarah Allen.

"List of Persons confirmed in St. George's Church
by the Rt. Revd. Thos. John Claggett, Bishop of the
Protestant Episcopal Church in Maryland, on Sunday
the 19th of June 1808"

Doctor Jacob Hall, William Hall, Thomas Hall, Jacob Washington Giles,
Mrs. Martha Giles, Aquila Hall, Peregrine Nowland, Rebecca Nowland,
Elizabeth Nowland, Benedict Hall, Isabella Hall, Milcah Hall, Harriot
Hall, Caroline Hall, Martha Matilda Hall, Mary Hall, John Hall,

Page 369

William Brooks Stokes, Elizabeth Griffith, George Griffith, John
Jolley, Paca Smith, Aquila Nelson, Robert Allen, Hannah Allen,
William Henry Allen, John Allen, Richard Nun Allen, Frances Smith,
Elizabeth Archer, Ebenezer Nun Allen, Sarah Ferrall, Cordelia
Phillips, Sarah Phillips Wilmer, Sarah Hughes, Martha Nelson.

"List of persons catechised in St. George's Church"

August 14, 1814	
Charlotte Lester	Samuel Griffith
Mary Ann Brown	Edward Griffith
Mary Wood	William Thomas
Clarissa Everist	William Smith
Benedict Hughes	Nimrod Garrettson
Henry Greenfield	Joshua Barnes
Henry Michael	John Cowan
Ethan Michael	Henry Taylor
	John Swan Everist

August 28, 1814	
Elizabeth Welch	George Nelson
Caroline Perryman	George Washington
Blanch Welch	Thomas Jefferson
Matthew Johnson Allen	Charles Perryman
	George Perryman

July 21, 1811	
Anne Eliza Chauncey	Benedict Charles Hall
Caroline Webster	Richard Deaver
Eliza Griffith	Benjamin Chauncey
Mirandia Chauncey	Otho Taylor
Lewis Griffith	Sylvester Taylor
	John Murphy

August 4, 1811	
Samuel Griffith	William Jones

Page 370

Marriage for Saint Paul's Parish Baltimore County, March 3, 1806,
Samuel Cummings Patrick and Mary Kipp (license same day), This
marriage returned to Dr. Bend, Rector of St. Paul's by me John Allen.

Marriages for St. James' Baltimore County - December 24, 1807,
Edward Fell Bond and Sarah Francklin Smith (license dame day).
November 29, 1809, Isaac Hitchcock and Sarah Clark (license
Harford County).

Registry of Marriages for Saint John's Parish from
the commencement of the Revd. John Allen's Ministry
in St. George's Parish, Harford Co., Maryland in 1795

November 17, 1796, George Chauncey & Rebecca Frances Dorsey.
February 14, 1797, William McComas and Mary McComas.
June 8, 1797, William Wilmer and Catharine Wetherall.
December 10, 1797, Robert Brazier and Sarah Davis.
April 12, 1798, William Allen and Hannah Bond.
June 21, 1798, William Duley and Elizabeth Kitely.
June 26, 1798, Joseph Cox and Elizabeth Shields.

November 15, 1798, James Maxwell Dorsey & Martha McComas.
November 22, 1798, John Wilson and Margaret Smith.
November 29, 1798, Joseph Brevitt and Cassandra Woodland.
December 2, 1798, Thomas Turner and Delia Corbin.
December 20, 1798, Nicholas York and Margaret Sutton.
May 12, 1799, Jonas Stevenson and Rachel Hughes.
May 16, 1799, Alexander Hellen and Susanna Durham.
May 21, 1799, James Walter Tolley and Susanna Howard.
May 23, 1799, Greenberry Debruler and Rachel Healy.
June 16, 1799, Walter Chilson and Hannah Martin.
August 1, 1799, John Magnus and Martha Morris.
September 5, 1799, Zenas Wells and Elizabeth Flanagan.
September 12, 1799, Henry Dawney and Martha Hill.
October 24, 1799, John Powell and Isabella Nesbitt.
October 24, 1799, Patrick Deegan and Polly McComas.

Page 371

January 7, 1800, Richard Touchstone and Sarah Touchstone.
January 23, 1800, George Stolinger and Ann Deaver.
May 29, 1800, Benjamin Wilmer and Margaret Crawford.
December 2, 1800, Andrew McCleary and Esther Israel.
March 26, 1801, William Wilson and Margaret Winstandley.
April 2, 1801, Isaac Kelly and Drusilla Durbin Nicolls.
April 9, 1801, James Wood and Elizabeth Maxwell.
April 26, 1801, Gilbert York and Mary Chilson.
May 26, 1801, George Bradford and Susanna McComas.
June 6, 1801, Thomas Hill and Martha Browning.
June 11, 1801, Thomas Spencer and Mary Nabb.
August 6, 1801, Edward Day of John, and Hannah Wilmer.
December 31, 1801, Daniel Ruff and Hannah Moffett.
March 18, 1802, Jeremiah Biddeson and Sarah Strong.
April 6, 1802, James Carroll and Susanna Lusbey.
November 18, 1802, William Billingslea and Elizabeth Waltham.
March 3, 1803, Benjamin Hill and Sarah Roberts.
August 18, 1803, John Winstandley and Cassandra Baker.
September 29, 1803, Jacob Wilson and Francis Thomas.
October 26, 1803, Robert Porter and Mary Cowan.
January 5, 1804, David Swift and Martha Roberts.
March 1, 1804, William Webster and Mary Hollis.
March 27, 1804, Samuel Taylor and Julia Walmsley.
April 26, 1804, Aquila Hughes and Ann Statis Gafford.
June 28, 1804, John Howlet and Betsey Smith.
July 30, 1804, Elisha Osborne and Hannah Reckhead.
December 6, 1804, James Maxwell Day and Rebecca Nabb.

Registry of Marriages for St. John's Parish commencing 1805

February 25, 1805, John Monks and Sarah Rebecca Lewis.
March 5, 1805, Andrew Thompson and Frances Day.
July 25, 1805, William Brazier and Elizabeth Saunders.

Page 372

January 30, 1806, Thomas William Bond and Sarah York Scott.
February 7, 1806, Gabriel Lostater and Julian Waskey.
April 1, 1806, Francis Delmas and Mary Walters.
April 1, 1806, William Partridge and Rosanna Wilmer.

April 3, 1806, Benjamin Lego and Elizabeth York.
May 1, 1806, John Yellott and Rebecca Ridgely Coleman.
November 27, 1806, Ephraim Swarts and Susanna Jones.
December 25, 1806, Ford Barns and Elizabeth Dutton.
February 12, 1807, John Hall and Charity Vanhorn.
June 18, 1807, John Stallions and Ann Whiteford.
June 25, 1807, Jacob Stallions and Ishabud Coffman.
February 25, 1808, Josiah Smith and Claracy Glanville.
June 30, 1808, John Wood and Charlotte Abbott.
February 14, 1810, William Dallam Lee and Ann Wilson.
May 24, 1810, Samuel Taylor and Sarah Stricklen.
October 19, 1813, James McCormick and Elizabeth Henderson.
Oct. 21, 1813, Richard Frisby Hollis and Catharine Theresa Norris.
May 26, 1814, Richard Shekel and Mary Spencer.

A copy of the above sent to Benj. Rumsey. Regr. of St. John's to the end of the year 1806 by me, John Allen, August 3rd, 1807.

"Saint John's Parish Funerals"

December 6, 1798, Elizabeth Allender.
June 30, 1799, John Rumsey.
July 17, 1799, John Beale Howard.
January 7, 1800, Catharine Wilmer.
September 3, 1800, Thomas Bond.
January 2, 1802, _____Nowland.

Conclusion to the end of the year 1804.

"Registry of Funerals for St. John's Parish commencing 1805"

July 14, 1809, Hannah Nun Allen.
July 9, 1811, Elizabeth Handy.
September 29, 1811, Zilfew Dorsey,
   wife of John Hammond Dorsey.
May 2, 1812, John Taylor Weston.
November 29, 1812, Rebecca Weston.
May 23, 1813, John Saunders.
November 11, 1814, Frances Howard.
   wife of Thomas Howard, dec'd.

"Registry of Funerals Havre de Grace Parish Harford Co."

March 26, 1811, Sarah Knight.

John Allen, Rector of St. George's Parish, Harford County.

"Baptisms during the Rectorship of S. W. Cramptons"

June 21, 1846
Hugh Christie, son of Robert & Elizabeth Walker, born May 18, 1846.

July 27, 1846
Catharine, daughter of George Blucher and Sarah Nichols Dunkell, born August 1, 1844.

George Augustus, son of George B. and Sarah N. Dunkel, born May 11, 1846.

October 25, 1846
Mary Josaphine Christie, born Sept. 11, 1846, of James & Ann.
Rebecca Newkirk Patterson, born Aug. 14, 1846, of W. A. & Sally S.
December 6, 1846
Mary Veazey Cowan, born Dec. 22, 1845, of John & Priscilla Ann.
Elizabeth Ann Chancey, born Sept. 14, 1846, of Benj. & Rebecca.
Louisa Ann Nelson, born Feb. 23, 1846, of Henry & Mary Amanda.

Page 374

December 30, 1846
Sarah Elizabeth, daughter of Joseph and Louisa Frisby (servants of Mr. Sidney Hall).
April 4, 1847
Mary Jane Turner, born Sept. 22, 1840, of Henry and Louisa.
Martha Caroline Turner, born Jan. 4, 1843, of same parents.
Lucy Ann Turner, born August 2, 1845, of same parents.
December 27, 1847
Hannah Jane Allander Hammond, of Henry & Fanny, aged about three years.
"The foregoing have been reported to the Convention of May 1848."

"Persons of color - Baptisms by S. W. Crampton"

July 10, 1848
Mary Martha Frisby, born ___ 16, 1848, of Henry and Eliza.
Charles Frisby, born April 1841, of William and Mary.
William Henry Hall, born June 1845, of Andrew and Mary.
July 11, 1848
Jacob Lewis, son of Nancy Rice, born August 13, 1841.
January 29, 1849
Harriet Jane Stephens, born Nov. 26, 1848, of John & Nancy.

"Baptisms of Whites"

October 27, 1848
Cordelia Phillips Patterson, born July 13, 1848, of William A. and Sally S.
January 23, 1849
John Abraham Canon, born Sept. 11, 1842, of John W. and Mary.
Thomas William Canon, born June 6, 1848, of same parents.
April 2, 1849
Mildred Hammond, born March 5, 1849, of Henry and Fanny.

Page 375   "Baptisms in St. George's Parish"

May 20, 1849
Eliza Jane Gilbert, 4 years of age, of Parker and Elizabeth.
Sarah Cordelia Gilbert, 5 years of age, of same parents.
John Franklin Gilbert, 6 years of age, of same parents.
John Franklin Noble, about 5 years old, of James & Elizabeth.
September 8, 1849
Jane Hepburn Ringgold, Francis Ringgold and Rachel Ringgold, children of John and Sarah Ringgold (no ages given in record).

September 16, 1849
Thomas Edward Turner, born June 20, 1848, of Henry & Louisa.

September 28, 1849
Miss Cornelia Crocket Slee, aged about 17 years.

May 4, 1850
Lizzie Polk, born Nov. 28, 1845, of Dr. John C. & Elizabeth O.
Mary Polk, born August 24, 1849, of same parents.

May 19, 1850
Mary Ann D. Myers, an adult.

June 16, 1850
Earnest Augustus Dunkel, born July 11, 1849, of John L. and Rebecca T.

September 22, 1850
Samuel Griffith, son of Dr. Septimus and Frances Davis.
Oliver Perry Myers, Nelson Myers, and George Washington Myers, sons of Christian and Mary Ann D. Myers.
Mary Isabella Wetherall, daughter of James and Susan.

October 16, 1850
Frances Barthia Patterson, born Aug. 4, 1850, of Wm. A. & Sally S.

December 1, 1850
Stephen Grimes Myers, son of Christian and Mary Ann Myers.
Isabella Myers, daughter of Christian and Mary Ann Myers.

"Confirmations by Bishop W. R. Whittingham"

August 27, 1846, Miss Sydney Williams, Mr. Sidney Hall.
November 1, 1846, Dr. Jacob A. Preston

Page 376   Deaths

January 22, 1846, Mr. Brooks, a hand on the railroad, caught between the cars and instantly killed.

October 2, 1846, Sally, daughter of Henry and Fanny Hammond, aged about 3 years.

February 5, 1847, Herman S. Thomas this day committed to the Tomb. He fell in the Battle of Monterey, September 23, 1846.

May 9, 1847
George B. Webster of Havre de Grace in the 29th year of his age.

"Deaths in St. George's Parish"

August 4, 1847, Miss Martha Jay, aged 76 years.
September 11, 1847, Mrs. Frances Nelson.
September 20, 1847, Mary Veasy, infant daughter of John and Priscilla Ann Cowan.
October 3, 1847, Mr. George Henderson,
November 1, 1847, Mrs. Semelia Ann Murphey.
December 24, 1847, Mrs. Mary Harris.
March 1, 1848, Rebecca Newkirk, daughter of W. A. & Sally S. Patterson.

March 6, 1848, Mary Martha Myers, aged 4 years 11 months and 10 days, daughter of C. H. and Mary Ann D. Myers.

March 8, 1848, Elizabeth Ann Myers, aged 2 years 3 months and 13 days, daughter of C. H. and M. Ann D. Myers.

"The foregoing have been reported to the Convention of May 1848."

Deaths (continued)

June 7, 1848, James Rice, a colored boy belonging to Mrs. Christie, aged about 10 years.
July 12, 1848, Mary Martha, daughter of Henry & Eliza Frisby.
July 27, 1848, Thomas Knight.
September 10, 1848, Harriet Newell, daughter of Henry & Eliza Knight, aged 4 years.
November 5, 1848, Col. Charles S. Sewell of Abington, aged 70.
March 28,_____, Mary Veazey.
April 2,_____, Mrs. Eliz. Casey, aged about 85.
May 20,_____, Mary Gilbert.

Page 377   "Marriages by S. W. Crampton, Rector of
            St. George's Parish"

January 15, 1846, William Tolly Wallis of Baltimore City to Miss Annie Tolly Hawkins.
November 4, 1847, John L. Dunkel of Baltimore City to Miss Rebecca L. Davidge.
"The foregoing have been reported to the Convention in May 1848."

"Marriages in St. George's Parish of persons of color"
May 25, 1849, George Frisby to Tinny Green.

"Marriages of persons of color by S. W. Crampton"
November 28, 1846, Charles Jones, servant man of Mr. E. Griffith, to Harriet, servant woman of Miss Silvers.
January 16, 1847, Philip T. Brown, a free man, to Martha Ringgold, a servant woman of Mr. M. Hawkins.
March 13, 1847, Israel Roberson, servant man of Mr. Mitchel, to Elizer Izen, a free woman.
May 26, 1847, Henry Frizby, servant man of Mr. G. Henderson, to Eliza Ringgold, servant woman of Mrs. I. A. Perryman.
"The foregoing have been entered in the journal of the Convention in May 1847."

"List of Communicants"

1846   Mrs. Caroline Preston, deceased.
1846   Mrs. Martha Hall, deceased.
1846   Mrs. Sarah Henderson, deceased.
1846   Mrs. Mary Ann Griffith, deceased.
1846   Mrs. Elizabeth Williams, deceased.
1846   Mrs. Rebecca Davage, removed.
1846   Miss Sidney Williams, removed.
1846   Mrs. Andrew Hall, deceased.
1846   Semelia Ann Murphey, deceased.
1846   Frances Nelson, deceased.

Page 378   Communicants (continued)
August 27, 1846
Mrs. Aquila Hall, removed.
Miss Sophia Hall. removed.
Miss Alverda Hall, removed.
Mrs. Cordelia Giles, deceased.
Miss Elizabeth Hall, removed.
Mrs. Eliz. Casey, deceased.

March 25, 1847, Col. Jacob Michael, deceased.

April 4, 1847, Mrs. Martha Jay, deceased.

Febr. 25, 1849, Miss Jannie I. Hepburn, removed.

April 8, 1849, Miss Frenetta F. Smith, deceased.
          Mrs. Mary Jay.

Sept. 8, 1849, Mrs. Sophia Hall, deceased.
          Sarah Ann Brooks, removed.

Nov. 4, 1849, Miss Hellen Davidge, removed.
          Mrs. Jane I. Dallam, removed.

1850, Mrs. Isabella A. Perryman, deceased.

May 19, 1850, Mrs. Mary Ann D. Myers, removed.
          Miss Maria M. Smith, deceased.

March 31, 1851, Miss Sarah B. Gilbert.
          Miss Rachel Jane Gilbert.
          Mr. Abner Gilbert, deceased.

"Deaths in St. George's Parish"

June 29, 1849, Charles Webster.
July 9, 1849, Elizabeth Troup, daughter of John L. and Rebecca L.
    Dunkel, aged about twelve months.
September 28, 1849, Miss Cornelia Crocket Slee.
October 15, 1849, Mrs._____Hall, wife of Andrew Hall, Jr.,
    died in Chicago, Illinois, buried in Baltimore County.
January 1, 1850, Mrs. Jane Gilbert.
March 19, 1850, Mrs. Elizabeth Williams, wife of George Williams.
March 14, 1850, Rachel, daughter of John and Sarah Ringgold.

Page 379

April 4, 1850, William Henry, son of Andrew and Mary Hall
          (servant woman of Mrs. Perryman).
October 11, 1850, John Wilson of Gunpowder Neck.
December 26, 1850, Garret V. Nelson.
January 28, 1851, George Washington, infant son of Christian
          and Mary Ann Myers.
February 4, 1850, Mr. David Macrackin, aged about 80 years.
March 8, 1850, Elizabeth McClure, daughter of John & Ann Martin.
April 7, 1850, Abner Gilbert.
May 18, 1850, Mr. Leonard Howard, aged about 62, died very suddenly.

Marriages in St. George's Parish by S. W. Crampton
July 9, 1850, Christian Linlop to Anna M. Henning.
January 16, 1851, Joseph Lee to Rosanna Towson.

Pages 379-380

"I believe the experience of the world will prove it, that a scandalous maintenance makes a scandalous ministry. Poverty and piety are not identical things - I have high ideas of the Office of the Ministry with Paul. I would magnify myself that I would like to see the finest genius and noblest talent in the country devoted to that noblest office. Of course, I rank piety as the first thing - but I am not one of those who think that God generally works by the weakest instruments. Though He may do so to show his power - For that cause God called forth the wisdom and statesmanship of Moses - the poetry of David - the imagination of Isaiah - the pathos of Jeremiah - the logic and eloquence of Paul - for that cause God sent down his own Angels from heaven - and more than that and above all for that cause God sent down his own blessed Son. I set the pulpit in the highest position which any man can occupy on earth and I desire - piety being granted - to see the first genius and noblest talent of our country consecrated to the service of my blessed master. I do not speak for myself and my existing brethren. We will very soon be mouldering in the dust."

                 S. W. Crampton

SURNAME INDEX

(Note: Index pages shown are microfilm pages.)

Abbott, 372
Abertcromby, 213
Acre, 243
Adair, 235
Adams, 197, 228, 284, 359
Addams, 4
Addison, 281
Adlin, 338
Adlum, 347, 350, 351
Adlur, 345
Ady, 154, 155, 281, 238, 311
Aikers, 357
Airs, 219, 225, 231, 262, 264
Aitken, 351
Albert, 328
Albudd, 264
Aldrutt, 265
Alen, 29
Alexander, 278
All, 353
Allam, 228
Allen, 23, 44, 67, 100, 119, 127,
    200, 203, 211, 244, 250, 272,
    288, 300, 303, 304, 306, 323,
    325, 328, 331, 335, 347, 352,
    359, 362, 363, 366, 367,
    368, 369, 370, 372, 373
Allender, 157, 158, 199, 266, 309,
    321, 324, 349, 355, 357, 360,
    372
Allexander, 214
Alleycock, 288
Allin, 100, 214, 259
Allinder, 158, 216, 262, 298
Almaney, 242
Almeny, 207
Almon, 258
Almoney, 260
Alms, 231
Amboy, 213
Amos, 62, 67, 69, 260, 286, 302
Amoss, 55, 63, 103, 113, 119, 147,
    152, 153, 167, 174, 198, 199,
    202, 220, 222, 228, 231, 206,
    263, 265, 266, 309, 310, 313
Anderson, 17, 97, 132, 189, 190,
    204, 206, 211, 212, 239,
    248, 257, 258, 259, 284,
    311, 315, 324, 330, 336
Andrew, 139, 147, 184, 185, 194,
    264
Andrews, 74, 224, 228, 336, 354,
    255
Andss, 263
Angell, 352
Annis, 350
Anotony, 320

Ansell, 225
Applebee, 202
Archer, 204, 338, 340,
    344, 354, 369
Ardy, 87
Armstron, 9
Armstrong, 10, 14, 23,
    24, 31, 33, 52, 65,
    77, 79, 89, 131, 146,
    170, 176, 191, 193,
    206, 208, 209, 214,
    225, 227, 228, 231,
    242, 244, 258, 264,
    328, 329, 343, 345,
    347, 351, 353, 354,
    357
Arnell, 112
Arnold, 41, 204, 248,
    347, 348, 358
Ash, 224
Ashen, 242
Asher, 66, 91, 122, 147,
    196, 199, 205, 209,
    222m 242m 244
Ashor, 205
Ashton, 307, 348
Ashtown, 309
Ashew, 265
Askew, 285
Aspey, 215
Asquith, 280
Assher, 26
Atherton, 17
Atkins, 258
Atkinson, 310
Atlar, 265
Auger, 213
Axter, 218
Ayton, 250

Back, 224
Backhouse, 263
Backwood, 323
Bacon, 131, 162, 216, 262
Badam, 34
Badwell, 228
Bailey, 235, 285, 300,
    336, 354, 370
Bain, 49, 174, 181
Baine, 177, 181
Baker, 14, 62, 83, 99,
    126, 129, 134, 137,
    150, 153, 157, 189,
    193, 197, 200, 202,
    213, 219, 222, 224,
    226, 230, 232, 238,
    241, 261, 262, 263,
    264, 269, 287, 301,
    303, 309, 313, 318, 371

(Index pages shown are microfilm pages.)

Baldwin, 310, 320, 353
Balch, 257
Banberry, 90
Bane, 222
Barber, 250
Barclay, 247
Bare, 326, 332, 355
Barham, 242
Barkabee, 205
Barkley, 232
Barnaby, 240
Barnes 325, 328, 330, 333,
344, 356, 357, 358,
362, 363, 364, 368,
369
Barney, 217, 262
Barns, 198, 211, 229, 304,
339, 342, 354, 360,
368, 372
Barr, 309, 311
Bartinn, 262
Bartley, 221, 326, 329, 332
Bartol, 334, 339,
Barton, 11, 12, 26, 53, 67,
68, 75, 76, 104, 122,
146, 162, 172, 201,
214, 215, 219, 220,
224, 225, 259, 260,
280, 281, 285, 291,
296
Bashet, 239
Baskett, 190
Baton, 225
Baughman, 350
Baxter, 287, 301, 320, 323
Baxton, 231
Bay, 225
Bayl, 201
Baylaff, 325
Bayless, 309
Bayley, 49, 50, 82, 88, 164,
208, 216, 217, 219,
223, 225, 230, 327,
339
Baylis, 353
Bayliss, 308
Bayly, 164
Bayne, 208, 250
Bays, 129
Beal, 258
Beally, 262
Beamer, 227
Beamsley, 208
Bean, 333, 334, 349
Beard, 223
Beatty, 358, 360, 364
Beaven, 242
Beaver, 199, 224, 227, 231

Beck, 37, 133, 134, 153, 197,
206, 209, 221, 222, 223,
242, 257
Beckhead, 371
Beek, 123
Beldem, 197
Bell, 145, 223
Bellance, 225
Bellows, 126
Bemer, 284
Benbo, 6
Bend, 370
Benkin, 227
Bennet, 242, 259, 331, 355
Bennett, 180, 207, 208, 242
Benson, 207, 242
Benton, 51
Berm, 190
Berret, 258
Berrey, 223
Berry, 4, 225
Berton, 11
Bevan, 239, 244, 258
Bevard, 309, 333, 350
Beven, 126, 199, 209, 211, 220
Bevens, 20, 80. 106, 108, 213
Bevon, 176, 179, 180, 184
Bickerton, 254
Biddeson, 196, 292, 297, 371
Biddeston, 260
Biddison, 292, 294, 297, 298
Biddle, 260
Bidison, 260
Bill, 262
Billingslea, 350, 371
Billingsley, 220, 222, 230, 264,
291
Birckhead, 317
Bird, 250
Birkhead, 287, 303
Birmer, 285
Bishop, 124, 125, 128, 185,
238, 248, 272, 365
Bishopp, 235, 236, 237
Blackburn, 266
Blackett, 201
Blacklidge, 29
Blackwalldren, 216
Blackwell, 161
Blake, 197, 329, 350, 351
Blond, 216
Blood, 225
Blunden, 219
Boarding, 192, 240
Bochley, 33
Body, 170, 192, 216, 344, 345
Bogan, 263
Bohon, 221

229

(Index pages shown are microfilm pages.)

Boice, 19
Boil, 325
Boland, 333
Bolster, 357
Bolton, 137
Bonaday, 215
Bonadee, 4
Bond, 4, 5, 9, 13, 17, 20, 36, 41, 53, 55, 63, 74, 82, 92, 95, 105, 151, 152, 153, 154, 174, 175, 179, 195, 196, 198, 201, 209, 210, 212, 213, 214, 216, 218, 219, 223, 227, 229, 230, 231, 233, 234, 238, 244, 258, 260, 263, 264, 269, 273, 282, 283, 292, 295, 301, 303, 304, 308, 365, 367, 370, 372 (and 354).
Bone, 218
Bonfield, 157
Bood, 224
Boone, 254
Boothby, 185, 188
Boram, 208
Bord, 227
Bordley, 235
Boreing, 146
Borewell, 241
Boring 262
Borns, 229
Borough, 103
Boseley, 6
Bosell, 212
Bosely, 232
Boseman, 159
Bosick, 260
Bosley, 5, 260, 261, 263
Bosman, 244, 266
Boston, 365
Boswell, 240, 241, 244
Bosworth, 249
Botts, 354
Boulson, 241
Bourn, 191
Bowen, 36, 208, 240
Bowers, 283
Bowing, 242
Bowles, 37, 275
Bowman, 352
Bown, 192
Bowyer, 343, 348, 354
Bowzer, 338, 339
Boyce, 235, 237, 262, 350
Boyd, 189, 190, 239, 332, 340, 350
Boyer, 341
Boyton, 312

Bozeley, 211
Bozley, 2, 146, 217, 219, 220, 225, 257, 258, 259, 262, 264, 223
Bozman, 201
Bozwell, 161, 193, 199
Bracket, 244
Bradfield, 195, 240
Bradford, 1, 13, 16, 17, 18, 19, 20, 21, 60, 61, 65, 66, 157, 190, 202, 226, 233, 234, 236, 274, 275, 278, 289, 301, 310, 349, 357, 358, 360, 371
Bradin, 264
Bradley, 220, 259, 323, 353
Bradshaw, 13, 17, 96
Brady, 349
Bragg, 110
Braham, 265
Braisher, 100, 114
Brammar, 101
Brandigan, 208
Branian, 279
Brannan, 223, 231, 259, 309
Braser, 249
Brazier, 304, 325, 349, 370, 371
Brereton, 164
Breton, 244
Brevitt, 370
Brewenton, 82
Brewer, 268, 346, 350, 368
Brian, 159, 195, 210, 229, 230
Brice, 372
Bridge, 309
Brierly, 204, 223, 228
Brierwood, 250
Briggs, 219
Bringingham, 328
Brisland, 334, 335, 353
Britain, 199
Broad, 77, 197, 243
Brock, 265
Brokley, 191, 239
Bronnell, 283
Brook, 270
Brooke, 244, 349, 359
Brooker, 201
Brookes, 343, 356
Brooks, 196, 241, 242, 253, 212, 331, 350, 356, 376, 378
Broom, 336, 353
Brown, 2, 93, 156, 159, 160, 166, 168, 175, 189, 192, 196, 203, 207, 209, 220,

(Index pages shown are microfilm pages.)

Brown (cont.), 221, 222, 226.
    228, 230, 234, 239, 240,
    241, 242, 262, 263, 265,
    268, 269, 283, 301, 323,
    324, 331, 339, 343, 344,
    346, 353, 356, 357, 358,
    359, 360, 361, 362, 363,
    369, 377
Browne, 237
Browning, 274, 289, 371
Brownly, 263
Bruff, 200, 244
Brusbanks. 81, 126, 152, 157,
    238
Bryan, 240
Buceton, 116
Buchanan, 99, 217, 225, 231, 236
Buck, 41, 44, 45, 143, 150, 173,
    224, 228, 263, 265, 295,
    298, 299, 300, 301, 302,
    307, 312, 313, 316, 318,
    319
Buckingham, 222
Buckley, 197, 263, 265
Budd, 282
Buegain, 196
Bull, 19, 21, 37, 54, 62, 64,
    77, 84, 85, 132, 143, 153,
    154, 165, 167, 168, 198,
    200, 206, 216, 219, 222,
    260, 291, 295, 365
Bullus, 310
Bunnell, 203
Bunting, 107
Burch, 166, 228
Burck, 249
Buredy, 190
Burgan, 196
Burges, 153, 199
Burgess, 244
Burk, 84, 162, 177, 197, 229,
    243, 255, 264
Burke, 191, 227, 329, 336, 343,
    349
Burkit, 8
Burnet, 257
Burnett, 257, 276
Burney, 29
Burns, 221, 351
Burton, 224, 257, 310
Bush, 194, 242
Bussey, 206
Buswell, 206
Butcher, 212
Butler, 194, 200, 203, 211, 241
Butlin, 265

Butram, 124, 238
Butteram, 2, 6
Butterworth, 147
Byass, 316
Byde, 257
Byfoot, 63, 64, 199, 244
Byford, 291
Byle, 261

Cable, 195
Caddle, 243, 250
Cadle, 53, 89, 110, 135, 143,
    198, 206, 224
Cain, 191, 216, 240, 258, 342,
    355
Calwell, 285
Calwill, 227
Camell, 4
Cameron, 17, 183, 221, 222
Cammall, 258
Cammel. 2, 143, 203
Cammell, 203, 221
Cammeron, 9, 12
Camoran, 96, 142, 227
Campbell, 175, 214, 217, 241,
    250
Campell, 2
Canaday, 221
Candle, 214
Candry, 244
Cane, 241.
Cannan, 84
Cannon, 84, 353, 354, 356,
    357, 358
Canoles, 309
Canon, 374
Cantler, 352, 354, 355
Cantwell, 202, 222, 231, 243
Capas, 224
Carback, 108, 198, 214, 217,
    223, 243
Carbel, 249
Cardel, 219
Carey, 240
Carlile, 20, 24, 27, 93, 150,
    154, 198, 201, 229,
    257, 335, 359, 361
Carlisle, 249
Carman, 225, 337, 352
Carr, 27, 258, 259, 279, 319
Carrall, 110
Carrol, 168, 260, 261, 266,
    282, 350
Carroll, 88, 110, 152, 161,
    163, 174, 221, 229,
    271, 287, 290, 310,
    318, 371

(Index pages shown are microfilm pages.) 232

Carsan, 240
Carson, 193
Cartee, 171, 202, 214
Carter, 173, 192, 193, 218, 226, 244, 260
Carthy, 264
Cartie, 45, 174
Carton, 326, 333
Cartwright, 266, 328
Carty, 4, 90, 102, 261, 264, 281, 351
Carver, 329
Carvil, 314
Cary, 319
Casey, 376, 378
Castle, 199
Caswell, 68, 127, 244
Caulfield, 325
Cauls, 118
Cavindire, 257
Chaberlane, 259
Chaeney, 112
Chainey, 136, 137
Chainy, 195
Chalk, 230
Chalke, 262
Chalson, 227
Chamberlin, 9
Chamberlain, 23, 24, 120, 215, 234, 235, 236, 286, 293, 294, 328, 329
Chamberlaine, 4, 58, 120, 223, 227, 334, 337, 353, 354
Chambrelane, 263, 265
Chambers, 88, 171, 197, 231, 243, 269, 302, 351
Chamney, 206
Chance, 168, 169, 173, 175, 181, 265, 350
Chancey, 333, 373
Chandley, 350
Chanley, 241
Chapman, 52, 222, 261, 313
Chauncey, 326, 328, 332, 342, 343, 344, 345, 346, 347, 348, 353, 354, 356, 357, 359, 361, 363, 364, 365, 369, 370
Chauncy, 359
Chenneworth, 40
Chenoweth, 42, 52
Chenowith, 42

Chesher, 104
Cheshere, 209
Chesolm, 331, 349
Cheverton, 239
Chew, 310, 319, 345, 348, 358
Chey, 249
Cheyne, 117, 127, 222, 234, 235, 240
Cheyrton, 190
Chields, 134
Chienie, 78
Chilcoat, 264
Childs, 134, 135, 138, 142, 147, 153, 154, 155, 174, 195, 205, 212, 224, 239, 241
Chilsom, 288
Chilson, 274, 289, 370, 371
Chine, 278
Chinworth, 275
Chinwoth, 229
Christeson, 160
Christian, 193
Christie, 210, 267, 362, 373, 376
Christison, 160
Christopher, 226
Churchman, 280
Chustee, 235
Chyne, 128
Claggett, 368
Clarage, 214
Clark, 4, 30, 100, 101, 154, 194, 199, 209, 212, 217, 219, 226, 227, 230, 231, 255, 258, 284, 298, 370
Clarke, 242, 258, 260, 261, 263, 264, 314, 358, 368
Clayton, 232
Clebedints, 224
Cleggett, 231
Clerk, 205, 244
Cleynard, 213
Cline, 350
Clinerown, 260
Cloggled, 263
Clybourn, 194
Clyburn, 242
Coale, 354
Coats, 325
Cock, 205
Cockey, 200
Cockin, 19
Cocknan, 310
Coeing, 232
Coffee, 201
Coffield, 334, 360
Coffill, 165

(Index pages shown are microfilm pages.)

Coffman, 271, 372
Cofield, 269
Cohen, 310
Coin, 189
Coldwell, 221
Cole, 5, 8, 58, 124, 192,
    198, 207, 209, 238, 243,
    258, 259, 263, 265, 331,
    335, 344, 349, 351, 352,
    356, 358
Colebeck, 263
Colegate, 98, 260
Coleman, 196, 228, 230, 267,
    271, 274, 279, 290,
    300, 302, 304, 306,
    307, 372
Coley, 261
Coligan, 264
Coligate, 263
Collason, 4
Collet, 211
Colletson, 208
Collett, 140, 147, 189, 198,
    243
Collins, 208, 215, 242, 259,
    263, 278, 282, 298,
    338, 342, 344, 355,
    357, 362
Collison, 261
Colls, 259
Combess, 334, 337, 344, 357
Combs, 228
Comoran, 96
Con, 186
Conden, 275
Condry, 92
Condon, 217
Conelly, 261
Coney, 230
Conly, 314
Conn, 281
Connelly, 260
Conner, 153, 222, 231
Conway, 222
Cook, 27, 206, 259, 349
Cooke, 265, 265
Cooley, 8, 27, 263
Coon, 275
Coop, 242
Cooper, 190, 226, 228, 284
Copas, 125, 130
Copass, 238
Cope, 194, 207, 241, 242
Copeland, 214
Copland, 80, 81, 93, 138,
    192, 195, 196, 219,
    221, 324, 350

Copperwhite, 216
Corback, 259
Corben, 242
Corbin, 146, 193, 195, 207,
    212, 217, 220, 222,
    230, 240, 264, 277,
    278, 370
Cord, 268, 281, 350, 355, 356
Cordsman, 242
Cornacle, 357
Corrothus, 231
Corse, 354
Corvin, 192, 193
Cosley, 192, 205
Costley, 123, 151, 171, 217, 229
Costly, 240
Costrall, 241
Cotteraell, 126
Cotteral, 258
Cotterell, 224
Cotterrell, 163, 194, 205
Cottrall, 239
Cottrell, 125
Coup, 194
Courtney, 316, 329, 352, 353, 354
Cowan, 5, 237, 257, 262, 283, 303,
    335, 339, 342, 352, 353, 369,
    371, 373, 376
Cowdray, 39
Cowdrey, 30, 31, 39, 96
Cowdry, 156, 200
Cowen, 279
Cox, 3, 4, 6, 42, 98, 124, 190,
    191, 204, 212, 239, 243, 259,
    271, 273, 305, 352, 354, 357,
    362, 365, 366, 370
Cozens, 229, 351
Crabson, 350, 355
Crabtree, 24, 36, 56, 195, 197,
    205, 209, 212, 220
Craft, 259
Crampton, 373, 378
Crane, 344, 349, 356
Crapson, 355
Craven, 306
Cravins, 268
Crawford, 84, 159, 201, 230,
    273, 289, 357, 371
Craws, 275
Crayton, 328
Criswell, 211
Crockett, 191, 192
Crofford, 17
Crokat, 239
Cromwell, 232, 260, 329, 350, 351
Cronin, 355
Crook, 215, 231, 236, 322

(Index pages shown are microfilm pages.)

Crooke, 265
crooks, 368
Crookshanks, 265
Crosby, 324
Cross. 115, 116, 145, 207,
    208, 218, 220, 221
Crouch, 216, 278
Crow, 228, 355
Croxal, 260
Crudgents, 208
Crutchinton, 232
Cullinson, 209
Cullison, 217, 264
Cullisson, 224
Cullister, 211
Cullum, 217, 220
Culver, 330, 336, 349
Culvert, 249
Cummin, 352
Cuninggam, 223
Cuningham, 313
Cununghame, 243
Cunningham, 258, 266, 286,
    327, 333, 336, 342,
    347, 348, 354, 358
Curbeck, 260
Curle, 255
Curley, 353
Curry, 281, 343, 351, 355
Cutchin, 3, 82, 189, 217

Dadd, 5
Dagg, 323
Dail, 262
Dale, 98, 323
Dallahide, 31, 39
Dallam, 101, 110, 111, 140,
    153, 154, 228, 234,
    245, 246, 250, 349,
    351, 361, 378
Dallas, 130, 226, 227, 298
Dallatude, 14
Dallerbride, 24
Dallerhide, 19
Dallerhyde, 206, 226
Danbe, 110
Danbie, 105
Danby, 72
Dandy, 20
Dannely, 263
Dannock, 125
Danton, 261
Darby, 72
Dargay, 288
Darnal, 214
Darram, 24, 25, 26

Daugh, 115
Daugherty, 353
Davage, 377
Davice, 186, 193, 200, 205, 212,
    214, 217, 218, 223, 224,
    226, 235
Davidge, 377, 378
Davies, 246, 276
Davinn, 263
Davinne, 260
Davis, 6, 33, 181, 191, 301,
    335, 339, 349, 364, 370, 375
Davise, 220
Davity, 262
Dawdrege, 244
Dawdridge, 17, 96
Dawes, 339, 340, 354
Dawney, 14, 31, 32, 39, 53, 120,
    239, 274, 288, 338, 343,
    370, 374
Daws, 226, 269, 283
Dawson, 259, 325, 355, 360
Day, 2, 3, 8, 9, 11, 19, 23, 24,
    25, 26, 41, 42, 43, 50, 53,
    63, 67, 68, 79, 80, 93, 124,
    127, 136, 149, 150, 154, 158,
    178, 196, 200, 218, 227, 233,
    234, 235, 236, 237, 250, 263,
    265, 266, 268, 269, 270, 274,
    276, 289, 294, 296, 297, 299,
    302, 304, 305, 308, 309, 313,
    314, 316, 317, 318, 319, 320,
    321, 325, 348, 350, 352, 366,
    371
Deadman, 155, 199, 207, 242, 244
Dean, 250, 252, 266, 349
Deane, 248
Deans, 127, 184, 253, 254
Deason, 93, 99, 103, 104, 124,
    131, 145, 146, 160, 195,
    198, 200, 203, 206, 228,
    230, 231, 238, 240, 241,
    243, 244
Deaton, 87
Deaver, 5, 213, 218, 273, 355,
    356, 369, 371, 354
Debrular, 279, 288
Debruler, 29, 46, 47, 48, 76,
    78, 137, 142, 156, 190,
    213, 226, 236, 262, 352,
    370
Decran, 330
Deegan, 370
Deel, 110
Deele, 103
Deeran, 334, 350, 361
Deeson, 262

(Index pages shown are microfilm pages.)

Deever, 20
Degeon, 352
Delany, 349
Delivett, 283
Dellerhide, 242
Delmas, 304, 372
Demaker, 281
Demett, 191, 216
Demitt, 8
Demmet, 208
Demmett, 51, 77, 115, 143, 160, 220, 227, 242, 225
Demmit, 77, 260
Demmitt, 77, 78, 134, 219, 295, 320
Demorce, 222, 231
Demors, 239
Demorse, 189, 190
Demoss, 59
Denboe, 109, 120, 139
Denbow, 211
Denmead, 309
Dennick, 243
Denton, 7, 8, 11, 13, 18, 24, 103, 106, 107, 122, 156, 161, 204, 228
Derbin, 7
Dering, 315
Desney, 44, 214, 228
Deson, 5, 6, 58, 59
Detter, 77, 213
Devans, 23
Dever, 5
Devlin, 329
Devoll. 209
Dew, 211
Dewson, 28, 38
Dey, 274
Dick, 226, 250, 324
Dickin, 258
Dickson, 217
Dikes, 214
Dimmitt, 295, 308, 318, 320, 321
Dimsdale, 211
Dimvutt, 316
Ditter, 75
Ditto, 10, 222, 226, 346
Divas, 30
Divers, 267, 291, 296, 297, 298, 306, 354, 282
Dives, 48, 106, 112, 144, 175, 181, 183, 184, 209, 223, 228, 229
Divine, 266
Dixon, 219

Dixson, 226
Doane, 320
Dobbins, 325
Dobson, 193, 240
Doce, 219
Donavan, 279
Donnel, 324, 326, 328, 333
Donovan, 326, 330, 353
Doolsacus, 333
Door, 229
Doover, 289
Dorcey, 261
Dormer, 350, 352, 359
Dorney, 78, 124, 136, 148, 189, 197, 198, 205, 217, 221, 230, 238, 243
Dorset, 340
Dorsey, 42, 113, 124, 149, 169, 175, 188, 189, 192, 234, 236, 238, 257, 260, 264, 270, 284, 300, 333, 350, 356, 361, 365, 370, 373
Dortridge, 169, 181, 199
Dotridge, 61
Doubfty, 220
Doubty, 182
Dougherty, 344, 352
Doughty, 272
Douglas, 311
Dowley, 88
Down, 122
Downes, 6, 12, 238
Downey, 212, 365
Downs, 124, 129, 208, 209, 276
Doyle, 191, 240, 351
Drake, 257
Dreston, 264
Drew, 144, 188, 357, 358
Drivett, 266
Druley, 129
Ducke, 260
Duer, 309
Duggle, 196
Duglas, 196
Duke, 202
Dukes, 214
Dulany, 39, 44, 81, 97, 144, 200, 350, 357
Duley, 370
Dulreple, 216
Dun, 247
Dunahue, 45, 61, 212
Duncan, 349
Dunkel, 373, 375, 377, 378
Dunkell, 373
Dunn, 45, 350, 353

(Index pages shown are microfilm pages.)

Dummick, 238
Dunning, 351
Dunnings, 333
Dunnock, 263
Dunsheath, 352
Dunstan, 276
Dunstone, 223
Durban, 282
Durbin, 40, 92, 125, 156, 157, 177, 190, 191, 212, 216, 217, 218, 264
Durham, 4, 17, 67, 82, 96, 102, 108, 192, 209, 228, 271, 279, 280, 288, 301, 302, 370
Durram, 21, 22
Dushan, 259
Duskin, 165, 203
Dutton, 152, 161, 163, 169, 177, 178, 191, 229, 304, 338, 352, 372
Dynes, 276

Earl, 123, 238
Easton, 259
Eddee, 125
Edward, 259
Edwards, 89, 197, 201, 208, 217, 220, 223, 243, 260, 262, 327
Edy, 134, 147, 159, 218, 230, 260, 261
Egle, 225
Egleston, 226, 227
Eights, 219
Elder, 226
Ellicott, 223, 225
Elledge, 75, 111
Ellenor, 284
Ellet. 345
Ellidge, 41, 67
Ellinder, 268, 280, 296, 298, 299
Ellinor, 302
Elliot, 9 242, 258
Elliott, 9, 58, 75, 83, 101, 121, 130, 131, 150, 155, 157, 196, 205, 206, 207, 208, 211, 212, 213, 216, 219, 222, 226, 364
Ellis, 327, 355
Ellison, 262
Ellot, 327
Ellott, 343
Ellwood, 197, 198, 243
Elrai, 338
Emeline (colored) et al., 312
Emes, 244

England, 249, 310
Enloes, 77, 99, 100, 114, 204, 210, 211, 215, 218, 221, 225
Enlove, 9
Enlow, 125, 293
Enlowe, 238
Enser, 151
Ensor, 2, 123, 186, 261, 263, 264
Enzer, 151
Enzor, 113, 145, 162, 167, 229
Erickson, 142, 144, 151, 161, 171, 193, 207, 234
Evans, 212, 215, 239, 265, 315, 320, 338, 346, 349, 358
Evens, 126
Everat, 262
Everet, 212
Everett, 109, 141, 200, 214, 332, 339, 350, 359, 360
Everist, 339, 340, 343, 354, 355, 357, 362, 363, 369
Everit, 67
Everitt, 141, 244, 284
Everrett, 213, 227
Everritt, 219
Eves, 165, 204
Evett, 351
Evins, 3, 262
Ewine, 203
Ewing, 306

Fairchild, 222
Falls, 308, 315, 316, 321
Fara, 243
Farlow, 224
Farmer, 240, 327
Farnell, 259
Faurnan, 222
Fawcet, 351
Fell, 181, 200, 211, 213, 218, 227
Ferguson, 261
Ferrall, 369
Few, 211
Fewgate, 85, 86
Fields, 228, 242, 257, 353
Finicum, 334
Finley, 253
Finnagan, 281
Fish, 228
Fisher, 330
Fitch, 211, 217
Fitchpatrick, 130

(Index pages shown are microfilm pages.)

Fitzsimmons, 222
Fiuer, 197
Fixson, 191
Flaharty, 345
Flaherty, 341
Flanagan, 171, 288, 295, 296, 297, 302, 361, 370
Flanagin, 171
Flannagen, 171, 214
Flannel, 243
Flannen, 197
Flanngin, 261
Fleetwood, 335
Fleming, 219, 228
Fletcher, 358
Fleury, 284
Flin, 242
Flincham, 296
Flindam, 300
Fling, 150
Flullen, 239
Foard, 310, 319, 320, 356
Foock, 309
Force, 311
Ford, 264, 281, 291, 306, 310, 312, 317
Foreacher, 229
Foreasey, 218
Foreasjute, 226
Foresight, 23
Forkner, 212
Forrest, 194, 242
Forsett, 262
Forwood, 279, 347, 352, 354, 364
Foster, 28, 111, 117, 199, 200, 244, 352, 357
Fowler, 167, 211, 229, 279
Fox, 197, 213, 350
Foy, 25
Fraisher, 134, 217
Frances, 313
Franklin, 213, 225, 233, 236, 237, 256, 263
Franks, 202
Frazer, 346, 347
Freeman, 37, 124, 139, 220, 223, 238
Freziel, 192
Frisby, 357, 361, 363, 374, 376, 377
Frissel, 203
Frissele, 163
Frissell, 19, 134, 163
Frissil, 14
Frissill, 134
Frizby, 377
Frizell, 241
Frizsell, 146

Frost, 199, 213, 222, 244, 253
Fugate, 22, 113, 200, 216
Fulford, 309, 348, 354, 364
Fulks, 219, 282
Fuller, 7, 72, 74, 79, 98, 112, 118, 145, 192, 211, 221, 222, 223, 224, 230, 240, 272, 308, 309, 365, 366
Fullerton, 278
Fulton, 11, 211, 308, 352, 354
Furness, 192

Gadd, 81, 105
Gaffin, 264
Gafford, 285, 303, 371
Gain, 239
Gaine, 191
Gairy, 358
Galaspie, 209
Gallaway, 182, 194, 201, 208, 215, 221
Gallion, 231, 286, 340, 356, 357, 358, 359
Gallop, 308, 309
Galloway, 19, 27, 39, 182, 190, 253, 278, 280, 291, 292, 297
Gallyhampton, 34, 222
Garaway, 353
Gardner, 45, 215, 218, 223, 230
Garland, 9, 47
Garretson, 127, 131, 199, 231, 358, 362, 363
Garrett, 144, 219, 223, 226, 271, 326, 359, 360
Garrettson, 69, 128, 369
Garrison, 260, 286
Garritt, 222
Gartside, 309
Gash, 225
Gassaway, 118, 234, 250
Gaton, 200, 202
Gatt, 264
Gay, 335, 347, 353, 127, 150, 234
Gazzoway, 359, 362
Geale, 359
Geary, 347, 364
Gebbs, 202
Gellard, 227
George, 221, 279
Gibbins, 160, 197, 209
Gibbs, 241
Gibson, 84, 222, 258, 263, 267, 328, 358
Giddins, 249

(Index pages shown are microfilm pages.)

Gilbert, 126, 200, 230, 239, 286, 325, 328, 329, 333, 342, 349, 350, 351, 352, 353, 354, 355, 359, 360, 361, 375, 376, 378, 379
Gilber, 311, 312
Giles, 187, 262, 283, 336, 337, 338, 354, 359, 362, 364, 368, 369
Gill, 217
Gillam, 277
Gillcoat, 263
Gillis, 229
Gillitt, 223
Ginkins, 265, 267, 280, 281, 301
Ginn, 213
Gist, 231
Gittings, 27, 120, 151, 168, 193, 221, 234, 235, 236, 237, 246, 276, 280, 282, 299, 302, 311, 312, 313, 315, 316, 317, 318, 320, 321
Giyton, 209
Gladen, 207
Glaron, 63
Glanville, 372
Glebe, 202
Gleed, 345
Godard, 219
Goddin, 326
Godsgrace, 160
Godman, 286
Goe. 280
Goff, 264
Gohon, 261
Golden, 123, 238
Golding, 144, 157, 260
Goldsmith, 85, 172
Goodbie, 212
Goodin, 310
Gooding, 229
Gordin, 221, 258, 262, 277, 350
Gorril, 345, 352
Gorsich, 264
Gorsouch, 313
Gorsuch, 6, 203, 217, 220, 261, 309, 311, 314, 316, 319, 321
Gosard, 204
Got, 240
Gott, 71, 189, 203, 211, 216, 220, 239, 241
Gould, 357
Gough, 266

Gouldsmith, 232, 257, 265
Gover, 330, 333, 349, 354, 368
Grace, 203, 331, 350
Graham, 209
Grahame, 242
Grant, 278
Grates, 226
Graves, 198, 226, 243, 269, 350
Gray, 202, 253, 269, 275, 323, 328, 332, 355
Grayham. 55, 274, 302
Green, 2, 19, 29, 30, 106, 108, 126, 192, 195, 196, 199, 203, 207, 208, 211, 215, 217, 218, 220, 224, 225, 229, 231, 240, 241, 257, 259, 260, 261, 275, 279, 294, 297, 302, 319, 355, 377 (also 239 and 265)
Greenfield, 46, 137, 284, 292, 333, 334, 361, 363, 369
Greenhall, 212, 292
Greenland, 353
Greenlee, 340, 344, 355, 356
Greenleefe, 206
Greenly, 331, 352
Greer, 20, 45, 46, 64, 99, 105, 119, 180, 193, 196, 201, 208, 223, 229, 231
Gregory, 218
Grey, 277, 331, 363
Grien, 246
Griffen, 244
Griffin, 80, 199, 207, 214, 230, 244, 253, 301
Griffis, 192
Griffith, 199, 301, 324, 335, 337, 339, 340, 342, 346, 351, 354, 355, 358, 361, 362, 363, 364, 369, 377
Grimes, 49, 114, 209, 277, 280, 296, 299
Grindal, 298
Grinin, 5
Groom, 198, 244
Groombridge, 227
Groome, 121
Groos, 3
Grooves, 263
Gross, 149
Grotto, 322
Grove, 26, 225
Grover, 27, 38, 155, 195, 204, 211, 221, 240, 241
Groves, 31, 95, 138, 205, 206, 209, 221, 229, 241, 242

(Index pages shown are microfilm pages.)

Grudgings, 261
Grunden, 283
Grundy, 233
Grupy, 310, 312, 314, 316, 317, 318, 319, 320, 321
Gubbin, 357
Gudgeon, 22, 33
Gudgins, 239
Guiton, 244
Gullam, 259
Gulliver, 260
Gunner, 102, 135
Gunnery, 39
Gunrey, 69
Gurnill, 264
Gutterredge, 219
Guyshard, 241
Guyton, 7, 20, 209, 211, 217, 223, 228, 275, 285, 292, 295, 309, 310, 314, 319, 320, 377
Gynn, 211
Gyton, 310

Haddington, 224
Hadisty, 258
Hadmington, 258
Hagarty, 326, 337, 341
Hagerty, 333, 349
Hail, 223
Hair, 275
Hakman, 89
Hale, 267
Haley, 271, 286
Hall, 51, 169, 179, 187, 195, 198, 216, 225, 240, 243, 254, 257, 258, 264, 265, 267, 268, 270, 287, 295, 297, 298, 309, 310, 314, 315, 316, 317, 321, 324, 326, 327, 329, 330, 334, 335, 336, 337, 338, 341, 350, 355, 356, 358, 360, 361, 362, 363, 364, 368, 369, 372, 374, 375, 377, 378, 379, 395
Hallam, 87, 88, 213
Hambleton, 207, 278, 282, 285, 325, 328
Hamby, 351, 352
Hamilton, 294
Hammelton, 193, 226, 227
Hammilton, 218, 219
Hammond, 196, 203, 241, 374, 376
Hampton, 276

Hanbury, 131
Hance, 191
Handerside, 262
Handland, 243
Handy, 363, 373
Hanks, 198
Hanna, 349, 351, 352
Hannah, 224, 225, 354
Hanson, 18, 58, 199, 275, 344, 356, 360
Hanway, 310
Harbert, 2
Hardesty, 215, 240
Harding, 227
Hardisty, 207, 218
Hardwick, 257
Hardy, 216
Hargisty, 154, 195
Hargrove, 325
Harkim, 262
Harlins, 262
Harman, 190
Harmpman, 263
Harp, 207, 349
Harper, 56, 218, 354
Harps, 198, 243
Harrard, 212
Harratt, 327
Harrett, 10
Harrington, 226, 293
Harrinton, 212
Harriott, 205
Harrice, 213
Harris, 35, 216, 220, 231, 262, 278, 339, 354, 366, 376
Harrit, 7
Harrod, 221
Harryman, 199, 204, 205, 213, 215, 218, 226, 265, 266
Harsh, 212, 213
Hart, 264, 266
Hartley, 302, 350
Hartly, 296
Harvard, 310
Harvey, 351
Harward, 331, 335, 347, 358
Harwood, 195, 240, 259, 267, 335, 352
Haryman, 262
Hatch, 8
Hatchcock, 12
Hatchman, 63, 233
Hatlin, 230
Hatten, 78, 213, 223, 228, 231, 323
Hattfield, 227

(Index pages shown are microfilm pages.)

Haughey, 352
Haulaway, 71, 116
Haundrix, 225
Hawkins, 190, 192, 222, 226, 265,
    347, 350, 358, 362, 364, 377
Hawlines, 264
Hayes, 34, 35, 60, 206, 278
Hays, 57, 92, 139, 149, 153,
    99, 203, 270, 356
Hayward, 358, 360
Healy, 370
Heath, 171, 263, 266
Hedington, 262
Heir, 220
Heirs, 223
Hildebroad, 208
Hellen, 288, 370
Helm, 223
Hely, 191, 239
Henallen, 126
Henderside, 255
Henderson, 232, 257, 325, 329,
    330, 346, 352, 354,
    358, 372, 376, 377
Henderton, 212
Hendon, 21, 104, 109, 195, 200,
    208, 223, 262, 266, 293
Hendress, 239
Hendrixson, 197, 218, 224, 225
Henley, 8, 193, 288
Henning, 379
Henry, 214
Henson, 323, 352
Hepburn, 378
Herbert, 214, 334, 351, 353, 357
Herington, 10
Hernly, 121, 179, 214, 215, 219,
    234
Heron, 207
Herring, 197, 241, 352
Herrington, 5, 9, 21, 198
Hewett, 198
Hewitt, 240
Hichcock, 2, 257
Hick, 260
Hickambottom, 4
Hickerson, 276
Hicks, 3, 6, 64, 65, 72, 75, 140,
    194, 198, 205, 208, 218,
    230, 231, 242
Hickson, 239
Higginbotham, 351
Higgins, 241
Higginson, 97, 137, 219
Higgs, 218
Hildebrand, 212
Hilhorn, 277

240

Hill, 29, 30, 39, 48, 92, 129,
    133, 166, 175, 190, 192,
    194, 211, 212, 219, 224,
    226, 230, 231, 239, 240,
    242, 261, 264, 274, 288,
    289, 303, 311, 366, 370,
    371
Hillen, 288, 370
Hillin, 222
Hilton, 130, 133, 218, 219,
    265, 277, 293, 294,
    296, 297, 298, 299
Hindon, 223, 229
Hines, 147, 172
Hinkes, 240
Hinton, 53
Hipkins, 2, 277, 305, 366
Hitccock, 9
Hitchcock, 12, 26, 39, 47, 72,
    74, 90, 110, 126,
    130, 133, 159, 164,
    185, 192, 224, 226,
    230, 238, 240
Hitely, 266
Hitton, 258
Hix, 86, 87, 189, 221,
Hobbs, 28, 353
Hobeard, 261
Hocraft, 264
Hodday, 257
Hodge, 253
Hogan, 160
Hogg, 204, 252
Hoggins, 325
Hognar, 225
Holding, 275
Holebrook, 258
Holland, 187, 213, 220, 221,
    226, 230, 261, 262,
    265, 266, 278, 286,
    311, 359
Hollaway, 250
Holles, 349, 350
Holley, 324, 342
Holliday, 229
Hollingsworth, 69, 267, 306, 309
Hollis, 198, 244, 303, 311, 323,
    328, 331, 336, 341, 344,
    346, 347, 354, 357, 358,
    359, 371, 372
Holloway, 221
Holmes, 329, 349
Holmoney, 220
Holt, 148, 192, 217, 234, 240,
    259, 261, 265
Homer, 326
Hooker, 211

(Index pages shown are microfilm pages.)

Hooper, 221, 228, 257, 262
Hope, 231
Hopham, 201
Hopkins, 4, 227, 230, 271,
    283, 327, 343, 357
Horn, 203
Horne, 226
Horner, 101, 134, 168, 183,
    204, 221, 223, 226,
    230, 266, 287
Horton, 158, 185, 212, 243
Hoskins, 309
Hougate, 61
House, 244
Householder, 257, 261
Housten, 217
How, 261
Howard, 13, 91, 92, 144, 177,
    187, 188, 195, 212,
    218, 220, 229, 232,
    235, 236, 237, 240,
    254, 265, 268, 270,
    271, 273, 282, 283,
    284, 287, 288, 291,
    298, 299, 300, 301,
    303, 307, 308, 309,
    310, 311, 315, 316,
    317, 319, 320, 321,
    352, 355, 356, 365,
    370, 372, 373, 379
Howles, 17
Howlet, 254, 371
Hows, 201
Huchens, 89
Hudson, 2, 200, 244, 255,
    300, 312, 365
Huet, 258
Huff, 261
Huggins, 68, 69, 71, 124, 131,
    192, 211, 240
Hughdell, 217, 222
Hughes, 177, 300, 303, 309, 311,
    313, 316, 318, 332, 335,
    337, 343, 352, 353, 354,
    356, 358, 361, 362, 365,
    369, 370, 371
Hughs, 112, 126, 153, 211, 214,
    228, 230, 231, 257, 258,
    259, 262, 264, 265, 311
Hughson, 217
Hugins, 238
Hugs, 261
Hugston, 263
Hunn, 46, 210
Hunt, 131, 134, 238, 262, 263,
    276
Hunter, 61, 103, 280

241

Husband, 280
Hutchens, 98, 100, 125, 131, 146,
    160, 165, 190, 224, 230
Hutchenson, 195, 201, 240
Hutchings, 38, 65
Hutchins, 146, 222, 224, 230,
    253, 266
Hutchison, 244
Hutton, 265
Hutton, 265
Huxson, 226
Hyat, 218
Hynes, 262

Inchman, 214
Ingham, 352
Ingram, 73, 119, 125, 143, 183,
    184, 189, 206, 213, 221,
    228, 229, 261
Ingrim, 238
Inloes, 310
Inmon, 149
Insor, 2
Israel, 273, 289, 371
Isham, 52, 91, 233
Isum, 11
Izen, 377

Jackman, 261, 262
Jackson, 17, 39, 40, 69, 80,
    106, 107, 118, 143, 154,
    199, 212, 213, 215, 218,
    220, 223, 224, 229, 244,
    258, 307, 311, 324, 351,
    353, 360
Jacob, 221
Jaman, 108
James, 40, 72, 73, 138, 156,
    179, 180, 191, 192, 193,
    196, 198, 201, 208, 210,
    213, 217, 218, 219, 220,
    221, 224, 227, 230, 235,
    238, 240, 241, 262, 265,
    299, 308
Jameson, 218
Jamison, 312, 355
Jarman, 102, 108, 137, 211, 213
Jarom, 259
Jarrett, 185, 207
Jarvis, 223, 302
Jawes, 100, 222
Jay, 376, 378
Jefferies, 325
Jefferson, 369
Jeffrey, 243
Jeffriys, 199

(Index pages shown are microfilm pages.)

Jellett, 335
Jemesom, 318
Jemmison, 351
Jenings, 114, 126, 193
Jenkins, 189, 231, 239, 283
Jennings, 238, 240, 249, 260
Jephs, 19
Jerman, 209, 211, 242
Jernes, 228
Jewel, 231
Jewells, 324
Johns, 214, 326, 338
Johnson, 9, 10, 60, 93, 110, 116,
    125, 137, 145, 147, 164,
    165, 168, 172, 177, 181,
    189, 190, 191, 200, 203,
    204, 205, 212, 214, 216,
    218, 220, 222, 223, 225,
    228, 235, 258, 259, 261,
    266, 281, 283, 285, 287,
    295, 306, 308, 319, 324,
    326, 327, 339, 340, 341,
    344, 345, 346, 351, 353,
    358, 362
Johnston, 250, 259
Johnstone, 91, 230
Jolley, 349, 369
Jonas, 257
Jones, 9, 12, 16, 50, 60, 72, 82,
    86, 88, 93, 102, 125, 140,
    160, 185, 191, 192, 193, 194,
    196, 197, 198, 202, 203, 206,
    208, 217, 220, 221, 222, 225,
    226, 229, 230, 233, 239, 240,
    242, 243, 262, 263, 264, 265,
    270, 276, 277, 283, 287, 304,
    309, 327, 341, 346, 349, 352,
    357, 358, 359, 372, 377
Jorden, 26
Judah, 252
Judd, 350
Judy, 227
Juel, 281

Kanasby, 6
Karson, 191
Kean, 353, 357
Keech, 308, 311, 315
Keen, 203, 211, 216
Keeth, 48
Keith, 189, 209, 239
Kell, 311
Kelley, 27, 38, 172, 208, 220,
    257, 264, 289
Kelly, 274, 333, 347, 348, 357, 371
Kelsey, 189, 222, 239
Kemp, 301

Kenhan, 190
Kenly, 309
Kennard, 309, 316
Kennedy, 357
Kenney, 353
Kenny, 355
Kern, 319
Kersey, 26, 162, 195, 201,
    202, 205
Key, 279
Keys, 204
Kidrack, 216
Kigeran, 314
Kiley, 209
Kimber, 244, 258
Kimberly, 178, 357
Kimble, 323, 331, 332, 333,
    342, 354, 355, 356,
    357, 362
Kimbley, 275
Kimbrin, 45
Kimler, 199
Kindle, 328
King, 106, 118, 133, 194,
    217, 222, 239, 264,
    308, 309, 319
Kingsley, 340
Kingstone, 209
Kinley, 309
Kinnedy, 253
Kinsley, 355
Kinzell, 287
Kipp, 370
Kirchen, 366
Kirk, 354, 358
Kiteley, 46
Kitely, 163, 189, 203, 224,
    229, 239, 241, 250, 370
Kitten, 224
Knapp, 213
Knight, 78, 204, 220, 225, 270,
    318, 325, 329, 334, 339,
    340, 342, 343, 344, 345,
    346, 347, 350, 354, 364,
    373, 376
Knoles, 134
Knowele, 197
Knowles, 131, 134
Knox, 213
Kobell, 240
Kug, 264
Kun 260

Lacy, 126
Lair, 125
Lake, 242
Lanagan, 353

(Index pages shown are microfilm pages.)   243

Lanardy, 216
Lancaster, 11, 354
Lane, 150, 159, 211, 220, 257
Langden, 280
Lare, 238
Latimore, 241
Lattamore, 230
Lattemore, 220
Law, 218
Lawder, 344, 364
Lawrance, 219
Lawrence, 285
Lawson, 71, 198, 213, 218, 227, 245, 249, 347
Lax, 221, 229
Leach, 197, 226, 261
Leadley, 283
Leagoe, 110
League, 118, 195, 218, 311
Lecester, 264
Ledgley, 229
Lee, 126, 210, 231, 239, 240, 258, 276, 309, 310, 311, 323, 324, 329, 333, 351, 353, 354, 355, 358, 372, 379
Leech, 213, 243
Leekins, 41
Leemon, 263
Lefne, 134
Legat, 244, 259
Legate, 209
Legatt, 114, 219, 224, 229, 257, 259
Leget, 276
Legett, 4, 255
Legatt, 212
Legget, 253
Leggett, 201
Leggot, 264
Lego, 372
Legoe, 22, 30, 31, 48, 50, 94, 116, 135, 205, 221, 224, 229, 231, 239, 241, 259, 260, 265
Legs, 304
Leigh, 355, 363
Lemmon, 227, 262, 341
Lendrum, 187, 250
Lennox, 161, 245
Lenox, 161, 226
Leshordie, 202
Lester, 351, 356, 369
Lewes, 231
Lewis, 236, 253, 263, 280, 304, 309, 310, 319, 352, 356, 363, 366, 367, 371

Leitch, 281
Limb, 220
Lin, 184, 232
Linchfield, 243
Linam, 287
Linde, 216
Lindsay, 243
Linlop, 379
Linsey, 242
Linzey, 197
Lisby, 67
Litle, 171, 206
Little, 180, 184, 204, 207, 213, 229, 258, 261, 284
Littlejohn, 204
Livingston, 359
Lloyd, 234, 310
Lockeord, 28
Lockery, 355
Lofferd, 221
Logan, 259
Logdin, 231
Loge, 214
Logg, 212
Lomax, 89, 212
Loney, 347, 354, 362
Long, 36, 95, 198, 205, 226, 232, 265, 279
Longman, 36
Lony, 192
Lord, 244
Lostater, 372
Lotton, 353
Lough, 5
Love, 63
Low, 37, 60, 72, 116, 134, 145, 190, 193, 194, 196, 199, 201, 209, 212, 224, 239, 242
Lowe, 23, 37, 68, 222, 242, 249
Lowen, 225
Lowery, 318
Loyd, 199
Lucas, 223, 282, 353
Luckey, 356
Ludley, 318
Lueester, 262
Lusbey, 371
Lusby, 140, 223, 228
Lyder, 261
Lymes, 259
Lynch, 194, 196, 211, 221, 224, 243, 270, 279, 281, 333, 334, 340, 356
Lynchfield, 198
Lynn, 195
Lyon, 194, 201, 206, 227, 228, 244

(Index pages shown are microfilm pages.)

Lyons, 357, 363
Lytle, 293, 294, 299, 356
Lyttle, 239

Macather, 293
McBlair, 310
McBride, 259
McCall, 266
McCandless, 363
McCannan, 285
McCaskey, 351
Macckelltons, 9
McClain, 351, 353
McClaskey, 346, 347
McClean, 273, 289
McCleary, 371
McClennan, 313
McClennel, 309
McClogan, 264
McClong, 227
McClongon, 222
McCloskey, 270
McComas, 66, 70, 76, 119, 160,
    189, 198, 204, 207, 217,
    219, 222, 223, 226, 228,
    234, 235, 238, 243, 249,
    274, 277, 284, 285, 286,
    288, 289, 294, 295, 300,
    301, 310, 322, 326, 330,
    331, 333, 341, 352, 353,
    365, 370, 371
McComass, 185
McCommass, 185
McComus, 25, 35, 38, 40, 41, 62,
    66
McConn, 309
McCormick, 358, 372
McCowen, 309
McCreary, 327
McCubbin, 106, 221, 267, 280,
    311, 312
McCubbins, 281, 283
McCulloch, 236, 245, 246
McCurdy, 318
McDaniel, 363
McDanile, 190
McDole, 352
McFaden, 176
McFadden, 176, 344
McFaddon, 336, 344, 357
McFee, 256
McFeel, 263
McGaberon, 262
McGall, 214
McGaw, 355
McGay, 358
McGee, 213

244

McGill, 168, 339, 349
McGonegal, 343
McGowan, 278, 333
McGowen, 295
McGowley, 274
McGrevey, 261
McGuire, 261
McIntire, 333
McKee, 329, 331
McKenley, 192, 220
McKenly, 198, 202, 243
McKennar, 271
McKenney, 145
McKibbin, 333, 336, 352
McKie, 352
McKinley, 211, 257
McKness, 241
McLain, 356
McLaughlin, 275, 325, 330, 334,
    337, 341, 350, 351, 368
McMar, 231
McMath, 281, 282
McNab, 326
McNamara, 217
McNeal, 270, 309
McNiece, 354
McNiel, 314
McPhail, 350, 352
McRackin, 379
Madden, 339
Madder, 353
Madewell, 145
Madrin, 309
Maffitt, 274, 290
Magaw, 334, 342, 353, 354,
    361, 363
Maggers, 213
Magnes, 288
Magness, 278
Magnus, 323, 357, 370
Magroth, 338
Mahon, 350, 352, 357
Mahone, 353
Mainard, 227
Mainer, 203, 209, 242
Mairer, 229
Major, 221
Majors, 225
Mallance, 243
Mallane, 198, 200
Mallaney, 261
Mallence, 244
Mallett, 259
Malsby, 353
Manby, 222
Manen, 49
Manes, 220
Marcer, 252

(Index pages shown are microfilm pages.)

March, 192, 260, 284, 309
Mariarte, 108
Marrer, 263
Marrica, 9
Marrikin, 11
Marryman, 221
Marsh, 134, 172, 206, 213, 222, 224, 228, 240
Marshal, 253
Marshall, 131, 154, 214, 230
Martin, 150, 159, 190, 199, 205, 209, 214, 218, 239, 244, 288, 290, 315, 317, 319, 331, 333, 351, 370, 379
Masey, 23
Maskel, 212
Maskell, 219
Mason, 67, 161, 191, 353
Masscey, 265
Massey, 23, 25, 70, 71, 219
Masters, 227
Matheny, 240
Mathers, 301
Mathews, 217, 227, 259, 281
Matthews, 6, 326, 328, 331, 336, 339, 342, 349, 350, 352, 356, 357, 359, 361, 362, 363, 367
Matticks, 350
Mattucks, 230
Maulsby, 280, 310
Maxwell, 12, 41, 42, 64, 127, 150, 151, 178, 188, 201, 212, 233, 234, 264, 268, 274, 278, 283, 289, 328, 365, 371
May, 219, 263
Mayer, 6
Mayes, 165
Maynadier, 309
Mayner, 213, 220
Mead, 1, 3, 30, 108, 129, 135, 136, 137, 152, 194, 209, 223, 238
Meade, 1
Meades, 1, 23
Meadows, 211
Meads, 1, 30, 93, 126, 136, 164, 239, 242
Meale, 219
Mears, 167, 206
Mecomas, 3, 6
Mecomus, 3, 53, 57
Medcalf, 86
Meed, 53, 94, 108, 111, 117, 118, 230
Meedes, 261

Meeds, 16, 213, 218
Meek, 226
Meeks, 358, 361
Meers, 224
Megumery, 146
Megummery, 146
Melloy, 211
Melton, 56
Menson, 224 Minson, 194, 241
Mercer, 227
Meridith, 236
Merredith, 173
Merrekin, 191
Merrica, 9
Merrideth, 173, 212, 218, 224
Merridith, 173
Merrikeen, 22, 23, 65
Merriken, 52, 60, 93, 95
Merrydeth, 259
Merryman, 212, 223, 226, 235, 259
Metheny, 90, 195
Mibbs, 226
Michael, 329, 332, 334, 344, 346, 347, 349, 350, 353, 354, 356, 361, 362, 363, 364, 369, 378
Middleditch, 323, 355
Middlemore, 33, 78, 250, 251, 252
Middleton, 283
Midlemore, 33
Miles, 21, 57, 60, 124, 127, 191, 197, 198, 217, 231, 232, 233, 243, 263, 265
Milham. 214
Milhews, 239
Milhughs, 130, 189, 199, 224
Milhuse, 126, 244
Miligan, 318
Milldews, 168
Miller, 197, 198, 204, 205, 213, 220, 228, 243, 250, 253, 318, 344, 348, 352, 354, 355, 356
Millhughs, 163
Millikin, 280
Mills, 275
Mitchel, 231, 257, 260, 264, 377
Mitchell, 83, 87, 101, 121, 222, 305, 331, 332, 333, 335, 337, 339, 342, 343, 344, 349, 350, 352, 355, 356, 366, 368
Miver, 197, 243
Miyon, 212
Mock, 258
Moffett, 371
Molton, 350

(Index pages shown are microfilm pages.) 246

Mires, 277
Miser, 218, 225
Monday, 258
Mongumry, 193
Monk, 74, 310, 319, 321, 322, 328
Monks, 270, 297, 304, 360, 364, 371
Montgomery, 240, 277, 357
Montjar, 323, 325, 328, 331, 341
Monts, 212
Mooberry, 328
Mooles, 257
Moon, 238
Moony, 212
Moore, 133, 153, 165, 216, 217, 220, 222, 229, 265, 286, 287, 302, 303, 318, 326, 342
Moores, 282, 301
More, 339, 350
Morehead, 215
Morel, 261
Moreton, 350
Morgan, 79, 190, 199, 244, 270, 271, 324, 345, 353, 357, 361, 366
Morioke, 264
Morris, 75, 126, 139, 197, 198, 199, 202, 220, 231, 239, 241, 243, 244, 263, 269, 288, 324, 325, 343, 355, 360, 370
Morrow, 10, 263
Morsel, 232
Morsell, 186
Mortimer, 204, 214, 220, 222
Morton, 261, 262
Moss, 208, 242
Mothby, 221
Mott, 309
Moulins, 239
Moxley, 356
Muckelderoay, 5
Mull, 368
Mullen, 189
Mulley, 277
Mulling, 223
Mulner, 265
Mungrum, 146
Munjar, 335
Mummukkhyam, 310
Munroe, 352
Murphey, 48, 180, 211, 212, 240, 244, 261, 266, 352, 376, 377
Murphy, 195, 199, 253, 356, 369

Murray, 277, 355
Murrey, 219, 230, 259, 283
Murrin, 238
Murry, 258
Mycas(Myers?), 340
Myers, 355, 375, 376, 378, 379

Nabb, 274, 289, 304, 371
Nairn, 243
Nairne, 23, 240
Narsh, 161
Nasbitt, 288
Nash, 161, 276
Neal, 277
Neale, 264
Nearn, 87, 147, 164, 195, 197, 204, 213, 262
Neil, 285
Neill, 286
Nellson, 16, 54
Nelman, 266
Nelson, 10, 23, 33, 327, 329, 335, 338, 341, 352, 355, 358, 360, 364, 369, 373, 376, 377, 379
Nesbitt, 370
Netcomb, 218
Nevins, 233
New, 227
Newes, 134
Newman, 195, 240
News, 134
Newton, 150, 162, 204
Nicholas, 140, 278
Nicholes, 206
Nicholas, 46, 88, 101, 138, 217, 224, 230, 242, 274, 280, 289
Nicholson, 201, 216, 236
Nicolls, 371
Niel, 243
Night, 350
Nixion, 223
Nixon, 88
Nixson, 88, 161, 172
Nobb, 289
Noble, 40, 375
Noland, 262, 263
Norington, 59
Norrington, 149, 200, 223, 244, 306
Norrinton, 19, 99, 111
Norris, 5, 8, 12, 13, 16, 20, 37, 53, 66, 67, 73, 76, 83, 86, 103, 106, 107, 120, 121, 122, 129, 130, 133, 138, 139, 140,

(Index pages shown are microfilm pages.)

Norris (continued) 147, 154, 156, 173, 174, 175, 182, 190, 191, 192, 201, 203, 207, 209, 211, 216, 220, 222, 223, 224, 226, 228, 230, 231, 234, 235, 236, 242, 258, 259, 261, 262, 263, 265, 269, 272, 275, 277, 280, 284, 301, 309, 311, 318, 357, 358, 367, 372
Norriss, 17
North, 224
Norton, 121, 265, 277
Nowel, 32
Nowland, 228, 269, 328, 341, 353, 355, 357, 358, 359, 363, 369
Nusewondon, 222
Nutterville, 279

Oakdin, 243
Oakley, 93, 131, 213, 220
O'Bond, 354
Obrian, 215
Obryan, 17
Ocian, 202
Odean, 125
O'Donil, 265
Oggdon, 198
Ogle, 234
O'Henry, 286
Oldham, 209
Oliver, 16, 342, 344, 357
O'Neal, 332
O'Neall, 126
O'Neil, 330, 337, 340
Onion, 42, 167, 175, 183, 249, 268, 277, 284, 298, 309, 311, 312, 319
Oram, 228, 259, 266
Orr, 327
Osborn, 45, 210, 297, 303, 357
Osborne, 323, 326, 327, 330, 334, 339, 340, 341, 346, 348, 349, 350, 353, 355, 356, 359, 360, 361, 362, 363, 368, 371
Otherson, 279
Otley, 349
Owen, 222
Owing, 229
Owings, 198

Paca, 1, 13, 19, 148, 225, 228, 230, 234, 235, 249, 351, 356, 357, 363
Packcow, 196
Padget, 63
Padgett, 63

Page, 264
Pain, 214
Pakt, 263
Palmer, 75, 202, 219, 222, 225, 228, 241, 259, 262, 323
Palmore, 125
Pardon, 265
Parish, 239, 260, 280
Parker, 105, 110, 134, 207, 214, 222, 224, 228, 242, 261, 264, 325
Parkes, 199
Parkew, 216
Parkinson, 243
Parks, 189, 196, 213, 222, 226, 239, 241, 243, 244
Parrish, 189, 208
Parsley, 190
Parson, 265
Parsons, 357
Partridge, 304, 372
Parwell, 230
Pasley, 239
Pasmore, 140, 238
Passine, 212
Patrick, 370
Patterson, 346, 347, 354, 357, 362, 373, 374, 375, 376
Patteson, 266
Peacock, 194, 208, 241, 245, 264
Peaifers, 254
Peak, 277
Peake, 5
Pearson, 6, 109
Peckon, 241
Pedder, 91
Pendegrass, 209
Penington, 4, 61
Penman, 201
Pennick, 258
Pennington, 229, 354
Penrice, 5
Perdere, 263
Perdue, 11, 130, 190, 194, 197, 209, 239, 242, 243, 258, 265, 300
Perigoe, 193, 240, 249
Periman, 358
Perkins, 282
Perkinson, 198
Perren, 209
Perrey, 231
Perrigoe, 159, 201
Perry, 283, 351
Perryman, 203, 358, 369, 377, 378
Person, 7, 8, 10, 12, 22
Petete, 3
Petetoe, 227

(Index pages shown are microfilm pages.)

Petit, 10, 249
Petite, 10
Petticoat, 262
Petty, 126, 239, 243
Philber, 232
Phillips, 86, 196, 199, 230, 241, 266, 346, 347, 348, 351, 354, 356, 361, 363, 369
Philpot, 260
Phipps, 186, 294
Phips, 276
Phraisher, 220
Phurmey, 209
Pickett, 2, 40, 41, 125, 148, 174, 203, 208, 214, 234
Pickitt, 230
Pierce, 315, 320
Pike, 190, 193, 205
Piles, 258
Pine, 204
Pines, 129, 130, 211, 225, 259
Pinion, 338
Pinkney, 337
Pinkstone, 149, 150
Pinox, 287
Pitts, 260
Plant, 242
Plow, 16
Plummer, 220
Poacock, 46
Poacocks, 100
Poccock, 229
Pocock, 177, 203, 212, 214, 216, 224, 253
Poess, 225
Pogue, 353, 355
Polard, 213
Polion, 61
Polk, 375
Poll, 310
Pollard, 206, 209, 212, 232
Pollet, 242
Polson, 243, 284
Poor, 207, 242
Popes, 217
Porrord, 222
Porter, 154, 197, 207, 241, 303, 340, 371
Potee, 34, 55, 141, 211, 212, 225, 257
Poteet, 67, 141, 151, 193, 197, 223, 225
Poteete, 55, 95
Poteett, 144
Potett, 126
Pottee, 34
Potteet, 124, 215

Potter, 207, 216
Poulson, 51, 110, 127, 157, 197, 200, 203, 220, 243
Powel, 239
Powell, 38, 190, 212, 288, 330, 370
Power, 171
Presburry, 266
Presbury, 4, 16, 20, 21, 25, 44, 47, 48, 62, 105, 106, 107, 166, 169, 177, 178, 179, 182, 183, 200, 202, 213, 214, 231, 233, 234, 236, 237, 262, 286, 351
Presgrove, 140
Preston, 3, 20, 22, 23, 27, 28, 32, 33, 40, 49, 55, 56, 78, 124, 198, 200, 204, 223, 236, 259, 261, 307, 375, 377
Price, 42, 90, 91, 122, 127, 142, 148, 152, 157, 194, 212, 216, 221, 223, 226, 230, 259, 260, 262, 264, 286, 330, 335, 336, 338, 343, 346, 347, 348, 353, 357
Prichett, 325, 328, 333, 359, 360
Prickett, 215, 223, 226
Prigg, 193, 199, 240, 324, 326, 329, 349, 352
Prine, 231, 263, 266
Pring, 242
Prington, 265
Prisley, 258
Pritcherd, 32
Procter, 265, 282
Progdon, 213
Prosper, 258
Prosser, 115, 133, 150, 160, 167, 208, 242, 350
Protser, 100
Prushman, 220
Prynne, 220
Purere, 263
Pustlay, 259
Puttee, 19, 35, 133, 214, 265
Pycraft, 40, 200
Pyke, 36
Pyles, 311, 317

Quine, 4, 77
Quinley, 222

Radford, 265
Railey, 219
Raine, 306
Ramage, 223

(Index pages shown are microfilm pages.)

Ramsey, 54, 141, 189, 190, 225, 239, 254
Rand, 351
Raven, 13, 15
Rawley, 108, 278
Rawlings, 95
Ray, 221, 330
Raynor, 209
Rea, 310, 314, 319
Read, 253, 254
Reason, 358
Reaven, 179, 196, 199, 204, 210, 211, 212, 213, 224, 228
Reaves, 249
Redman, 352
Reed, 188, 276, 279, 357
Rees, 327
Reeves, 113, 200, 213, 240, 244
Reevsm 226
Regan, 346
Rench, 213
Reneher, 124
Renshaw, 249, 259, 276, 367
Reynolds, 311, 315, 317, 320
Rhoades, 75, 111, 119, 368
Rhodes, 5, 10, 33, 34, 41, 55, 61, 65, 134, 142, 160, 191, 205, 211, 219, 239, 257, 265 (and 228)
Rhodons, 61
Rice, 28, 204, 207, 222, 338, 374, 376
Rich, 219
Richard, 250
Richards, 211, 261
Richardson, 19, 20, 36, 37, 70, 102, 144, 152, 192, 207, 214, 218, 221, 224, 227, 231, 241, 261, 265, 271, 293, 301, 356, 358
Ricket, 258
Rickets, 209
Ricketts, 44, 89, 151, 157, 161, 163, 171, 217, 309
Rickitts, 231, 236
Riddle, 207
Rider, 126, 201, 238, 343, 356
Ridesole, 182
Rieley, 357
Riely, 345, 357
Rigbee, 225
Rigbie, 206, 218, 228
Rigden, 335
Rigdon, 261, 264, 327, 349, 355, 356
Riggin, 357
Right, 6
Riley, 220

Ringgold, 375, 377, 378
Riset, 242
Ristau, 266
Risteau, 21, 123, 179, 194, 196, 232, 245, 292, 319, 320, 348, 362
Ristieu, 204
Ristone, 196, 224, 241
Ristow, 258
Roach, 211, 282
Roades, 10
Robb, 278
Robenson, 197
Roberson, 19, 57, 58, 60, 244, 377
Roberts, 3, 4, 40, 49, 69, 70, 84, 88, 125, 157, 172, 209, 212, 214, 220, 229, 233, 238, 249, 257, 281, 303, 350, 371
Robertson, 48, 75, 82, 92, 176, 197, 199, 200, 205, 218, 273, 365
Robeson, 205, 231
Robinett, 302
Robinson, 2, 4, 6, 11, 196, 257, 293, 301, 317, 326, 356
Robison, 88, 257, 260, 334, 350
Rochold, 80
Rock, 255, 258, 279
Rocker, 263
Rockhold, 80, 142, 198, 211, 224, 225, 231, 243, 255, 262, 277, 358
Rodenheizer, 325
Rodes, 5, 15, 258, 337
Rodgers, 351, 356, 362
Roe, 86, 196, 198
Rogen, 225
Rogers, 35, 214, 218, 220, 237, 267, 269, 334, 349, 353, 354
Roggers, 5
Rollans, 7
Rollar, 8
Roller, 3
Rollo, 26, 68, 73, 94, 212, 218, 233
Ronay, 353
Rooke, 261
Rooms, 220
Roose, 266
Root, 326
Rose, 213, 264
Ross, 229, 258, 352
Roun, 316, 319
Rouse, 318
Row, 217, 222, 243, 270, 272, 365

(Index pages shown are microfilm pages.)

Rowan, 186, 232
Rowe, 203, 212
Rowing, 180, 203
Rowings, 166, 213
Rown, 310
Rownes, 241
Rozomister, 224
Ruby, 228
Ruff, 139, 143, 171, 200, 207, 216, 274, 290, 323, 358, 360, 371
Rullns, 320
Rumpley, 263
Rumsay, 308, 309, 312, 316, 317, 320
Rumsey, 51, 187, 237, 265, 287, 296, 299, 302, 303, 305, 306, 307, 308, 310, 316, 317, 318, 319, 320, 321, 322, 359, 366, 372
Run, 228
Ruse, 222
Rush, 281
Russel, 155, 156, 202, 229, 245
Russell, 213, 355
Rusy, 318
Ruth, 219
Rutledge, 130, 137, 145, 196, 209, 222, 225, 227, 228, 229, 231, 242, 243, 255
Rutlege, 258
Rutlidge, 260, 263, 265
Ruvis, 260
Rivut, 312
Ryley, 207, 211, 212, 226
Ryon, 199
Rynoo, 257
Ryston, 241

Saddon, 226
Sadler, 283, 310, 312, 316, 320, 321
Sadlers, 257
St. Clair, 270, 317, 351
Salter, 209
Sampson, 241, 258, 356
Samson, 43, 44, 196, 198, 207, 212, 218, 220, 229
Sandage, 204
Sandeford, 253
Sanders, 272, 278
Sanderson, 281
Sandige, 241
Sandy, 211
Sank, 262
Sappington, 309
Sattle, 230
Sattler, 311

250

Saunders, 184, 198, 228, 231, 253, 266, 270, 304, 325, 356, 365, 371, 373
Savage, 159
Savin, 360
Savors, 145
Savory, 120, 234
Says, 265
Sacntly, 268
Scarborough, 327, 329
Scarbrough, 286
Scarf, 206, 209, 218, 219, 253
Scarff, 181, 183, 225, 260
Scharf, 194
Schott, 7
Scickermore, 9
Scimmons, 102, 112, 144, 159, 167, 207
Scimons, 144
Scofield, 277
Scoles, 229
Scot, 7, 21, 253
Scotland, 198
Scott, 7, 9, 21, 24, 26, 36, 51, 52, 59, 62, 73, 94, 99, 115, 119, 120, 129, 133, 138, 139, 147, 161, 162, 198, 199, 211, 215, 219, 220, 229, 231, 232, 234, 235, 243, 244, 259, 260, 261, 264, 271, 284, 285, 286, 290, 297, 304, 310, 311, 317, 318, 349, 359, 372
Scotter, 222
Scotty, 259
Scovall, 337
Scurrey, 136, 164
Seal, 270
Seale, 184
Sears, 203, 361
Seemmons, 98
Sevan, 183
Sewell, 296, 366, 367, 376
Shadows, 199, 244
Shaffer, 310
Shafford, 257
Shannem, 202
Sharp, 206, 229
Sharpe, 252
Shaw. 109, 199, 201, 202, 221, 225, 244
Shay, 357
Shea, 260
Sheapard, 21
Shearswood, 354
Sheerswood, 305, 366
Shekel, 372
Shelby, 261

(Index pages shown are microfilm pages.)   251

Sheldon, 221, 232, 257
Shelly, 254
Shelvey, 226
Shepard, 90, 194, 208, 241, 249
Sheppard, 62, 64, 73, 77, 88,
    94, 96, 97, 114, 124
Shepperd, 103, 112, 216
Sheredine, 285, 286, 306
Sherelock, 104
Shewbridge, 139, 140
Shidle, 349
Shields, 218, 221, 268, 305, 328,
    348, 366, 370
Shipley, 117
Shipton, 183, 184, 217
Shoats, 264
Shody, 353
Shoebridge, 75
Short, 286
Shoudy, 279
Showdy, 211
Sickelmore, 223, 266
Sickemore, 7, 8, 11
Sicklemore, 4, 84, 97, 208, 213
Silvers, 377
Simkine, 242
Simmons, 20, 24, 118, 215, 223,
    226, 230, 231, 233
Simons, 6, 15
Sinclair, 241, 326
Sinclare, 216
Sindall. 192
Sing, 197
Sinklar, 231, 226
Sinkler, 196, 204, 227, 231, 258
Skarabon, 194
Skeerer, 48
Skinner, 254
Skinnoni, 202
Skipen, 242
Skipper, 209
Skipton, 215
Slade, 4, 19, 43, 54, 55, 60, 74,
    170, 197, 209, 222, 224,
    229, 257, 259, 310, 353
Slades, 345
Slaids, 346
Slater, 212
Slaughter, 206
Slee, 375, 378
Sligh, 295
Slowin, 261
Small, 266, 309, 339, 342, 347,
    351, 355
Smalley, 91
Smart, 62, 175

Smith, 8, 16, 40, 42, 64, 68,
    73, 75, 88, 92, 123, 124,
    129, 139, 148, 151, 155,
    163, 166, 172, 174, 189,
    193, 194, 206, 209, 215,
    216, 217, 226, 227, 230,
    232, 235, 239, 241, 242,
    257, 258, 261, 262, 265,
    266, 282, 283, 286, 302,
    303, 307, 324, 327, 329,
    331, 335, 337, 341, 343,
    345, 346, 350, 351, 357,
    358, 361, 369, 370, 371,
    372, 378
Smithers, 191
Smithson, 54, 101, 138, 218,
    228, 229, 230, 275, 284,
    290, 302, 355
Sneed, 315, 317
Snody, 364
Somner, 92, 249
Sostater, 304
Soullivin, 263
Sparks, 223, 260
Spear, 285, 365
Spears, 365
Speer, 183
Spencer, 181, 217, 274, 276,
    289, 331, 371, 372
Sprucebanks, 356
Sprusbanks, 81
Sresbury, 21
Stackey, 65
Stafford, 264
Stallings, 328, 349
Stallions, 353, 372
Standafar, 58, 96
Standeford, 73, 74, 79, 80, 81,
    89, 90, 102, 104, 116,
    121, 131, 140, 141, 144,
    145, 146, 155, 188, 189,
    192, 201, 202, 205, 207,
    212, 213, 214, 218, 221,
    224, 227, 229, 230, 233
Standerline, 157
Standiford, 90, 111, 114, 116,
    188, 191, 257, 259, 261,
    262, 263, 265, 266, 275,
    307, 310
Standove, 19
Standton, 103
Stanley, 263
Stansbury, 170, 189, 194, 196,
    204, 213, 221, 228, 242,
    259, 263, 282, 299, 306
Stark, 364

(Index pages shown are microfilm pages.)

Starkey, 99, 126, 133, 138, 149, 180, 181, 182, 192, 208, 215, 216, 228, 229, 234, 250, 291
Starkeys, 249
Starr, 309
Steadman, 194
Stearns, 316
Steedman, 241
Steel, 190, 239, 258, 325, 330, 332, 335, 342
Steele, 353
Stephens, 89, 124, 191, 206, 261, 374
Stephenson, 47, 162, 352
Steven, 22
Stevens, 5, 22, 177, 202, 203, 214, 231, 238, 241, 249, 257
Stevenson, 162, 205, 225, 228, 283, 288, 350, 359, 360, 370
Stevert, 211
Steward, 241, 242, 276
Stewart, 194, 203, 221, 226, 266, 358, 360, 363
Stiles, 244, 352
Stileve, 199
Stockdale, 349
Stocksdale, 287
Stockton, 358
Stokes, 78, 194, 210, 213, 227, 356, 364, 368, 369
Stolinger, 273, 289, 371
Stollcup, 353
Stone, 218, 260
Stotts, 220
Stout, 2
Stover, 309
Street, 213, 265
Stricker, 349
Strickland, 283
Stricklen, 357, 372
Strong, 269, 357, 371
Stroud, 327
Stubs, 205
Studart, 266
Stump, 356
Sullivan, 247
Sumarts, 279
Summers, 229
Summon, 309
Summons, 74, 124
Sunderland, 344
Sunk, 229
Surnard, 241

Suter, 330, 332, 337
Sutten, 253
Sutton, 191, 195, 197, 220, 224, 239, 257, 263, 347, 351, 354, 358, 370
Swain, 353
Swaine, 350
Swan, 51, 166, 225, 227, 229
Swann, 318, 319, 320
Swarts, 304, 372
Sweeting, 49, 259
Swift, 14, 28, 218, 303, 371
Swinard, 196
Sye, 212
Symmonds, 212
Symons, 235
Sympson, 124
Symson, 199
Synkins, 208

Tailor, 62
Talbee, 49, 90, 130, 133, 176, 211, 225
Talbot, 61
Talbott, 40, 61, 65, 66, 67, 72, 105, 108, 186, 208, 209, 211, 215, 216, 224, 225, 229, 230, 237, 259, 260, 261, 265
Tarman, 23
Tate, 217, 231, 241
Tayler, 5, 8, 11, 37, 49, 63, 243
Taylor, 5, 7, 16, 18, 19, 22, 31, 37, 53, 59, 65, 92, 95, 96, 103, 118, 133, 145, 147, 158, 173, 174, 176, 191, 193, 195, 198, 202, 207, 211, 216, 218, 219, 220, 223, 225, 227, 229, 234, 240, 257, 259, 261, 265, 276, 279, 282, 285, 300, 301, 303, 305, 331, 332, 336, 341, 344, 347, 351, 352, 353, 354, 355, 356, 357, 358, 365, 366, 369, 372
Tayman, 164, 202, 238, 241, 244
Teat, 204
Teate, 207
Temple, 38
Templeton, 349
Tenent, 42
Thaker, 214
Thayer, 243
Thesbord, 264

(Index pages shown are microfilm pages.)

Thine, 260
Thomas, 77, 141, 165, 203, 225, 227, 241, 258, 260, 265, 268, 303, 334, 341, 342, 343, 351, 353, 355, 369, 371, 376
Thompson, 161, 192, 207, 209, 217, 229, 241, 243, 260, 263, 265, 270, 276, 290, 304, 309, 318, 325, 351, 354, 355, 371
Thomson, 75, 228, 342, 353
Thornberry, 215
Thornbury, 191, 239
Thornhill, 194, 242, 261
Thornton, 210, 269
Thorp, 220
Thrap, 219, 276
Thrift, 18, 20, 29, 162, 163, 205, 213, 218, 225, 227, 262, 269, 271
Thrist, 6
Thurston, 160
Thyler, 198
Tibbett, 219
Tibbs, 60, 61
Tilley, 196
Timmons, 192
Tinecum, 268
Tipper, 222
Tipton, 225, 228, 261, 264
Todd, 207, 215, 266
Toder, 240
Tolley, 69, 127, 128, 147, 150, 169, 170, 178, 213, 218, 233, 234, 236, 237, 246, 250, 282, 288, 307, 308, 316, 370
Tomkins, 228, 327
Tomley, 190
Tomlin, 239
Tomson, 352
Tongue, 201
Toomy, 185, 232, 257
Tootle, 271
Torrence, 309
Touchstone, 273, 289, 330, 358, 371
Tower, 262
Townsend, 257
Townsley, 355
Towson, 49, 218, 263, 379
Trago, 352, 354
Tragor, 357
Trapnell, 257
Trasey, 260
Travers, 253
Travis, 239

Treadaway, 331, 365
Tredway, 316
Treble, 212
Tredway, 66, 191, 221, 272
Tredwell, 47, 169, 205
Trevis, 189, 230
Trew, 195
Tridge, 190
Trigger, 169, 358
Troit, 258
Trotten, 192
Truelove, 353
Truss, 273, 365
Tucker, 201, 219, 223
Tuckin, 224
Tuder, 4, 88, 182, 193, 213, 217, 220, 226
Tudor, 280, 281, 309
Tunis, 47, 48, 49, 173, 212, 231, 232
Turbel, 192
Turk, 292, 296, 347, 358
Turner, 51, 52, 126, 178, 179, 239, 268, 269, 278, 310, 320, 334, 357, 367, 370, 374, 375
Turnpace, 292
Turret, 117
Twifard, 342
Twine, 5
Tydings, 286

Ullman, 318
Underwood, 126, 239
Upsal, 258

Vance, 287, 323
Vanhorn, 278, 372
Vanhorne, 232
Vansick, 350
Vansicle, 326, 354, 356, 357, 361, 364
Vanzant, 354
Vasey, 57
Vaughan, 258
Vaughn, 225
Vaunce, 193
Veasey, 358
Veazey, 376
Venney, 207
Vershon, 266
Vernun, 215
Vincent, 222, 357
Vine, 64, 76, 77, 209, 242
Viteau, 230

(Index pages shown are microfilm pages.)

Waaler, 130
Waddham, 207
Wade, 334
Wagstar, 243
Waits, 219, 282
Walker, 6, 220, 227, 264, 373
Walkins, 339
Wallace, 240
Waller, 240
Wallis, 195, 266, 377
Wallix, 94
Walmoley, 371
Wamsley, 305, 366
Walters, 2, 36, 287, 304, 372
Waltham, 92, 185, 186, 201, 210, 235, 250, 263, 268, 284, 371
Walton, 201, 209, 223, 240
Wana, 300
Wane, 262, 310
Wantland, 224, 259
Ward, 7, 8, 10, 11, 12, 53, 63, 76, 91, 103, 113, 126, 140, 142, 149, 180, 181, 183, 198, 216, 220, 224, 229, 239, 242, 243, 255, 261, 301
Wardrop, 250
Wareham, 329, 330, 334
Wareing, 209
Warfield, 349
Warhorn, 242
Warner, 236
Warrant, 221
Warrel, 117, 143, 145, 156
Warrell, 117
Warren, 91, 203, 241, 336
Warrick, 214
Warring, 242
Warrington, 176
Washington, 369
Waskey, 304, 372
Waters, 197, 269, 275, 277, 280, 287
Wathusd, 259
Wation, 231
Watkins, 42, 59, 102, 129, 141, 146, 164, 194, 201, 205, 211, 213, 215, 223, 229, 249, 259, 260, 275, 285, 310, 320, 336
Watson, 26, 40, 162, 215, 260
Watters, 166, 167, 168, 175, 209, 213, 216, 219, 226, 227, 230, 235, 236, 237, 309
Watts, 221, 346
Wattson, 221, 259
Way, 326, 327
Waylon, 9

Wear, 279
Webb, 226, 308, 328, 330, 337, 340, 350
Webber, 208
Webster, 211, 223, 228, 266, 268, 303, 323, 326, 329, 356, 357, 360, 369, 371, 376, 378
Weecks, 155
Weekes, 238
Weeks, 2, 258, 295, 345
Ween, 219
Weir, 214
Welch, 193, 221, 222, 369
Welcher, 201, 226, 228
Welkinson, 227
Wells, 19, 124, 198, 211, 243, 259, 288, 328, 370
Welmoth, 223
Welsh, 369
Welsley, 303
West, 19, 41, 228, 267, 286, 306, 319, 338, 351, 352, 360
Westcomb, 219, 222
Westerman, 201
Westfield, 266
Weston, 373
Westwood, 34, 115
Wetherall, 45, 219, 233, 237, 370, 375
Whaland, 241, 243
Whaleland, 61
Wharrington, 159
Wharton, 8, 192, 195, 203, 240
Whaylon, 52
Whayson, 13
Whealand, 85, 110, 117, 142, 152, 162, 195, 197, 200, 205, 221, 226, 229, 230, 231, 244
Wheals, 202
Wheatley, 83, 219
Wheatly, 258
Wheeks, 262
Wheeler, 204, 224, 263, 264, 349, 357
Whelar, 265
Whey, 259
Wheylon, 15
Whicks, 227, 230
Whild, 141
Whiley, 264
Whips, 125, 249
Whistler, 319
Whitacar, 5, 6,
Whitaker, 111, 194, 195, 198, 209, 211, 215, 219, 225, 240, 241, 261, 263, 271,

(Index pages shown are microfilm pages.)   255

Whitaker (continued) 277, 291,
    295, 350, 355, 366
White, 5, 85, 109, 117, 135,
    143, 145, 154, 167, 173,
    182, 196, 202, 203, 212,
    213, 214, 216, 223, 228,
    229, 239, 241, 242, 243,
    250, 257, 261, 268, 286,
    329, 331
Whiteaker, 198, 207
Whiteford, 372
Whitehead, 68, 73, 131, 177,
    200, 229, 244, 257
Whiteley, 229
Whitemore, 226
Whitford, 285
Whithead, 8
Whitington, 206
Whittacar, 4
Whittaker, 302
Wiat, 264
Wicks, 159, 226, 262, 277
    125
Wiggfield, 226
Wiggin, 194
Wilb, 259
Wilcher, 260
Wiley, 243, 354
Wilford, 230
Wilkins, 223
Wilkinson, 153, 160, 196, 218,
    221, 242, 264
Wilkson, 160
Willard, 263
Williams, 7, 91, 195, 198, 199,
    202, 207, 209, 211, 218,
    228, 240, 241, 243, 250,
    255, 257, 259, 262, 306,
    307, 309, 311, 318, 336,
    351, 352, 354, 355, 375,
    377, 378
Williamson, 49, 217, 225
Willion, 225, 260
Willis, 258
Willmer, 268
Willmott, 133, 151, 234, 235,
    258, 362
Willson, 23, 101, 102, 193, 196,
    219, 226, 257, 260
Wilmer, 231, 267, 269, 271, 273,
    274, 289, 303, 304, 306,
    328, 356, 365, 369, 370,
    371, 372
Wilmot, 168
Wilmott, 163, 359
Wilson, 241, 262, 271, 274, 280,
    284, 289, 301, 303, 310,
    314, 315, 316, 317, 320,

Wilson (continued) 327, 331, 339,
    349, 351, 353, 356, 357,
    371, 372, 369
Winchester, 354
Winks, 225
Winstandley, 303, 371
Winstandry, 289
Wiseley, 17
Witheral, 24, 25
Witherall, 25, 286
Wittacre, 19, 25, 38, 64
Wittam, 13
Wittame, 13
Woaler, 231
Wodgworth, 140, 141
Wood, 200, 205, 211, 218, 219,
    223, 226, 229, 230, 241,
    244, 254, 257, 260, 274,
    289, 309, 311, 328, 330,
    334, 341, 349, 353, 357,
    358, 363, 369, 371, 372
Woodard, 202
Woodcock, 220
Wooden, 74, 106, 296
Woodland, 220, 261, 265, 282,
    282
Woodlow, 262
Wooling, 175
Wooller, 101
Woolley, 82
Woolling, 44, 49, 214, 215,
    217, 223, 225
Worbleton, 205
Wordgworth, 141, 154, 155, 219,
    232
Wordsworth, 217
Worrall, 275
Worthington, 114, 216, 218, 221,
    258, 284, 306, 356
Wright, 17, 26, 38, 74, 77, 79,
    89, 100, 115, 116, 119, 125,
    136, 155, 164, 193, 206, 212,
    214, 215, 216, 218, 221, 222,
    223, 224, 227, 228, 229, 230,
    233, 236, 238, 240, 241, 264,
    271, 279, 301, 302, 306, 325,
    330, 336, 340, 351, 353, 371
Wrongs, 263   (also 226)
Wuskitt, 227
Wyle, 132, 187, 197, 198, 207,
    211, 212, 218, 225, 226,
    227, 232, 234, 257, 258,
    260

Yarley, 285
Yates, 243
Yearks, 222
Yearly, 230

(Index pages shown are microfilm pages.)

Yeates, 157, 197, 203
Yeats, 117, 189, 190, 191, 239
Yellott, 304, 306, 309, 367, 372
Yeo, 212
Yoark, 2, 3
Yokely, 333, 358
York, 2, 10, 17, 20, 21, 22, 37, 50,
    52, 76, 78, 124, 125, 136, 161,
    163, 204, 223, 226, 227, 230,
    238, 263, 266, 269, 271, 274,
    289, 304, 351, 370, 371, 372
Yorke, 10, 11, 352
Young, 99, 118, 206, 211, 213, 214,
    227, 231, 234, 235, 237, 258,
    265, 268, 284, 350
Youngblood, 202

Zara, 350

Other books by the author:

A Closer Look at St. John's Parish Registers [Baltimore County, Maryland], 1701-1801
A Collection of Maryland Church Records
A Guide to Genealogical Research in Maryland: 5th Edition, Revised and Enlarged
Abstracts of the Ledgers and Accounts of the Bush Store and Rock Run Store, 1759-1771
Abstracts of the Orphans Court Proceedings of Harford County, 1778-1800
Abstracts of Wills, Harford County, Maryland, 1800-1805
Baltimore City [Maryland] Deaths and Burials, 1834-1840
Baltimore County, Maryland, Overseers of Roads, 1693-1793
Bastardy Cases in Baltimore County, Maryland, 1673-1783
Bastardy Cases in Harford County, Maryland, 1774-1844
Bible and Family Records of Harford County, Maryland Families: Volume V
Children of Harford County: Indentures and Guardianships, 1801-1830
Colonial Delaware Soldiers and Sailors, 1638-1776
Colonial Families of the Eastern Shore of Maryland Volumes 5, 6, 7, 8, 9, 11, 12, 13, 14, and 16
Colonial Maryland Soldiers and Sailors, 1634-1734
Dr. John Archer's First Medical Ledger, 1767-1769, Annotated Abstracts
Early Anglican Records of Cecil County
Early Harford Countians, Individuals Living in Harford County, Maryland in Its Formative Years Volume 1: A to K, Volume 2: L to Z, and Volume 3: Supplement
Harford County Taxpayers in 1870, 1872 and 1883
Harford County, Maryland Divorce Cases, 1827-1912: An Annotated Index
Heirs and Legatees of Harford County, Maryland, 1774-1802
Heirs and Legatees of Harford County, Maryland, 1802-1846
Inhabitants of Baltimore County, Maryland, 1763-1774
Inhabitants of Cecil County, Maryland, 1649-1774
Inhabitants of Harford County, Maryland, 1791-1800
Inhabitants of Kent County, Maryland, 1637-1787
Joseph A. Pennington & Co., Havre De Grace, Maryland Funeral Home Records: Volume II, 1877-1882, 1893-1900
Maryland Bible Records, Volume 1: Baltimore and Harford Counties
Maryland Bible Records, Volume 2: Baltimore and Harford Counties
Maryland Bible Records, Volume 3: Carroll County
Maryland Bible Records, Volume 4: Eastern Shore
Maryland Deponents, 1634-1799
Maryland Deponents: Volume 3, 1634-1776
Maryland Public Service Records, 1775-1783: A Compendium of Men and Women of Maryland Who Rendered Aid in Support of the American Cause against Great Britain during the Revolutionary War
Marylanders to Carolina: Migration of Marylanders to North Carolina and South Carolina prior to 1800

Marylanders to Kentucky, 1775-1825

Methodist Records of Baltimore City, Maryland: Volume 1, 1799-1829

Methodist Records of Baltimore City, Maryland: Volume 2, 1830-1839

Methodist Records of Baltimore City, Maryland: Volume 3, 1840-1850 (East City Station)

More Maryland Deponents, 1716-1799

More Marylanders to Carolina: Migration of Marylanders to North Carolina and South Carolina prior to 1800

More Marylanders to Kentucky, 1778-1828

Outpensioners of Harford County, Maryland, 1856-1896

Presbyterian Records of Baltimore City, Maryland, 1765-1840

Quaker Records of Baltimore and Harford Counties, Maryland, 1801-1825

Quaker Records of Northern Maryland, 1716-1800

Quaker Records of Southern Maryland, 1658-1800

Revolutionary Patriots of Anne Arundel County, Maryland

Revolutionary Patriots of Baltimore Town and Baltimore County, 1775-1783

Revolutionary Patriots of Calvert and St. Mary's Counties, Maryland, 1775-1783

Revolutionary Patriots of Caroline County, Maryland, 1775-1783

Revolutionary Patriots of Cecil County, Maryland

Revolutionary Patriots of Delaware, 1775-1783

Revolutionary Patriots of Dorchester County, Maryland, 1775-1783

Revolutionary Patriots of Frederick County, Maryland, 1775-1783

Revolutionary Patriots of Harford County, Maryland, 1775-1783

Revolutionary Patriots of Kent and Queen Anne's Counties

Revolutionary Patriots of Lancaster County, Pennsylvania

Revolutionary Patriots of Maryland, 1775-1783: A Supplement

Revolutionary Patriots of Maryland, 1775-1783: Second Supplement

Revolutionary Patriots of Montgomery County, Maryland, 1776-1783

Revolutionary Patriots of Prince George's County, Maryland, 1775-1783

Revolutionary Patriots of Talbot County, Maryland, 1775-1783

Revolutionary Patriots of Worcester and Somerset Counties, Maryland, 1775-1783

Revolutionary Patriots of Washington County, Maryland, 1776-1783

St. George's (Old Spesutia) Parish, Harford County, Maryland: Church and Cemetery Records, 1820-1920

St. John's and St. George's Parish Registers, 1696-1851

Survey Field Book of David and William Clark in Harford County, Maryland, 1770-1812

The Crenshaws of Kentucky, 1800-1995

The Delaware Militia in the War of 1812

Union Chapel United Methodist Church Cemetery Tombstone Inscriptions, Wilna, Harford County, Maryland

www.ingramcontent.com/pod-product-compliance
Lightning Source LLC
Chambersburg PA
CBHW050135170426
43197CB00011B/1850